Praise for *Python Polars: The Definitive Guide*

Jeroen and Thijs have done an excellent job—not only teaching you the ins and outs of Polars but also helping you unlearn habits from other tools like pandas. They really bring out the power of expressions, which are key to using Polars effectively, guiding you toward a more declarative, functional approach to data processing. As you work through this book, I'm sure you'll gain a deep understanding of Polars and discover fresh ways to approach data processing.

—*Ritchie Vink, Creator of Polars (excerpt from the Foreword)*

Polars has become a rising star in the Python data ecosystem, showing what's possible in a next-generation data frame library. Jeroen and Thijs have written a timely and essential resource to help you take advantage of everything Polars has to offer.

—*Wes McKinney, Creator of pandas,*
Principal Architect, Posit PBC

Polars has brought a ton of much-needed innovation to the data frame world with its much more streamlined API and efficient implementation. As a result, the capabilities of data analysis in Python are pushed to new heights. We also greatly enjoy Ritchie and team as a part of the Amsterdam data ecosystem.

I greatly respect Jeroen's commitment to teaching data science in an accessible way, whether it be on the command line or elsewhere. His and Thijs's book is a testament to this commitment, and I recommend it to the data science community.

—*Hannes Mühleisen, Cocreator of DuckDB*

Polars is emerging as one of the leading data frameworks in Python, especially for time series analysis and forecasting. It is now fully integrated with libraries like Nixtla's MLForecast and StatsForecast, allowing for the creation of forecasts at scale with high performance.

Jeroen and Thijs have done an excellent job of establishing a solid foundation for both new practitioners who wish to learn how to process data with Python and experienced users looking to transition from pandas to Polars.

—*Rami Krispin, Senior Manager,*
Data Science and Engineering at Apple

The depth that Jeroen and Thijs went into in order to produce this phenomenally good book is impressive. There are some pretty good Polars books out there, but this is the best one. They don't just repeat what's in the user guide—they go above and beyond: in-depth explanations of expressions, (friendly) comparisons with other tools, an example of how to go beyond what Polars offers out-of-the-box with a geocoding plugin! Whether you're new to Polars or want to improve your understanding of it, I wholeheartedly recommend this book.

—*Marco Gorelli, Senior Software Engineer at Quansight,*
Core Contributor to Polars and pandas, Creator of Narwhals

Python Polars:
The Definitive Guide

*Transforming, Analyzing, and Visualizing Data
with a Fast and Expressive DataFrame API*

Jeroen Janssens and Thijs Nieuwdorp

O'REILLY®

Python Polars: The Definitive Guide

by Jeroen Janssens and Thijs Nieuwdorp

Copyright © 2025 Jeroen Janssens and Thijs Nieuwdorp. All rights reserved.

Published by O'Reilly Media, Inc., 1005 Gravenstein Highway North, Sebastopol, CA 95472.

O'Reilly books may be purchased for educational, business, or sales promotional use. Online editions are also available for most titles (*http://oreilly.com*). For more information, contact our corporate/institutional sales department: 800-998-9938 or *corporate@oreilly.com*.

Acquisitions Editor: Aaron Black
Development Editor: Sarah Grey
Production Editor: Jonathon Owen
Copyeditor: Sonia Saruba
Proofreader: Miah Sandvik

Indexer: WordCo Indexing Services, Inc.
Interior Designer: David Futato
Cover Designer: Karen Montgomery
Illustrator: Kate Dullea

February 2025:   First Edition

Revision History for the First Edition

2025-02-19:   First Release

See *http://oreilly.com/catalog/errata.csp?isbn=9781098156084* for release details.

978-1-098-15608-4

[LSI]

Table of Contents

Part II. Form

Part III. Express

Part V.   Advance

Foreword

It was never meant to be this serious.

In December 2019, I became a dad, and then the pandemic hit. This left me dazed; juggling life with a newborn and trying to hold on to a sense of "me." In a burst of new-dad sleep deprivation, I figured I'd take on a new project. Honestly, it started as nothing more than a hobby.

At work, I had to join two CSV files while programming in Rust, and it felt like way more hassle than it should have been. I wondered if there were easier ways to get it done than setting up SQLite. So, as one often does in software development, I decided to try my hand at creating my own join algorithm.

At the time, I was pretty new to Rust and didn't know much about optimizing performance. So as a proud writer of my first join algorithm, I learned that my implementation was much slower than pandas. This unsatisfying result planted the seed of what would later become Polars.

This led me down a path of researching database engines, learning Rust, and a lot of trial and error over the next year and a half. As I learned more about databases, algorithms, performance, memory, unsafe code, etc., my goals shifted. I went from just wanting to make a faster join than pandas to building a DataFrame package for Rust, and eventually, a high-performance query engine that could rival the state of the art in the Python landscape.

I drew inspiration from pandas' strengths and weaknesses, the declarative approaches of SQL and PySpark, functional programming principles, and the rigor of Rust's type system. At first, I even thought I'd model it directly on the pandas API. But I quickly realized that limiting myself that way hurt my creative drive and would only lead to a less effective tool. When I decided to let go of this constraint and merged the lazy and eager APIs into one expression-based API, the project was molding into something people might now recognize as Polars.

On March 15, 2021, I released this as a research project on PyPI. I was able to evolve this pet project into a full-fledged DataFrame processing package called Polars. Eventually, Polars' success enabled me to secure funding and start my own company, Polars Inc.

Today, Polars is its own company—something I'm proud of—and it's a constant source of energy for me. Finally, a lot of the ideas I have can come to fruition (not all of them, but hey, I'm ambitious). With Polars, my hope is to create one DataFrame API that works across the board, whether you're dealing with small or big data, all on the same tech stack.

Together with a dedicated team at Polars Inc. and a growing, enthusiastic community of contributors, we're tackling many interesting technical challenges. Each scale comes with its own set of challenges, and finding solutions for these tough problems so that millions of users have a better experience is incredibly rewarding. One challenge involves accurately handling time zones. This may sound trivial, but dealing with time zone conversions and ensuring consistency across different systems is notoriously difficult. A big technical challenge we're currently facing is translating the DataFrame API into a full streaming model. This transition requires rethinking how operations—such as computing the mean or accessing the last row—will work in a streaming context, as opposed to in-memory batch processing. I'm confident that we'll rise to these challenges.

Over time, Polars has grown beyond my initial expectations. It's been incredibly rewarding to see it used in surprising scenarios, such as finite element method simulations involving 1,500 joins. Users have also employed Polars for metaprogramming tasks, generating complex queries that would be impractical to write by hand.

Looking ahead, the future of Polars is exciting. We're focused on extending its streaming capabilities, allowing you to process huge datasets on your own laptop. We're also working on creating a distributed cloud environment to do fast distributed computing on massive datasets. Another key goal is to support extension types, paving the way, for example, for geospatial data types. These developments aim to make Polars a go-to tool for data processing—from tiny datasets that fit in memory to massive datasets that require distributed computing. On top of that, we'll keep investing in the user experience through improvements like error messages that inform you up front when a query will eventually fail.

I'm really glad you're holding *Python Polars: The Definitive Guide* by Jeroen Janssens and Thijs Nieuwdorp. I know Jeroen and Thijs well from our days at Xomnia, where we shared a lot of training sessions, company trips, drinks, ideas—the whole mix. When Jeroen first suggested I write a book, I had to thank him—my energy was all going into Polars—but I wholeheartedly supported him when he decided to take up the challenge with Thijs. Then, on a company trip to Jordan, both Jeroen and

Thijs held me to it, and I ended up spending hours on the bus explaining—and occasionally defending—my design choices for Polars.

Jeroen and Thijs have done an excellent job—not only teaching you the ins and outs of Polars but also helping you unlearn habits from other tools like pandas. They really bring out the power of expressions, which are key to using Polars effectively, guiding you toward a more declarative, functional approach to data processing. As you work through this book, I'm sure you'll gain a deep understanding of Polars and discover fresh ways to approach data processing.

Enjoy the read, follow along with the examples, and take your data analysis skills to a new level.

— Ritchie Vink, Creator of Polars
Amsterdam, November 2024

Preface

Polars has quickly emerged as one of the most exciting innovations in the Python data ecosystem. With its blazingly-fast performance, expressive API, and ability to handle massive datasets, it's become a powerful alternative to traditional tools like pandas. Built with efficiency in mind, Polars leverages Rust for its backend to offer great speeds, especially when it comes to multi-core and GPU acceleration. Whether you're working with large-scale data wrangling, complex transformations, or real-time analysis, Polars has shown that it can handle the toughest challenges with ease.

We first learned about Polars through our colleague, Ritchie Vink, the creator of Polars, at Xomnia in Amsterdam. This was back in 2022, when Polars wasn't as well-known as it is now. Intrigued by Ritchie's enthusiasm and explanation of some of its features, we decided to give it a try. We were hooked. The elegant syntax and the impressive speed stood out immediately. It was a stark contrast to the complexity and performance limitations we had encountered with other tools. Polars felt like a breath of fresh air—simple, yet powerful. We could see that this was something special.

Soon after, we had the perfect opportunity to put Polars to the test. We were working together on the same team at Alliander, the largest utility company in the Netherlands. A particular data pipeline needed to be scaled up so that it would process the entire electrical grid on a weekly basis. Unfortunately, because it was implemented in a combination of R and Python with pandas, this was infeasible. Thanks to a minimal viable benchmark with Polars, we managed to convince the team to reimplement the entire pipeline using Polars. As a result, we were able to drastically improve the performance of the pipeline while reducing memory consumption. The impact was immediate and transformative, not only saving the project but also cementing our belief in Polars' potential.

This success convinced us that Polars deserved a book so that this package and our hard-won knowledge could be shared with a larger audience. Fast-forward a year and a half, and here's the result: *Python Polars: The Definitive Guide*. We hope that by reading this book, you'll be equipped to achieve similar success in your own projects.

Who This Book Is For

This book is designed for anyone looking to leverage the power of Polars in Python to transform, analyze, and visualize data more efficiently and effectively. Whether you're a seasoned data analyst, a data engineer, or even someone new to the world of data science, you'll find valuable insights and practical examples that can be applied directly to real-world challenges. To illustrate the diverse ways in which Polars can benefit different users, let's take a look at two key personas: Hanna, a seasoned data analyst, and Kosjo, an experienced data engineer.

Hanna: The Data Analyst

Hanna is a seasoned data analyst. She's comfortable with Python and has a good grasp of pandas but occasionally struggles with its syntax and feels there must be a more elegant way to perform certain operations. Like many analysts, she regularly tackles exploratory data analysis (EDA) tasks that involve cleaning, transforming, and summarizing large datasets. However, she often finds herself battling with pandas' sometimes complex and unintuitive syntax, especially when it comes to performing more advanced data manipulations or scaling her work to larger datasets.

For someone like Hanna, this book offers a streamlined, more intuitive alternative to pandas, with the added benefit of being able to handle data at a larger scale without sacrificing speed or readability. Polars provides a more Pythonic and performant way to perform the types of analyses Hanna does daily. By learning Polars, Hanna can simplify her workflow, write more elegant code, and unlock greater performance in her exploratory data analysis tasks.

Kosjo: The Data Engineer

Kosjo is an experienced data engineer, tasked with processing large volumes of data and building pipelines that support complex data workflows. They are highly skilled in Python and work with various technologies to ensure smooth data movement and processing. As part of their role, Kosjo is often responsible for optimizing processes to reduce infrastructure costs, especially when working with big data. This means reducing the time and resources required for heavy transformations without having to manage a distributed computing cluster.

Polars can help Kosjo achieve these goals. It is designed for speed and performance, especially when dealing with large datasets or intensive transformations. Its parallel execution model allows Kosjo to process data faster than traditional pandas, while its intuitive API keeps development simple. This book will guide Kosjo through leveraging Polars for complex data engineering tasks, enabling them to scale their workflows efficiently without the overhead of distributed systems or dealing with complex setup configurations.

A Broader Audience

In addition to these two personas, this book is also for data scientists, software engineers, and anyone else working with Python who is looking to explore the capabilities of Polars. Whether you're handling small to medium-sized datasets or need to process terabytes of data, Polars offers a unified, high-performance approach to working with data. If you're looking for a faster, more elegant way to analyze and manipulate your data without compromising on readability, this book will serve as a valuable resource to enhance your data-handling skills.

In summary, whether you're looking to improve your day-to-day data analysis or streamline your data engineering workflows, *Python Polars: The Definitive Guide* is designed to help you unlock the full potential of Polars and solve data challenges with speed and elegance.

Get More Out of This Book

We also have a website, *polarsguide.com*, where you can connect with us on LinkedIn, join the Polars Discord server, and get access to our GitHub repo full of scripts and datasets to help you get the most out of this book.

Conventions Used in This Book

The following typographical conventions are used in this book:

Italic
Indicates new terms, URLs, directory names, and filenames.

`Constant width`
Used for program listings, as well as within paragraphs to refer to program elements such as variable or function names, databases, data types, environment variables, statements, and keywords.

`Constant width bold`
Shows commands or other text that should be typed literally by the user.

`Constant width italic`
Shows text that should be replaced with user-supplied values or by values determined by context.

This element signifies a tip or suggestion.

 This element signifies a general note.

 This element indicates a warning or caution.

O'Reilly Online Learning

 For more than 40 years, *O'Reilly Media* has provided technology and business training, knowledge, and insight to help companies succeed.

Our unique network of experts and innovators share their knowledge and expertise through books, articles, and our online learning platform. O'Reilly's online learning platform gives you on-demand access to live training courses, in-depth learning paths, interactive coding environments, and a vast collection of text and video from O'Reilly and 200+ other publishers. For more information, visit *https://oreilly.com*.

How to Contact Us

Please address comments and questions concerning this book to the publisher:

O'Reilly Media, Inc.
1005 Gravenstein Highway North
Sebastopol, CA 95472
800-889-8969 (in the United States or Canada)
707-827-7019 (international or local)
707-829-0104 (fax)
support@oreilly.com
https://oreilly.com/about/contact.html

We have a web page for this book, where we list errata, examples, and any additional information. You can access this page at *https://oreil.ly/PythonPolars*.

For news and information about our books and courses, visit *https://oreilly.com*.

Find us on LinkedIn: *https://linkedin.com/company/oreilly-media*

Watch us on YouTube: *https://youtube.com/oreillymedia*

Acknowledgments

Writing *Python Polars: The Definitive Guide* has been an incredible journey—one that would not have been possible without the support and encouragement of so many people.

A heartfelt thank you to Ritchie Vink, the creator of Polars, for his guidance and for sharing his vision during many talks over the course of writing this book. His innovative work on Polars has been a constant source of inspiration, and his willingness to engage in deep discussions about design choices has significantly enhanced our understanding. We are truly honored that you wrote the foreword to this book.

We're deeply grateful to Sarah Grey, our development editor at O'Reilly. Her sharp linguistic skills, thoughtful advice, and encouraging nudges have been indispensable. A big thank you to Aaron Black, our acquisitions editor, for believing in this project, and to Jonathon Owen, our production editor, for guiding it across the finish line. Working with O'Reilly was once again a pleasure, particularly thanks to David Futato, Emilia Philip, Karen Montgomery, Kate Dullea, Kristen Brown, Miah Sandvik, Sharon Cordesse, Sonia Saruba, and many other colleagues operating behind the scenes.

Special thanks to our technical reviewers—Bram Timmers, Christine Stinger, David Langerveld, James Males, Marco Gorelli, and Stijn de Gooijer—for your thorough analysis and constructive feedback. Your expertise and attention to detail have greatly improved the quality and depth of this book. Of course, any remaining errors are entirely our own responsibility.

To our colleagues and friends at Xomnia, thank you for fostering an environment of learning and collaboration. This is the place where Ritchie Vink started working on Polars; where Jeroen, Thijs, and Ritchie met; and where the idea for this book was born. In particular we would like to thank Cheryl Zandvliet, Jordi Hompes, and Tim Paauw for their support. To our team members of IILS at Alliander: a big thank you for giving us the opportunity to put our Polars knowledge to the test and apply it to a meaningful use case.

We had the pleasure of collaborating with NVIDIA and Dell Technologies to benchmark Polars on the GPU. The results are documented in the Appendix. Thank you

Crystal Cook, Dylan Filkins, Irina Shekhovtsova, Jamil Semaan, Jenn Yonemitsu, Mark Cai, Nick Becker, and Travis Wells for making this possible. A special thanks to Logan Lawler for going above and beyond to ensure we had all the necessary hardware.

We want to acknowledge the vibrant Polars community. Your enthusiasm, contributions, and feedback have not only advanced the development of Polars but have also motivated us to dive deeper into its capabilities. We particularly appreciate each and every contribution, however small, by the following generous people: Adam Johnson, Alex Birch, Alexander Beedie, Alexandru Bernea, Alvin Wanyeki, Andy Terra, Arnaud Vennin, Barbera Droste, Bradley Grant, Carlos Scheidegger, Christian Heinze, Dean MacGregor, Dom Yarnell, Frits Van der Woude, Gert Hulselmans, Guillaume Rischard, Hannes Mühleisen, Hassan Kibirige, Hella Haanstra, Isabel Fernandez Escapa, Jake VanderPlas, James Powell, Jeroen "Junior" Siebers, John Sandall, Josko de Boer, Liam Brannigan, Marcos Detry, Marnix van Lieshout, Marysia Winkels, Matt Harrison, Matt Shepit, Michael Chow, Mine Çetinkaya-Rundel, Ollie Dapper, Orson Peters, Owen Prough, Peter Wang, Rami Krispin, Richard Iannone, Romano Vacca, Thomas Aarholt, Thomas M. Ahern, Tomara Youngblood, Vincent D. Warmerdam, Wes McKinney, William van Lith, Yu Ri Tan, and Yuki Kakegawa.

On a personal note, we would like to thank our family and friends. Jeroen thanks his wife Esther, his daughter Florien, and his son Olivier for letting him disappear many nights and weekends. Thank you for being so supportive while making sure that he doesn't forget what truly matters.

Thijs thanks Paula, whose support caused him to pick up the (figurative) pen in the first place and kept the ink flowing when it was tough. Thank you for the countless cups of tea that warmed the spirit and for patiently listening to endless rants and raves about Polars.

Lastly, to you, the reader of this book—thank you for your interest in Polars. This book exists because of you and for you. We hope it will enhance your data processing skills and open up new possibilities.

## PART I

Begin

## CHAPTER 1

Introducing Polars

In 2022, we found ourselves in the middle of a challenging project for a client. Their data pipeline was growing out of control. The codebase was a mix of Python and R, with the Python side relying heavily on the pandas package for wrangling all the data. Over time, three major issues emerged: the code was becoming increasingly difficult to maintain, performance had slowed to a crawl, and memory consumption had skyrocketed to over 500 GB. These problems were stifling productivity and pushing the limits of the infrastructure.

Back then, Polars was still relatively unknown, but we had experimented with it and seen some promising results. Convincing the rest of the team to migrate both the pandas and R code to Polars wasn't easy, but once the switch was made, the impact was immediate. The new data pipeline was much faster, and the memory footprint shrank to just 40 GB—a fraction of what it used to be.

Thanks to this success, we're fully convinced of the power of Polars. We wrote this book, *Python Polars: The Definitive Guide*, to share with you what we've learned and help you unlock the same potential in your data workflows.

In this introductory chapter, you'll learn:

- The main features of Polars
- Why Polars is fast and popular
- How Polars compares to other data processing packages
- Why you should use Polars
- How we have organized this book
- Why we focus on Python Polars

In addition, we'll demonstrate Polars' capabilities through a showcase, where we transform, analyze, and visualize data related to bike trips in New York City.

What Is This Thing Called Polars?

Polars is a high-performance data processing package designed for efficient handling of large-scale datasets. What started as a side project by Ritchie Vink to learn Rust and to better understand data processing has now grown into a popular package.[1] Data scientists, data engineers, and software developers use it to perform data analysis, create data visualizations, and build data-intensive applications used in production.

Key Features

Here are some key features of Polars:

Speed and efficiency
  Written in Rust and leveraging decades of database research, Polars is engineered for speed and performance. Thanks to parallel processing and memory optimization techniques, it can process large datasets significantly faster than other data processing packages, often 10 to 100 times faster for common operations.

DataFrame structure
  Polars uses DataFrames as its core data structure. A *DataFrame* is a two-dimensional data structure composed of rows and columns, similar to a spreadsheet or database table. Polars DataFrames are immutable, promoting functional-style operations and ensuring thread safety.

Expressive API
  Polars provides an intuitive and concise syntax for data processing tasks, making it easy to learn, use, and maintain.

Key Concepts

Key concepts you'll become familiar with in this book include:

Lazy evaluation
  Polars employs "lazy" evaluation, where operations are built into an optimized execution plan and executed only when needed. This approach minimizes unnecessary work and can lead to substantial performance gains.

---

1 Refer to the Foreword for additional backstory on how Polars came to be.

Expressions

Polars uses expressions to define operations on DataFrames. These expressions are composable, allowing users to create complex data pipelines, built from basic building blocks.

Query optimization

Polars automatically optimizes the execution plan for efficient resource use, based on expressions and data characteristics.

Advantages

Here is a quick rundown of Polars' main advantages:

Performance

Thanks to its efficient algorithms, parallel execution engine, and use of vectorization with Single Instruction, Multiple Data (SIMD), Polars is designed to take full advantage of modern hardware. It can optionally leverage NVIDIA GPUs to further improve performance. (We benchmark the difference the GPU makes in the Appendix.)

Memory efficiency

Polars requires less memory than other data processing packages.

Interoperability

Built on Apache Arrow, a standardized columnar memory format for flat and hierarchical data, Polars offers excellent interoperability with other data processing tools and packages. It can be used directly in Rust and has language bindings for Python, R, SQL, JavaScript, and Julia. In a moment we'll explain why this book focuses on Python specifically.

Streaming capabilities

Polars can process data in chunks, allowing for out-of-core computations on datasets that don't fit in memory.

In summary, Polars is a powerful package for transforming and analyzing data, particularly suited for pipelines where performance and efficiency are crucial.

Why You Should Use Polars

"Come for the speed, stay for the API" is a popular saying within the Polars community. It nicely captures the two main reasons for choosing Polars: performance and usability. Let's dive into those two reasons. After that, we'll also address the popularity of Polars.

Performance

First and foremost, you should use Polars for its outstanding performance. Figure 1-1 shows, for a number of data processing packages, the duration (in seconds) for running a variety of queries. These queries come from a standardized set of benchmarks and include reading the data from disk.

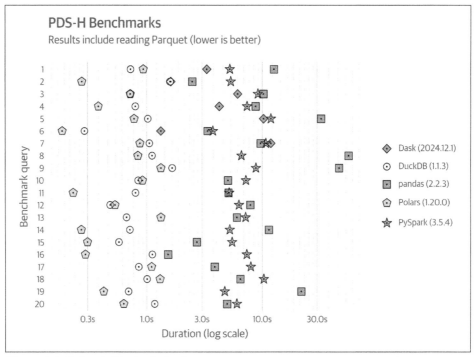

Figure 1-1. Polars is blazingly fast[2]

Polars often outperforms the other packages: Dask, DuckDB, pandas, and PySpark.

Usability

While performance may be the initial draw, many users find themselves staying with Polars due to its well-designed API. The Polars API is characterized by:

---

2 Dask failed on queries 8-20. pandas took 56.3 s on query 8 and took 46.5 s on query 9. More information: *https://github.com/TNieuwdorp/polars-benchmark*.

Consistency

Operations behave predictably across different data types and structures and are based on the data processing grammar that you already know.

Expressiveness

Polars offers its own expression system that allows you to create complex data transformations in a concise and readable way.

Functional approach

The API encourages a functional programming style, which fits well with data processing and makes your code easy to read, write, and maintain.

Eager and lazy APIs

You can choose and easily switch between eager execution for quick, ad hoc results and lazy evaluation for optimized performance, depending on your needs. You'll get a preview of both APIs in the showcase at the end of this chapter.

The combination of performance and usability has led to Polars gaining popularity at a fast pace, as we'll discuss next.

Popularity

You should never choose a particular piece of software just because it's popular. It can cause you to miss out on options that might better fit your needs, as popularity doesn't always mean it's the best choice. On the other hand, picking something that isn't well-known or well-maintained can lead to issues such as limited community support, security risks, and lack of updates, making it a less reliable option in the long run.

Luckily, Polars is very much actively maintained (with a new release nearly every week on GitHub (*https://oreil.ly/RkDWA*)), and its community is growing rapidly (with a Discord server[3] that currently has over five thousand members). From our own experience, we can say that bugs are fixed quickly and that questions are addressed kindly and swiftly.

There's no perfect measure for the popularity of an open source project. The number of GitHub stars is, however, a good indicator of a project's visibility and community interest. It reflects how many people find it noteworthy or potentially useful. Figure 1-2 shows the number of GitHub stars for a variety of Python packages for processing data.

---

3 You are welcome to join the Discord server at *https://discord.gg/4qf7UVDZmd*.

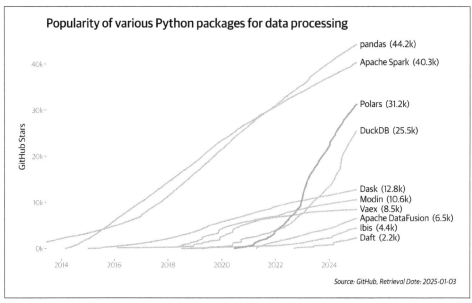

Figure 1-2. Popularity of various Python data processing packages, expressed in GitHub stars

Apache Spark and pandas, two projects that have been around for over 10 years, have the highest number of GitHub stars. Polars, which is one of the youngest projects, comes in at third place. If these three projects maintain their current trajectory, then Polars is set to overtake both pandas and Apache Spark within the next few years. In short, Polars is here to stay, and is worth the time to learn.

Sustainability

Because of the way Polars is designed, it efficiently computes queries. According to research done by Felix Nahrstedt et al. (2024) (*https://oreil.ly/jcHci*), Polars consumes 63% of the energy needed by pandas on the TPC-H benchmark and uses eight times less energy than pandas on synthetic data. In an age when there is more and more data to process, doing so sustainably becomes increasingly important. Polars sets an example for processing data with a low carbon footprint.

Polars Compared to Other Data Processing Packages

Of course, Polars isn't the only package for processing data. In this section we provide an overview of how Polars compares to other popular data processing packages in Python. We highlight the strengths and weaknesses of each, helping you understand where Polars fits in the landscape of data processing tools.

pandas

pandas is the most widely used data processing package for Python. It provides data structures like DataFrames and Series, along with a rich set of functions for data analysis, cleaning, and transformation.

Compared to pandas, Polars offers significantly better performance, especially for large datasets. Polars is built on Rust and uses Apache Arrow for memory management, allowing it to process data much faster than pandas does. While pandas uses eager execution by default, Polars provides both eager and lazy execution options, enabling query optimization. However, pandas still has a larger ecosystem and better integration with other data science packages.

Dask

Dask is a package for parallel computing in Python. It extends the functionality of NumPy, pandas, and scikit-learn to distributed computing systems. Dask is particularly useful for processing datasets that are too large to fit in memory.

Like Dask, Polars supports parallel processing and can handle large datasets. However, Polars is designed for single-machine use, while Dask focuses on distributed computing. Polars generally offers better performance for operations that can fit in memory, while Dask excels at processing truly massive datasets across multiple machines.

DuckDB

DuckDB is an in-process SQL OLAP database management system. It's designed to be fast and efficient for analytical queries on structured data. DuckDB can be embedded directly in applications and supports SQL queries.

Both Polars and DuckDB are optimized for analytical workloads and offer excellent performance. Polars provides a more Pythonic API, while DuckDB uses SQL for querying.

PySpark

PySpark is the Python API for Apache Spark, a distributed computing system designed for big data processing. It provides a wide range of functionalities, including SQL queries, machine learning, and graph processing. PySpark is particularly useful for processing very large datasets across clusters of computers.

While PySpark is designed for distributed computing, Polars focuses on single-machine performance. Polars generally offers faster performance for datasets that can fit on a single machine. However, PySpark is more suitable for truly massive datasets that require distributed processing across multiple computers. Polars is easier to set up and use than the more complex PySpark ecosystem.

Why We Focus on Python Polars

Since Polars is built in Rust and has language bindings for Python, R, SQL, JavaScript, and Julia, you might be wondering why we focus on its Python API.

According to the 2024 Stack Overflow Developer Survey,[4] Python is the most popular programming language among respondents who are learning to code, and the fourth most popular among professional developers. This is not surprising, since Python is known for its simplicity, readability, and versatility and is widely used in data science, machine learning, web development, and more.

This popularity is reflected in the Polars community, where the Python API is the most complete, most used, and most often updated API. Furthermore, Python is widely regarded as the language of choice for data analysis and data processing, and most data scientists and data engineers are familiar with it.

How This Book Is Organized

This book contains 18 chapters, spread over five parts and an appendix. Each chapter starts with a short introduction of the things we'll discuss and concludes with key takeaways.

Part I, "Begin"
> The first part, "Begin," contains the first three chapters of the book. These chapters are meant to introduce you to Polars, get you up and running, and help you start using it yourself.
>
> Chapter 1, this chapter, discusses what Polars is, explains why you should use it, and demonstrates its capabilities through a showcase. Chapter 2 covers everything you need to get started with Polars, including instructions on how to install Polars and how to get the code and data used in this book. If you have any experience using pandas, then Chapter 3 will help you transition to Polars by explaining and showing the differences between the two packages.

Part II, "Form"
> The name of the second part, "Form," has two meanings, as it's about both the *form* of data structures and data types as well as *forming* DataFrames from some source. In other words, you'll learn how to read and write data, and how this data is stored and handled in Polars.
>
> Chapter 4 provides an overview of the data structures and data types that Polars supports and how missing data is handled. Chapter 5 explains the difference between the eager API, which is used for quick results, and the lazy API, which

---

4 See *https://survey.stackoverflow.co/2024* for the full report.

is used for optimized performance. Chapter 6 covers how to read and write data from and to various file formats, such as CSV, Parquet, and Arrow.

Part III, "Express"

Expressions play a central role within Polars, so it's only fitting that this third part, "Express," is in the middle of the book.

Chapter 7 starts with examples of where expressions are used, provides a formal definition of an expression, and explains how you can create them. Chapter 8 enumerates the many methods for continuing expressions, including mathematical operations, working with missing values, applying smoothing, and summarizing. Chapter 9 shows how to combine multiple expressions using, for example, arithmetic and Boolean logic.

Part IV, "Transform"

Once you understand expressions, you can incorporate them into functions and methods to transform your data, which is what this fourth part, "Transform," is all about.

Chapter 10 explains how to select and create columns and work with column names and selectors. Chapter 11 shows the different ways of filtering and sorting rows. Chapter 12 covers how to work with textual, temporal, and nested data types. Chapter 13 goes into grouping, aggregating, and summarizing data. Chapter 14 explains how to combine different DataFrames using joins and concatenations. Chapter 15 shows how to reshape data, through (un)pivoting, stacking, and extending.

Part V, "Advance"

The last part of this book, "Advance," contains a variety of more advanced topics.

Chapter 16 explains how to visualize data using a selection of visualization packages, including Altair, hvPlot, and plotnine. Chapter 17 shows how you can extend Polars with custom Python functions and your own Rust plugins. Chapter 18 looks behind the curtains of Polars, explaining how it's built, how it works under the hood, and why it's so fast.

The book concludes with an appendix that covers how to leverage the power of GPUs to accelerate Polars, offering insights into maximizing performance.

An ETL Showcase

Now that you've learned where Polars comes from and how it will benefit you, it's time to see it in action. We've prepared an extract-transform-load (ETL) showcase, in which we're going to demonstrate the capabilities of Polars by transforming, analyzing, and visualizing data related to bike trips in New York City.

Strictly speaking, ETL is about extracting, transforming, and loading data, but we have added two data visualization bonuses.

The outline of this showcase is as follows. First, we import the required packages. Second, we download the raw data. Third, we clean this raw data and enrich it with new columns. Finally, we write the data to Parquet files so that we can reuse it in later chapters.

Don't Worry About the Syntax

The purpose of this showcase is to give you a taste of what Polars looks like. There will be lots of new syntax and concepts that you're not yet familiar with. Don't worry about this; everything will be explained throughout the course of this book. You don't have to run these code snippets yourself. Instead, just read and enjoy the ride.

Let's get started.

Extract

The first step of this ETL showcase is to *extract* the data. We are going to use two different sources: one is about the bike trips themselves, and the other is about New York City's neighborhoods and boroughs. However, we first need to import the packages that we're going to use for this showcase.

Import packages

Obviously, we will need Polars itself. For the geographical operations in this showcase, we've made a custom plugin that you can import as `polars_geo`. We'll explain how to compile and install this plugin in Chapter 17. We also need the plotnine package, which we're going to use to create a couple of data visualizations:

```
import polars as pl      ❶
import polars_geo
from plotnine import *   ❷
```

❶   It's customary to import Polars as the alias `pl`.

❷   In Python scripts, it's not recommended to import all the functions of a package into the global namespace, like we do here. In ad hoc notebooks and in this showcase, however, it's OK because it allows us to use the functions within the plotnine package without having to type the package name, which is much more convenient.

Let's move on to the next step, which is to download and extract the bike trips.

Download and extract Citi Bike trips

The data that we're going to use comes from Citi Bike, New York City's public bike rental system. This system offers bikes that you can hire for short trips up to 30 or 45 minutes, depending on whether you're a member. The data is freely available from their website.[5]

The following commands download the ZIP file, extract the CSV file, and remove the ZIP file (as it's no longer needed):

```
! curl -sO https://s3.amazonaws.com/tripdata/202403-citibike-tripdata.csv.zip
! unzip -o 202403-citibike-tripdata.csv.zip "*.csv" -x "*/*" -d data/citibike/
! rm -f 202403-citibike-tripdata.csv.zip
```

Shell Commands

These shell commands are not Python code. In Jupyter, the exclamation mark (!) causes these commands to be executed by a shell rather than the Python interpreter. If you're on Windows, or if you're not comfortable running commands like this, you can download and extract the data manually:

1. Visit the Citi Bike website (*https://oreil.ly/SZc7e*).
2. Click on the link "downloadable files of Citi Bike trip data."
3. Download the ZIP file *202403-citibike-tripdata.csv.zip*.
4. Extract the ZIP file.
5. Move the CSV file to the *data/citibike* subdirectory.

Let's continue to the next step, which is to load this CSV file into a Polars DataFrame.

Read Citi Bike trips into a Polars DataFrame

Before we read any raw data into a Polars DataFrame, we always like to inspect it first. We'll count the number of lines in this CSV file using wc and print the first six lines using head:

```
! wc -l data/citibike/202403-citibike-tripdata.csv
! head -n 6 data/citibike/202403-citibike-tripdata.csv

2663296 data/citibike/202403-citibike-tripdata.csv
"ride_id","rideable_type","started_at","ended_at","start_station_name","start_s…
"62021B31AF42943E","electric_bike","2024-03-13 15:57:41.800","2024-03-13 16:07:…
"EC7BE9D296FFD072","electric_bike","2024-03-16 10:25:46.114","2024-03-16 10:30:…
"EC85C0EEC95157BB","classic_bike","2024-03-20 19:20:49.818","2024-03-20 19:28:0…
```

```
"9DDE9AF5606B4E0F","classic_bike","2024-03-13 20:31:12.599","2024-03-13 20:40:3…
"E4446F457328C5FE","electric_bike","2024-03-16 10:50:11.535","2024-03-16 10:53:…
```

It appears that we have over 2.6 million rows, where each row is one bike trip. The CSV file seems to be well formatted, with a header, and a comma as the separator.

When we first tried to read this CSV file into Polars, we found two problematic columns. The values stored in columns start_station_id and end_station_id are in fact Strings, but Polars assumes that they are numbers, because in the first few rows, they look like numbers. Specifying the types manually for these two columns solves this. Let's read the CSV file into a DataFrame called trips and print the number of rows:

```
trips = pl.read_csv(  ❶
    "data/citibike/202403-citibike-tripdata.csv",
    try_parse_dates=True,
    schema_overrides={
        "start_station_id": pl.String,
        "end_station_id": pl.String,
    },
).sort(  ❷
    "started_at"
)

trips.height
```

❶ You'll learn about reading data in Chapter 6.

❷ You'll learn about sorting rows in Chapter 11.

```
2663295
```

Here's what the DataFrame looks like. Because it's too wide to comfortably show on the page, we use print() three times to show all the columns:

```
print(trips[:, :4])
print(trips[:, 4:8])
print(trips[:, 8:])
```

```
shape: (2_663_295, 4)
```

ride_id	rideable_type	started_at	ended_at
---	---	---	---
str	str	datetime[μs]	datetime[μs]
9EC2AD5F3F8C8B57	classic_bike	2024-02-29 00:20…	2024-03-01 01:20…
C76D82D96516BDC2	classic_bike	2024-02-29 07:54…	2024-03-01 08:54…
…	…	…	…
D8B20517A4AB7D60	classic_bike	2024-03-31 23:56…	2024-03-31 23:57…
6BC5FAFEAC948FB1	electric_bike	2024-03-31 23:57…	2024-03-31 23:59…

```
shape: (2_663_295, 4)
```

start_station_na...	start_station_id	end_station_name	end_station_id
str	str	str	str
61 St & 39 Ave	6307.07	null	null
E 54 St & 1 Ave	6608.09	null	null
...	...	...	...
Division St & Bo...	5270.08	Division St & Bo...	5270.08
Montrose Ave & B...	5068.02	Humboldt St & Va...	4956.02

shape: (2_663_295, 5)

start_lat	start_lng	end_lat	end_lng	member_casual
f64	f64	f64	f64	str
40.7471	-73.9028	null	null	member
40.756265	-73.964179	null	null	member
...	...	...	...	...
40.714193	-73.996732	40.714193	-73.996732	member
40.707678	-73.940297	40.703172	-73.940636	member

Not a bad start. The DataFrame trips has a variety of columns, including time-stamps, categories, names, and coordinates. This will allow us to produce plenty of interesting analyses and data visualizations.

Read in neighborhoods from GeoJSON

New York City is a large place, with many neighborhoods spread over five boroughs: The Bronx, Brooklyn, Manhattan, Staten Island, and Queens. Our trips DataFrame lacks this information. If we were to add the neighborhood and borough where each trip starts and ends, we would be able to compare boroughs with each other or answer questions such as "What is the busiest neighborhood in Manhattan?"

To add this information, we are going to read a GeoJSON file that contains all the boroughs and neighborhoods of New York City. The raw data, which is on GitHub (*https://oreil.ly/uUcM4*), looks like this:[6]

```
! python -m json.tool data/citibike/nyc-neighborhoods.geojson
{
    "type": "FeatureCollection",
    "crs": {
        "type": "name",
        "properties": {
            "name": "urn:ogc:def:crs:OGC:1.3:CRS84"
```

---

6 The original filename is *custom-pedia-cities-nyc-Mar2018.geojson*.

```
            }
    },
    "features": [
        {
            "type": "Feature",
            "properties": {
                "neighborhood": "Allerton",
                "boroughCode": "2",
                "borough": "Bronx",
                "X.id": "http://nyc.pediacities.com/Resource/Neighborhood/Aller…"
            },
            "geometry": {
                "type": "Polygon",
                "coordinates": [
                    [
                        [
                            -73.84859700000018,
                            40.871670000000115
                        ],
                        [
                            -73.84582253683678,
                            40.870239076236174
                        ],
… with 134240 more lines
```

This deeply nested structure contains all the information we need. The areas are stored as *polygons*, which are sequences of coordinates. We transform this deeply nested structure into a rectangular form: that is, a DataFrame.

```
neighborhoods = (
    pl.read_json("data/citibike/nyc-neighborhoods.geojson")
    .select("features")
    .explode("features")  ❶
    .unnest("features")
    .unnest("properties")
    .select("neighborhood", "borough", "geometry")
    .unnest("geometry")
    .with_columns(polygon=pl.col("coordinates").list.first())
    .select("neighborhood", "borough", "polygon")
    .filter(pl.col("borough") != "Staten Island")  ❷
    .sort("neighborhood")
)

neighborhoods
```

❶ You'll learn about reshaping nested data structures in Chapter 15.

❷ Staten Island doesn't have any Citi Bike stations.

```
shape: (258, 3)
┌─────────────────┬──────────┬────────────────────────────────────────────────┐
│ neighborhood    │ borough  │ polygon                                        │
│ ---             │ ---      │ ---                                            │
│ str             │ str      │ list[list[f64]]                                │
╞═════════════════╪══════════╪════════════════════════════════════════════════╡
│ Allerton        │ Bronx    │ [[-73.848597, 40.87167], [-73.845823, 40.87023…│
│ Alley Pond Park │ Queens   │ [[-73.743333, 40.738883], [-73.743714, 40.7394…│
│ Arverne         │ Queens   │ [[-73.789535, 40.599972], [-73.789541, 40.5999…│
│ Astoria         │ Queens   │ [[-73.901603, 40.76777], [-73.902696, 40.76688…│
│ Bath Beach      │ Brooklyn │ [[-73.99381, 40.60195], [-73.99962, 40.596469]…│
│ …               │ …        │ …                                              │
│ Williamsburg    │ Brooklyn │ [[-73.957572, 40.725097], [-73.952998, 40.7222…│
│ Windsor Terrace │ Brooklyn │ [[-73.980061, 40.660753], [-73.979878, 40.6607…│
│ Woodhaven       │ Queens   │ [[-73.86233, 40.695962], [-73.856544, 40.69707…│
│ Woodlawn        │ Bronx    │ [[-73.859468, 40.900517], [-73.85926, 40.90033…│
│ Woodside        │ Queens   │ [[-73.900866, 40.757674], [-73.90014, 40.75615…│
└─────────────────┴──────────┴────────────────────────────────────────────────┘
```

We now have a clean DataFrame with 258 neighborhoods, the boroughs in which they are located, and their polygons. If a neighborhood consists of multiple separate areas (that is, multiple polygons), it will appear multiple times in this DataFrame. Before we use this `neighborhoods` DataFrame to add information to the `trips` DataFrame, we first want to visualize it so that we have some context.

Bonus: Visualizing Neighborhoods and Stations

To visualize the neighborhoods of New York City and all the Citi Bike stations, we are going to use the plotnine package (*https://plotnine.org*). plotnine expects the DataFrame in a long format—that is, one row per coordinate—so we have some wrangling to do:

```python
neighborhoods_coords = (
    neighborhoods.with_row_index("id")
    .explode("polygon")
    .with_columns(
        lon=pl.col("polygon").list.first(),
        lat=pl.col("polygon").list.last(),
    )
    .drop("polygon")
)

neighborhoods_coords
```

```
shape: (27_569, 5)
```

id	neighborhood	borough	lon	lat
u32	str	str	f64	f64
0	Allerton	Bronx	-73.848597	40.87167
0	Allerton	Bronx	-73.845823	40.870239
0	Allerton	Bronx	-73.854559	40.859954
0	Allerton	Bronx	-73.854665	40.859586
0	Allerton	Bronx	-73.856389	40.857594
…	…	…	…	…
257	Woodside	Queens	-73.910618	40.755476
257	Woodside	Queens	-73.90907	40.757565
257	Woodside	Queens	-73.907828	40.756999
257	Woodside	Queens	-73.90737	40.756988
257	Woodside	Queens	-73.900866	40.757674

To get the coordinates of the stations, we calculate, per station, the median coordinates of the start location of each bike trip:

```
stations = (
    trips.group_by(station=pl.col("start_station_name"))
    .agg(  ❶
        lon=pl.col("start_lng").median(),
        lat=pl.col("start_lat").median(),
    )
    .sort("station")
    .drop_nulls()
)
stations
```

❶ You'll learn about aggregation in Chapter 13.

```
shape: (2_143, 3)
```

station	lon	lat
str	f64	f64
1 Ave & E 110 St	-73.938203	40.792327
1 Ave & E 16 St	-73.981656	40.732219
1 Ave & E 18 St	-73.980544	40.733876
1 Ave & E 30 St	-73.975361	40.741457
1 Ave & E 38 St	-73.971822	40.746202
…	…	…
Wyckoff Ave & Stanhope St	-73.917914	40.703545
Wyckoff St & 3 Ave	-73.982586	40.682755
Wythe Ave & Metropolitan Ave	-73.963198	40.716887
Wythe Ave & N 13 St	-73.957099	40.722741
Yankee Ferry Terminal	-74.016756	40.687066

The following code snippet contains the plotnine code to produce Figure 1-3. Each dot is a bike station. The four colors indicate the boroughs. The shading of the neighborhoods is only used to make them visually more separate; it has no meaning:

```
(
    ggplot(neighborhoods_coords, aes(x="lon", y="lat", group="id"))
    + geom_polygon(aes(alpha="neighborhood", fill="borough"), color="white")
    + geom_point(stations, size=0.1)
    + scale_x_continuous(expand=(0, 0))
    + scale_y_continuous(expand=(0, 0, 0, 0.01))
    + scale_alpha_ordinal(range=(0.3, 1))
    + scale_fill_brewer(type="qual", palette=2)
    + guides(alpha=False)
    + labs(
        title="New York City neighborhoods and Citi Bike stations",
        subtitle="2,143 stations across 106 neighborhoods",
        caption="Source: https://citibikenyc.com/system-data",
        fill="Borough",
    )
    + theme_void(base_family="Guardian Sans", base_size=14)
    + theme(
        dpi=300,
        figure_size=(7, 9),
        plot_background=element_rect(fill="white", color="white"),
        plot_caption=element_text(style="italic"),
        plot_margin=0.01,
        plot_title=element_text(ha="left"),
    )
)
```

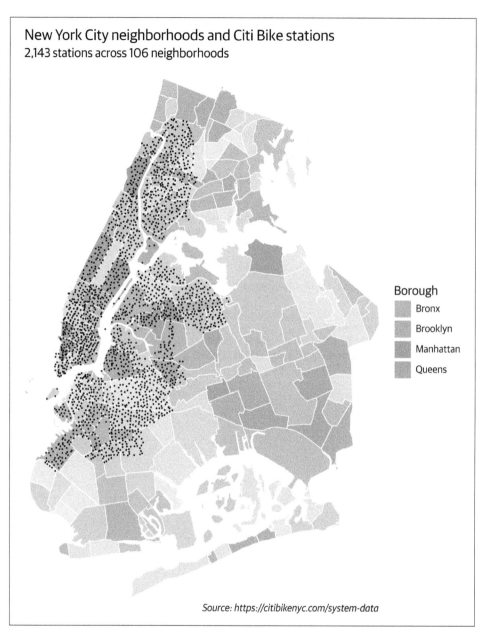

Figure 1-3. New York City neighborhoods and Citi Bike stations

Isn't New York City beautiful?

Transform

No dataset is perfect and neither is ours. That's why the second step of this ETL showcase is to *transform* the data. We'll start with the columns and subsequently clean up the rows. We will also be adding some new columns along the way.

Clean up columns

The following snippet cleans up the columns of our `trips` DataFrame in these ways:

- It gets rid of the columns `ride_id`, `start_station_id`, and `end_station_id`, because we don't need them.
- It shortens the column names so that they're easier to work with.
- It turns `bike_type` and `rider_type` into categories, which better reflects the data types of these columns.
- It adds a new column called `duration`, which is based on the start and end times of the bike trip.

```
trips = trips.select(
    bike_type=pl.col("rideable_type")
    .str.split("_")
    .list.get(0)
    .cast(pl.Categorical),  ❶
    rider_type=pl.col("member_casual").cast(pl.Categorical),
    datetime_start=pl.col("started_at"),
    datetime_end=pl.col("ended_at"),
    station_start=pl.col("start_station_name"),
    station_end=pl.col("end_station_name"),
    lon_start=pl.col("start_lng"),
    lat_start=pl.col("start_lat"),
    lon_end=pl.col("end_lng"),
    lat_end=pl.col("end_lat"),
).with_columns(  ❷
    duration=(pl.col("datetime_end") - pl.col("datetime_start"))
)

trips.columns
```

❶ You'll learn about expressions in Chapter 7.

❷ You'll learn about selecting and creating columns in Chapter 10.

```
['bike_type',
 'rider_type',
 'datetime_start',
 'datetime_end',
 'station_start',
 'station_end',
```

```
    'lon_start',
    'lat_start',
    'lon_end',
    'lat_end',
    'duration']
```

Let's continue with the rows of the `trips` DataFrame.

Clean up rows

You may have noticed that some of the rows are missing values. Because we have plenty of data anyway, it doesn't hurt to remove those rows. If you have very little data, then you may want to use a different strategy, such as imputing the missing values with, say, the average value or the most common value.

There are a few bike trips that started in February and ended in March. It'll make our analyses and visualizations cleaner if we remove those trips as well. Finally, let's also remove all bike rides that started and ended at the same bike station and had a duration of less than five minutes, as those are not actually trips:

```
trips = (
    trips.drop_nulls()
    .filter(  ❶
        (pl.col("datetime_start") >= pl.date(2024, 3, 1))
        & (pl.col("datetime_end") < pl.date(2024, 4, 1))
    )
    .filter(
        ~(
            (pl.col("station_start") == pl.col("station_end"))
            & (pl.col("duration").dt.total_seconds() < 5 * 60)
        )
    )
)

trips.height
```

❶ You'll learn about filtering rows in Chapter 11.

```
2639170
```

The DataFrame `trips` still has more than 2.6 million rows, which is plenty.

Add trip distance

The distance of a bike trip would be interesting to have because we could then correlate it with, say, the duration. We don't have the actual bike routes available to us, so the best that we can do is take the start and end coordinates and then calculate what is known as the *Haversine distance*.[7]

The Haversine distance can be calculated using the methods that Polars provides, but we would like to use an existing crate called geo. There's just one thing: this crate is created in Rust, not in Python. So we have created a custom package, specifically for this book, that turns the geo crate into a Polars plugin. This allows us to calculate the Haversine distance as if it were a Polars method.

The method `Expr.geo.haversine_distance()` expects a coordinate, meaning a longitude–latitude pair:

```
trips = trips.with_columns(
    distance=pl.concat_list("lon_start", "lat_start").geo.haversine_distance(
        pl.concat_list("lon_end", "lat_end")
    )
    / 1000  ❶
)

trips.select(
    "lon_start",
    "lon_end",
    "lat_start",
    "lat_end",
    "distance",
    "duration",
)
```

❶ The result of the geo Haversine method is reported in meters. Then we divide by one thousand to get kilometers. You'll learn more about our custom plugin in Chapter 17.

shape: (2_639_170, 6)

lon_start	lon_end	lat_start	lat_end	distance	duration
f64	f64	f64	f64	f64	duration[µs]
-73.995071	-74.007319	40.749614	40.707065	4.842569	27m 36s 805ms
-73.896576	-73.927311	40.816459	40.810893	2.659582	9m 25s 264ms
-73.988559	-73.989186	40.746424	40.742869	0.398795	3m 29s 483ms
-73.995208	-74.013219	40.749653	40.705945	5.09153	30m 56s 960ms
-73.957559	-73.979881	40.69067	40.668663	3.08728	11m 32s 483ms
…	…	…	…	…	…
-73.974552	-73.977724	40.729848	40.729387	0.272175	1m 41s 374ms
-73.971092	-73.965269	40.763505	40.763126	0.492269	3m 30s 363ms
-73.959621	-73.955151	40.808625	40.81	0.406138	1m 46s 248ms
-73.965971	-73.962644	40.712996	40.712605	0.283781	1m 43s 906ms

---

7 The Haversine distance is the shortest distance between two points on a sphere.

```
| -73.940297 | -73.940636 | 40.707678 | 40.703172 | 0.501835 | 2m 6s 109ms |
```

Keep in mind that the Haversine distance is "as the crow flies," not as the biker rides. Still, this gives us a decent approximation of the trip distance.

Add borough and neighborhood

Previously, we obtained the coordinates of the stations and the polygons of the neighborhoods. To determine in which neighborhood each station lies, we need to test whether every coordinate is in every polygon. This method is not perfect. Some stations do not match; some match more than once. This has to do with the borders of the neighborhood.

Again, we can use our custom plugin for this, because it also has a method called Expr.geo.point_in_polygon():

```
stations = (
    stations.with_columns(point=pl.concat_list("lon", "lat"))
    .join(neighborhoods, how="cross")
    .with_columns(
        in_neighborhood=pl.col("point").geo.point_in_polygon(pl.col("polygon"))
    )
    .filter(pl.col("in_neighborhood"))
    .unique("station")
    .select(
        "station",
        "borough",
        "neighborhood",
    )
)

stations

shape: (2_133, 3)
```

station	borough	neighborhood
str	str	str
1 Ave & E 110 St	Manhattan	East Harlem
1 Ave & E 16 St	Manhattan	Stuyvesant Town
1 Ave & E 18 St	Manhattan	Stuyvesant Town
1 Ave & E 30 St	Manhattan	Kips Bay
1 Ave & E 38 St	Manhattan	Murray Hill
…	…	…
Wyckoff Ave & Stanhope St	Brooklyn	Bushwick
Wyckoff St & 3 Ave	Brooklyn	Gowanus
Wythe Ave & Metropolitan Ave	Brooklyn	Williamsburg
Wythe Ave & N 13 St	Brooklyn	Williamsburg
Yankee Ferry Terminal	Manhattan	Governors Island

We can add this information to the `trips` DataFrame by joining on the `station` column twice: once with `station_start` and once with `station_end`:

```
trips = (
    trips.join(
        stations.select(pl.all().name.suffix("_start")), on="station_start"
    )
    .join(stations.select(pl.all().name.suffix("_end")), on="station_end")
    .select(
        "bike_type",
        "rider_type",
        "datetime_start",
        "datetime_end",
        "duration",
        "station_start",
        "station_end",
        "neighborhood_start",
        "neighborhood_end",
        "borough_start",
        "borough_end",
        "lat_start",
        "lon_start",
        "lat_end",
        "lon_end",
        "distance",
    )
)
```

Here's what the final DataFrame looks like:

```
print(trips[:, :4])
print(trips[:, 4:7])
print(trips[:, 7:11])
print(trips[:, 11:])
```

shape: (2_638_971, 4)

bike_type	rider_type	datetime_start	datetime_end
cat	cat	datetime[μs]	datetime[μs]
electric	member	2024-03-01 00:00:02.490	2024-03-01 00:27:39.295
electric	member	2024-03-01 00:00:04.120	2024-03-01 00:09:29.384
…	…	…	…
electric	member	2024-03-31 23:55:41.173	2024-03-31 23:57:25.079
electric	member	2024-03-31 23:57:16.025	2024-03-31 23:59:22.134

shape: (2_638_971, 3)

duration	station_start	station_end
duration[μs]	str	str

27m 36s 805ms	W 30 St & 8 Ave	Maiden Ln & Pearl St
9m 25s 264ms	Longwood Ave & Southern Blvd	Lincoln Ave & E 138 St
…	…	…
1m 43s 906ms	S 4 St & Wythe Ave	S 3 St & Bedford Ave
2m 6s 109ms	Montrose Ave & Bushwick Ave	Humboldt St & Varet St

shape: (2_638_971, 4)

neighborhood_start	neighborhood_end	borough_start	borough_end
str	str	str	str
Chelsea	Financial District	Manhattan	Manhattan
Longwood	Mott Haven	Bronx	Bronx
…	…	…	…
Williamsburg	Williamsburg	Brooklyn	Brooklyn
Williamsburg	Williamsburg	Brooklyn	Brooklyn

shape: (2_638_971, 5)

lat_start	lon_start	lat_end	lon_end	distance
f64	f64	f64	f64	f64
40.749614	-73.995071	40.707065	-74.007319	4.842569
40.816459	-73.896576	40.810893	-73.927311	2.659582
…	…	…	…	…
40.712996	-73.965971	40.712605	-73.962644	0.283781
40.707678	-73.940297	40.703172	-73.940636	0.501835

Before we continue with the third and final step of the ETL showcase, we would like to share one more data visualization.

Bonus: Visualizing Daily Trips per Borough

Now that we have this information, we can analyze and visualize all sorts of interesting things, such as the number of trips per day per borough:

```
trips_per_hour = trips.group_by_dynamic(
    "datetime_start", group_by="borough_start", every="1d"
).agg(num_trips=pl.len())

trips_per_hour
```

shape: (124, 3)

borough_start	datetime_start	num_trips
str	datetime[µs]	u32
Manhattan	2024-03-01 00:00:00	56434

```
| Manhattan    | 2024-03-02 00:00:00 | 17450 |
| Manhattan    | 2024-03-03 00:00:00 | 69195 |
| Manhattan    | 2024-03-04 00:00:00 | 63734 |
| Manhattan    | 2024-03-05 00:00:00 | 33309 |
| ...          | ...                 | ...   |
| Queens       | 2024-03-27 00:00:00 | 6232  |
| Queens       | 2024-03-28 00:00:00 | 3770  |
| Queens       | 2024-03-29 00:00:00 | 6637  |
| Queens       | 2024-03-30 00:00:00 | 6583  |
| Queens       | 2024-03-31 00:00:00 | 6237  |
```

Again, we will be using plotnine to create the visualization (see Figure 1-4):

```python
from mizani.labels import label_comma

(
    ggplot(
        trips_per_hour,
        aes(x="datetime_start", y="num_trips", fill="borough_start"),
    )
    + geom_area()
    + scale_fill_brewer(type="qual", palette=2)
    + scale_x_datetime(date_labels="%-d", date_breaks="1 day", expand=(0, 0))
    + scale_y_continuous(labels=label_comma(), expand=(0, 0))
    + labs(
        x="March 2024",
        fill="Borough",
        y="Trips per day",
        title="Citi Bike trips per day in March 2024",
        subtitle="On March 23, nearly 10 cm of rain fell in NYC",
    )
    + theme_tufte(base_family="Guardian Sans", base_size=14)
    + theme(
        axis_ticks_major=element_line(color="white"),
        figure_size=(8, 5),
        legend_position="top",
        plot_background=element_rect(fill="white", color="white"),
        plot_caption=element_text(style="italic"),
        plot_title=element_text(ha="left"),
    )
)
```

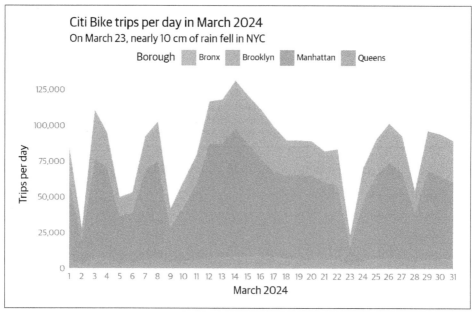

Figure 1-4. Citi Bike trips per day in March 2024

There will be many more data visualizations made with many other packages in Chapter 16.

Load

The third and final step of this ETL showcase is to load the data. In other words, we are going to write the data back to disk.

Write partitions

Instead of writing back a CSV file, we will use the Parquet file format. Parquet provides several advantages over CSV:

- It includes the data type for each column, known as the *schema*.
- It uses columnar storage instead of row-based, enabling faster, optimized reads.
- Data is organized into chunks with embedded statistics, allowing for efficient skipping of unnecessary data.
- It applies compression, reducing the overall storage footprint.

Instead of writing a single Parquet file, we are going to write one file for each day. This way, each file is small enough to be hosted on GitHub, which is necessary to share the data easily with you.

Each filename starts with the String `trips`, followed by a dash (-) and the date:

```
trips_parts = (
    trips.sort("datetime_start")
    .with_columns(date=pl.col("datetime_start").dt.date().cast(pl.String))
    .partition_by(["date"], as_dict=True, include_key=False)
)

for key, df in trips_parts.items():
    df.write_parquet(f"data/citibike/trips-{key[0]}.parquet")
```

Verify

Let's verify that the previous code snippet produced 31 Parquet files using `ls`:

```
! ls -1 data/citibike/*.parquet
```

```
data/citibike/trips-2024-03-01.parquet
data/citibike/trips-2024-03-02.parquet
data/citibike/trips-2024-03-03.parquet
data/citibike/trips-2024-03-04.parquet
data/citibike/trips-2024-03-05.parquet
… with 26 more lines
```

Using *globbing*,[8] we can easily read all the Parquet files into a single DataFrame:

```
pl.read_parquet("data/citibike/*.parquet").height
```

```
2638971
```

Excellent. We'll use this data later in Chapter 16 to create many exciting data visualizations. Now that data has been *loaded*, we could conclude this ETL showcase. However, there is just one more bonus that we would like to share, which enables you to make the entire ETL showcase faster.

Bonus: Becoming Faster by Being Lazy

Up till now, we have been using Polars' so-called *eager* API. Eager in this context means that commands are executed straightaway. Polars is already fast relative to its competitors. If we use Polars' *lazy* API, our calculations can sometimes be even faster.

With the lazy API, we're not operating directly on a DataFrame. Instead, we're building a recipe of instructions. When we are ready, we tell Polars to execute it. Before Polars actually does so, it will first optimize this recipe.

As for our showcase, being completely lazy is slightly less efficient than being eager. That's because certain parts would need to be computed twice, because Polars doesn't know how to cache the results. The following code snippet fixes this using lazy

---

8 *Globbing* is a pattern-matching technique used to select filenames based on wildcard characters like * and ?.

execution in some parts, then turning them into DataFrames so that these results are properly cached. It's all of the preceding code, with just a few minor changes:

```
trips = (
    pl.scan_csv(
        "data/citibike/202403-citibike-tripdata.csv",  ❶
        try_parse_dates=True,
        schema_overrides={
            "start_station_id": pl.String,
            "end_station_id": pl.String,
        },
    )
    .select(
        bike_type=pl.col("rideable_type").str.split("_").list.get(0),
        rider_type=pl.col("member_casual"),
        datetime_start=pl.col("started_at"),
        datetime_end=pl.col("ended_at"),
        station_start=pl.col("start_station_name"),
        station_end=pl.col("end_station_name"),
        lon_start=pl.col("start_lng"),
        lat_start=pl.col("start_lat"),
        lon_end=pl.col("end_lng"),
        lat_end=pl.col("end_lat"),
    )
    .with_columns(duration=(pl.col("datetime_end") - pl.col("datetime_start")))
    .drop_nulls()
    .filter(
        ~(
            (pl.col("station_start") == pl.col("station_end"))
            & (pl.col("duration").dt.total_seconds() < 5 * 60)
        )
    )
    .with_columns(
        distance=pl.concat_list(
            "lon_start", "lat_start"
        ).geo.haversine_distance(pl.concat_list("lon_end", "lat_end"))
        / 1000
    )
).collect()  ❷

neighborhoods = (
    pl.read_json("data/citibike/nyc-neighborhoods.geojson")
    .lazy()  ❸
    .select("features")
    .explode("features")
    .unnest("features")
    .unnest("properties")
    .select("neighborhood", "borough", "geometry")
    .unnest("geometry")
    .with_columns(polygon=pl.col("coordinates").list.first())
    .select("neighborhood", "borough", "polygon")
    .sort("neighborhood")
```

```
        .filter(pl.col("borough") != "Staten Island")
)

stations = (
    trips.lazy()
    .group_by(station=pl.col("station_start"))
    .agg(
        lat=pl.col("lat_start").median(),
        lon=pl.col("lon_start").median(),
    )
    .with_columns(point=pl.concat_list("lon", "lat"))
    .drop_nulls()
    .join(neighborhoods, how="cross")
    .with_columns(
        in_neighborhood=pl.col("point").geo.point_in_polygon(pl.col("polygon"))
    )
    .filter(pl.col("in_neighborhood"))
    .unique("station")
    .select(
        pl.col("station"),
        pl.col("borough"),
        pl.col("neighborhood"),
    )
).collect()

trips = (
    trips.join(
        stations.select(pl.all().name.suffix("_start")), on="station_start"
    )
    .join(stations.select(pl.all().name.suffix("_end")), on="station_end")
    .select(
        "bike_type",
        "rider_type",
        "datetime_start",
        "datetime_end",
        "duration",
        "station_start",
        "station_end",
        "neighborhood_start",
        "neighborhood_end",
        "borough_start",
        "borough_end",
        "lat_start",
        "lon_start",
        "lat_end",
        "lon_end",
        "distance",
    )
)

trips.height
```

❶ The function `pl.scan_csv()` returns a LazyFrame, making all the subsequent methods lazy.

❷ The method `lf.collect()` turns a LazyFrame into a DataFrame.

❸ The method `df.lazy()` turns a DataFrame into a LazyFrame.

2639179

For a single month of bike trips, Polars doesn't speed up much, because the point-in-polygon test is dominating the timing. However, when we take a year's worth of bike trips, the lazy approach is 33% faster than the eager approach. That's a substantial speedup for just a couple of code changes.

You'll learn more about eager and lazy APIs in Chapter 5.

Takeaways

In this chapter you've learned that:

- Polars is a blazingly fast DataFrame package with a focus on performance and ease of use through an intuitive API.
- Polars is written in Rust and has bindings for Python, R, JavaScript, and Julia.
- The Python version is the most mature and most used version of Polars.
- Polars is a very popular Python package, as measured by the number of GitHub stars.
- Polars is, in many cases, faster than its competitors.
- When using the lazy API, Polars can be even faster.
- Polars is great for transforming, analyzing, and visualizing data.

In the next chapter, we will show how to install Polars and how to get started with it. Additionally, we talk about how you can follow along with the code examples in this book.

## CHAPTER 2

Getting Started

To explore all the exciting features Polars has to offer, you'll need to get it up and running first.

In this chapter, you'll:

- Set up your working environment
- Install all the necessary dependencies for following along with the examples in this book into a virtual environment using uv
- Learn how to start and use JupyterLab, the environment in which you'll be running the code examples in this book
- Learn how to install Polars and its optional dependencies for your own projects
- Learn how to configure Polars to your liking
- See how to compile Polars from source, and what to do in edge cases where you're working with very large datasets or older processors

It's recommended that you follow along with the code examples in this book. Learning new packages tends to stick much better when you're playing around with what you've learned, as opposed to just reading about the possibilities.

Setting Up Your Environment

To follow along in this book, you will need to set up an environment. We will first download the project files. After that we will install uv, the tool required to get up and running. uv is an extremely fast Python package and project manager written in Rust. Using uv you'll install the project dependencies needed to follow along with the examples in the book.

Downloading the Project

It's possible to download the project files in two ways. The first way is by installing Git. The second is by downloading the project files as a ZIP file.

- Installing using Git:

  To easily stay in sync with any changes that may come, we recommend using Git. You can install Git as instructed on this page (*https://oreil.ly/FS0GY*).

  When up and running, you can run:

  ```
  $ git clone https://github.com/jeroenjanssens/python-polars-
  the-definitive-guide
  ```

- Installing through a ZIP file:

  On the GitHub repository, you can download all files as a ZIP file by clicking the green Code button in the middle of the screen.

  You'll see a Download ZIP button at the bottom of the popup that you can use to download the files, as shown in Figure 2-1.

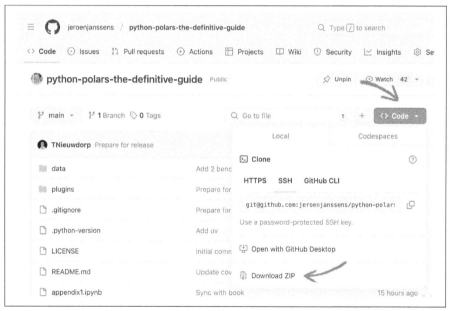

Figure 2-1. The Download ZIP button on GitHub

After downloading the ZIP file, you can extract it to a directory of your choice.

Now that the project files are on your system, we can set up our environment. For this we use uv.

Installing uv

You can find the up-to-date information on how to install uv on this page (*https://oreil.ly/48Hwl*).

The recommended way is to use the standalone installer, which can be installed as follows:

- For Linux and macOS, you can install uv by running the following command in your favorite command-line interface:

  ```
  $ curl -LsSf https://astral.sh/uv/install.sh | sh
  ```

- If you use Windows, you can install uv by running the following command in PowerShell:

  ```
  PS C:\Users\You> powershell -ExecutionPolicy ByPass -c
  "irm https://astral.sh/uv/install.ps1 | iex"
  ```

Dollars, Exclamation Marks, and Percentages

Some code snippets start with a dollar sign ($) or PS >. This is known as the prompt and is not part of the command. The prompt is there to indicate that the command should be run in a Linux or macOS terminal (in case of $) or Windows PowerShell (in case of PS >). Do *not* include the prompt itself when running the command.

On the other hand, when you see an exclamation mark (!) or a percentage sign (%) in front of a command, it means that the command is meant to be run in Jupyter Notebook. These characters *should* be included.

Installing the Project

With uv installed, we can get our project up and running in no time using the following command:

```
$ uv sync
```

Working with the Virtual Environment

uv creates a *virtual environment* for you and installs all the dependencies that are needed to run the code examples in this book. A virtual environment is a self-contained directory that contains a Python installation for a particular version of Python, plus a number of additional packages. This way you can work on multiple projects with different dependencies without them interfering with each other. There are two ways to work with the virtual environment:

- The recommended way is to prefix your commands with uv run, for example, uv run jupyter lab to launch Jupyter using your virtual environment. This works on all operating systems.
- The other way is to activate the virtual environment, as shown here, and then run all subsequent commands normally.
  — You can activate the virtual environment in macOS and Linux by running:

    ```
    $ source .venv/bin/activate
    ```

  — And you can activate it in Windows by running:

    ```
    PS > .venv\Scripts\activate
    ```

Any time you come back to work on this project, you'll need to run the preceding commands to get your environment up and running again.

Verifying Your Installation

Throughout the book we use Polars version 1.20.0. Run the following code in a new notebook to check which version of Polars you're using:

```
import polars as pl

pl.show_versions()

--------Version info---------
Polars:                1.20.0
Index type:            UInt32
Platform:              macOS-14.5-arm64-arm-64bit
Python:                3.12.6 (main, Sep  9 2024, 21:36:32) [Clang 18.1.8 ]
LTS CPU:               False

----Optional dependencies----
Azure CLI              2.67.0
adbc_driver_manager    1.2.0
altair                 5.4.1
azure.identity         <not installed>
boto3                  <not installed>
cloudpickle            3.1.0
connectorx             0.4.0
deltalake              0.21.0
fastexcel              0.12.0
fsspec                 2024.10.0
gevent                 24.11.1
google.auth            <not installed>
great_tables           0.14.0
matplotlib             3.9.2
nest_asyncio           1.6.0
numpy                  2.1.3
```

```
openpyxl        3.1.5
pandas          2.2.3
pyarrow         18.0.0
pydantic        2.9.2
pyiceberg       0.7.1
sqlalchemy      2.0.36
torch           <not installed>
xlsx2csv        0.8.3
xlsxwriter      3.2.0
```

Crash Course in JupyterLab

To run the code examples in this book you'll need to use Jupyter. Jupyter is a web-based interactive development environment of notebooks, code, and data. To start working with Polars, you can open any of the chapters' notebooks in the menu on the left, or you can create your own notebook by clicking the Python 3 Notebook button in the launcher.

To start Jupyter, you can run the following command in the terminal:

```
$ uv run jupyter lab
```

This opens a window in the browser with the Jupyter interface. If this does not pop up, you need to copy the URL that will be printed in the terminal. It will look something like *http://127.0.0.1:8888/lab?token=....* Click it, or copy and paste it into a browser window to connect to the Jupyter server inside the container. This will open up JupyterLab in your browser, in which you can get to work.

To work in a Jupyter notebook, you'll need to know some basics. Jupyter content is loaded in cells. These cells can be marked as different programming languages, but also as Markdown. In this book you will mostly work with Python code cells.

To navigate and edit these cells, Jupyter knows two modes: command mode and edit mode.

Command mode
> The default mode when opening a notebook or while pressing Esc when in a cell. When it's active, the selected cell has a blue border and no cursor inside of it. Command mode is used to edit the notebook as a whole, or add, delete, or edit cell types in the notebook.

Edit mode
> Can be activated by pressing Enter when on a selected cell. In this mode, the selected cell gets a green border. Edit mode is used to write in cells.

Keyboard Shortcuts

There are a few important shortcuts you should know. Table 2-1 lists shortcuts that can be run in any mode, Table 2-2 lists shortcuts that can be run in command mode, and Table 2-3 lists shortcuts that can be run in edit mode.

Any mode

The shortcuts in Table 2-1 can always be run, regardless of what mode you're in.

Table 2-1. Shortcuts usable in any mode

Shortcut key	Effect
Shift + Enter	Run the selected cell, and select the cell below.
Ctrl + Enter	Run the selected cell, and don't move the selection.
Alt + Enter	Run the selected cell, and insert a new cell below.
Ctrl + S	Save the notebook.

Command mode

The shortcuts in Table 2-2 can be run when you're in command mode.

Table 2-2. Shortcuts usable in command mode

Shortcut key	Action
Enter	Switch to Edit Mode.
Up / K	Select the cell above.
Down / J	Select the cell below.
A	Insert a new cell above the current cell.
B	Insert a new cell below the current cell.
D, D (press the key twice)	Delete the selected cell.
Z	Undo cell deletion.
M	Change the cell type to Markdown.
Y	Change the cell type to Code.

Edit mode

The shortcuts in Table 2-3 can be run when you're in edit mode.

Table 2-3. Shortcuts usable in edit mode

Shortcut key	Action
Esc	Switch to command mode.
Ctrl + Shift + -	Split the current cell at cursor.

Keep these shortcuts handy, and in no time you'll fly across the screen in any Jupyter notebook.

Additionally, Jupyter has a few special symbols that can be used in code cells. An exclamation mark (!) before a command tells the Jupyter kernel to run the command following it in a bash session, instead of interpreting it as Python. For example, you can list the contents of the current directory by using the exclamation mark:

```
! ls
```

Another special symbol that can be used is the percent sign (%). The percent sign is a special feature of the IPython kernel called a *magic*. Magics are built-in commands designed to solve various common problems. These are not part of the Python language, but they're features of the IPython shell. Magics come in two kinds:

Line magics
> These are preceded by a single percent sign (%) and work a lot like shell commands. For example, you use `%cat` to display the contents of a file.

Cell magics
> These are preceded by two percent signs (%%). Examples are `%%time`, which times how long the code in that cell takes to run, and `%%bash`, which we'll use later to execute multiple bash commands in one go.

To see all other commands the IPython shell has to offer, you can run `%lsmagic`.

Jupyter Notebook Versus JupyterLab

JupyterLab is the latest web-based interactive development environment for notebooks, code, and data. Originally, Jupyter started as just notebook files, but it has since created a layer on top of that called JupyterLab. It allows you to work with documents and activities such as Jupyter notebooks, text editors, terminals, and custom components from a single browser-based interface. In this book we'll use JupyterLab to run the code examples.

Installing Polars on Other Projects

Although we've already set up our environment, it's still good to know the general way of installing Polars for your own projects. The latest information on how to install Polars can always be found on the GitHub page (*https://oreil.ly/pmSuC*) and the User Guide (*https://oreil.ly/fnG2A*). The following section is based on those instructions at the time of writing.

Polars works with optional dependencies for different use cases. Polars supports a lot of optional dependencies. These optional dependencies are organized into groups, which we'll discuss.

All Optional Dependencies

All optional dependencies can be installed together with Polars by using the following bracket notation. To install the latest Polars version with all of its dependencies, you can run the following command in a terminal:

```
$ uv pip install 'polars[all]'
```

Lots of uv

Throughout this book, you'll see us use the command-line tool uv. We currently find it the fastest and most ergonomic tool to manage Python environments. If you want, you can still use `pip` or `conda` instead. For example, to install all Polars dependencies using `pip`, run:

```
$ pip install 'polars[all]'
```

And to install using conda, run:

```
$ conda install -c conda-forge polars
```

Optional Dependencies for Interoperability

To work with other DataFrame packages, the dependencies in Table 2-4 can be installed with Polars.

Table 2-4. Optional Polars dependencies for interoperability with other DataFrame packages

Tag	Description
pandas	Convert data to and from pandas DataFrames/Series.
numpy	Convert data to and from NumPy arrays.
pyarrow	Convert data to and from PyArrow tables/arrays.
pydantic	Convert data from Pydantic models to Polars.

Optional Dependencies for Working with Spreadsheets

The dependencies in Table 2-5 allow for working with Excel or other spreadsheet formats. You can install them all with the excel tag.

Table 2-5. Optional Polars dependencies for working with spreadsheet files

Tag	Description
excel	Install *all* supported Excel engines.
calamine	Read from Excel files with the calamine engine.
openpyxl	Read from Excel files with the openpyxl engine.
xlsx2csv	Read from Excel files with the xlsx2csv engine.
xlsxwriter	Write to Excel files with the XlsxWriter engine.

Optional Dependencies for Working with Databases

In Table 2-6 you can find the dependencies that allow you to seamlessly connect with databases and load your data from there. You can install them all with the `database` tag.

Table 2-6. Optional Polars dependencies for connecting with databases

Tag	Description
database	Install all supported database engines.
adbc	Read from and write to databases with the Arrow Database Connectivity (ADBC) engine.
connectorx	Read from databases with the ConnectorX engine.
sqlalchemy	Write to databases with the SQLAlchemy engine.

Optional Dependencies for Working with Remote Filesystems

If you want to connect to a remote filesystem, Polars allows you to do so by using the `fsspec` package, shown in Table 2-7.

Table 2-7. Optional Polars dependency for connecting with cloud platforms

Tag	Description
fsspec	Read from and write to remote filesystems.

Optional Dependencies for Other I/O Formats

In a world with more I/O formats than you thought existed, Polars uses some dependencies to read from those formats shown in Table 2-8.

Table 2-8. Optional Polars dependencies for working with even more I/O

Tag	Description
deltalake	Read from and write to Delta tables.
iceberg	Read from Apache Iceberg tables.

Optional Dependencies for Extra Functionality

Besides dependencies for loading data from different sources, Polars also sports a set of optional dependencies for functionalities that aren't standard. These can be found in Table 2-9.

Table 2-9. Optional Polars dependencies for additional functionality

Tag	Description
async	Collect LazyFrames asynchronously.
cloudpickle	Extended pickle functionality to serialize user-defined functions.
graph	Visualize LazyFrames as a graph.
plot	Plot DataFrames through the plot namespace.
style	Style DataFrames through the style namespace.
timezone	Time zone support.[a]

[a] Time zone support is only needed if you use Python < 3.9 on Windows.

Installing Optional Dependencies

If you want to install a subset of the dependencies, you can install it in the following way:

```
$ uv pip install 'polars[pandas,numpy]'
```

If you only want to install the base package, the best way to install the latest version of Polars is as follows:

```
$ uv pip install polars
```

Configuring Polars

Generally, Polars works out of the box with sensible defaults. This makes using the configuration settings a more advanced topic. However it can be useful to know how to configure Polars to your liking.

Polars provides a number of configuration settings. These options allow you to enable alpha features, change the formatting of printed tables, set logging levels, and set the streaming chunk size. In the polars.Config class you can find the following settings and some additional ones that we won't cover. A complete overview can be found in the online Polars documentation (*https://oreil.ly/CI7Rq*). Table 2-10 is an excerpt from that documentation showing the most important configuration settings.

Table 2-10. A few notable Polars configuration settings

Method	Description
`pl.Config.set_decimal_separator(…)`	Set the decimal separator character.
`pl.Config.set_float_precision(…)`	Control the number of decimal places displayed for floating-point values.
`pl.Config.set_fmt_str_lengths(…)`	Set the number of characters used to display String values.
`pl.Config.set_tbl_cols(…)`	Set the number of columns that are visible when displaying tables.
`pl.Config.set_tbl_formatting(…)`	Set the table formatting style.
`pl.Config.set_tbl_rows(…)`	Set the max number of rows used to draw the table (both DataFrame and Series).
`pl.Config.set_tbl_width_chars(…)`	Set the maximum width of a table in characters.
`pl.Config.set_thousands_separator(…)`	Set the thousands grouping separator character.
`pl.Config.set_verbose(…)`	Enable additional verbose/debug logging.

These config options can be changed, saved, and loaded as a JSON String or file using the `pl.Config.load()`, `pl.Config.load_from_file()`, `pl.Config.save()`, and `pl.Config.save_to_file()` functions. To see the current state, you can call `pl.Config.state()`. To restore all settings back to the defaults, you can call `pl.Config.restore_defaults()`.

Temporary Configuration Using a Context Manager

To run a specific scope of code with a different configuration, you can use a *context manager*. A context manager is a construct in Python that allows for precise creation and removal of resources. The context for which resources are defined is indicated by calling the context manager using the `with` keyword, and indenting the scope of code that should be affected by it. In Polars' case, only the code within the scope of the context manager will be executed with the given configuration, after which it returns to the previous settings:

```
with pl.Config() as cfg:
    cfg.set_verbose(True)
    # Polars operation for which you want to see the verbose logging

# Code outside of the scope is not affected
```

A more concise approach is to pass the options directly as arguments to the `Config()` constructor. If you use this approach, you can omit the `set_` part of the option:

```
with pl.Config(verbose=True):
    # Polars operation you want to see the verbose logging of
    pass
```

To showcase some of the formatting configuration settings, you're going to generate your first DataFrame. A DataFrame is a two-dimensional data structure representing data as a table with rows and columns. This is one of the main data structures that is used in Polars. Later on in this book, we'll introduce you to all structures in more depth.

In the following code, we've made a short function that is able to generate a random String with a length that can be set. After that we create a dictionary that has the keys column_1 to column_20 and 5 rows of randomly generated Strings with a length of 50 characters:

```
import random
import string


def generate_random_string(length: int) -> str:
    return "".join(random.choice(string.ascii_letters) for i in range(length))


data = {}
for i in range(1, 11):
    data[f"column_{i}"] = [generate_random_string(50) for _ in range(5)]  ❶

df = pl.DataFrame(data)
```

❶ We use an *f-string* here to dynamically create column names. F-strings are the preferred way of weaving variables into a String and have been available since Python version 3.6.

Let's see what this DataFrame looks like:

```
df

shape: (5, 10)
┌────────────┬────────────┬────────────┬─────┬────────────┬────────────┬────────────┐
│ column_1   │ column_2   │ column_3   │ ... │ column_8   │ column_9   │ column_10  │
│ ---        │ ---        │ ---        │     │ ---        │ ---        │ ---        │
│ str        │ str        │ str        │     │ str        │ str        │ str        │
╞════════════╪════════════╪════════════╪═════╪════════════╪════════════╪════════════╡
│ NITxKLUkXv │ vrLgRRjGXL │ ErZIZfRrEq │ ... │ beymgYVfd  │ bIghJrUqO  │ HGdFNGSPa  │
│ yOYxtzSnWQ │ QPcPJFsbjj │ jUgWnjTSkj │     │ LsnHFrZmS  │ JqRwQUErd  │ BmfvCdhzj  │
│ ...        │ ...        │ ...        │     │ Vg...      │ Zq...      │ vl...      │
│ MqZmJeOHNK │ ubSBwYOgYk │ HQdUpgsJus │ ... │ eCkqtkOlh  │ WAXfTTOBr  │ vMRyUWIKs  │
│ XceAPNdRbO │ fTatOQmkRm │ uscqAuvSfP │     │ sGftkqIII  │ PsfVWUnPQ  │ NxGcuadnN  │
│ ...        │ ...        │ ...        │     │ ox...      │ Fu...      │ Iq...      │
│ HlXQdVFTVL │ ybaZRpdIJh │ VtnYHFRNNA │ ... │ LPZvTIIwV  │ SkjhgiCfk  │ WFNCaqjtg  │
│ DbZHFIWPUw │ PzrHJsjSaA │ KCTLizyVyl │     │ UqtjLJOoU  │ eDxeEcShL  │ aEadCeEDR  │
│ ...        │ ...        │ ...        │     │ jW...      │ Rg...      │ Aw...      │
│ dODwyenwQR │ BmfJOHYZkA │ JbXtfyUyNG │ ... │ NOtdYhuJy  │ dbjtoFjvZ  │ yQFKPBjQV  │
│ PMqTnmiEzN │ oMfoGlBbBH │ DXbgdKpXjo │     │ yTiStIGcI  │ NZlgFFPGW  │ vjgyHvJrC  │
│ ...        │ ...        │ ...        │     │ jZ...      │ EW...      │ jA...      │
└────────────┴────────────┴────────────┴─────┴────────────┴────────────┴────────────┘
```

```
| IuXzwotCLy | cZzaPcRNBU | vTlcINzgBB | … | kLtrJblaW | ZxIcqHlie | WpcBNWzeo |
| OyjNrWVpyT | DfuMHNCJGn | zoCWOeoaTT |   | xtcSpyOnC | MgqgEqCXh | OXJFltrfa |
| …          | …          | …          |   | ow…       | DU…       | uf…       |
```

Unfortunately, the standard DataFrame output doesn't fit in this book. Say you want to make it fit, but you still want to see as many columns as possible by shrinking the text that is displayed. In that case you can set the amount of columns shown to −1 (to print all of them) and lower the String length that is displayed to 4.

```python
with pl.Config(tbl_cols=-1, fmt_str_lengths=4):
    print(df)
```

shape: (5, 10)

```
| col  | colu… | colu… | colu… | colu… | colu… | colu… | colu… | colu… | colu… |
| u…   | ---   | ---   | ---   | ---   | ---   | ---   | ---   | ---   | ---   |
| ---  | str   | str   | str   | str   | str   | str   | str   | str   | str   |
| str  |       |       |       |       |       |       |       |       |       |
|======|=======|=======|=======|=======|=======|=======|=======|=======|=======|
| NIT  | vrLg… | ErZI… | aXoG… | zQXd… | BqAF… | PrRN… | beym… | bIgh… | HGdF… |
| X…   |       |       |       |       |       |       |       |       |       |
| MqZ  | ubSB… | HQdU… | jvRg… | zcDr… | Pees… | Zqsj… | eCkq… | WAXf… | vMRy… |
| m…   |       |       |       |       |       |       |       |       |       |
| HlX  | ybaZ… | VtnY… | JFHN… | EXzX… | aBdy… | QkOA… | LPZv… | Skjh… | WFNC… |
| Q…   |       |       |       |       |       |       |       |       |       |
| dOD  | BmfJ… | JbXt… | rHAq… | pwJO… | oRCW… | OgCG… | NOtd… | dbjt… | yQFK… |
| w…   |       |       |       |       |       |       |       |       |       |
| IuX  | cZza… | vTlc… | JNjW… | OEuZ… | AXWe… | eQTy… | kLtr… | ZxIc… | WpcB… |
| z…   |       |       |       |       |       |       |       |       |       |
```

Compact, yet it shows all of the columns. Perfect.

It's All About Context

Context managers contain two key methods under the hood. They consist of an __enter__ and __exit__ that are respectively called before and after running the code within the indicated context. A small example would be:

```
class YourContextManager:
    def __enter__(self):
        print("Entering context")

    def __exit__(self, type, value, traceback):
        print("Exiting context")


with YourContextManager():
    print("Your code")
Entering context
Your code
Exiting context
```

One of the popular uses of a context manager is to read from files, which can be done like this:

```
with open("data/fruit.csv", "r") as file:
    print(file.readline())
```

Local Configuration Using a Decorator

If you want to change configuration settings during a specific function call, you can decorate that function with the pl.Config() decorator. Just as in the context manager, you can omit the set_ part of the option.

```
@pl.Config(ascii_tables=True)
def write_ascii_frame_to_stdout(df: pl.DataFrame) -> None:
    print(str(df))


@pl.Config(verbose=True)
def function_that_im_debugging(df: pl.DataFrame) -> None:
    # Polars operation for which you want to see the verbose logging
    pass
```

Compiling Polars from Scratch

Compiling Polars from source has several advantages. Although unlikely in the case of Polars, because there are frequent releases, compiling from source allows access to the latest changes right away. Compiling from source allows you to make changes to the source code, recompile it yourself, and make use of your own custom functionality. (If it's a useful addition for everyone, be sure to contribute it to the project.) If you're working on a nonstandard architecture, compiling the code yourself is sometimes even required, because a precompiled version may not be available. And if you really know what you're doing, it's possible to tweak compiler optimizations when compiling your own code, potentially resulting in more efficient or faster software for your use case.

The steps required to compile Polars from source are as follows:

1. Install the Rust compiler by following the instructions on the download page (*https://oreil.ly/n7jMz*).

2. Install maturin, a zero-configuration package that helps build and publish Rust crates with Python bindings. You can install it from the Unix command line by running:

   ```
   $ uv pip install maturin
   ```

   It's important that you install it into the virtual environment of the project you're working on.

3. Compile the binary. There are two ways of compiling the binary:

   - If you're prioritizing runtime performance over build time length (for example, building the package once and running it with maximum performance):

     ```
     $ maturin develop --release -m py-polars/Cargo.toml --
       -C target-cpu=native
     ```

   - If you're prioritizing faster build times over fast performance (for example, in the case of developing and testing changes):

     ```
     $ maturin develop --release -m py-polars/Cargo.toml --
       -C codegen-units=16 -C lto=thin -C target-cpu=native
     ```

Crates, Packages, and Module Names

The Rust *crate* that implements the Python bindings is called py-polars, to distinguish itself from the wrapped Rust crate Polars. However, because both the Python *package* and the Python *module* are named polars, you can conveniently run uv pip install polars and import polars.

Edge Case: Very Large Datasets

If you'll be working with very large datasets that exceed 4.2 billion rows, you will need to install Polars in a different way. Internally, Polars uses a 32-bit integer representation to keep track of the data. If the dataset grows larger than that, Polars has to be compiled with a bigidx feature flag so the internal representation can reflect that. Additionally, it can be installed using uv pip install polars-u64-idx. This might cause a loss of performance if you don't actually need support for such large datasets.

Edge Case: Processors Lacking AVX Support

Advanced Vector Extensions (AVX) refers to a set of extensions that was made to the x86 instruction set architecture. These extensions allow for more complex and efficient computation operations at the CPU level. This set of features was first implemented on Intel and AMD CPUs that were shipped in 2011. These features are unfortunately not available on earlier processors. If you're working with a chipset that doesn't support AVX, you will need to install polars-lts-cpu. This package can also be found on PyPI and can be installed with `uv pip install polars-lts-cpu`.

Can't Have It Both Ways

Installing both `polars` and `polars-lts-cpu` will result in strange errors when importing and using Polars.

Takeaways

In this chapter you've learned how to:

- Set up your environment using uv and Git
- Run the code examples in JupyterLab
- Install Polars and optional dependencies
- Tweak the configuration of Polars to make it just right
- Compile Polars from source, and when you might want to do that

This will allow you to run Polars yourself and start exploring the opportunities it brings. In the next chapter you can dive right into that by taking a closer look at the similarities and differences when Polars is compared to the popular DataFrame package pandas.

## CHAPTER 3

Moving from pandas to Polars

There is a good chance that you already have experience with pandas. If you don't, you can safely skip this chapter. If you do, we encourage you to read this chapter; it will make the rest of the book easier to follow.

In this chapter we want to make sure that your transition from pandas to Polars is as smooth as possible by highlighting the similarities and, more importantly, the differences between these two packages.

Ever since Polars took off, it has been compared to pandas. While the comparison is often in favour of Polars, not everybody is equally respectful about this. We cannot abide this. The reason is that data scientists actually owe pandas a lot. Without pandas, there would probably be no Polars. We even think it's safe to say that without pandas, Python wouldn't be such a popular language for working with data. We'll focus on the similarities and differences of these two packages as objectively as possible.

In this chapter, you'll learn:

- What pandas and Polars have in common
- How the syntax and output of both packages differ in appearance
- Which pandas concepts you need to unlearn
- How common operations are performed in both packages

We will focus on the user experience, rather than the underlying mechanics, and we won't compare the performance of pandas and Polars in this chapter. The instructions to get any files you might need are in Chapter 2. We assume that you have the files in the *data* subdirectory.

Animals

Throughout this chapter we're using a CSV file called *data/animals.csv*, which is about 10 animals and some of their properties, like habitat, lifespan, and weight. It's small, but large enough for the purposes of this chapter. The raw data looks like this:

```
! cat data/animals.csv

animal,class,habitat,diet,lifespan,status,features,weight
dolphin,mammal,oceans/rivers,carnivore,40,least concern,high intelligence,150
duck,bird,wetlands,omnivore,8,least concern,waterproof feathers,3
elephant,mammal,savannah,herbivore,60,endangered,large ears and trunk,8000
ibis,bird,wetlands,omnivore,16,least concern,"long, curved bill",1
impala,mammal,savannah,herbivore,12,least concern,"long, curved horns",70
kudu,mammal,savannah,herbivore,15,least concern,spiral horns,250
narwhal,mammal,arctic ocean,carnivore,40,near threatened,"long, spiral tusk",
panda,mammal,forests,herbivore,20,vulnerable,black and white coloration,100
polar bear,mammal,arctic,carnivore,25,vulnerable,thick fur and blubber,720
ray,fish,oceans,carnivore,20,"","flat, disc-shaped body",90
```

The raw data is important to consider because both packages will read this slightly differently. Notice that we're missing the narwhal's weight (the line ends with a comma) and for the ray, we have an empty value for its status (two double quotes, to be precise). Can you guess how pandas deals with those two values? You'll find out soon. But first, let's consider what pandas and Polars have in common.

Similarities to Recognize

From a high level, pandas and Polars have a lot in common. Both:

- Are Python packages for manipulating structured data[1]
- Offer the DataFrame as their main data structure
- Have defined the DataFrame as made up of (potentially multiple) Series, where each Series must have the same number of values, and the values within a Series must have the same data type
- Support a variety of data types, such as Booleans, Integers, Floats, Strings, Categoricals, dates, times, and durations
- Have a very large API (that is, many functions and methods) to perform operations on DataFrames and Series
- Can read from, and write to, a variety of file formats and databases

---

1 As the title of this book suggests, we're focusing on Python Polars. Technically, Polars is written in Rust and offers bindings for Python, R, JavaScript, and Julia.

- Can be used in Jupyter Notebooks and offer an HTML representation
- Begin with the letter "p"

What's in a Name?

The name "pandas" has nothing to do with the animal—it is derived from "Panel Data," a three-dimensional DataFrame. Since pandas version 0.20.0, which was released in May 2017, the Panel data structure has been deprecated; the name obviously stuck. Nowadays, the two main data structures in pandas are the Series and the DataFrame, similar to Polars.

Ritchie Vink, its creator, chose the name "Polars" for two reasons: First, because a polar bear is stronger than a panda bear. Second, because it ends with "rs," a nod to the Rust programming language, in which Polars is implemented.

These points should give you quite a solid foundation to start your transition from pandas to Polars. After all, these are quite a few concepts that you don't have to learn from scratch.

Now it's time to consider the differences between pandas and Polars. We'll start at the beginning: their appearances.

Appearances to Appreciate

As with every first encounter in life, your initial opinion will be based on appearance. Because you are familiar with pandas, Polars may appear strange at first. Let's address this head on.

Import both pandas and Polars as follows:

```
import pandas as pd
import polars as pl
```

That's right: instead of using pd as your starting point, you'll have to get used to using pl. Now you're ready to examine how Polars looks, both from a code perspective and an output perspective, and compare that to pandas.

Differences in Code

Let's read our CSV file *data/animals.csv* and create both a pandas DataFrame, called animals_pd, and a Polars DataFrame, called animals_pl:

```
animals_pd = pd.read_csv("data/animals.csv", sep=",", header=0)
animals_pl = pl.read_csv("data/animals.csv", separator=",", has_header=True)
```

```
print(f"{type(animals_pd) = }")
print(f"{type(animals_pl) = }")

type(animals_pd) = <class 'pandas.core.frame.DataFrame'>
type(animals_pl) = <class 'polars.dataframe.frame.DataFrame'>
```

Even though these functions have the same name, read_csv(), they accept different arguments (for instance, sep versus separator) and produce different types.

You Got This

There are many more situations where you'll encounter these small differences, and they can make your transition to Polars a lot more challenging at first. It's good to be aware of this. At the same time, trust us when we say that things will be alright. You got this.

Let's look at how pandas and Polars display their DataFrames and Series.

Differences in Display

When you work inside a Jupyter Notebook, DataFrames are displayed nicely using some HTML and CSS. Figures 3-1 and 3-2 show two screenshots of how a pandas and a Polars DataFrame are displayed in a Jupyter Notebook.

[3]:	animals_pd							
[3]:	**animal**	**class**	**habitat**	**diet**	**lifespan**	**status**	**features**	**weight**
0	dolphin	mammal	oceans/rivers	carnivore	40	least concern	high intelligence	150.0
1	duck	bird	wetlands	omnivore	8	least concern	waterproof feathers	3.0
2	elephant	mammal	savannah	herbivore	60	endangered	large ears and trunk	8000.0
3	ibis	bird	wetlands	omnivore	16	least concern	long, curved bill	1.0
4	impala	mammal	savannah	herbivore	12	least concern	long, curved horns	70.0
5	kudu	mammal	savannah	herbivore	15	least concern	spiral horns	250.0
6	narwhal	mammal	arctic ocean	carnivore	40	near threatened	long, spiral tusk	NaN
7	panda	mammal	forests	herbivore	20	vulnerable	black and white coloration	100.0
8	polar bear	mammal	arctic	carnivore	25	vulnerable	thick fur and blubber	720.0
9	ray	fish	oceans	carnivore	20	NaN	flat, disc-shaped body	90.0

Figure 3-1. A screenshot of a pandas DataFrame in a Jupyter Notebook

```
[4]:  animals_pl

[4]:  shape: (10, 8)
```

animal	class	habitat	diet	lifespan	status	features	weight
str	str	str	str	i64	str	str	i64
"dolphin"	"mammal"	"oceans/rivers"	"carnivore"	40	"least concern"	"high intelligence"	150
"duck"	"bird"	"wetlands"	"omnivore"	8	"least concern"	"waterproof feathers"	3
"elephant"	"mammal"	"savannah"	"herbivore"	60	"endangered"	"large ears and trunk"	8000
"ibis"	"bird"	"wetlands"	"omnivore"	16	"least concern"	"long, curved bill"	1
"impala"	"mammal"	"savannah"	"herbivore"	12	"least concern"	"long, curved horns"	70
"kudu"	"mammal"	"savannah"	"herbivore"	15	"least concern"	"spiral horns"	250
"narwhal"	"mammal"	"arctic ocean"	"carnivore"	40	"near threatened"	"long, spiral tusk"	null
"panda"	"mammal"	"forests"	"herbivore"	20	"vulnerable"	"black and white coloration"	100
"polar bear"	"mammal"	"arctic"	"carnivore"	25	"vulnerable"	"thick fur and blubber"	720
"ray"	"fish"	"oceans"	"carnivore"	20	""	"flat, disc-shaped body"	90

Figure 3-2. A screenshot of a Polars DataFrame in a Jupyter Notebook

Notice the following differences between the two screenshots:

- pandas displays the values, whereas Polars also displays the shape, that is, the number of rows and columns, of the DataFrame.

- pandas prints the Index, numbers zero through nine, on the left side, whereas Polars does not.

- pandas shows the column names, whereas Polars also shows the data type of the column.

- pandas displays the two missing values as NaN, whereas Polars displays null for the missing weight and two double quotes for the missing status.

- pandas displays Strings as is, while Polars displays double quotes around them.

When you use Python inside a terminal, you'll see a textual representation instead of an HTML representation. The same holds for this book. Here's how that looks in both pandas and Polars:

```
animals_pd
        animal   class        habitat       diet  lifespan           status  \
0      dolphin  mammal  oceans/rivers  carnivore        40     least concern
1         duck    bird       wetlands   omnivore         8     least concern
2     elephant  mammal       savannah  herbivore        60        endangered
3         ibis    bird       wetlands   omnivore        16     least concern
4       impala  mammal       savannah  herbivore        12     least concern
5         kudu  mammal       savannah  herbivore        15     least concern
6      narwhal  mammal   arctic ocean  carnivore        40   near threatened
7        panda  mammal        forests  herbivore        20        vulnerable
8    polar bear  mammal         arctic  carnivore        25        vulnerable
```

```
9      ray   fish       oceans carnivore    20           NaN

                 features  weight
0         high intelligence   150.0
1       waterproof feathers     3.0
2       large ears and trunk 8000.0
3         long, curved bill     1.0
4        long, curved horns    70.0
5               spiral horns   250.0
6         long, spiral tusk     NaN
7   black and white coloration 100.0
8       thick fur and blubber   720.0
9     flat, disc-shaped body    90.0
```

animals_pl

shape: (10, 8)

animal	class	habitat	diet	lifespan	status	features	weight
str	str	str	str	i64	str	str	i64
dolphin	mammal	oceans/ rivers	carnivore	40	least concern	high intelligence	150
duck	bird	wetlands	omnivore	8	least concern	waterproof feathers	3
elephant	mammal	savannah	herbivore	60	endangered	large ears and trunk	8000
ibis	bird	wetlands	omnivore	16	least concern	long, curved bill	1
impala	mammal	savannah	herbivore	12	least concern	long, curved horns	70
kudu	mammal	savannah	herbivore	15	least concern	spiral horns	250
narwhal	mammal	arctic ocean	carnivore	40	near threatened	long, spiral tusk	null
panda	mammal	forests	herbivore	20	vulnerable	black and white colo…	100
polar bear	mammal	arctic	carnivore	25	vulnerable	thick fur and blubbe…	720
ray	fish	oceans	carnivore	20		flat, disc-sh	90

Apparently, the two DataFrames are too wide to fit comfortably on one screen. Each package uses a different strategy to deal with this. pandas first prints as many columns as possible, and then continues below that. Notice that the Index is printed twice. Polars prints all the columns next to each other, but wraps the text inside each column so that each row takes up multiple lines. Some long values in the features column are truncated. Again, Polars prints the shape of the DataFrame and the data types of each column. By default, Polars adds borders. In the textual representation, as opposed to the HTML representation, Polars does not surround Strings with double quotes.

For the sake of completeness, let's see how a pandas Series and a Polars Series look if we extract a single column as a Series:

```
animals_pd["animal"]
```

```
0         dolphin
1            duck
2        elephant
3            ibis
4          impala
5            kudu
6         narwhal
7           panda
8      polar bear
9             ray
Name: animal, dtype: object
```

```
animals_pl.get_column("animal")
```

```
shape: (10,)
Series: 'animal' [str]
[
        "dolphin"
        "duck"
        "elephant"
        "ibis"
        "impala"
        "kudu"
        "narwhal"
        "panda"
        "polar bear"
        "ray"
]
```

Again we see that pandas prints the Index. We also now see the data type that pandas has assigned to this Series, namely object.

pandas does not have an HTML representation of a Series, while Polars does. This means a pandas Series looks like the preceding textual representation, while the Polars Series looks like the HTML representation of a DataFrame, as shown in Figure 3-2.

For the remainder of this chapter—and book—we're going to be using the textual representations of DataFrames. To make the `animals_pd` and `animals_pl` Data-Frames fit more comfortably on the page, we're going to remove three columns:

```
animals_pd = animals_pd.drop(columns=["habitat", "diet", "features"])
animals_pd
```

```
     animal   class  lifespan           status  weight
0   dolphin  mammal        40     least concern   150.0
1      duck    bird         8     least concern     3.0
2  elephant  mammal        60        endangered  8000.0
3      ibis    bird        16     least concern     1.0
4    impala  mammal        12     least concern    70.0
5      kudu  mammal        15     least concern   250.0
6   narwhal  mammal        40   near threatened     NaN
7     panda  mammal        20        vulnerable   100.0
8 polar bear  mammal       25        vulnerable   720.0
9       ray    fish        20               NaN    90.0
```

```
animals_pl = animals_pl.drop("habitat", "diet", "features")
animals_pl
```

shape: (10, 5)

animal	class	lifespan	status	weight
str	str	i64	str	i64
dolphin	mammal	40	least concern	150
duck	bird	8	least concern	3
elephant	mammal	60	endangered	8000
ibis	bird	16	least concern	1
impala	mammal	12	least concern	70
kudu	mammal	15	least concern	250
narwhal	mammal	40	near threatened	null
panda	mammal	20	vulnerable	100
polar bear	mammal	25	vulnerable	720
ray	fish	20		90

Some of the differences in appearance are purely aesthetic, such as using double quotes and borders. Many of these aesthetics can be configured. Other differences in appearance have to do with underlying concepts, such as the Index.

Concepts to Unlearn

Unlearning concepts is perhaps the most difficult aspect of transitioning from pandas to Polars. These concepts influence how you think about working with a DataFrame and define the API that is available to you.

If you don't take the time to do this, then you'll be at a disadvantage compared to someone who is starting from scratch. In the next five sections we will look at the following concepts: the Index, axes, indexing and slicing, eagerness, and relaxedness.

Index

The first thing you can forget about is the Index. A pandas DataFrame always has an Index and sometimes even a MultiIndex. Many DataFrames just have a RangeIndex, including our `animals_pd` DataFrame:

```
animals_pd.index
```

```
RangeIndex(start=0, stop=10, step=1)
```

Certain methods, including aggregation, change the Index:

```
animals_agg_pd = animals_pd.groupby(["class", "status"])[["weight"]].mean()
animals_agg_pd
```

```
                               weight
class   status
bird    least concern         2.000000
mammal  endangered         8000.000000
        least concern       156.666667
        near threatened             NaN
        vulnerable          410.000000
```

You can verify that the previous code snippet creates a MultiIndex based on the columns `class` and `status`:

```
animals_agg_pd.index
```

```
MultiIndex([(  'bird',    'least concern'),
            ('mammal',       'endangered'),
            ('mammal',    'least concern'),
            ('mammal', 'near threatened'),
            ('mammal',       'vulnerable')],
           names=['class', 'status'])
```

Because many users find an Index difficult to work with, they want to get rid of it. You can pass `as_index=False` to `df.groupby()` to avoid this behavior, but you've probably used the `df.reset_index()` method more than once to turn an Index or MultiIndex into columns:

```
animals_agg_pd.reset_index()
```

```
    class          status      weight
0    bird    least concern    2.000000
1  mammal       endangered 8000.000000
2  mammal    least concern  156.666667
3  mammal  near threatened         NaN
4  mammal       vulnerable  410.000000
```

Polars DataFrames do not have an Index, let alone a MultiIndex—only columns. Here is the output of the same aggregation in Polars (don't worry about the syntax for now):

```
animals_pl.group_by(["class", "status"]).agg(pl.col("weight").mean())
```

shape: (6, 3)

class	status	weight
str	str	f64
--------	-----------------	------------
mammal	least concern	156.666667
bird	least concern	2.0
mammal	endangered	8000.0
mammal	near threatened	null
mammal	vulnerable	410.0
fish		90.0

Notice that Polars includes a row for the class fish, whereas pandas does not. We'll come back to this.

Having no Index means that the following pandas DataFrame methods have no equivalents in Polars: df.align(), df.droplevel(), df.reindex(), df.rename_axis(), df.reset_index(), df.set_axis(), df.set_index(), df.sort_index(), df.stack(), df.swapaxis(), df.swaplevel(), and df.unstack().

Axes

The second thing you can forget about are axes. pandas DataFrames have two axes: rows and columns.

Many pandas DataFrame methods can operate on either rows or columns, including df.drop(), df.dropna(), df.filter(), df.rename(), df.shift(), df.sort_index(), and df.sort_values(). These methods accept the axis argument, for which the default value is "0" or "rows". It's not uncommon to forget to specify the axis, which can then lead to an error, for example when trying to drop the column weight:

```
animals_pd.drop("weight")

KeyError: "['weight'] not found in axis"
```

pandas assumes that you want to drop rows that have the Index value "weight". To operate on columns, you either specify axis=1 or axis="columns". Alternatively, you can sometimes use the keyword argument columns (as we did in the beginning of this chapter when we dropped three columns). So to actually drop the column weight, you can do the following:

```
animals_pd.drop("weight", axis=1)

        animal   class  lifespan           status
0       dolphin  mammal        40    least concern
1          duck    bird         8    least concern
2      elephant  mammal        60       endangered
3          ibis    bird        16    least concern
4        impala  mammal        12    least concern
5          kudu  mammal        15    least concern
6       narwhal  mammal        40  near threatened
7         panda  mammal        20       vulnerable
8    polar bear  mammal        25       vulnerable
9           ray    fish        20              NaN
```

Of course, Polars DataFrames also have rows and columns; it's just that you don't have to worry about specifying which axis you want to operate on. Polars methods always operate on either the columns (such as df.drop() and df.rename()) or the rows (such as df.filter(), df.sort(), and df.drop_nulls()).

Indexing and Slicing

pandas code usually contains many brackets in the form of df[]. These brackets allow you to index and slice rows and columns. They are used when selecting columns, slicing rows, filtering rows, creating new columns, updating existing columns, and extracting values.

For example, to select the columns animal and class:

```
animals_pd[["animal", "class"]]

        animal   class
0       dolphin  mammal
1          duck    bird
2      elephant  mammal
3          ibis    bird
4        impala  mammal
5          kudu  mammal
6       narwhal  mammal
7         panda  mammal
8    polar bear  mammal
9           ray    fish
```

Or to keep only animals that are endangered:

```
animals_pd[animals_pd["status"] == "endangered"]

      animal   class  lifespan      status  weight
2   elephant  mammal        60  endangered  8000.0
```

Or to show the first three rows of the DataFrame:

```
animals_pd[:3]

      animal   class  lifespan         status  weight
0    dolphin  mammal        40  least concern   150.0
1       duck    bird         8  least concern     3.0
2   elephant  mammal        60     endangered  8000.0
```

Or to update an existing column:

```
animals_pd["weight"] = animals_pd["weight"] * 1000
```

In pandas, the brackets can also be preceded by a property:

- Use df.at[] to access a single value for a row/column pair by label.
- Use df.iat[] to access a single value for a row/column pair by integer position.
- Use df.loc[] to access a group of rows and columns by labels.
- Use df.iloc[] to access a group of rows and columns by integer positions.

Besides these various flavors of brackets, pandas also has the methods df.xs(), df.get(), and df.filter(). The number of ways to access rows and columns, combined with their flexibility and overlap in functionality, can be overwhelming.

Polars has none of this. Well, it does support the basic flavor of brackets, mostly for compatibility reasons. The general rule in Polars is: don't use brackets. Polars offers specific methods to accomplish the same thing. This not only makes your code more readable, but also allows Polars to optimize your computations when you're in lazy mode (which you'll learn about in Chapter 5).

Leave Those Brackets Alone

As mentioned, the general rule in Polars is to avoid using brackets. The exception to this rule is that brackets are useful when you want to do a one-off inspection of certain rows or columns.

For example, in Chapter 16, we use slicing to comfortably print all the columns of a wide DataFrame:

```
print(trips[:, :4])
print(trips[:, 4:7])
print(trips[:, 7:11])
print(trips[:, 11:])
```

Besides this, there's no reason to use brackets in your Polars code.

Another effect of the Index is that in pandas, column assignments are automatically aligned by the existing Index of the DataFrame. Take, for example, the following column:

```
animals_pd["weight"]
```

```
0      150.0
1        3.0
2     8000.0
3        1.0
4       70.0
5      250.0
6        NaN
7      100.0
8      720.0
9       90.0
Name: weight, dtype: float64
```

Now, if you want to sort the values in this column and place them back in the original DataFrame, you could do the following:

```
animals_pd["weight"] = animals_pd["weight"].sort_values()
```

However, because these new values are aligned by the existing Index, the original DataFrame doesn't change, even though this runs an expensive sort:

```
animals_pd["weight"]
```

```
0      150.0
1        3.0
2     8000.0
3        1.0
4       70.0
5      250.0
6        NaN
7      100.0
8      720.0
9       90.0
Name: weight, dtype: float64
```

This is an unexpected side effect of the Index.

Eagerness

With pandas, every operation is eager and many happen in place. *Eager* means that every operation is executed immediately. *In place* means that the operation does not return a new DataFrame, but modifies the existing one. You saw an example of this earlier, when we updated the weight column.

With Polars, none of the operations are in place by default.[2]

Besides eager mode, Polars also supports lazy queries. With a lazy query, you start with a LazyFrame (instead of a DataFrame), specify all the operations you want to perform, and then finalize with a `lf.collect()` call. Polars then optimizes the query and executes it.

Here's an example where we specify a lazy query that reads in the CSV file *data/animals.csv*, calculates the mean weight for each class, and then keeps only the row where class is equal to mammal:

```
lazy_query = (
    pl.scan_csv("data/animals.csv")
    .group_by("class")
    .agg(pl.col("weight").mean())
    .filter(pl.col("class") == "mammal")
)
```

The `pl.scan_csv()` function doesn't read the file straight away.

You can see what happens under the hood by showing the *query plan*. A query plan contains the computational steps that will be run when executing your query. It is read from bottom to top. We'll give you a detailed explanation of the query plan in Chapter 18, because it requires more knowledge on how Polars works. In the meanwhile, we'll give a glimpse to show you a big advantage of Polars: its optimizer.

Here's the unoptimized (naive) query plan (see Figure 3-3):

```
lazy_query.show_graph(optimized=False)
```

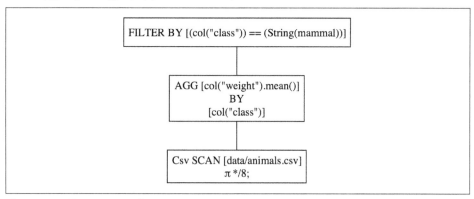

Figure 3-3. Naive query plan

And here's the optimized query plan (see Figure 3-4):

---

2 In Polars, only a few operations are done in place, such as `Series.extend()`, or `df.hstack()` and `df.shrink_to_fit()`, if you specify `in_place=True`.

```
lazy_query.show_graph()
```

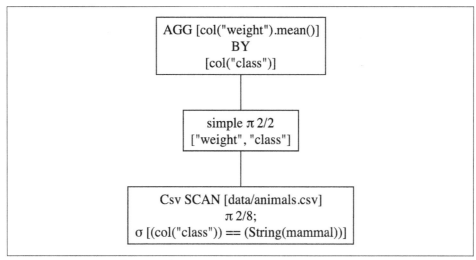

Figure 3-4. Optimized query plan

Polars recognizes that it's faster to filter before aggregation. The step where it reads the file already contains the filter. This saves time in two ways. First, it only reads the necessary data. Second, subsequent steps only have to process what you'll actually need. Using the `lf.collect()` method, we materialize the DataFrame:

```
lazy_query.collect()

shape: (1, 2)
```

class	weight
---	---
str	f64
mammal	1548.333333

You'll learn more about the lazy API in Chapter 5. Using the lazy API on such a small dataset doesn't do it justice, but it gets the point across. Even when you don't use the lazy API, your Polars code will look similar, with many methods and (hopefully) zero brackets.

Relaxedness

The last concept you need to forget about is the relaxedness of pandas. In other words, get comfortable with the strictness of Polars.

This is not so much a single concept as it is a collection of various properties. Here's an incomplete list:

- pandas allows you to use date Strings when working with dates and times. In Polars, you have to use a Python `datetime` data type, or Polars' own Date or Datetime data types. You'll learn all about these data types in Chapter 12.

- pandas allows column names to be other data types than Strings. In Polars, only String names are allowed.

- pandas has many ways to display or work with missing values: `None`, `NaN`, `NA`, `<NA>`, `NaT`, and `np.nan`, which also depend on the data type. Polars distinguishes between missing values (`null`) and invalid numbers (`NaN`, which stands for "Not a Number"), and these apply in the same way regardless of the data type.

- As a result, pandas converts Integer columns to Floats when missing values are introduced (although this doesn't happen with the new Arrow data types). This is because the Integer data type cannot contain missing values. Polars does not do this, as it supports missing values in all data types.

- pandas quietly drops rows with missing values when aggregating (see the previous aggregation example). Polars keeps all groups.

- In pandas, columns can fall back to the data type Object even when they're actually Strings and Floats. Polars never falls back to generic Python Objects.

- In pandas, you can compare Boolean Series with Integers. With Polars, you can only compare Boolean Series with Booleans (and Boolean Series).

- In pandas, you can have multiple columns with the same name. In Polars, column names must be unique.

- In pandas, methods and properties such as `df.loc[]` return a Series instead of a DataFrame when only a single value is passed (unless there are multiple columns with the same name, in which case it *does* return a DataFrame). Polars returns a DataFrame with one row.

- In pandas, `df.sum(axis=0)` returns a Series. In Polars, the same operation returns a one-row DataFrame.

As you will learn in this book, this strictness will get you a lot in return, such as fast feedback on whether a query will fail, a guarantee that results will be correct, and a number of optimizations. In short: Polars being stricter is, in our opinion, a feature rather than a bug.

Syntax to Forget

Once you've managed to unlearn these concepts, it comes down to the smaller things such as different names for functions, methods, and arguments. It can be quite annoying to forget the pandas syntax (where necessary), but often the documentation is enough to quickly fix these kinds of issues.

Lost in Translation

You might be tempted to translate your existing pandas code to Polars by going over the lines one by one. This is like translating a Dutch expression to English word for word, which *puts no sods on the dike*.[3] In other words, this is generally not a good idea. The reason is that you'll end up with code that's not idiomatic, or worse, not performant.

Common Operations Side By Side

In the next few sections we're going to look at common DataFrame operations and compare how they're done in both pandas and Polars. This list is not complete, but it should give you an idea of how these two packages approach things differently. We'll also highlight any differences in output.

Removing duplicate values

Let's remove rows so that the `class` column only contains unique values. With pandas:

```
animals_pd.drop_duplicates(subset="class")
```

```
     animal   class  lifespan          status  weight
0   dolphin  mammal        40   least concern   150.0
1      duck    bird         8   least concern     3.0
9       ray    fish        20             NaN    90.0
```

And with Polars:

```
animals_pl.unique(subset="class")
```

```
shape: (3, 5)
```

animal	class	lifespan	status	weight
---	---	---	---	---
str	str	i64	str	i64
dolphin	mammal	40	least concern	150
duck	bird	8	least concern	3
ray	fish	20		90

Note the different method name: pandas uses `df.drop_duplicates()`, while Polars uses `df.unique()`.

---

3 "That puts no sods on the dike" is a direct translation of the Dutch expression "Dat zet geen zoden aan de dijk." This means that something is inadequate or doesn't contribute to solving the problem.

Also note that Polars does not maintain the order of the rows (ray appears before duck). This is because Polars runs queries in parallel, which can reorder things because of their timing. You can change that by specifying maintain_order=True, which is more expensive to run.

Removing missing values

Let's remove any rows for which the weight is missing. With pandas:

```
animals_pd.dropna(subset="weight")
```

```
        animal   class  lifespan         status  weight
0      dolphin  mammal        40  least concern   150.0
1         duck    bird         8  least concern     3.0
2     elephant  mammal        60     endangered  8000.0
3         ibis    bird        16  least concern     1.0
4       impala  mammal        12  least concern    70.0
5         kudu  mammal        15  least concern   250.0
7        panda  mammal        20     vulnerable   100.0
8   polar bear  mammal        25     vulnerable   720.0
9          ray    fish        20            NaN    90.0
```

And with Polars:

```
animals_pl.drop_nulls(subset="weight")
```

```
shape: (9, 5)
┌────────────┬────────┬──────────┬───────────────┬────────┐
│ animal     │ class  │ lifespan │ status        │ weight │
│ ---        │ ---    │ ---      │ ---           │ ---    │
│ str        │ str    │ i64      │ str           │ i64    │
╞════════════╪════════╪══════════╪═══════════════╪════════╡
│ dolphin    │ mammal │ 40       │ least concern │ 150    │
│ duck       │ bird   │ 8        │ least concern │ 3      │
│ elephant   │ mammal │ 60       │ endangered    │ 8000   │
│ ibis       │ bird   │ 16       │ least concern │ 1      │
│ impala     │ mammal │ 12       │ least concern │ 70     │
│ kudu       │ mammal │ 15       │ least concern │ 250    │
│ panda      │ mammal │ 20       │ vulnerable    │ 100    │
│ polar bear │ mammal │ 25       │ vulnerable    │ 720    │
│ ray        │ fish   │ 20       │               │ 90     │
└────────────┴────────┴──────────┴───────────────┴────────┘
```

Notice the different method names: pd.df.dropna() versus pl.df.drop_nulls().

Sorting rows

Let's sort the DataFrame according to the weight column in descending order (heaviest animals first). In pandas:

```
animals_pd.sort_values("weight", ascending=False)
```

```
      animal   class  lifespan          status  weight
2    elephant  mammal        60      endangered  8000.0
8  polar bear  mammal        25      vulnerable   720.0
5        kudu  mammal        15   least concern   250.0
0     dolphin  mammal        40   least concern   150.0
7       panda  mammal        20      vulnerable   100.0
9         ray    fish        20             NaN    90.0
4      impala  mammal        12   least concern    70.0
1        duck    bird         8   least concern     3.0
3        ibis    bird        16   least concern     1.0
6     narwhal  mammal        40  near threatened     NaN
```

And in Polars:

```
animals_pl.sort("weight", descending=True)
```

```
shape: (10, 5)
┌────────────┬────────┬──────────┬─────────────────┬────────┐
│ animal     ┆ class  ┆ lifespan ┆ status          ┆ weight │
│ ---        ┆ ---    ┆ ---      ┆ ---             ┆ ---    │
│ str        ┆ str    ┆ i64      ┆ str             ┆ i64    │
╞════════════╪════════╪══════════╪═════════════════╪════════╡
│ narwhal    ┆ mammal ┆ 40       ┆ near threatened ┆ null   │
│ elephant   ┆ mammal ┆ 60       ┆ endangered      ┆ 8000   │
│ polar bear ┆ mammal ┆ 25       ┆ vulnerable      ┆ 720    │
│ kudu       ┆ mammal ┆ 15       ┆ least concern   ┆ 250    │
│ dolphin    ┆ mammal ┆ 40       ┆ least concern   ┆ 150    │
│ panda      ┆ mammal ┆ 20       ┆ vulnerable      ┆ 100    │
│ ray        ┆ fish   ┆ 20       ┆                 ┆ 90     │
│ impala     ┆ mammal ┆ 12       ┆ least concern   ┆ 70     │
│ duck       ┆ bird   ┆ 8        ┆ least concern   ┆ 3      │
│ ibis       ┆ bird   ┆ 16       ┆ least concern   ┆ 1      │
└────────────┴────────┴──────────┴─────────────────┴────────┘
```

Note the difference in method name, df.sort_values() versus df.sort(), and the argument used to reverse the sort order: ascending=False versus descending=True. Also, pandas puts missing values last, whereas Polars puts them first. This can be changed by specifying nulls_last=True.

Casting an existing column

Let's convert the data type of the column lifespan from an Integer to a Float. With pandas:

```
animals_pd.assign(lifespan=animals_pd["lifespan"].astype(float))
```

```
     animal   class  lifespan          status  weight
0   dolphin  mammal      40.0   least concern   150.0
1      duck    bird       8.0   least concern     3.0
2  elephant  mammal      60.0      endangered  8000.0
3      ibis    bird      16.0   least concern     1.0
4    impala  mammal      12.0   least concern    70.0
5      kudu  mammal      15.0   least concern   250.0
```

```
6     narwhal  mammal   40.0  near threatened    NaN
7       panda  mammal   20.0       vulnerable  100.0
8  polar bear  mammal   25.0       vulnerable  720.0
9         ray    fish   20.0              NaN   90.0
```

In practice, most pandas code changes the column directly through assignment (=) instead of using the df.assign() method.

And with Polars:

```
animals_pl.with_columns(pl.col("lifespan").cast(pl.Float64))
```

```
shape: (10, 5)
```

animal	class	lifespan	status	weight
---	---	---	---	---
str	str	f64	str	i64
dolphin	mammal	40.0	least concern	150
duck	bird	8.0	least concern	3
elephant	mammal	60.0	endangered	8000
ibis	bird	16.0	least concern	1
impala	mammal	12.0	least concern	70
kudu	mammal	15.0	least concern	250
narwhal	mammal	40.0	near threatened	null
panda	mammal	20.0	vulnerable	100
polar bear	mammal	25.0	vulnerable	720
ray	fish	20.0		90

Polars uses the pl.col() function to create an expression. Expressions are a big topic in Polars, and you'll learn all about them in Part III, "Express".

Aggregating rows

Let's aggregate the rows by the columns class and status, then compute the mean weight per group. You've already seen this example, but it's worth repeating. With pandas:

```
animals_pd.groupby(["class", "status"])[["weight"]].mean()
```

```
                          weight
class  status
bird   least concern     2.000000
mammal endangered     8000.000000
       least concern    156.666667
       near threatened         NaN
       vulnerable       410.000000
```

And with Polars:

```
animals_pl.group_by("class", "status").agg(pl.col("weight").mean())
```

---

shape: (6, 3)

class	status	weight
str	str	f64
mammal	least concern	156.666667
bird	least concern	2.0
mammal	endangered	8000.0
mammal	near threatened	null
mammal	vulnerable	410.0
fish		90.0

The method name is slightly different: pandas uses df.groupby(), while Polars uses df.group_by() (note the underscore). pandas creates a MultiIndex based on the class and status columns, whereas Polars keeps them as columns. Again, Polars uses an expression inside the df.GroupBy.agg() method. This coincidentally allows you to build your own complex aggregations, while pandas is limited to a list of predetermined aggregations: (min, max, first, mean, std, and a few others). You'll learn everything about aggregations in Polars in Chapter 13.

To and From pandas

Luckily, it is very easy to step between pandas and Polars. The easiest way to explore if Polars can bring something to your use case is by swapping out a piece of the pipeline with Polars and benchmarking the difference in performance it might bring you. When you're coming from a pandas DataFrame, going to Polars looks like the following:

```
animals_pl = pl.DataFrame(animals_pd)

animals_pl
```

shape: (10, 5)

animal	class	lifespan	status	weight
str	str	i64	str	f64
dolphin	mammal	40	least concern	150.0
duck	bird	8	least concern	3.0
elephant	mammal	60	endangered	8000.0
ibis	bird	16	least concern	1.0
impala	mammal	12	least concern	70.0
kudu	mammal	15	least concern	250.0
narwhal	mammal	40	near threatened	null
panda	mammal	20	vulnerable	100.0
polar bear	mammal	25	vulnerable	720.0

```
| ray       | fish  | 20  | null            | 90.0  |
```

This allows you to start working with the DataFrame using Polars. The moment you want to go back again, you can do so by running the following:

```
there_and_back_again_df = animals_pl.to_pandas()

there_and_back_again_df
```

```
        animal   class  lifespan           status  weight
0      dolphin  mammal        40    least concern   150.0
1         duck    bird         8    least concern     3.0
2     elephant  mammal        60       endangered  8000.0
3         ibis    bird        16    least concern     1.0
4       impala  mammal        12    least concern    70.0
5         kudu  mammal        15    least concern   250.0
6      narwhal  mammal        40  near threatened     NaN
7        panda  mammal        20       vulnerable   100.0
8   polar bear  mammal        25       vulnerable   720.0
9          ray    fish        20             None    90.0
```

This allows you to easily swap between DataFrame packages whenever you want.

Takeaways

In this chapter we've looked at the similarities and differences between pandas and Polars. The key takeaways are:

- Without pandas there would probably be no Polars.
- pandas and Polars have, at a high level, a few things in common.
- On the outside, a Polars DataFrame appears quite similar to a pandas one, but includes useful information such as its shape and the data types of its columns.
- You can forget about a couple of pandas-specific concepts, such as the Index, axes, indexing, slicing, eagerness, and relaxedness.
- There are many methods and arguments that have different names, which can be confusing and even frustrating.
- For some operations, the output can be slightly different as well.
- It's easy to move between a pandas DataFrame and a Polars DataFrame.

We realize it's a bold thing to ask you to forget what you know about pandas. We'll make it up to you by showing the ease of use and beauty of Polars in the remaining parts of the book.

## PART II

Form

## CHAPTER 4

Data Structures and Data Types

Now that you've been properly introduced, it's time to focus on how Polars works.

Data comes in many shapes and sizes, all of which need to be stored in proper structures in order to work with them. To accommodate all the data you'll be working with, Polars implements the Arrow memory specification, which provides a vast array of data types.

In this chapter you'll learn about:

- The structures Polars uses to store data
- The different data types that are available
- Some of the data types that aren't so straightforward

Let's start the beautiful journey of learning about Polars.

The instructions to get any files you might need are in Chapter 2. We assume that you have the files in the *data* subdirectory.

Series, DataFrames, and LazyFrames

Polars stores all of its data in a *Series* or a *DataFrame*.

A Series is a one-dimensional data structure that holds a sequence of values. All values in a Series have the same data type, like Integers, Floats, or Strings. Series *can* exist on their own, but they're most commonly used as columns in a DataFrame.

An example of a Series is the following:

```
sales_series = pl.Series("sales", [150.00, 300.00, 250.00])

sales_series
```

```
shape: (3,)
Series: 'sales' [f64]
[
        150.0
        300.0
        250.0
]
```

A DataFrame is a two-dimensional data structure that organizes data in a table format, with rows and columns. Internally, it's represented as a sequence of multiple Series, each with the same length. To dive deeper into the inner workings of Series and DataFrames, refer to Chapter 18.

Here's an example of a DataFrame that incorporates the Series you just made:

```
sales_df = pl.DataFrame(
    {
        "sales": sales_series,
        "customer_id": [24, 25, 26],
    }
)

sales_df
```

```
shape: (3, 2)
┌─────────┬─────────────┐
│ sales   ┆ customer_id │
│ ---     ┆ ---         │
│ f64     ┆ i64         │
╞═════════╪═════════════╡
│ 150.0   ┆ 24          │
│ 300.0   ┆ 25          │
│ 250.0   ┆ 26          │
└─────────┴─────────────┘
```

A *LazyFrame* resembles a DataFrame but holds no data.[1] While a DataFrame stores data directly in memory, a LazyFrame contains only instructions for reading and processing data. None of the read operations or transformations applied to a LazyFrame are executed immediately; instead, they are deferred until needed, hence the term "lazy" evaluation. Until evaluation, a LazyFrame remains a blueprint for generating a DataFrame—a query graph representing the computational steps. This query graph enables the optimizer to refine and optimize the planned computations, ensuring efficient execution when finally evaluated.

Here's an example of a LazyFrame (see Figure 4-1):

---

[1] A LazyFrame can hold data when you turn a DataFrame lazy using df.lazy(). In this case, the source DataFrame is stored in the LazyFrame itself. Besides that, a LazyFrame can contain metadata about the source data to allow the optimizer to perform its magic.

```
lazy_df = pl.scan_csv("data/fruit.csv").with_columns(
    is_heavy=pl.col("weight") > 200
)

lazy_df.show_graph()
```

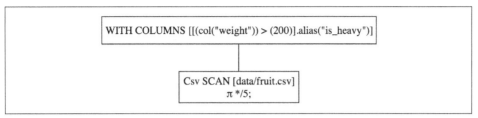

Figure 4-1. LazyFrame query graph

This blueprint turns into a DataFrame once you execute it with a method like `lf.collect()`.

We will dive deeper into the usage of the two eager and lazy APIs in Chapter 5.

Data Types

To store data efficiently, Polars implements the Apache Arrow memory specification. In Chapter 18 you can read more about what Arrow is and how it works. In short, Arrow is a columnar memory format for flat and hierarchical data, organized for efficient analytic operations on modern hardware like CPUs and GPUs. This means that Polars stores your data in a way that allows for optimal performance when processing it.

Polars has implemented the data types shown in Table 4-1. Most of these are based on the data types defined by the Arrow specification.[2] Some data types occur multiple times with different bit sizes. This allows you to store data that fits within the range with a smaller memory footprint.

Table 4-1. Data types available in Polars

Group	Type	Details	Range
	DataType	Base class for all Polars data types.	
Numeric	Decimal	Decimal 128-bit type with an optional precision and non-negative scale.	Can exactly represent 38 significant digits.
	Float32	32-bit floating-point type.	-3.4e+38 to 3.4e+38

---

2 Polars sometimes deviates from the Arrow specification. For instance, Polars has implemented its own String data type for additional performance gains. Arrow also doesn't have the Object and Unknown data types. See *https://arrow.apache.org/docs/python/api/datatypes.html*.

Group	Type	Details	Range
	Float64	64-bit floating-point type.	-1.7e+308 to 1.7e+308
	Int8	8-bit signed Integer type.	-128 to 128
	Int16	16-bit signed Integer type.	-32,768 to 32,767
	Int32	32-bit signed Integer type.	-2,147,483,648 to 2,147,483,647
	Int64	64-bit signed Integer type.	-9,223,372,036,854,775,808 to 9,223,372,036,854,775,807
	UInt8	8-bit unsigned Integer type.	0 to 255
	UInt16	16-bit unsigned Integer type.	0 to 65,535
	UInt32	32-bit unsigned Integer type.	0 to 4,294,967,295
	UInt64	64-bit unsigned Integer type.	0 to 1.8446744e+19
Temporal	Date	Calendar date type. Uses the Arrow date32 data type, which represents the number of days since Unix epoch 1970-01-01 as int32.	-5877641-06-24 to 5879610-09-09
	Datetime	Calendar date and time type. Exact timestamp encoded with int64 since Unix epoch. Default unit is microseconds.	
	Duration	Time duration/delta type.	
	Time	Time of day type.	
Nested	Array	Fixed-length List data type.	
	List	Variable-length List data type.	
	Struct	Struct type.	
String	String	UTF-8 encoded String type of variable length.	
	Categorical	A categorical encoding of a set of Strings. Allows for more efficient memory usage if a Series contains few unique Strings.	
	Enum	A categorical encoding of a set of Strings that is fixed. The categories must be known and defined beforehand.	
Other	Boolean	Boolean type taking 1 bit of space.	True or False
	Binary	Binary type with variable-length bytes.	
	Null	Type representing Null/None values.	
	Object	Type for wrapping arbitrary Python objects.	
	Unknown[a]	Type representing data type values that could not be determined statically.	

[a] The documentation lists the Unknown data type. This data type is only used internally as a placeholder and should not be used in your code.

Object Stowaways

Sometimes you need to add arbitrary Python objects to a Data-Frame. For example, you want to store multiple machine learning models in a column. In this case you can use the Object data type.

The downside is that this data cannot be processed using the normal functions. Moreover, none of the optimizations are used, because Polars does not use Python to look at what the data represents. As a result, an Object column can be seen as a passenger in the DataFrame, which is passed on in, say, join operations, but does not take part in optimized calculations.

Using Objects is generally discouraged when the data can be represented by another data type, but there can be use cases for it.

Nested Data Types

Polars has three nested data types: Array, List, and Struct. These data types enable Polars to manage complex data structures efficiently within a DataFrame. The Array data type represents fixed-size collections where each element holds the same data type, commonly used for compact storage and predictable indexing. The List data type is more flexible, allowing variable-length collections within each row. Lastly, the Struct data type lets users store and access related fields as a single entity, encapsulating multiple named fields in a column.

An Array is a collection of elements that are of the same data type. Within a Series, each Array must have the same shape. The shape can of be any dimension. For example, to store the pixels of RGB images with a size of 640 by 480, you would use three dimensions. You can specify the inner data type and the shape of an Array as follows:

```
coordinates = pl.DataFrame(
    [
        pl.Series("point_2d", [[1, 3], [2, 5]]),
        pl.Series("point_3d", [[1, 7, 3], [8, 1, 0]]),
    ],
    schema={
        "point_2d": pl.Array(shape=2, inner=pl.Int64),
        "point_3d": pl.Array(shape=3, inner=pl.Int64),
    },
)

coordinates
```

```
shape: (2, 2)
┌───────────────┬───────────────┐
│ point_2d      │ point_3d      │
│ ---           │ ---           │
│ array[i64, 2] │ array[i64, 3] │
```

| [1, 3] | [1, 7, 3] |
| [2, 5] | [8, 1, 0] |

A List is comparable to an Array in that it is a collection of elements of the same data type. However in contrast to the Array, a List does not have to have the same length on every row. Note that it's different from the Python `list` which can contain multiple data types. It is possible to store Python lists in the Series by making the data type Object. The only argument List takes is what data type it contains.

Here's how you can create a DataFrame with two List columns. Because we're not specifying a schema like we did in the previous example, the inner data types are inferred from the data:

```
weather_readings = pl.DataFrame(
    {
        "temperature": [[72.5, 75.0, 77.3], [68.0, 70.2]],
        "wind_speed": [[15, 20], [10, 12, 14, 16]],
    }
)

weather_readings

shape: (2, 2)
```

temperature	wind_speed
list[f64]	list[i64]
[72.5, 75.0, 77.3]	[15, 20]
[68.0, 70.2]	[10, 12, … 16]

Lastly, there's the Struct data type. A Struct is often used to work multiple Series at once. Here's an example that shows how Structs can be created using Python dictionaries:

```
rating_series = pl.Series(
    "ratings",
    [
        {"Movie": "Cars", "Theatre": "NE", "Avg_Rating": 4.5},
        {"Movie": "Toy Story", "Theatre": "ME", "Avg_Rating": 4.9},
    ],
)
rating_series

shape: (2,)
Series: 'ratings' [struct[3]]
[
        {"Cars","NE",4.5}
        {"Toy Story","ME",4.9}
]
```

We discuss working with List, Array, and Struct data types in more detail in Chapter 12.

Missing Values

In Polars, missing data is always represented as null. This holds for *all* data types, including the numerical ones.[3] Information about missing values is stored in metadata of the Series.

Additionally, whether a value is missing is stored in its *validity bitmap*, which is a bit that is set to 1 if the value is present and 0 if it is missing. This lets you cheaply check how many values are missing in a Series, using methods like df.null_count() and Expr.is_null().

To demonstrate this, we'll create a DataFrame with some missing values:

```
missing_df = pl.DataFrame(
    {
        "value": [None, 2, 3, 4, None, None, 7, 8, 9, None],
    },
)
missing_df
```

```
shape: (10, 1)
┌───────┐
│ value │
│ ---   │
│ i64   │
╞═══════╡
│ null  │
│ 2     │
│ 3     │
│ 4     │
│ null  │
│ null  │
│ 7     │
│ 8     │
│ 9     │
│ null  │
└───────┘
```

You can fill in missing data using the Expr.fill_null() method, which you can call in four ways:

- Using a single value
- Using a fill strategy

---

3 Except the Null data type itself, which cannot be missing.

- Using an expression
- Using an interpolation

Not a Number but Not Missing Either

NaN (meaning "not a number") values are not considered missing data in Polars. These values are used for the Float data types to represent the result of an operation that is not a number.

Consequently, NaN values are not counted as null values in methods like df.null_count() or Expr.fill_null(). As an alternative, use Expr.is_nan() and Expr.fill_nan() to work with these values.

The following example shows how you can fill with a single value:

```
missing_df.with_columns(filled_with_single=pl.col("value").fill_null(-1))
```

```
shape: (10, 2)
┌───────┬───────────────────┐
│ value │ filled_with_single │
│ ---   │ ---               │
│ i64   │ i64               │
╞═══════╪═══════════════════╡
│ null  │ -1                │
│ 2     │ 2                 │
│ 3     │ 3                 │
│ 4     │ 4                 │
│ null  │ -1                │
│ null  │ -1                │
│ 7     │ 7                 │
│ 8     │ 8                 │
│ 9     │ 9                 │
│ null  │ -1                │
└───────┴───────────────────┘
```

The second way is to use a *fill strategy*. A fill strategy allows you to pick an imputation strategy out of the following list:

forward
Fill with the previous non-null value.

backward
Fill with the next non-null value.

min
Fill with the minimum value of the Series.

max

Fill with the maximum value of the Series.

mean

Fill with the mean of the Series. Note that this mean is cast to the data type of the Series, which in the case of an Integer means that the part behind the decimal mark is cut off.

zero

Fill with 0.

one

Fill with 1.

In the following example, you'll see all of these strategies next to each other:

```
missing_df.with_columns(
    forward=pl.col("value").fill_null(strategy="forward"),
    backward=pl.col("value").fill_null(strategy="backward"),
    min=pl.col("value").fill_null(strategy="min"),
    max=pl.col("value").fill_null(strategy="max"),
    mean=pl.col("value").fill_null(strategy="mean"),
    zero=pl.col("value").fill_null(strategy="zero"),
    one=pl.col("value").fill_null(strategy="one"),
)
```

shape: (10, 8)

value	forward	backward	min	max	mean	zero	one
i64	i64	i64	i64	i64	i64	i64	i64
null	null	2	2	9	5	0	1
2	2	2	2	2	2	2	2
3	3	3	3	3	3	3	3
4	4	4	4	4	4	4	4
null	4	7	2	9	5	0	1
null	4	7	2	9	5	0	1
7	7	7	7	7	7	7	7
8	8	8	8	8	8	8	8
9	9	9	9	9	9	9	9
null	9	null	2	9	5	0	1

The third way of filling null values is with an expression like pl.col("value").mean(). Expressions won't be fully explained until Chapter 7, but we wanted to at least show an example of how this would work:

```
missing_df.with_columns(
    expression_mean=pl.col("value").fill_null(pl.col("value").mean())
)
```

shape: (10, 2)

```
┌───────┬─────────────────┐
│ value │ expression_mean │
│ ---   │ ---             │
│ i64   │ f64             │
╞═══════╪═════════════════╡
│ null  │ 5.5             │
│ 2     │ 2.0             │
│ 3     │ 3.0             │
│ 4     │ 4.0             │
│ null  │ 5.5             │
│ null  │ 5.5             │
│ 7     │ 7.0             │
│ 8     │ 8.0             │
│ 9     │ 9.0             │
│ null  │ 5.5             │
└───────┴─────────────────┘
```

We showcase more ways of filling null values using expressions in Chapter 8. The fourth and final way of filling nulls is with an interpolation method like df.interpolate():

```
missing_df.interpolate()
```

shape: (10, 1)

```
┌───────┐
│ value │
│ ---   │
│ f64   │
╞═══════╡
│ null  │
│ 2.0   │
│ 3.0   │
│ 4.0   │
│ 5.0   │
│ 6.0   │
│ 7.0   │
│ 8.0   │
│ 9.0   │
│ null  │
└───────┘
```

Floats: How Do They Work?

A Float data type is a floating-point number format. Its precision is determined by the number of bits used to represent it. The default precision in Polars is double-precision, which uses 64 bits. This level of precision is available by using the Float64 data type. Additionally, there's also the Float32 data type. This single-precision floating-point number uses 32 bits, allowing for a smaller memory footprint, at the cost of precision.

To explain how a floating-point number works, we'll assume the 32-bit variant. The 32 bits contain the following information:

- The 1st bit represents the sign bit (0 for positive, 1 for negative).
- The 2nd-9th bits represent the exponent by which the fraction is multiplied.
- The 10th-32nd bits represent the fraction with an implicit leading 1 before the binary representation.

The formula for calculating the value of a Float32 is given by:

$$x = (-1)^{sign} * (1 + fraction) * 2^{(exponent - bias)}$$

The bias for Float32 is a constant value of 127. This means that the actual exponent value in decimal form is obtained by subtracting this bias from the exponent's binary representation. The reason a Float uses a bias is that the negative exponents generated from the subtraction of the bias ensure it can represent both very large and very tiny numbers efficiently.

As an example, consider the following Float in bits:

0 10000010 10100000000000000000000

Where:

0
> Means the Float is positive.

10000010
> The *exponent* in binary, which is 130 in decimal.

10100000000000000000000
> This is the *fraction* part in binary. It's calculated by adding an implicit leading 1 (for normalized numbers) to the binary digits, interpreted as follows: 1 (the implicit leading 1) plus $1 * 2^{-1}$ (the first digit, representing 0.5) plus $0 * 2^{-2}$ (the second digit, ignored since it's 0) plus $1 * 2^{-3}$ (the third digit, representing 0.125). Subsequent digits are zeros and do not contribute to the value. Therefore, the fraction equals $1 + 0.5 + 0.125 = 1.625$.

Plugging these values in to the formula gives:

- $x = (-1)^{0} * (1 + 0.5 + 0.125) * 2^{(130 - 127)}$
- $x = 1 * 1.625 * 8$
- $x = 13$

Data Type Conversion

There are situations where you need to change the data type of a column or Series. For example, you just read a CSV file, and there's a column which is incorrectly inferred as a String, and should be numeric.

For this, you can use either the Expr.cast() or the df.cast() methods.

The Expr.cast() method changes the data type of one column (technically, an expression) to the one provided as an argument. Here's an example that demonstrates why having the right data type matters:

```
string_df = pl.DataFrame({"id": ["10000", "20000", "30000"]})
print(string_df)
print(f"Estimated size: {string_df.estimated_size('b')} bytes")

shape: (3, 1)
┌───────┐
│ id    │
│ ---   │
│ str   │
╞═══════╡
│ 10000 │
│ 20000 │
│ 30000 │
└───────┘
Estimated size: 15 bytes
```

However, you know that this column only contains numeric data types, which can be stored more efficiently. Changing the data type would look like this:

```
int_df = string_df.select(pl.col("id").cast(pl.UInt16))
print(int_df)
print(f"Estimated size: {int_df.estimated_size('b')} bytes")

shape: (3, 1)
┌───────┐
│ id    │
│ ---   │
│ u16   │
╞═══════╡
│ 10000 │
│ 20000 │
│ 30000 │
└───────┘
Estimated size: 6 bytes
```

We just reduced the used memory by more than 60%. Using the optimal data types can provide a lot of performance advantages.

Table 4-1 shows the ranges of each data type, where applicable. Memory usage can be optimized by casting to the smallest size of a data type that still fits the data.

In the preceding example, you used the `Expr.cast()` method for expressions. You can also use the `df.cast()` method on a DataFrame. In that case, you can cast multiple Series at once by specifying either a single data type or a dictionary of column-type pairs. The keys can be column names or column selectors. Here are the ways to use the `df.cast()` method, starting with casting everything to one data type:

```
data_types_df = pl.DataFrame(
    {
        "id": [10000, 20000, 30000],
        "value": [1.0, 2.0, 3.0],
        "value2": ["1", "2", "3"],
    }
)
```

```
data_types_df.cast(pl.UInt16)
```

shape: (3, 3)

id	value	value2
u16	u16	u16
10000	1	1
20000	2	2
30000	3	3

Or with a dictionary, to cast certain Series differently:

```
data_types_df.cast({"id": pl.UInt16, "value": pl.Float32, "value2": pl.UInt8})
```

shape: (3, 3)

id	value	value2
u16	f32	u8
10000	1.0	1
20000	2.0	2
30000	3.0	3

You can also cast specific data types to others, as follows. Let's cast all Float64 values to Float32, and all String values to UInt8:

```
data_types_df.cast({pl.Float64: pl.Float32, pl.String: pl.UInt8})
```

shape: (3, 3)

id	value	value2
i64	f32	u8
10000	1.0	1

```
| 20000 | 2.0  | 2     |
| 30000 | 3.0  | 3     |
```

Lastly, you can use column selectors:

```
import polars.selectors as cs

data_types_df.cast({cs.numeric(): pl.UInt16})

shape: (3, 3)
```

```
| id    | value | value2 |
| ---   | ---   | ---    |
| u16   | u16   | str    |
|       |       |        |
| 10000 | 1     | 1      |
| 20000 | 2     | 2      |
| 30000 | 3     | 3      |
```

We'll explore the column selectors in more detail in Chapter 10.

Basic casting doesn't always magically work. In some cases, special methods need to be used because data cannot be parsed without extra knowledge. One of the examples is when parsing a Datetime from a String. In Chapter 12 you'll read about methods that allow for this more advanced casting.

Takeaways

In this chapter you learned about:

- The structures Polars provides for working with data: Series, DataFrame, and LazyFrames.
- The different data types Polars offers for data storage.
- Some data types that offer their own special operations, such a textual, nested, and temporal data types. We'll dive deeper into these specifics in Chapter 12.
- The way missing data is handled in Polars.
- Changing data types using the `Expr.cast()` and `df.cast()` methods.

This knowledge can be used to fill our DataFrames. In the next chapter you'll dive into the different APIs that Polars offers to work on this data.

## CHAPTER 5

Eager and Lazy APIs

Now that you have an understanding of the data structures and data types available in Polars, we will look at the two different *application programming interfaces* (APIs) to interact with that data: the eager API and the lazy API. Each API addresses specific use cases and has unique performance characteristics. Understanding these APIs is critical to using Polars' data processing and analysis capabilities effectively.

In this chapter, you'll learn:

- That the eager API uses an immediate execution model, ideal for data exploration and iterative tasks

- That the lazy API defers the execution of data transformations until necessary, which allows for comprehensively optimizing queries and improving performance, especially in large-scale and performance-sensitive scenarios

- About which API fits with which use cases and how to choose the right one for your needs

The instructions to get any files you might need are in Chapter 2. We assume that you have the files in the *data* subdirectory.

Eager API: DataFrame

The eager API in Polars operates on an immediate execution model, where each function is executed sequentially, line by line, on the dataset. This approach is particularly effective for data exploration and iterative analysis, as it allows for direct interaction with the data at every step. You can execute functions on intermediate results, providing immediate feedback and insights, which is invaluable for making informed decisions about subsequent queries. This execution style is very similar to the experience offered by packages like pandas, making it a familiar and intuitive choice for those transitioning from or accustomed to the pandas workflow.

In this example, we'll explore the eager API of Polars through a practical application. We have a dataset of taxi trips, and our goal is to analyze the data to derive the top three vendors by revenue per distance traveled. Let's break down the process step by step to understand how the eager API facilitates this analysis. Note that we use the %%time cell magic to time and print how long the code execution takes:

```
%%time
trips = pl.read_parquet("data/taxi/yellow_tripdata_*.parquet")  ❶
sum_per_vendor = trips.group_by("VendorID").sum()  ❷

income_per_distance_per_vendor = sum_per_vendor.select(
    "VendorID",
    income_per_distance=pl.col("total_amount") / pl.col("trip_distance"),
)

top_three = income_per_distance_per_vendor.sort(  ❸
    by="income_per_distance", descending=True
).head(3)

top_three
```

❶ This reads all the Parquet files that match the *glob pattern*. A glob pattern is a String definition used to specify groups of filenames by matching patterns. We'll dive deeper into this in Chapter 6 on reading and writing data. For now, it is sufficient to know that the dataset consists of several files, which Polars reads into a DataFrame in one go. The function pl.read_parquet() returns a DataFrame which is executed using the eager API.

❷ All columns are summed by VendorID, so you can calculate with total amounts.

❸ From these sums you can calculate the average income per distance traveled for all trips per vendor.

```
CPU times: user 9.45 s, sys: 8.7 s, total: 18.1 s
Wall time: 8.52 s
shape: (3, 2)
┌──────────┬─────────────────────┐
│ VendorID │ income_per_distance │
│ ---      │ ---                 │
│ i64      │ f64                 │
╞══════════╪═════════════════════╡
│ 1        │ 6.434789            │
│ 6        │ 5.296493            │
│ 5        │ 4.731557            │
└──────────┴─────────────────────┘
```

After the data is sorted, you can select the top three, answering our earlier question: "Who are the top three vendors by revenue per distance traveled?"

When doing this kind of analysis, it's often better to tackle the main problem in smaller parts. This way, you get to see the data at each step, which helps you make better choices for the next steps.

Lazy API: LazyFrame

The lazy API defers executing all selection, filtering, and manipulation until the moment it is actually needed. This gives the query engine more information about what data and transformations are actually needed, and allows for a bunch of optimizations that heavily increase performance. The best uses cases for the lazy API include big and complex datasets and performance-critical applications where speed is of the essence.

The lazy API applies various optimizations to improve the performance of data processing. These optimizations primarily focus on reducing the amount of data that needs to be processed and minimizing the number of operations required to achieve the desired result. The reduction of data that is being processed is achieved by not even reading data from the source in the first place, which occurs at the scan level. That is done in three main ways:

- Only reading columns that are needed
- Filtering out rows that are not needed
- Only reading parts of the column that are needed for the query

These optimizations are all applied behind the scenes by the query planner and optimizer. For more details on the optimizations applied by the lazy API, see Chapter 18. The main takeaway of the lazy API is that it works smarter, not harder.

In addition, the lazy API can catch data type errors before processing the data. (These are also known as SchemaErrors.) The query plan contains the knowledge of what needs to happen at each step along the way and what the result should look like.

Take the next example. You'll make a LazyFrame that contains names and ages of three people. If you take the age Series, which contains the Int64 data type, and treat it as a String, you'll immediately get an error before any calculation is done:

```
names_lf = pl.LazyFrame(
    {"name": ["Alice", "Bob", "Charlie"], "age": [25, 30, 35]}
)

erroneous_query = names_lf.with_columns(
    sliced_age=pl.col("age").str.slice(1, 3)
)
```

```
result_df = erroneous_query.collect()

SchemaError: invalid series dtype: expected `String`, got `i64` for series with
name `age`
```

This allows queries to fail fast and provide a short feedback loop that improves programming efficiency. If you were working on large datasets with long-running queries, it could've taken you hours to run into the error.

Performance Differences

We recommend you try executing identical queries using both the lazy and eager APIs. It's a good way to see the profound optimization benefits. Let's examine the eager query we ran earlier on a dataset of taxi trip records stored in Parquet format:

```
%%time
trips = pl.scan_parquet("data/taxi/yellow_tripdata_*.parquet")
sum_per_vendor = trips.group_by("VendorID").sum()

income_per_distance_per_vendor = sum_per_vendor.select(
    "VendorID",
    income_per_distance=pl.col("total_amount") / pl.col("trip_distance"),
)

top_three = income_per_distance_per_vendor.sort(
    by="income_per_distance", descending=True
).head(3)

top_three.collect()
```

```
CPU times: user 2.01 s, sys: 301 ms, total: 2.31 s
Wall time: 592 ms
shape: (3, 2)
```

VendorID	income_per_distance
i64	f64
1	6.434789
6	5.296493
5	4.731557

This returns the same DataFrame, but the lazy API does it about 10 times faster than the eager API. Now that's what we call blazingly fast.

In Polars, a LazyFrame is evaluated and converted into a DataFrame only when you invoke the lf.collect() method. While this lazy evaluation offers efficiency gains, it's crucial to note that subsequent calls to lf.collect() will recompute the

LazyFrame from scratch. This means the same calculations will be run multiple times, which you want to prevent.

We'll make a small LazyFrame with two columns of three rows and act like it's a very big dataset with long calculation times:

```
lf = pl.LazyFrame({"col1": [1, 2, 3], "col2": [4, 5, 6]})

# ... Some heavy computation ...

print(lf.collect())

print(lf.with_columns(pl.col("col1") + 1).collect())  ❶
```

❶ This line recalculates the LazyFrame from scratch.

```
shape: (3, 2)
┌──────┬──────┐
│ col1 │ col2 │
│ ---  │ ---  │
│ i64  │ i64  │
╞══════╪══════╡
│ 1    │ 4    │
│ 2    │ 5    │
│ 3    │ 6    │
└──────┴──────┘
shape: (3, 2)
┌──────┬──────┐
│ col1 │ col2 │
│ ---  │ ---  │
│ i64  │ i64  │
╞══════╪══════╡
│ 2    │ 4    │
│ 3    │ 5    │
│ 4    │ 6    │
└──────┴──────┘
```

At the end of this chapter we'll give you a trick to prevent recalculation by "caching" the intermittent result.

Functionality Differences

The big difference between a LazyFrame and a DataFrame is that in a LazyFrame, the data is not available until it's collected. This means certain functionalities will not be available. We'll go through the different types of operations in the next section and point out the differences.

Attributes

Of all the *attributes* that are available to a DataFrame, the LazyFrame lacks `shape`, `height`, and `flags`, as shown in Table 5-1. The first two describe the number of Series and rows the DataFrame has, which can only be given once the data is available. `flags` is a dictionary containing indicators like whether a Series is sorted, which is used internally for optimizations.

Table 5-1. Attributes of DataFrames versus LazyFrames

Attribute	DataFrame	LazyFrame
.columns	✓	✓
.dtypes	✓	✓
.flags	✓	
.height	✓	
.schema	✓	✓
.shape	✓	
.width	✓	✓

Aggregation Methods

Table 5-2 lists both *vertical aggregation* methods and *horizontal aggregation* methods. The latter have names that end with `_horizontal`.

All the vertical aggregation methods, such as `df.max()`, can be applied to both DataFrames and LazyFrames. These methods don't require the query engine to have knowledge about the data up front, and will be added to the query plan to be executed upon data collection.

Horizontal aggregation methods, such as `df.sum_horizontal()`, are applied row-wise across columns. These methods do require the query engine to have knowledge about the data up front. As such, the horizontal aggregation methods are only available to DataFrames.

Table 5-2. Aggregation methods of DataFrames versus LazyFrames

Method	DataFrame	LazyFrame
.count()	✓	✓
.max()	✓	✓
.max_horizontal()	✓	
.mean()	✓	✓
.mean_horizontal(…)	✓	
.median()	✓	✓

Method	DataFrame	LazyFrame
.min()	✓	✓
.min_horizontal()	✓	
.product()	✓	
.quantile(…)	✓	✓
.std(…)	✓	✓
.sum()	✓	✓
.sum_horizontal(…)	✓	
.var(…)	✓	✓

Additionally, the df.product() method is only available for DataFrames.

Computation Methods

DataFrames have the *computation* methods df.fold() and df.hash_rows(), while a LazyFrame doesn't have computation methods at all. Both of these computations are row-wise reductions. df.fold() allows you to provide a method that reduces two columns to one, while df.hash_rows() just hashes all the information on a row to a UInt64 value.

Descriptive Methods

The only *descriptive* methods a LazyFrame has are lf.explain() and lf.show_graph() to showcase the query plan, as shown in Table 5-3. A DataFrame has a lot of methods to showcase specifics about the data, such as df.describe() and df.estimated_size().

Table 5-3. Descriptive methods of DataFrames versus LazyFrames

Method	DataFrame	LazyFrame
.approx_n_unique()	✓	
.describe(…)	✓	[a]
.estimated_size(…)	✓	
.explain(…)		✓
.glimpse()	✓	
.is_duplicated()	✓	
.is_empty()	✓	
.is_unique()	✓	
.n_chunks()	✓	
.n_unique(…)	✓	

Method	DataFrame	LazyFrame
.null_count()	✓	✓
.show_graph(…)		✓

[a] LazyFrame technically has the lf.describe() operation, but this collects the results to gather it.

GroupBy Methods

All the methods you can apply to a *group* in the GroupBy context are the same in both LazyFrames and DataFrames, except that a DataFrame lets you iterate over the groups, as shown in Table 5-4.

Table 5-4. GroupBy methods of DataFrames versus LazyFrames

Method	DataFrame	LazyFrame
.__iter__()	✓	
.agg(…)	✓	✓
.all()	✓	✓
.count()	✓	✓
.first()	✓	✓
.head(…)	✓	✓
.last()	✓	✓
.len()	✓	✓
.map_groups(…)	✓	✓
.max()	✓	✓
.mean()	✓	✓
.median()	✓	✓
.min()	✓	✓
.n_unique()	✓	✓
.quantile(…)	✓	✓
.sum()	✓	✓
.tail(…)	✓	✓

Exporting Methods

A DataFrame has several options of exporting the data to different formats (see Table 5-5). Since a LazyFrame doesn't have any data, there's no possibility for exports.

Table 5-5. Export methods for DataFrames

Method	Description
df.to_arrow(…)	Collect the underlying Arrow arrays in an Arrow table.
df.to_dict(…)	Convert DataFrame to a dictionary mapping Series name to values.
df.to_dicts()	Convert every row to a dictionary of Python-native values.
df.to_init_repr(…)	Convert DataFrame to instantiable String representation.
df.to_jax(…)	Convert DataFrame to a JAX array, or dict of JAX arrays.
df.to_numpy(…)	Convert this DataFrame to a NumPy ndarray.
df.to_pandas(…)	Convert this DataFrame to a pandas DataFrame.
df.to_struct(…)	Convert a DataFrame to a Series of type Struct.
df.to_torch(…)	Convert DataFrame to a PyTorch tensor, dataset, or dictionary of tensors.

DataFrames and LazyFrames also have a `.serialize()` method, which can be considered a way of exporting data.

Manipulation and Selection Methods

The *manipulation* and *selection* methods are the most important ones. They contain the core functionality of data manipulation. Table 5-6 shows the many differences between the two APIs.

Table 5-6. Manipulation methods of DataFrames versus LazyFrames

Method	DataFrame	LazyFrame
.bottom_k(…)	✓	✓
.cast(…)	✓	✓
.clear(…)	✓	✓
.clone()	✓	✓
.drop(…)	✓	✓
.drop_in_place(…)	✓	
.drop_nulls(…)	✓	✓
.explode(…)	✓	✓
.extend(…)	✓	
.fill_nan(…)	✓	✓
.fill_null(…)	✓	✓
.filter(…)	✓	✓
.first()		✓
.gather_every(…)	✓	✓

Method	DataFrame	LazyFrame
.get_column(…)	✓	
.get_column_index(…)	✓	
.get_columns()	✓	
.group_by(…)	✓	✓
.group_by_dynamic(…)	✓	✓
.head(…)	✓	✓
.hstack(…)	✓	
.insert_column(…)	✓	
.inspect(…)		✓
.interpolate()	✓	✓
.item(…)	✓	
.iter_columns()	✓	
.iter_rows()	✓	
.iter_slices(…)	✓	
.join(…)	✓	✓
.join_asof(…)	✓	✓
.join_where(…)	✓	✓
.last()		✓
.limit(…)	✓	✓
.melt(…)	✓	✓
.merge_sorted(…)	✓	✓
.partition_by()	✓	
.pipe(…)	✓	
.pivot(…)	✓	
.rechunk()	✓	
.rename(…)	✓	✓
.replace_column(…)	✓	
.reverse()	✓	✓
.rolling(…)	✓	✓
.row(…)	✓	
.rows(…)	✓	
.rows_by_key(…)	✓	
.sample(…)	✓	
.select(…)	✓	✓
.select_seq(…)	✓	✓
.set_sorted(…)	✓	✓

Method	DataFrame	LazyFrame
.shift(…)	✓	✓
.shrink_to_fit(…)	✓	
.slice(…)	✓	✓
.sort(…)	✓	✓
.sql(…)	✓	✓
.tail(…)	✓	✓
.to_dummies(…)	✓	
.to_series(…)	✓	
.top_k(…)	✓	✓
.transpose(…)	✓	
.unique(…)	✓	✓
.unnest(…)	✓	✓
.unpivot(…)	✓	✓
.unstack(…)	✓	
.update(…)	✓	✓
.upsample(…)	✓	
.vstack(…)	✓	
.with_columns(…)	✓	✓
.with_columns_seq(…)	✓	✓
.with_context(…)		✓
.with_row_count(…)	✓	✓
.with_row_index(…)	✓	✓

Miscellaneous Methods

The *miscellaneous* methods are the ones that don't fit in any of the other categories. These are shown in Table 5-7.

Table 5-7. Miscellaneous methods of DataFrames versus LazyFrames

Method	DataFrame	LazyFrame
.cache()		✓
.collect(…)		✓
.collect_async()		✓
.collect_schema()	✓	✓
.corr(…)	✓	
.equals(…)	✓	
.lazy()	✓	✓

Method	DataFrame	LazyFrame
.map_batches(…)		✓
.map_rows(…)	✓	
.pipe(…)		✓
.profile(…)		✓

Unstable Out-of-Core Computation

The lazy API offers a special mode to do computations *out of core*: that is, processing data that would be too large to fit into RAM by doing the calculations on *chunks* of data instead. The amazing thing about supporting out-of-core computation is that it moves the barrier for processing data from the size of your RAM to the size of your hard disk, which can be a difference of orders of magnitude. You can trigger this mode by passing streaming=True to the lf.collect() method to collect the end result to RAM, or you can write the results to disk using lf.sink_csv(), lf.sink_ipc(), lf.sink_parquet(), or lf.sink_ndjson(). If you use lf.collect(streaming=True), the end result must fit in RAM.

In streaming mode, the API reads the data in chunks of rows. This chunk size is determined by Polars based on your hardware and the dataset you're working with. This API is used in the exact same way as the lazy API, but the execution model under the hood is different.

This mode is experimental at the time of writing and will not be covered further in this edition of the book.

Tips and Tricks

In this section we'll cover some tips and tricks. Most of these will be very practical in your day-to-day usage of Polars. This is typically the kind of information that you won't find in the documentation but that can make your life a lot easier.

Going from LazyFrame to DataFrame and Vice Versa

You can switch from one API to the other with a single command, as shown in Figure 5-1.

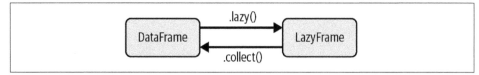

Figure 5-1. Two methods to switch between APIs

You can go from the eager API to the lazy API by adding `df.lazy()` behind a DataFrame or methods returning a DataFrame. This results in no computation, but tells the query planner to use the data in memory as a starting point for a new query plan.

You can go from the lazy to eager API by calling `lf.collect()` on a LazyFrame or a function returning a LazyFrame. This executes the query plan built for that LazyFrame, triggering computation. Afterwards, the result will be stored in RAM. If you're using streaming mode and not calling `lf.collect()`, but calling `lf.sink_parquet()` instead, the result is written to disk, preventing out-of-memory errors.

Joining a DataFrame with a LazyFrame

When you perform joins in Polars, the data structures involved *must be of the same type*. To be specific, you cannot directly join a DataFrame with a LazyFrame. You might want to do this if, for example, you've got a small DataFrame with metadata that you want to join with a large dataset that you've got in a LazyFrame.

Here's a snippet that would result in an error:

```
big_sales_data = pl.LazyFrame(
    {"sale_id": [101, 102, 103], "amount": [250, 150, 300]}
)

sales_metadata = pl.DataFrame(
    {"sale_id": [101, 102, 103], "category": ["A", "B", "A"]}
)

big_sales_data.join(sales_metadata, on="sale_id").collect()

TypeError: expected `other` join table to be a LazyFrame, not a 'DataFrame'
```

Fortunately, resolving this is straightforward. You can either make the DataFrame lazy by appending `df.lazy()`, or materialize the LazyFrame using `lf.collect()`. We advise sticking with the lazy API for better performance and efficiency.

Here's how to successfully perform the join by making the DataFrame lazy:

```
big_sales_data = pl.LazyFrame(
    {"sale_id": [101, 102, 103], "amount": [250, 150, 300]}
)

sales_metadata = pl.DataFrame(
    {"sale_id": [101, 102, 103], "category": ["A", "B", "A"]}
)

big_sales_data.join(sales_metadata.lazy(), on="sale_id").collect()

shape: (3, 3)
```

```
┌─────────┬────────┬──────────┐
│ sale_id │ amount │ category │
```

```
| ---   | ---   | ---  |
| i64   | i64   | str  |
|=======|=======|======|
| 101   | 250   | A    |
| 102   | 150   | B    |
| 103   | 300   | A    |
```

Where in the first output you got an error, you now get a valid LazyFrame.

Caching Intermittent Results

LazyFrames are smart, but they're not magic. If it's calculated one time, and you don't save it either to disk or to a variable in memory, it will need to be recalculated the next time you call on it. To avoid unnecessarily recomputations, you can *cache* the LazyFrame. Caching is done by calling `lf.collect().lazy()` after the heavy computation and saving the result to a variable. This will evaluate the LazyFrame, keep it in memory, and return a new LazyFrame pointing to the materialized data stored in RAM.

Here's how you can optimize the preceding example. (We're not so much concerned with the actual timing here, but more about the idea that steps have to be recomputed.)

```
lf = pl.LazyFrame({"col1": [1, 2, 3], "col2": [4, 5, 6]})

# ... Some heavy computation ...

lf = lf.collect().lazy()   ❶
print(lf.collect())

print(lf.with_columns(pl.col("col1") + 1).collect())   ❷
```

❶ Cache the LazyFrame.

❷ This line makes use of the cached LazyFrame.

```
shape: (3, 2)
┌──────┬──────┐
│ col1 │ col2 │
│ ---  │ ---  │
│ i64  │ i64  │
╞══════╪══════╡
│ 1    │ 4    │
│ 2    │ 5    │
│ 3    │ 6    │
└──────┴──────┘
shape: (3, 2)
┌──────┬──────┐
│ col1 │ col2 │
```

```
|  ---  |  ---  |
|  i64  |  i64  |
╞═══════╪═══════╡
|   2   |   4   |
|   3   |   5   |
|   4   |   6   |
└───────┴───────┘
```

If you hadn't cached the LazyFrame, the second `lf.collect()` call would've recalcu-lated the LazyFrame from scratch. This pattern can be a lifesaver when dealing with resource-intensive computations, as it enables you to leverage the benefits of lazy evaluation while mitigating its computational drawbacks.

Takeaways

In this chapter we've covered eager and lazy APIs in Polars. Among other things, you learned about:

- The eager API, which immediately executes queries and is accessed through the DataFrame API. That makes it most useful for iterative calculations and data exploration.
- The lazy API, which defers execution to optimize the work it needs to do and is accessed through the LazyFrame API. That makes it most useful for when you want the most performance of your calculation and when you don't need the intermittent results.
- How LazyFrames don't contain data, while DataFrames do, and that they have some differences in functionality because of that.
- The lazy API streaming mode, which lets you calculate out-of-core with larger-than-RAM datasets.
- Some practical tips, like how use caching to avoid calculating the same Lazy-Frame multiple times, and how to join DataFrames and LazyFrames.

With this knowledge, you can determine which is the perfect API for your use case. Now it's time to learn to load data from files into the structures we've talked about in this chapter. The next chapter is about reading and writing data to and from different file formats.

## CHAPTER 6

Reading and Writing Data

Now that you've seen some essential concepts such as data types and the different APIs, you're ready to learn about working with external data sources. That includes reading data from files and databases into Polars. We'll also cover how to write your results to files and databases. By the end of this chapter, you'll be able to start working with your own data. We encourage you to start using your own data as soon as possible, because it will make learning about Polars not only more enjoyable but also more effective.

External data can come in all sorts of ways from all sorts of places. Because of this, Polars has over 30 functions related to reading data, and those functions accept many arguments. It would be challenging and, more importantly, extremely boring to cover every function and every argument in this chapter. That's what the official API documentation (*https://oreil.ly/kuLtC*) is for. We'll give a quick overview of the formats Polars supports, together with the relevant methods to work with them. In the rest of the chapter, we will focus on the formats and situations that you're most likely to encounter.

In this chapter, you'll learn how to:

- Read and write data in many formats, including CSV, Excel, and Parquet
- Handle multiple files efficiently using globbing
- Correctly read missing values
- Deal with character encodings
- Read data eagerly and lazily

You'll be using a couple of additional packages:

- xlsx2csv to read Excel spreadsheets
- chardet to determine the character encoding of a file
- ConnectorX to connect to databases
- pyarrow to read PyArrow datasets

Chapter 2 has instructions for how to install these packages.

In order to demonstrate working with various data formats, this chapter uses a lot of datasets. The instructions to get the corresponding files are in Chapter 2. We assume that you have the files in the *data* subdirectory.

Format Overview

Polars supports many formats. You can find an overview of these formats and their corresponding read functions and write methods in Table 6-1. For brevity's sake, we've omitted the `pl.` and `df.` prefixes in the table. Names that start with `read_` and `scan_` are top-level functions. Names that start with `write_` and `sink_` are DataFrame and LazyFrame methods. Not all options of reading and writing are supported for all data formats.

Table 6-1. Supported I/O formats in Polars and the corresponding read functions and write methods

Format	Read (`pl.`)	Read lazy (`pl.`)	Write (`df.`)	Write streaming (`df.`)
Avro	`read_avro()`		`write_avro()`	
Clipboard	`read_clipboard()`		`write_clipboard()`	
CSV	`read_csv()` `read_csv_batched()`	`scan_csv()`	`write_csv()`	`sink_csv()`
Database	`read_database()` `read_database_uri()`		`write_database()`	
Delta Lake	`read_delta()`	`scan_delta()`	`write_delta()`	
Excel/ODS	`read_excel()` `read_ods()`		`write_excel()`	
Feather/IPC	`read_ipc()` `read_ipc_schema()` `read_ipc_stream()`	`scan_ipc()`	`write_ipc()` `write_ipc_stream()`	`sink_ipc()`
Iceberg		`scan_iceberg()`		
JSON	`read_json()` `read_ndjson()`	`scan_ndjson()`	`write_json()` `write_ndjson()`	`sink_ndjson()`

Format	Read (pl.)	Read lazy (pl.)	Write (df.)	Write streaming (df.)
Parquet	read_parquet() read_par quet_schema()	scan_parquet()	write_parquet()	sink_parquet()
PyArrow Dataset[a]		scan_pyar row_dataset(…)		

[a] This is not an actual data format. Instead, Polars can use the PyArrow reader to parse datasets that correspond to the format pyarrow can read.

Reading CSV Files

We'll start with comma-separated values (CSV), the file format that is perhaps most prevalent in programming, data analysis, and scientific research. Despite its prevalence, it's not without its flaws. When you're handed a file with the extension *.csv*, there's no knowing what's inside:

- Is the delimiter a comma, a tab, a semicolon, or something else?
- Is the character encoding UTF-8, ASCII, or something else?
- Is there a header with column names? How many lines is it?
- How are missing values represented?
- Are values properly quoted?

Polars can handle all these situations, but there might be some trial and error involved.

Imagine, for a moment, that you have a straightforward CSV file such as *data/penguins.csv*. Before you immediately start loading this data into Polars, let's have a look at the raw contents of the file using the command-line tool cat:[1]

```
! cat data/penguins.csv

"rowid","species","island","bill_length_mm","bill_depth_mm","flipper_length_mm"…
"1","Adelie","Torgersen",39.1,18.7,181,3750,"male",2007
"2","Adelie","Torgersen",39.5,17.4,186,3800,"female",2007
"3","Adelie","Torgersen",40.3,18,195,3250,"female",2007
"4","Adelie","Torgersen",NA,NA,NA,NA,NA,2007
"5","Adelie","Torgersen",36.7,19.3,193,3450,"female",2007
"6","Adelie","Torgersen",39.3,20.6,190,3650,"male",2007
"7","Adelie","Torgersen",38.9,17.8,181,3625,"female",2007
"8","Adelie","Torgersen",39.2,19.6,195,4675,"male",2007
"9","Adelie","Torgersen",34.1,18.1,193,3475,NA,2007
… with 335 more lines
```

---

1 If you're on Windows and cat doesn't seem to work, you can use type instead.

At first glance, this CSV file appears to be straightforward indeed. The first line is a header and the delimiter is a comma, which matches Polars' defaults. Moreover, the character encoding is compatible with UTF-8 (more on this later). This makes us feel confident enough to read the dataset into a Polars DataFrame:

```
penguins = pl.read_csv("data/penguins.csv")
penguins
```

shape: (344, 9)

rowid	species	island	...	body_mass_g	sex	year
---	---	---		---	---	---
i64	str	str		str	str	i64
1	Adelie	Torgersen	...	3750	male	2007
2	Adelie	Torgersen	...	3800	female	2007
3	Adelie	Torgersen	...	3250	female	2007
4	Adelie	Torgersen	...	NA	NA	2007
5	Adelie	Torgersen	...	3450	female	2007
...	...	...	...	...	...	...
340	Chinstrap	Dream	...	4000	male	2009
341	Chinstrap	Dream	...	3400	female	2009
342	Chinstrap	Dream	...	3775	male	2009
343	Chinstrap	Dream	...	4100	male	2009
344	Chinstrap	Dream	...	3775	female	2009

It looks like this CSV file has been read correctly, except for one thing: NA values are not interpreted as missing values, as you can see in the body_mass_g column, row 4. You'll fix that in the next section.

If your CSV file is different, then perhaps the arguments listed in Table 6-2 can help.

Table 6-2. Common arguments for the function pl.read_csv()

Argument	Description
source	Path to a file or a file-like object.
has_header	Indicate if the first row of dataset is a header or not.
columns	Columns to select. Accepts a list of column indices (starting at zero) or a list of column names.
separator	Single-byte character to use as delimiter in the file.
skip_rows	Start reading after a certain number of lines.
null_values	Values to interpret as null values.
encoding	Default of utf8. utf8-lossy means that invalid UTF-8 values are replaced with ◆ characters. When using other encodings than utf8 or utf8-lossy, the input is first decoded in memory with Python.

Parsing Missing Values Correctly

It's quite common for a dataset to have missing values. Unfortunately for plain-text formats such as CSV, there's no standard way to represent these. Representations that we've seen in the wild include NULL, Nil, None, NA, N/A, NaN, 999999, and the empty String.

By default, Polars only interprets empty Strings as missing values. Any other representations need to be passed explicitly as a String (or a list of Strings) to the null_values argument. So let's fix those missing values in *data/penguins.csv*:

```
penguins = pl.read_csv("data/penguins.csv", null_values="NA")
penguins
```

shape: (344, 9)

rowid	species	island	...	body_mass_g	sex	year
i64	str	str		i64	str	i64
1	Adelie	Torgersen	...	3750	male	2007
2	Adelie	Torgersen	...	3800	female	2007
3	Adelie	Torgersen	...	3250	female	2007
4	Adelie	Torgersen	...	null	null	2007
5	Adelie	Torgersen	...	3450	female	2007
...	...	...	...	...	...	...
340	Chinstrap	Dream	...	4000	male	2009
341	Chinstrap	Dream	...	3400	female	2009
342	Chinstrap	Dream	...	3775	male	2009
343	Chinstrap	Dream	...	4100	male	2009
344	Chinstrap	Dream	...	3775	female	2009

DataFrames in This Book Versus Jupyter Notebook

When DataFrames are rendered in ASCII, such as in this book, all Strings are displayed without quotes. That means you won't be able to check visually whether missing values are interpreted correctly.

When you're using Jupyter Notebook, you'll get an HTML rendering of a DataFrame, as shown in Figure 3-2. Here, missing values are displayed as null without quotes, whereas regular Strings are displayed with quotes.

If you're not sure whether all missing values have been parsed correctly, you can count them programmatically using the df.null_count() method:

```
penguins.null_count().transpose(   ❶
    include_header=True, column_names=["null_count"]
)
```

❶ You transpose the output to get a better overview of all the counts.

```
shape: (9, 2)
┌──────────────────┬────────────┐
│ column           │ null_count │
│ ---              │ ---        │
│ str              │ u32        │
╞══════════════════╪════════════╡
│ rowid            │ 0          │
│ species          │ 0          │
│ island           │ 0          │
│ bill_length_mm   │ 2          │
│ bill_depth_mm    │ 2          │
│ flipper_length_mm│ 2          │
│ body_mass_g      │ 2          │
│ sex              │ 11         │
│ year             │ 0          │
└──────────────────┴────────────┘
```

In Chapter 4 we discuss various strategies for dealing with missing values.

Reading Files with Encodings Other Than UTF-8

Every text file has a certain *character encoding*. A character encoding is a system that assigns unique codes to individual characters in a set, allowing them to be represented and processed by computers.

Polars assumes that the CSV file is encoded in UTF-8, which is a widely used encoding. UTF-8 can represent any character in the Unicode standard, which includes a vast range of characters from a multitude of languages, both modern and historic, as well as a wide array of symbols.

If you try to read a CSV file with a different encoding than UTF-8, you'll ideally[2] get an error, just like we get here with *data/directors.csv*:

```
pl.read_csv("data/directors.csv")

ComputeError: invalid utf-8 sequence
```

Apparently, *data/directors.csv* is not encoded in UTF-8.

If you start guessing the encoding, you could end up using one that doesn't upset Polars, but the bytes in your file could still get interpreted incorrectly. If you're not familiar with the language, then it's difficult to spot that something's off.

---

2 We say "ideally" because then it's clear that you haven't specified the correct encoding.

Now let's imagine you're told that your file contains the names of directors, including some Asian names. Your best guess is to try an encoding common for Chinese characters:

```
pl.read_csv("data/directors.csv", encoding="EUC-CN")
```

```
shape: (4, 3)
```

name	born	country
str	i64	str
考侯	1930	泣塑
Verhoeven	1938	オランダ
弟宏	1942	泣塑
Tarantino	1963	势柜

That worked. Or did it? When you verify this by translating (using, for example, your favorite search engine) the first country from Chinese to English, it says "Weeping plastic." What? That's no country we've ever heard of!

Instead of guessing the encoding, it's better to let the chardet package detect it. The following function returns the encoding for a given filename. Let's apply this function to our CSV file:

```
import chardet


def detect_encoding(filename: str) -> str:
    """Return the most probable character encoding for a file."""

    with open(filename, "rb") as f:
        raw_data = f.read()
        result = chardet.detect(raw_data)
        return result["encoding"]


detect_encoding("data/directors.csv")
```

```
'EUC-JP'
```

So chardet detected a different encoding—one that's often used for Japanese characters. Let's try the EUC-JP encoding with Polars:

```
pl.read_csv("data/directors.csv", encoding="EUC-JP")
```

```
shape: (4, 3)
```

name	born	country
str	i64	str

```
| 深作      | 1930 | 日本     |
| Verhoeven | 1938 | オランダ |
| 宮崎      | 1942 | 日本     |
| Tarantino | 1963 | 米国     |
```

Now this is correct. Trust us, we checked it.

Conclusion: you'd better not guess the encoding of a file. This holds not just for CSV files, but for all text-based files, including JSON, XML, and HTML.

Reading Excel Spreadsheets

While CSV is common in data-heavy, programmatic, and analytical contexts, Excel spreadsheets are common in business contexts, which often involve manual data inspection, data entry, and basic analyses.

They can contain complex data, markup, formulas, and charts. Although useful for business applications, these features can hamper reading the spreadsheet into Polars. Ideally, the spreadsheet would only contain data in a rectangular shape, just like a CSV file.

To read Excel spreadsheets into a DataFrame, Polars can use the calamine, xlsx2csv, or openpyxl package. (Instructions on how to install these packages can be found in Chapter 2.) The calamine package is the default and is a Rust-based package that serializes and deserializes spreadsheets impressively fast. The xlsx2csv package converts the Excel file to an in-memory CSV file using the `pl.read_csv()` functionality of Polars. The openpyxl package is significantly slower than the other two, but supports automatic type inference, making it useful for some edge cases where the other packages fail to successfully read an Excel file. In our examples you'll work with calamine, which is the default.

Let's read *data/top-2000-2023.xlsx*, which is a spreadsheet from Top2000, an annual Dutch radio program. It contains the two thousand most popular songs as voted by the station's listeners in 2023.

```
songs = pl.read_excel("data/top2000-2023.xlsx")   ❶
songs
```

❶ The Dutch column names translate to position, title, artist, and year. (Fun fact: Dutch is, after Frisian, the closest relative of English.)

```
shape: (2_000, 4)
```

positie	titel	artiest	jaar
i64	str	str	i64
1	Bohemian Rhapsody	Queen	1975

```
| 2    | Roller Coaster       | Danny Vera     | 2019 |
| 3    | Hotel California     | Eagles         | 1977 |
| 4    | Piano Man            | Billy Joel     | 1974 |
| 5    | Fix You              | Coldplay       | 2005 |
| …    | …                    | …              | …    |
| 1996 | Charlie Brown        | Coldplay       | 2011 |
| 1997 | Beast Of Burden      | Bette Midler   | 1984 |
| 1998 | It Was A Very Good Y… | Frank Sinatra  | 1968 |
| 1999 | Hou Van Mij          | 3JS            | 2008 |
| 2000 | Drivers License      | Olivia Rodrigo | 2021 |
```

Table 6-3 lists some commonly used arguments.

Table 6-3. Common arguments for the function `pl.read_excel()`

Argument	Description
source	Path to a file or a file-like object.
sheet_id	Sheet number to convert (0 for all sheets). Defaults to 1 if neither this nor sheet_name are specified. If multiple sheets are selected, the function will return a dictionary with the sheet name as key, and the DataFrame as value.
sheet_name	Sheet name to convert. Cannot be used in conjunction with sheet_id.
engine	The package used to process the Excel file. Can be calamine, xlsx2csv, or openpyxl.
engine_options	Additional options passed to the engine's constructor function. (Doesn't work for calamine.)
read_options	Additional options passed to the engine's function reading the file. (Doesn't work for openpyxl.)
has_header	Whether the file uses a header for the table.

If you find that `pl.read_excel()` doesn't work with your spreadsheet files out of the box, we recommend you try the openpyxl or xlsx2csv engine and tweak the `engine_options` as needed. You can refer to the documentation (*https://oreil.ly/a4yCp*) for advanced options.

Working with Multiple Files

If your data is spread across multiple files and those files all have the same format and schema, you might be able to read them all at once.

For instance, let's consider daily stock information for three companies: ASML Holding N.V. (ASML), NVIDIA Corporation (NVDA), and Taiwan Semiconductor Manufacturing Company Limited (TSM). The data is split across multiple CSV files, such that you have one file per company per year. The files are named according to the pattern *data/stock/<symbol>/<year>.csv*. For example: *data/stock/nvda/2010.csv* and *data/stock/asml/2022.csv*.

Because these files have the same format and schema, you can use a *globbing pattern*. Globbing patterns can contain special characters which act as wildcards, such as:

- Asterisks (*), which match zero or more characters in a String. For example, the pattern *.csv will match any filename that ends in *.csv*.

- Question marks (?), which match exactly one character. For example, the pattern file?.csv will match files like *file1.csv* or *fileA.csv* but not *file12.csv*.

- Square brackets ([]), which match one character of a certain set or a range. For example, file-[ab].csv matches *file-a.csv* and *file-b.csv*. The pattern file-[0-9].csv matches *file-0.csv*, *file-1.csv*, *file-2.csv*, up to *file-9.csv*.

To read NVIDIA stock data for years 2010 through 2019, use the following pattern:

```
pl.read_csv("data/stock/nvda/201?.csv")
```

shape: (2_516, 8)

symbol	date	open	...	close	adj close	volume
str	str	f64		f64	f64	i64
NVDA	2010-01-04	4.6275	...	4.6225	4.240429	80020400
NVDA	2010-01-05	4.605	...	4.69	4.30235	72864800
NVDA	2010-01-06	4.6875	...	4.72	4.32987	64916800
NVDA	2010-01-07	4.695	...	4.6275	4.245015	54779200
NVDA	2010-01-08	4.59	...	4.6375	4.254189	47816800
...	...	...	...	...	...	...
NVDA	2019-12-24	59.549999	...	59.654999	59.422798	13886400
NVDA	2019-12-26	59.689999	...	59.797501	59.564739	18285200
NVDA	2019-12-27	59.950001	...	59.217499	58.987	25464400
NVDA	2019-12-30	58.997501	...	58.080002	57.853928	25805600
NVDA	2019-12-31	57.724998	...	58.825001	58.596027	23100400

To read all CSV files in the *data/stock* directory, use two asterisks because they're located in different subdirectories:

```
all_stocks = pl.read_csv("data/stock/**/*.csv")
all_stocks
```

shape: (18_476, 8)

symbol	date	open	...	close	adj close	volume
str	str	f64		f64	f64	i64
ASML	1999-01-04	11.765625	...	12.140625	7.522523	1801867
ASML	1999-01-05	11.859375	...	13.96875	8.655257	8241600
ASML	1999-01-06	14.25	...	16.875	10.456018	16400267
ASML	1999-01-07	14.742188	...	16.851563	10.441495	17722133

ASML	1999-01-08	16.078125	...	15.796875	9.787995	10696000
...	...	...	...	...	...	...
TSM	2023-06-26	102.019997	...	100.110001	99.125954	8560000
TSM	2023-06-27	101.150002	...	102.080002	101.076591	9732000
TSM	2023-06-28	100.5	...	100.919998	99.927986	8160900
TSM	2023-06-29	101.339996	...	100.639999	99.650742	7383900
TSM	2023-06-30	101.400002	...	100.919998	99.927986	11701700

If you cannot express the files you wish to read through a globbing pattern, you can use a manual approach:

1. Construct a list of filenames to read.

2. Read those files using the appropriate Polars function (e.g., `pl.read_csv()`).

3. Combine the Polars DataFrames using the `pl.concat()` function.

Here's an example where you read all ASML stock data from leap years:

```
import calendar

filenames = [
    f"data/stock/asml/{year}.csv"
    for year in range(1999, 2024)
    if calendar.isleap(year)
]

filenames
```

```
['data/stock/asml/2000.csv',
 'data/stock/asml/2004.csv',
 'data/stock/asml/2008.csv',
 'data/stock/asml/2012.csv',
 'data/stock/asml/2016.csv',
 'data/stock/asml/2020.csv']
```

```
pl.concat(pl.read_csv(f) for f in filenames)
```

shape: (1_512, 8)

symbol	date	open	...	close	adj close	volume
---	---	---		---	---	---
str	str	f64		f64	f64	i64
ASML	2000-01-03	43.875	...	43.640625	27.040424	1121600
ASML	2000-01-04	41.953125	...	40.734375	25.239666	968800
ASML	2000-01-05	39.28125	...	39.609375	24.542597	1458133
ASML	2000-01-06	36.75	...	37.171875	23.032274	3517867
ASML	2000-01-07	36.867188	...	38.015625	23.555077	1631200
...	...	...	...	...	...	...
ASML	2020-12-24	478.950012	...	483.089996	468.836365	271900
ASML	2020-12-28	487.140015	...	480.23999	466.070496	449300
ASML	2020-12-29	489.450012	...	484.01001	469.729218	377200

```
| ASML   | 2020-12-30 | 488.130005 | … | 489.910004 | 475.455231 | 381900 |
| ASML   | 2020-12-31 | 490.0      | … | 487.720001 | 473.329803 | 312700 |
```

We discuss the `pl.concat()` function in more detail in Chapter 14.

Reading Parquet

The Parquet format is a columnar storage file format optimized for use in big data processing frameworks like Apache Spark, DuckDB, and, of course, Polars. While Parquet is designed for efficient on-disk storage, it complements the Apache Arrow in-memory format that Polars is built on by having a comparable columnar data representation, allowing seamless transitions between disk and memory, which we'll discuss in Chapter 18.

Compared to row-based formats like CSV and Excel, Parquet is more efficient at reading and writing large datasets, especially when querying specific columns. Additionally, Parquet supports complex nested data structures, while CSV and Excel are generally flat, making Parquet a more versatile choice for complex datasets. Parquet files also include the schema of the data, eliminating the kinds of errors that you saw when reading CSV files.

Here's an example using trip data from yellow cabs in New York City:

```
%%time
trips = pl.read_parquet("data/taxi/yellow_tripdata_*.parquet")
trips
```

```
CPU times: user 2 µs, sys: 0 ns, total: 2 µs
Wall time: 4.05 µs
shape: (39_656_098, 19)
```

VendorID	tpep_pickup_datetime	…	congestion_surcharge	airport_fee
---	---		---	---
i64	datetime[ns]		f64	f64
1	2022-01-01 00:35:40	…	2.5	0.0
1	2022-01-01 00:33:43	…	0.0	0.0
2	2022-01-01 00:53:21	…	0.0	0.0
2	2022-01-01 00:25:21	…	2.5	0.0
2	2022-01-01 00:36:48	…	2.5	0.0
…	…	…	…	…
2	2022-12-31 23:46:00	…	null	null
2	2022-12-31 23:13:24	…	null	null
2	2022-12-31 23:00:49	…	null	null
1	2022-12-31 23:02:50	…	null	null
2	2022-12-31 23:00:15	…	null	null

The Need for Speed

On our modest laptops, reading nearly 40 million rows with `pl.read_parquet()` takes only a few microseconds. You can measure the time it takes on your machine using Jupyter's `%time` magic.

Table 6-4 lists some commonly used arguments for reading Parquet files.

Table 6-4. Common arguments for the function `pl.read_parquet()`

Argument	Description
source	Path to a file or a file-like object. If the path is a directory, files in that directory will all be read.
columns	Columns to select. Accepts a list of column indices (starting at zero) or a list of column names.
n_rows	Stop reading from Parquet file after reading n_rows. Only valid when use_pyarrow=False.
use_pyarrow	Use PyArrow instead of the Rust-native Parquet reader. The PyArrow reader is more stable (default: False).

Parquet's speed and robustness make it, in our humble opinion, the best file format when working with DataFrames. You'll be seeing a lot more of it in the rest of this book.

Reading JSON and NDJSON

In this section we discuss how to read JavaScript Object Notation (JSON), and its cousin Newline Delimited JSON (NDJSON).

JSON

JSON is a text format that is easy for humans to read and write, and easy for machines to parse and generate. Unlike CSV and Excel, JSON can contain nested data structures. This flexibility makes it a popular choice for APIs, NoSQL databases, and configuration files.

Let's look at the raw contents of *data/pokedex.json*:

```
! cat data/pokedex.json
{
  "pokemon": [{
    "id": 1,
    "num": "001",
    "name": "Bulbasaur",
    "img": "http://www.serebii.net/pokemongo/pokemon/001.png",
    "type": [
```

```
      "Grass",
      "Poison"
    ],
    "height": "0.71 m",
    "weight": "6.9 kg",
    "candy": "Bulbasaur Candy",
    "candy_count": 25,
    "egg": "2 km",
    "spawn_chance": 0.69,
    "avg_spawns": 69,
    "spawn_time": "20:00",
    "multipliers": [1.58],
    "weaknesses": [
      "Fire",
      "Ice",
      "Flying",
      "Psychic"
    ],
    "next_evolution": [{
      "num": "002",
      "name": "Ivysaur"
    }, {
      "num": "003",
      "name": "Venusaur"
    }]
  }, {
… with 4053 more lines
```

This JSON file starts and ends with a curly brace, meaning that the entire file is one JSON object. Those curly braces are precisely what allows JSON to be highly nested.

The object has one key, pokemon, which contains a list of objects. The first 33 lines show also the first Pokemon object, namely Bulbasaur. This object, in turn, has some keys that contain other objects. Again, this flexibility has many advantages, but as you'll see next, also poses some challenges when reading it with Polars.

So let's see what happens when you read this JSON file into a Polars DataFrame:

```
pokedex = pl.read_json("data/pokedex.json")
pokedex
```

shape: (1, 1)

pokemon
list[struct[17]]
[{1,"001","Bulbasaur","http://www.serebii.net/pokemongo/pokemon/001.png",["Grass", "Poison"],"0.71 m","6.9 kg","Bulbasaur Candy","2 km",0.69,69.0,"20:0…

Notice how everything is read as a single value? That's because the JSON object has only one key, called pokemon, whose value is a list of objects. Polars doesn't make any assumptions as to how to flatten a nested structure into a rectangular shape.

Luckily, Polars offers two methods to flatten the data manually: df.explode(), which is used to turn every item in a list into a new row, and df.unnest(), which is used to turn every key of an object into a new column. We'll discuss these two methods in more detail in Chapter 12. For now, let's flatten the pokedex to some extent:

```
(
    pokedex.explode("pokemon")
    .unnest("pokemon")
    .select("id", "name", "type", "height", "weight")
)
```

shape: (151, 5)

id	name	type	height	weight
i64	str	list[str]	str	str
1	Bulbasaur	["Grass", "Poison"]	0.71 m	6.9 kg
2	Ivysaur	["Grass", "Poison"]	0.99 m	13.0 kg
3	Venusaur	["Grass", "Poison"]	2.01 m	100.0 kg
4	Charmander	["Fire"]	0.61 m	8.5 kg
5	Charmeleon	["Fire"]	1.09 m	19.0 kg
…	…	…	…	…
147	Dratini	["Dragon"]	1.80 m	3.3 kg
148	Dragonair	["Dragon"]	3.99 m	16.5 kg
149	Dragonite	["Dragon", "Flying"]	2.21 m	210.0 kg
150	Mewtwo	["Psychic"]	2.01 m	122.0 kg
151	Mew	["Psychic"]	0.41 m	4.0 kg

Table 6-5 lists some commonly used arguments for reading JSON and NDJSON, which we cover next.

Table 6-5. Common arguments for the functions pl.read_json() and pl.read_ndjson()

Argument	Description
source	Path to a file or a file-like object.
schema	The DataFrame schema may be declared in several ways. (1) As a dictionary of {name: type} pairs; if type is None, it will be auto-inferred. (2) As a list of column names; in this case, types are automatically inferred. (3) As a list of (name, type) pairs; this is equivalent to the dictionary form.
schema_overrides	Support type specification or override one or more columns. Note that any types inferred from the schema argument will be overridden. Underlying data, the names given here will overwrite them.

NDJSON

NDJSON is a convenient format for storing or streaming structured data to be processed one record at a time. It's essentially a collection of JSON objects, separated by newline characters.

Each line in an NDJSON dataset is a valid JSON object, but the file as a whole is not a valid JSON array because the newline characters are not part of the JSON syntax. This format is beneficial because it allows you to add to the dataset easily and read the data efficiently, line by line, which can be particularly useful in streaming scenarios or when dealing with large datasets that cannot fit into memory all at once. NDJSON is used in settings from log files to RESTful APIs.

We've prepared *data/wikimedia.ndjson* by listening to the stream of the Wikimedia API for a while and slightly cleaning it up. Here are the first five lines of that file:

```
! cat data/wikimedia.ndjson
```

```
{"$schema":"/mediawiki/recentchange/1.0.0","meta":{"uri":"https://en.wikipedia.…
{"$schema":"/mediawiki/recentchange/1.0.0","meta":{"uri":"https://en.wikipedia.…
{"$schema":"/mediawiki/recentchange/1.0.0","meta":{"uri":"https://en.wikipedia.…
{"$schema":"/mediawiki/recentchange/1.0.0","meta":{"uri":"https://en.wikipedia.…
{"$schema":"/mediawiki/recentchange/1.0.0","meta":{"uri":"https://en.wikipedia.…
… with 95 more lines
```

Again, every line is a single JSON object. Let's have a closer look at the first one:

```
from json import loads
from pprint import pprint

with open("data/wikimedia.ndjson") as f:
    pprint(loads(f.readline()))
```

```
{'$schema': '/mediawiki/recentchange/1.0.0',
 'bot': False,
 'comment': '/* League champions, runners-up and play-off finalists */',
 'id': 1659529639,
 'length': {'new': 91166, 'old': 91108},
 'meta': {'domain': 'en.wikipedia.org',
          'dt': '2023-07-29T07:51:39Z',
          'id': '0416300b-980c-45bb-b0a2-c9d7a9e2b7eb',
          'offset': 4820784717,
          'partition': 0,
          'request_id': 'ea0541fb-4e72-4fc3-82f0-6c26651b2043',
          'stream': 'mediawiki.recentchange',
          'topic': 'eqiad.mediawiki.recentchange',
          'uri': 'https://en.wikipedia.org/wiki/EFL_Championship'},
 'minor': False,
 'namespace': 0,
 'notify_url': 'https://en.wikipedia.org/w/index.php?diff=1167689309&oldid=1166…
 'parsedcomment': '<span dir="auto"><span class="autocomment"><a '
                  'href="/wiki/EFL_Championship#League_champions,_runners-up_an…
```

```
                    'title="EFL Championship">→\u200eLeague champions, '
                    'runners-up and play-off finalists</a></span></span>',
  'revision': {'new': 1167689309, 'old': 1166824248},
  'server_name': 'en.wikipedia.org',
  'server_script_path': '/w',
  'server_url': 'https://en.wikipedia.org',
  'timestamp': 1690617099,
  'title': 'EFL Championship',
  'title_url': 'https://en.wikipedia.org/wiki/EFL_Championship',
  'type': 'edit',
  'user': '87.12.215.232',
  'wiki': 'enwiki'}
```

Notice that this JSON object is slightly nested. Three keys, namely length, meta, and revision, have multiple keys and values. Let's see how Polars loads this data using the pl.read_ndjson() function:

```
wikimedia = pl.read_ndjson("data/wikimedia.ndjson")
wikimedia
```

shape: (100, 20)

| $schema | meta | … | wiki | parsedcomment |
| --- | --- | | --- | --- |
str	struct[9]		str	str
/mediawiki/recentc…	{"https://en.wikip…	…	enwiki	<span dir="auto"><…
/mediawiki/recentc…	{"https://en.wikip…	…	enwiki	
/mediawiki/recentc…	{"https://en.wikip…	…	enwiki	<span dir="auto"><…
/mediawiki/recentc…	{"https://en.wikip…	…	enwiki	Nominated for dele…
/mediawiki/recentc…	{"https://en.wikip…	…	enwiki	Rescuing 1 sources…
…	…	…	…	…
/mediawiki/recentc…	{"https://en.wikip…	…	enwiki	<span dir="auto"><…
/mediawiki/recentc…	{"https://en.wikip…	…	enwiki	Ce
/mediawiki/recentc…	{"https://en.wikip…	…	enwiki	
/mediawiki/recentc…	{"https://en.wikip…	…	enwiki	
/mediawiki/recentc…	{"https://en.wikip…	…	enwiki	<span dir="auto"><…

Just as with the pokedex, you can use the df.unnest() method to turn the keys into new columns.

```
(
    wikimedia.rename({"id": "edit_id"})
    .unnest("meta")
    .select("timestamp", "title", "user", "comment")
)
```

shape: (100, 4)

timestamp	title	user	comment
i64	str	str	str

```
| 1690617099 | EFL Championship   | 87.12.215.232     | /* League champio… |
| 1690617102 | Lim Sang-choon     | Preferwiki        |                    |
| 1690617104 | Higher             | Ss112             | /* Albums */ add   |
| 1690617104 | International Pok… | Piotrus           | Nominated for del… |
| 1690617105 | Abdul Hamid Khan … | InternetArchiveBo… | Rescuing 1 source… |
| …          | …                  | …                 | …                  |
| 1690617238 | Havering Resident… | MRSC              | /* 2018 election … |
| 1690617235 | Olha Kharlan       | 2603:7000:2101:AA… | Ce                 |
| 1690617238 | Mukim Kota Batu    | Pangalau          |                    |
| 1690617239 | User:IDK1213safas… | 94.101.29.27      |                    |
| 1690617234 | List of bus route… | Pedroperezhumbert… | /* Non-TfL bus ro… |
```

Note that you need to rename the `id` column to `edit_id` because otherwise `df.unn est()` fails, complaining about duplicate column names. Polars requires that all column names are unique in order to apply expressions more efficiently. This sometimes requires renaming columns before they end up in your DataFrame twice. In this case the `meta` struct, containing an `id` field, is turned into a column, while there already is a column called `id`.

Other File Formats

Polars also supports the formats Arrow IPC (Feather version 2), Apache Avro, Delta Lake tables, and PyArrow datasets. For these formats, use the `pl.read_ipc()`, `pl.read_avro()`, `pl.read_delta`, and `pl.scan_pyarrow_dataset()` functions, respectively.

If you have a file that's not supported by Polars, then perhaps pandas can lend a hand. pandas has been around for over 14 years, so it's not surprising that it supports more formats. You can convert a pandas DataFrame to a Polars DataFrame using `pl.from_pandas()`. Here's an example of reading a table from an HTML page:

```
import pandas as pd

url = "https://en.wikipedia.org/wiki/List_of_Latin_abbreviations"
pl.from_pandas(pd.read_html(url)[0])  ❶
```

❶ Because the page contains multiple tables, you need to select the right one.

```
shape: (63, 4)
```

abbreviation	Latin	translation	usage and notes
str	str	str	str
AD	anno Domini	"in the year of t…	Used to label or …
a.i.	ad interim	"temporarily"	Used in business …
a.m.	ante meridiem	"before midday"[1…	Used on the twelv…

ca. c.	circa	"around", "about"...	Used with dates t...
Cap.	capitulus	"chapter"	Used before a cha...
...	...	...	...
SOS	si opus sit	"if there is need...	A prescription in...
sic	sic	"thus"	Used when quoting...
stat.	statim	"immediately"	Often used in med...
viz.	videlicet	"namely", "to wit...	In contradistinct...
vs. v.	versus	"against"	Sometimes is not ...

Besides HTML, pandas (not Polars) offers support for reading fixed-width text files, HDF5, ORC, SAS, SPSS, Stata, XML, and other formats. Some of these formats require an additional package to be installed. For instance, the preceding HTML example requires the lxml package. See the I/O Tools section in the pandas User Guide (*https://oreil.ly/FEYZK*) for more information.

Querying Databases

Polars provides a convenient way to interface with relational databases using the pl.read_database() function. This function allows you to execute SQL queries directly and retrieve the results as a DataFrame. Polars supports retrieving data from various relational databases, including Postgres, MS SQL, MySQL, Oracle, SQLite, and BigQuery.

The pl.read_database() function needs an SQL query and a connection String. The connection String allows you to specify the database's type, its location, and, if needed, your credentials. For example, the connection String to a Postgres database follows the pattern: postgres://username:password@server:port/database.

A database usually runs somewhere else (or at least in a separate process) and usually requires credentials. An SQLite database, however, is just a single local file. So, to keep things easy for ourselves, you're going to use an SQLite database to demonstrate how Polars can query databases. The process is the same for the other types of databases, except that you need to specify a different connection String and perhaps use a different SQL dialect.

You'll use the Sakila database, a sample database originally developed by the MySQL development team and ported to SQLite (*https://oreil.ly/GT3Rf*) by Bradley Grant. The following query selects 10 imaginary film titles, along with a category, rating, and length for each:

```
pl.read_database_uri(
    query="""
    SELECT
        f.film_id,
        f.title,
        c.name AS category,
        f.rating,
```

```
        f.length / 60.0 AS length
    FROM
        film AS f,
        film_category AS fc,
        category AS c
    WHERE
        fc.film_id = f.film_id
        AND fc.category_id = c.category_id
    LIMIT 10
    """,
    uri="sqlite:::data/sakila.db",
)
```

shape: (10, 5)

film_id	title	category	rating	length
i64	str	str	str	f64
---------	------------------	-------------	--------	----------
1	ACADEMY DINOSAUR	Documentary	PG	1.433333
2	ACE GOLDFINGER	Horror	G	0.8
3	ADAPTATION HOLES	Documentary	NC-17	0.833333
4	AFFAIR PREJUDICE	Horror	G	1.95
5	AFRICAN EGG	Family	G	2.166667
6	AGENT TRUMAN	Foreign	PG	2.816667
7	AIRPLANE SIERRA	Comedy	PG-13	1.033333
8	AIRPORT POLLOCK	Horror	R	0.9
9	ALABAMA DEVIL	Horror	PG-13	1.9
10	ALADDIN CALENDAR	Sports	NC-17	1.05

If SQL is not your cup of tea but you still need to read from a database, you can use one or more SELECT * FROM table queries to select everything and continue in Polars. The following three SQL queries and Polars code produce the same result as the preceding single SQL query:

```
db = "sqlite:::data/sakila.db"
films = pl.read_database_uri("SELECT * FROM film", db)
film_categories = pl.read_database_uri("SELECT * FROM film_category", db)
categories = pl.read_database_uri("SELECT * FROM category", db)

(
    films.join(film_categories, on="film_id", suffix="_fc")
    .join(categories, on="category_id", suffix="_c")
    .select(
        "film_id",
        "title",
        pl.col("name").alias("category"),
        "rating",
        pl.col("length") / 60,
    )
    .limit(10)
)
```

```
shape: (10, 5)
┌─────────┬──────────────────┬─────────────┬────────┬──────────┐
│ film_id │ title            │ category    │ rating │ length   │
│ ---     │ ---              │ ---         │ ---    │ ---      │
│ i64     │ str              │ str         │ str    │ f64      │
╞═════════╪══════════════════╪═════════════╪════════╪══════════╡
│ 1       │ ACADEMY DINOSAUR │ Documentary │ PG     │ 1.433333 │
│ 2       │ ACE GOLDFINGER   │ Horror      │ G      │ 0.8      │
│ 3       │ ADAPTATION HOLES │ Documentary │ NC-17  │ 0.833333 │
│ 4       │ AFFAIR PREJUDICE │ Horror      │ G      │ 1.95     │
│ 5       │ AFRICAN EGG      │ Family      │ G      │ 2.166667 │
│ 6       │ AGENT TRUMAN     │ Foreign     │ PG     │ 2.816667 │
│ 7       │ AIRPLANE SIERRA  │ Comedy      │ PG-13  │ 1.033333 │
│ 8       │ AIRPORT POLLOCK  │ Horror      │ R      │ 0.9      │
│ 9       │ ALABAMA DEVIL    │ Horror      │ PG-13  │ 1.9      │
│ 10      │ ALADDIN CALENDAR │ Sports      │ NC-17  │ 1.05     │
└─────────┴──────────────────┴─────────────┴────────┴──────────┘
```

When you take this approach, consider how much data will be transferred. For a better performance, it's usually a good idea to let the database do as much work as possible and select only the columns you need.

Writing Data

Python Polars offers a wide range of methods when it comes to writing data to a file. Understanding the nuances of each format helps you to make an informed decision tailored to your specific data needs.

CSV Format

One of the most popular choices for writing is the CSV format. CSV stands out for its universal recognition and compatibility with a vast array of software and tools. To save a DataFrame in this format, you can use the df.write_csv() method:

```
all_stocks.write_csv("data/all_stocks.csv")
```

Table 6-6 lists some frequently used arguments for writing CSV files.

Table 6-6. Common arguments for the method df.write_csv()

Argument	Description
file	File path to write the DataFrame to. If set to None (default), the output is returned as a String instead.
include_header	Whether to include a header (default: True).
separator	Character to separate CSV fields (default: ,).
quote	Character to use for quoting values (default: ").
null_value	String to represent missing values (default: empty String).

Since CSV is a text-based format, it's easily readable by humans. However, as you've seen, it does come with some challenges related to encoding, missing data, and schema inference.

Excel Format

If you're looking to write data in a format familiar to many business users, the Excel format is an optimal choice. The method `df.write_excel("filename.xlsx")` accomplishes this:

```
all_stocks.write_excel("data/all_stocks.xlsx")
```

Table 6-7 lists some frequently used arguments for writing Excel files.

Table 6-7. Common arguments for the method `df.write_excel()`

Argument	Description
worksheet	Name of target worksheet (default: Sheet1).
position	Table position in Excel notation (e.g., "A1"), or a (row,col) Integer tuple.
table_style	A named Excel table style, such as "Table Style Medium 4", or a dictionary of {"key":value} options containing one or more of the following keys: style, first_column, last_column, banded_columns, and banded_rows.
column_widths	A {colname:int} dict or single Integer that sets (or overrides if auto-fitting) table column widths in Integer pixel units. If given as an Integer, the same value is used for all table columns.

Excel's primary advantage lies in its support for multisheet workbooks and its capability to incorporate styling and formulas directly into the data. Nevertheless, it is a binary format, which means direct human readability is compromised. Moreover, it's not the best choice for very large datasets, as performance can be an issue.

Parquet Format

If your DataFrame is large and you need an efficient read/write mechanism, the Parquet format is ideal. Using the `df.write_parquet("filename.parquet")` method, you can save data in this columnar storage format:

```
all_stocks.write_parquet("data/all_stocks.parquet")
```

Table 6-8 lists some frequently used arguments for writing Parquet files.

Table 6-8. Common arguments for the method df.write_parquet()

Argument	Description
file	File path to which the DataFrame should be written.
compression	Choose zstd for good compression performance. Choose lz4 for fast compression and decompression. Choose snappy for more backwards compatibility guarantees when you deal with older Parquet readers.
compression_level	The level of compression to use. Higher compression means smaller files on disk. Each algorithm tends to have its own range to select from. Be sure to check the documentation if you'd like to use this.

Parquet is designed for efficiency; it compresses data for optimal storage and supports intricate nested data structures. Furthermore, it retains the schema information, allowing for consistent data retrieval. However, Parquet isn't as universally recognized as CSV or Excel, so you might need specific tools or packages to read the data.

Other Considerations

Polars also supports writing to other formats like Avro and JSON. When determining the appropriate format, it's essential to weigh factors like the data's intended use, compatibility with other software, the size of the dataset, and the intricacy of the required data structures.

Takeaways

In this chapter, you've learned:

- That Polars provides extensive functionality to read and write data in various formats (e.g., CSV, Excel, Parquet, JSON)
- How Polars supports efficient reading/writing, lazy loading, and handling of complex data structures (e.g., nested JSON, Parquet)
- That packages like calamine, chardet, and ConnectorX assist with specific tasks like Excel reading, encoding detection, and database connections
- How to handle issues like missing values, character encoding, and file format specifics (e.g., delimiters in CSV) using tailored options in Polars
- How to use globbing to read multiple files with matching patterns, and how df.explode() and df.unnest() functions help manage nested data
- That for large datasets, Parquet is preferred over CSV and Excel in terms of performance

With these functions under your belt, you should have no problem applying the upcoming topics and code samples to your own data.

## PART III

Express

## CHAPTER 7

Beginning Expressions

The goal of this chapter is to introduce expressions, which are what makes the Polars API so powerful and elegant. This chapter forms the basis for the remaining chapters of Part III, "Express", where we go into more detail regarding specific expressions and how to use them.

Polars Expressions Versus Regular Expressions

Polars expressions should not be confused with regular expressions. A *regular expression*, or *regex*, is a sequence of characters that is used to match text. For example, the regex `[Pp](ol|and)ar?s` matches both `pandas` and `Polars`, but it doesn't match `panda` or `polaris`. A few Polars methods do accept regexes, such as `pl.col()` for selecting columns, and `Expr.str.replace()` for replacing values. The interactive website RegExr (*https://regexr.com*) by Grant Skinner and the book *Introducing Regular Expressions* by Michael Fitzgerald (O'Reilly) are useful resources for learning more about regexes.

Expressions, in Polars, are reusable building blocks that enable you to perform many data-wrangling tasks, including selecting existing columns, creating new columns, filtering rows on a condition, and calculating aggregations. In short, they pop up everywhere.

Expressions have so much to offer that we've split their discussion into three chapters, as pictured in Figure 7-1. In Chapter 13 we cover various methods that are accessible through so-called namespaces (explained in the next section).

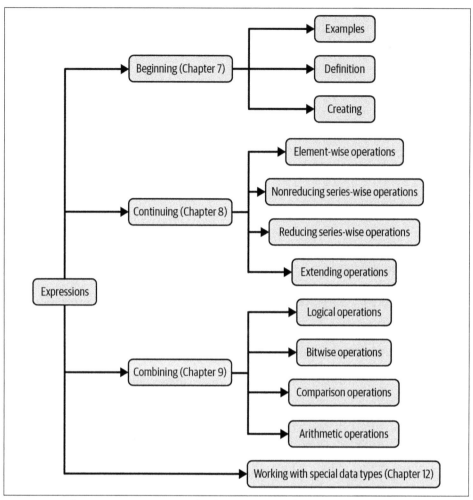

Figure 7-1. The many expression methods are organized into three chapters

In this chapter you'll learn:

- What expressions are
- Where expressions can be used
- How to create expressions from existing columns
- How to create expressions from literal values
- How to create expressions from ranges
- How to rename expressions
- Why expressions are the recommended way of working with Polars

The instructions to get any files you might need are in Chapter 2. We assume that you have the files in the *data* subdirectory.

Examples First, Definition Later

Without context, it's hard to grasp the abstract concept of an expression. That's why before you dive into the definition and further explanation, we'll show some examples so you can get an idea of how it works. After that we will explore its precise definition and break it down into its different components.

Afterwards, in Chapters 8 and 9 you'll learn how to expand expressions and how to combine them, respectively.

Methods and Namespaces

The pl.Expr class, which represents a Polars expression, has about 350 methods (!) at the time of writing. More than a hundred expression methods are accessible through *namespaces*: groups of methods that each deal with a particular data type.

For example, the Expr.str namespace has methods for working with Strings, the Expr.dt namespace has methods for working with temporal values, and the Expr.cat namespace has methods for working with categories. These types and their associated methods are covered in Chapter 12. In this chapter we'll focus on the fundamentals and more general methods of expressions.

Expressions by Example

Expressions really shine when they're being applied. That may sound obvious, but expressions by themselves don't do anything. They're lazy, just like LazyFrames. In practice, expressions are applied by passing them as arguments to some DataFrame or LazyFrame method.

Before we dive into the details of expressions, we're going to demonstrate expressions through some examples:

- Selecting columns with the method df.select()
- Creating new columns with the method df.with_columns()
- Filtering rows with the method df.filter()
- Aggregating with the method df.group_by()
- Sorting rows with the method df.sort()

As you're going through these examples, keep in mind that it's not the methods but the expressions that matter most. Each method will be covered in more detail in its own chapter.

We'll use the following DataFrame about 10 delicious fruits[1] from around the world:

```
fruit = pl.read_csv("data/fruit.csv")
fruit
```

shape: (10, 5)

name	weight	color	is_round	origin
str	i64	str	bool	str
Avocado	200	green	false	South America
Banana	120	yellow	false	Asia
Blueberry	1	blue	false	North America
Cantaloupe	2500	orange	true	Africa
Cranberry	2	red	false	North America
Elderberry	1	black	false	Europe
Orange	130	orange	true	Asia
Papaya	1000	orange	false	South America
Peach	150	orange	true	Asia
Watermelon	5000	green	true	Africa

The methods we demonstrate are also available for LazyFrames, but since we're only dealing with 10 rows, a DataFrame will do just fine. And since we don't have to materialize the result with the method lf.collect(), it keeps the examples shorter.

Selecting Columns with Expressions

You can select one or more existing columns from a DataFrame using the method df.select(). Any columns not mentioned in the expressions are dropped from the output. Additionally, any expressions in the df.select() method resulting in new columns will create a new column in the resulting DataFrame. The following code snippet selects the fruit's name, color, origin, weight (in kilograms), and is_round:

```
fruit.select(
    pl.col("name"),          ❶
    pl.col("^.*or.*$"),      ❷
    pl.col("weight") / 1000, ❸
    "is_round",              ❹
)
```

---

1 Yes, avocado is actually a fruit—a large single-seeded berry, to be precise.

❶ The function pl.col() is the most common way to start an expression. The argument is a String that refers to an existing column—in this case, name.

❷ pl.col() also accepts regular expressions as arguments. This regular expression matches the two columns color and origin, because their names both contain the String or.

❸ You can perform arithmetic (addition, subtraction, multiplication, and division) on expressions using the operators you're already familiar with. (We'll discuss performing arithmetic further in Chapter 9.) Notice how Polars automatically casts the weight column from an Integer (i64) to a Float (f64) to allow for fractional weights.

❹ The method df.select() also accepts Strings to refer to existing columns. This might be convenient because you have to type less. However, since a String is not an expression, you won't be able to apply any arithmetic or other operations to it.

```
shape: (10, 5)
```

name	color	origin	weight	is_round
str	str	str	f64	bool
Avocado	green	South America	0.2	false
Banana	yellow	Asia	0.12	false
Blueberry	blue	North America	0.001	false
Cantaloupe	orange	Africa	2.5	true
Cranberry	red	North America	0.002	false
Elderberry	black	Europe	0.001	false
Orange	orange	Asia	0.13	true
Papaya	orange	South America	1.0	false
Peach	orange	Asia	0.15	true
Watermelon	green	Africa	5.0	true

Creating New Columns with Expressions

With the method df.with_columns() you can create one or more columns, either based on existing columns or from scratch, and add these to the existing DataFrame. In this example we add two columns to our fruit DataFrame: one that indicates whether a fruit is a fruit (which is obviously always True) and one that indicates whether a fruit is a berry (based on its name):

```
fruit.with_columns(
    pl.lit(True).alias("is_fruit"),  ❶
    is_berry=pl.col("name").str.ends_with("berry"),  ❷
)
```

❶ With the function `pl.lit()` you start an expression based on a literal value, such as `True`. The method `Expr.alias()` allows you to name new columns and rename existing columns.

❷ The `Expr.str.ends_with()` method is one the many String methods in the `str` namespace. As mentioned, these will be covered in Chapter 12. Here we use the keyword syntax, instead of the `Expr.alias()` method, to specify the column name `is_berry`.

shape: (10, 7)

name	weight	color	is_round	origin	is_fruit	is_berry
str	i64	str	bool	str	bool	bool
Avocado	200	green	false	South Amer…	true	false
Banana	120	yellow	false	Asia	true	false
Blueberry	1	blue	false	North Amer…	true	true
Cantaloupe	2500	orange	true	Africa	true	false
Cranberry	2	red	false	North Amer…	true	true
Elderberry	1	black	false	Europe	true	true
Orange	130	orange	true	Asia	true	false
Papaya	1000	orange	false	South Amer…	true	false
Peach	150	orange	true	Asia	true	false
Watermelon	5000	green	true	Africa	true	false

Naming Columns

In the previous example we used two ways to specify the name of the column.

First, we used the `Expr.alias()` method to rename the expression, which, in turn, determines the name of the column. In this case, the name is tied to the expression itself, regardless of where it is used.

Second, we used the keyword syntax to specify the name of the new column directly. In that case, the name is local to the context where the expression is used.

There are situations where the keyword syntax is not possible. When you start using a keyword, all the subsequent arguments (expressions) must be keyword arguments as well. The keyword must be a valid Python name, meaning that it cannot start with a number, can only contain alphanumeric characters and underscores, and cannot be a reserved keyword in Python, such as `class` and `except`.

When both ways are used, the keyword takes precedence over the name of the expression. We generally prefer the keyword syntax for its clarity and brevity.

Filtering Rows with Expressions

To filter rows based on an expression, use the method `df.filter()`. Only rows for which the expression evaluates to `True` are kept. This example only keeps fruits that weigh more than 1,000 grams *and* are round:

```
fruit.filter(
    (pl.col("weight") > 1000)  ❶
    & pl.col("is_round")  ❷
)
```

❶ Existing columns can be turned into Boolean ones using comparison operators, such as the greater than (>) operator.

❷ Here we combine two expressions using the logical AND (&) operator. The output is `True` if and only if both expressions are `True`. (We discuss logical operators in Chapter 9.)

```
shape: (2, 5)
┌────────────┬────────┬────────┬──────────┬────────┐
│ name       │ weight │ color  │ is_round │ origin │
│ ---        │ ---    │ ---    │ ---      │ ---    │
│ str        │ i64    │ str    │ bool     │ str    │
╞════════════╪════════╪════════╪══════════╪════════╡
│ Cantaloupe │ 2500   │ orange │ true     │ Africa │
│ Watermelon │ 5000   │ green  │ true     │ Africa │
└────────────┴────────┴────────┴──────────┴────────┘
```

Aggregating with Expressions

Aggregation typically involves creating groups of rows, then summarizing each group into one row. This example creates groups based on the last part of the `origin` column, then calculates the number of fruits per group and their average weight. Note that it uses expressions in two different places: in determining the groups, and then in summarizing the groups:

```
fruit.group_by(pl.col("origin").str.split(" ").list.last()).agg(  ❶
    pl.len(),  ❷
    average_weight=pl.col("weight").mean()  ❸
)
```

❶ Each unique value of this expression (the last part of the `origin` column) leads to one group.

❷ The expression created by the function `pl.len()` returns the number of rows in the group.

❸ The method `Expr.mean()` is one of many that summarize data—turning multiple values into one.

```
shape: (4, 3)
```

origin	len	average_weight
str	u32	f64
America	4	300.75
Asia	3	133.333333
Africa	2	3750.0
Europe	1	1.0

Embarrassingly Parallel

We don't want to get ahead of ourselves too much, but we're pretty excited to let you know that multiple expressions are executed in parallel—as is the case with both the aggregation and selection examples. This is one of the reasons why Polars is so blazingly fast.

Sorting Rows with Expressions

To rearrange a DataFrame based on one or more columns, use the method `df.sort()`. This example sorts the fruits based on the lengths of their names:

```
fruit.sort(
    pl.col("name").str.len_bytes(),  ❶ ❷
    descending=True,  ❸
)
```

❶ The `str` namespace has no `len()`, because there are two ways of determining length: `len_bytes()` or `len_chars()`. We'll explain the difference in Chapter 12.

❷ You can sort on an expression that's not actually present in the `fruits` DataFrame. (While the names are present, their *lengths* are not.) It's not necessary to explicitly add a new column if you only want to use it for sorting.

❸ For ascending order (the default), remove this argument or set it to `False`.

```
shape: (10, 5)
```

name	weight	color	is_round	origin
str	i64	str	bool	str
Cantaloupe	2500	orange	true	Africa
Elderberry	1		black	false	Europe

```
| Watermelon | 5000 | green  | true  | Africa        |
| Blueberry  | 1    | blue   | false | North America |
| Cranberry  | 2    | red    | false | North America |
| Avocado    | 200  | green  | false | South America |
| Banana     | 120  | yellow | false | Asia          |
| Orange     | 130  | orange | true  | Asia          |
| Papaya     | 1000 | orange | false | South America |
| Peach      | 150  | orange | true  | Asia          |
```

The Definition of an Expression

Now that you've seen some concrete examples of expressions and how they can be applied, it's time to define what exactly an expression is.

> ## Expression Definition
>
> An expression is a tree of operations that describe how to construct one or more Series.

Let's break this definition down into five parts:

Series

> Recall from Chapter 4 that a Series is an array of values with the same data type, such as `pl.Float64` for 64-bit Floats or `pl.String` for Strings. You can think of a Series as a column in a DataFrame, but keep in mind that a Series can exist on its own and is therefore not *always* part of a DataFrame.

Tree of operations

> An expression can consist of: a single operation, multiple operations in a linear sequence, and multiple operations organized in a tree-like structure.

> Figure 7-2 shows three example expressions. If these expressions were to be executed, they would produce three columns with the values 3, 8, and 4, respectively. Note that the third diagram in Figure 7-2 is indeed tree-like.

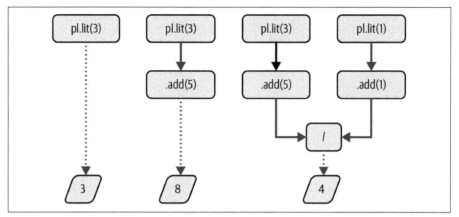

Figure 7-2. An expression is a tree of operations

Generally speaking, all expressions are tree-like, but they don't necessarily have branches or parents.

Describe

An expression is just a description; it doesn't construct any Series by itself, nor does it have a method to execute itself. Expressions are only executed when passed as arguments to functions such as pl.select() and methods such as df.group_by(). Then one or more Series are constructed.

If you think of an expression as a recipe, then the operations would be the steps, and the functions and methods would be the cooks.

Construct

You don't always see the Series that's being constructed. Whether the constructed Series becomes (or become) part of the DataFrame will depend on the function or method executing the expression. An example of where this is not the case is the function pl.filter(). The constructed Series is only used to determine which rows of the DataFrame should be kept; it doesn't become a new column. The word *construct* should also be taken with a grain of salt: if the expression only consists of a single operation that references an existing column in a Data-Frame, then no Series is actually being constructed.

One or more

A single expression can describe the construction of more than one Series. For example, the function pl.all() refers to all columns in a DataFrame. The expression pl.all().mul(10).name.suffix("_times_10") multiplies the values in all existing columns by 10 and adds _times_10 to their names:

```
(
    pl.DataFrame({"a": [1, 2, 3], "b": [0.4, 0.5, 0.6]}).with_columns(
        pl.all().mul(10).name.suffix("_times_10")
```

```
        )
    )
    shape: (3, 4)
```

a	b	a_times_10	b_times_10
i64	f64	i64	f64
1	0.4	10	4.0
2	0.5	20	5.0
3	0.6	30	6.0

With the method `Expr.meta.has_multiple_outputs()`, you can check whether an expression describes the potential construction of multiple Series. The `Expr.meta` namespace will be further covered in Chapter 18:

```
pl.all().mul(10).name.suffix("_times_10").meta.has_multiple_outputs()
```

```
True
```

Whether multiple Series are actually constructed depends on the DataFrame to which they're applied. If the DataFrame only has one Series (i.e., column) to begin with, `pl.all()` will only construct one Series.

Properties of Expressions

It's one thing to know the definition of expressions; it's another thing to understand how they work in practice. Here are a couple of properties of expressions worth mentioning:

Lazy
Expressions are lazy: by themselves, they don't do anything. Perhaps being lazy is their most important property, because without it, they wouldn't have the other four properties we're about to mention.

Function and data dependent
Expressions depend on both the function that executes them and the DataFrame (or LazyFrame) onto which they are applied. The function determines what happens to the Series being constructed; the DataFrame determines the type and length of the Series.

To demonstrate, let's pass the same expression (`is_orange`) to three different functions (methods), shown here alongside their output:

```
is_orange = (pl.col("color") == "orange").alias("is_orange")
```

```
fruit.with_columns(is_orange)
```

```
shape: (10, 6)
```

name	weight	color	is_round	origin	is_orange
str	i64	str	bool	str	bool
Avocado	200	green	false	South America	false
Banana	120	yellow	false	Asia	false
Blueberry	1	blue	false	North America	false
Cantaloupe	2500	orange	true	Africa	true
Cranberry	2	red	false	North America	false
Elderberry	1	black	false	Europe	false
Orange	130	orange	true	Asia	true
Papaya	1000	orange	false	South America	true
Peach	150	orange	true	Asia	true
Watermelon	5000	green	true	Africa	false

```
fruit.filter(is_orange)
shape: (4, 5)
```

name	weight	color	is_round	origin
str	i64	str	bool	str
Cantaloupe	2500	orange	true	Africa
Orange	130	orange	true	Asia
Papaya	1000	orange	false	South America
Peach	150	orange	true	Asia

```
fruit.group_by(is_orange).len()
shape: (2, 2)
```

is_orange	len
bool	u32
false	6
true	4

The key takeaway is that you'll use the same syntax to accomplish different tasks. This ties into the next property of expressions: reusability.

Reusable

Expressions are Python objects. In the previous example, we created the expression object is_orange and reused it by passing it to different methods of the fruit DataFrame. Taking this further, there's nothing stopping us from using the same expression on a completely different DataFrame:

```
flowers = pl.DataFrame(
    {
        "name": ["Tiger lily", "Blue flag", "African marigold"],
        "latin": ["Lilium columbianum", "Iris versicolor", "Tagetes erecta"],
        "color": ["orange", "purple", "orange"],
    }
)

flowers.filter(is_orange)
```

```
shape: (2, 3)
┌─────────────────┬────────────────────┬────────┐
│ name            │ latin              │ color  │
│ ---             │ ---                │ ---    │
│ str             │ str                │ str    │
╞═════════════════╪════════════════════╪════════╡
│ Tiger lily      │ Lilium columbianum │ orange │
│ African marigold│ Tagetes erecta     │ orange │
└─────────────────┴────────────────────┴────────┘
```

Expressive

Expressions are, indeed, expressive for two reasons. First, a single expression can operate on multiple Series (columns) simultaneously, allowing for concise, powerful transformations across different columns without needing repetitive code. Second, expressions are flexible, enabling complex operations like arithmetic, String manipulation, and filtering to be easily composed and chained in a readable, compact form. This expressiveness enables you to articulate your data transformations effectively.

Efficient

Because expressions are lazy, you can optimize them before you execute them. Polars will minimize the number of computations required to construct the Series by analyzing the operations in the expression. Moreover, when a function is given multiple expressions, they are executed in parallel.

To summarize, expressions have many favorable properties. Let's continue with creating expressions.

Creating Expressions

Each expression starts with a first operation. Generally speaking, a new expression is created using a function that doesn't depend on another expression. Once you have an expression, you can continue to build on it with many methods and combine it with other expressions using inline operators (discussed in the next two chapters). Let's look at the various ways in which we can create one, starting with existing columns.

From Existing Columns

The most common way to create an expression is to reference one or more existing columns in the DataFrame. After all, most often you want to transform the data you already have. This can be done with the function pl.col(), which accepts column names, regular expressions, and data types. Here are a few examples.

For demonstration purposes, we execute the expressions using the method df.select() and get the list of column names via the df.columns attribute. You can reference a particular column by passing its name:

```
fruit.select(pl.col("color")).columns
```

```
['color']
```

If the DataFrame has no column with that particular name, Polars will raise an exception:

```
fruit.select(pl.col("is_smelly")).columns
```

```
ColumnNotFoundError: is_smelly

Resolved plan until failure:

        ---> FAILED HERE RESOLVING 'select' <---
DF ["name", "weight", "color", "is_round"]; PROJECT */5 COLUMNS
```

Regular expressions are especially useful for referencing multiple columns whose names have a common pattern. To do so, the regular expression has to start with a caret (^) and end with a dollar sign ($):

```
fruit.select(pl.col("^.*or.*$")).columns
```

```
['color', 'origin']
```

With pl.col("*") or the convenient alias pl.all(), you can reference all columns:

```
fruit.select(pl.all()).columns
```

```
['name', 'weight', 'color', 'is_round', 'origin']
```

You can reference all columns with a particular data type (for example, pl.String for Strings):

```
fruit.select(pl.col(pl.String)).columns
```

```
['name', 'color', 'origin']
```

You can give pl.col() multiple column names or data types:

```
fruit.select(pl.col(pl.Boolean, pl.Int64)).columns
```

```
['weight', 'is_round']
```

Or you can pass them as a list, if that's more convenient:

```
fruit.select(pl.col(["name", "color"])).columns
```

```
['name', 'color']
```

Column Selectors

An additional feature from which you can start expressions in Polars are column selectors. These are the recommended way to select columns based on their properties (such as selecting all numerical columns, or columns of a specific data types, etc.) We will dive into how these work in Chapter 10.

From Literal Values

To create a new expression based on some other Python value, you can use the function pl.lit(). *Lit* is short for "literal." The next few examples execute the expressions using the pl.select() function, which starts with a new, empty DataFrame:

```
pl.select(pl.lit(42))
```

```
shape: (1, 1)
┌─────────┐
│ literal │
│ ---     │
│ i32     │
╞═════════╡
│ 42      │
└─────────┘
```

Notice that the column name is literally literal. You can give this column a better name using the method Expr.alias():

```
pl.select(pl.lit(42).alias("answer"))
```

```
shape: (1, 1)
┌────────┐
│ answer │
│ ---    │
│ i32    │
╞════════╡
│ 42     │
└────────┘
```

Alternatively, you can specify a different column name by using the following keyword syntax:

```
pl.select(answer=pl.lit(42))
```

When you execute these expressions using the function pl.select(), the constructed Series have only one value. However, when you execute the same expression to a nonempty DataFrame, the length of the Series will be equal to the number of rows, because all columns in a Polars DataFrame must have the same length:

```
fruit.with_columns(planet=pl.lit("Earth"))
```

shape: (10, 6)

name	weight	color	is_round	origin	planet
str	i64	str	bool	str	str
Avocado	200	green	false	South America	Earth
Banana	120	yellow	false	Asia	Earth
Blueberry	1	blue	false	North America	Earth
Cantaloupe	2500	orange	true	Africa	Earth
Cranberry	2	red	false	North America	Earth
Elderberry	1	black	false	Europe	Earth
Orange	130	orange	true	Asia	Earth
Papaya	1000	orange	false	South America	Earth
Peach	150	orange	true	Asia	Earth
Watermelon	5000	green	true	Africa	Earth

As you can see, the value Earth is repeated such that the length of the Series planet is equal to the number of rows in the DataFrame. Values are only repeated automatically if you pass a single value to the function pl.lit(). When you pass more than one value, but fewer values than there are rows, you get an error:

```
fruit.with_columns(pl.lit(pl.Series([False, True])).alias("row_is_even"))
```

```
ShapeError: unable to add a column of length 2 to a DataFrame of height 10
```

Also, the list of values [False, True] is first turned into a Series using the pl.Ser ies() constructor. Otherwise, Polars will create a list column such that each row has these two values:

```
fruit.with_columns(row_is_even=pl.lit([False, True]))
```

shape: (10, 6)

name	weight	color	is_round	origin	row_is_even
str	i64	str	bool	str	list[bool]
Avocado	200	green	false	South America	[false, true]
Banana	120	yellow	false	Asia	[false, true]
…	…	…	…	…	…
Peach	150	orange	true	Asia	[false, true]
Watermelon	5000	green	true	Africa	[false, true]

To repeat values explicitly, for a fixed number of times, you can use the function pl.repeat(). The functions pl.zeros() and pl.ones() are aliases for pl.repeat(0.0) and pl.repeat(1.0), respectively:

```
pl.select(pl.repeat("Ella", 3).alias("umbrella"), pl.zeros(3), pl.ones(3))
```

```
shape: (3, 3)
┌──────────┬───────┬──────┐
│ umbrella │ zeros │ ones │
│ ---      │ ---   │ ---  │
│ str      │ f64   │ f64  │
╞══════════╪═══════╪══════╡
│ Ella     │ 0.0   │ 1.0  │
│ Ella     │ 0.0   │ 1.0  │
│ Ella     │ 0.0   │ 1.0  │
└──────────┴───────┴──────┘
```

Keep in mind that the length of each Series must be the same; otherwise you'll get an error:

```
fruit.with_columns(planet=pl.repeat("Earth", 9))

ShapeError: unable to add a column of length 9 to a DataFrame of height 10
```

From Ranges

Polars offers a couple of convenient functions for creating ranges of Integers, Dates, Times, and Datetimes. They are listed in Table 7-1.

Table 7-1. Functions for creating ranges

Function	Description
pl.arange(…)	A range of integers. Alias of pl.int_range(…).
pl.date_range(…)	A range of dates.
pl.date_ranges(…)	Each element is a range of dates.
pl.datetime_range(…)	A range of Datetimes.
pl.datetime_ranges(…)	Each element is a range of Datetimes.
pl.int_range(…)	A range of integers.
pl.int_ranges(…)	Each element is a range of integers.
pl.time_range(…)	A range of times.
pl.time_ranges(…)	Each element is a range of times.

The following example demonstrates the functions pl.int_range(), its alias pl.arange(), and pl.int_ranges(). It also includes a sneak peek to the method Expr.list.len(), which calculates the number of elements in each list in the int_range column:

```
pl.select(
    start=pl.int_range(0, 5), end=pl.arange(0, 10, 2).pow(2)
).with_columns(int_range=pl.int_ranges("start", "end")).with_columns(
    range_length=pl.col("int_range").list.len()
)
```

```
shape: (5, 4)
```

start	end	int_range	range_length
i64	i64	list[i64]	u32
0	0	[]	0
1	4	[1, 2, 3]	3
2	16	[2, 3, … 15]	14
3	36	[3, 4, … 35]	33
4	64	[4, 5, … 63]	60

Note that the function `pl.int_ranges()` generates a Series where each element is a list of integers. The functions `pl.date_ranges`, `pl.datetime_ranges`, and `pl.time_ranges()` work similarly, but for dates, Datetimes, and times, respectively:

```
pl.select(
    start=pl.date_range(pl.date(1985, 10, 21), pl.date(1985, 10, 26)),
    end=pl.repeat(pl.date(2021, 10, 21), 6),
).with_columns(range=pl.datetime_ranges("start", "end", interval="1h"))
```

```
shape: (6, 3)
```

start	end	range
date	date	list[datetime[μs]]
1985-10-21	2021-10-21	[1985-10-21 00:00:00, 1985-10-21 01:00:00, …
1985-10-22	2021-10-21	[1985-10-22 00:00:00, 1985-10-22 01:00:00, …
1985-10-23	2021-10-21	[1985-10-23 00:00:00, 1985-10-23 01:00:00, …
1985-10-24	2021-10-21	[1985-10-24 00:00:00, 1985-10-24 01:00:00, …
1985-10-25	2021-10-21	[1985-10-25 00:00:00, 1985-10-25 01:00:00, …
1985-10-26	2021-10-21	[1985-10-26 00:00:00, 1985-10-26 01:00:00, …

In Chapter 12 we cover working with temporal data (such as dates and times) in more detail.

Other Functions to Create Expressions

There are many functions to create expressions. Unfortunately, we're not able to cover all of them in this chapter. However, to give you an idea of the possibilities, we'll briefly mention a couple of functions, what they do, and where we'll cover them in more detail.

First, the function `pl.len()` is used, as the name implies, for counting the length of the column. It's most often used when aggregating using the method `df.group_by()`. This is covered in Chapter 13.

Second, the function `pl.element()` represents a single element in a list. It is used in combination with the method `Expr.list.eval()` to apply an expression to each element in a list. We explain this is further detail in Chapter 12.

Renaming Expressions

Renaming an expression—which eventually determines the name of the Series that will be constructed—happens very often. There are various reasons why you would want to rename an expression, including:

- To better express what the column is about
- To avoid duplicate column names
- To clean up a column name
- To change the default column name

Good Names

Having good expression names is just as important as having good variable names in general. They can drastically influence the quality of your code. We personally recommend using column names that are all lowercase, using underscores to separate words. This is also known as *snake_case*.

The most common method to change the name of an expression is `Expr.alias()`. Additional methods that are concerned with the name of an expression are available within the `Expr.name` namespace (see Table 7-2). The methods `Expr.name.map_fields()`, `Expr.name.prefix_fields()`, and `Expr.name.suffix_fields()` can only be used when the data type of the expression is `pl.Struct`.

Table 7-2. Methods for renaming expressions

Method	Description
`Expr.alias(…)`	Rename the expression.
`Expr.name.keep()`	Keep the original root name of the expression.
`Expr.name.map(…)`	Rename the expression by mapping a function over the root name.
`Expr.name.prefix(…)`	Add a prefix to the root column name of the expression.
`Expr.name.suffix(…)`	Add a suffix to the root column name of the expression.
`Expr.name.to_lowercase()`	Make the root column name lowercase.
`Expr.name.to_uppercase()`	Make the root column name uppercase.
`Expr.name.map_fields(…)`	Rename fields of a struct by mapping a function over the field name.

Method	Description
Expr.name.prefix_fields(…)	Add a prefix to all field names of a struct.
Expr.name.suffix_fields(…)	Add a suffix to all field names of a struct.

To illustrate, consider this small DataFrame with some arbitrary column names:

```
df = pl.DataFrame({"text": "value", "An integer": 5040, "BOOLEAN": True})
df
```

```
shape: (1, 3)
┌───────┬────────────┬─────────┐
│ text  │ An integer │ BOOLEAN │
│ ---   │ ---        │ ---     │
│ str   │ i64        │ bool    │
╞═══════╪════════════╪═════════╡
│ value │ 5040       │ true    │
└───────┴────────────┴─────────┘
```

We can change these column names with various methods:

```
df.select(
    pl.col("text").name.to_uppercase(),
    pl.col("An integer").alias("int"),
    pl.col("BOOLEAN").name.to_lowercase(),
)
```

```
shape: (1, 3)
┌───────┬──────┬─────────┐
│ TEXT  │ int  │ boolean │
│ ---   │ ---  │ ---     │
│ str   │ i64  │ bool    │
╞═══════╪══════╪═════════╡
│ value │ 5040 │ true    │
└───────┴──────┴─────────┘
```

Chaining Naming Operations

At the time of writing, Polars allows only one naming operation per expression. So the following is not allowed:

```
df.select(
    pl.all()
    .name.to_lowercase()
    .name.map(lambda s: s.replace(" ", "_"))
)

InvalidOperationError: 'Expr: .rename_alias(col("text"))'
not allowed in this context/location

Resolved plan until failure:

        ---> FAILED HERE RESOLVING 'select' <---
DF ["text", "An integer", "BOOLEAN"]; PROJECT */3 COLUMNS
```

A solution is to combine all the operations into one (anonymous) function and then apply that with the `Expr.name.map()` method:

```
df.select(
    pl.all().name.map(lambda s: s.lower().replace(" ", "_"))
)
shape: (1, 3)
```

text	an_integer	boolean
str	i64	bool
value	5040	true

This restriction may be lifted in a future version of Polars.

Expressions Are Idiomatic

You already know that expressions are lazy and that they need to be executed in order to be useful. We understand that it may take time to get used to this, especially if you're used to a nonlazy (eager) way of working using packages, such as pandas.

So here's a word of caution. All expression methods and inline operations are also available for Series. For instance, the filtering rows example from earlier, which uses expressions, can be rewritten to use Series directly:

```
fruit.filter((fruit["weight"] > 1000) & fruit["is_round"])

shape: (2, 5)
```

name	weight	color	is_round	origin
str	i64	str	bool	str

| Cantaloupe | 2500 | orange | true | Africa |
| Watermelon | 5000 | green | true | Africa |

If you have experience with pandas, then this syntax will look familiar, and you might be tempted to write this way when using Polars.

While the preceding code produces the same results as the original example, it runs suboptimally. The condition is evaluated before the `df.filter()` method is applied. Because it's not an expression, the optimizer can't make optimizations. Moreover, the two components are executed serially rather than in parallel.

This becomes even more clear when you apply multiple methods to a LazyFrame. Here's an example that uses expressions:

```
(
    fruit.lazy()
    .filter((pl.col("weight") > 1000) & pl.col("is_round"))
    .with_columns(is_berry=pl.col("name").str.ends_with("berry"))
    .collect()
)
```

shape: (2, 6)

name	weight	color	is_round	origin	is_berry
str	i64	str	bool	str	bool
Cantaloupe	2500	orange	true	Africa	false
Watermelon	5000	green	true	Africa	false

Now an example without expressions:

```
(
    fruit.lazy()
    .filter((fruit["weight"] > 1000) & fruit["is_round"])
    .with_columns(is_berry=fruit["name"].str.ends_with("berry"))
    .collect()
)
```

```
ShapeError: unable to add a column of length 10 to a DataFrame of height 2
```

That's right: Polars can't optimize the execution plan, and *now* you also have to be careful to apply the methods in the correct order to avoid an error. (The reason for the error is that the method `df.filter()` reduces the DataFrame to 2 rows, whereas the variable `fruit` still refers to a DataFrame with 10 rows.)

For these reasons, we always encourage you to use expressions. Being lazy pays off in Polars.

Takeaways

In this chapter, we've introduced expressions in Polars and their core uses. You have learned that:

- Expressions in Polars are reusable, lazy building blocks that allow for efficient data manipulation, including selecting, filtering, and creating new columns.

- Expressions are flexible and enable complex operations like arithmetic, comparisons, and String manipulations, making them highly versatile.

- You can create expressions from existing columns, literal values, or ranges, providing powerful methods for transforming and managing data.

- Polars optimizes expressions, executing them in parallel, which leads to faster and more efficient data processing.

- Renaming expressions is essential for clarity and avoiding duplicate column names, and can be easily done using methods like `Expr.alias()` or the keyword syntax.

- It is recommended to use expressions over direct Series operations for better performance and parallel execution.

In the next chapter, we will explore how to expand on expressions by combining them for more advanced data manipulation.

## CHAPTER 8

Continuing Expressions

In the previous chapter you learned how to begin an expression from scratch. A bare expression only gets you so far. In this chapter, you'll learn how to continue an expression by adding additional operations (or methods).

More specifically, you'll learn how to:

- Perform mathematical transformations
- Work with missing values
- Apply smoothing to values
- Select specific values
- Summarize values using statistics

A Plethora of Methods

There are more than 138 methods discussed in this chapter. It's not possible to explain and demonstrate every single method in full detail. Please refer to the Polars API Reference (*https://oreil.ly/ jZkWd*) for more details and examples.

For some code snippets in this chapter, we use the math and numpy modules for accessing certain constants, such as math.pi, and for generating random values:

```
import math
import numpy as np

print(f"{math.pi=}")
rng = np.random.default_rng(1729)
print(f"{rng.random()=}")
```

```
math.pi=3.141592653589793
rng.random()=0.03074202960516803
```

Let's get into how this chapter is structured.

The instructions to get any files you might need are in Chapter 2. We assume that you have the files in the *data* subdirectory.

Types of Operations

Rather than presenting 138 methods as one long list, we've organized them into five sections according to which inputs they use and the shape of their output. Within those five sections we've grouped methods into categories when applicable. Methods that do not fall into any category are placed in the section "Other Operations." Figure 8-1 shows the types of operations for continuing expressions.

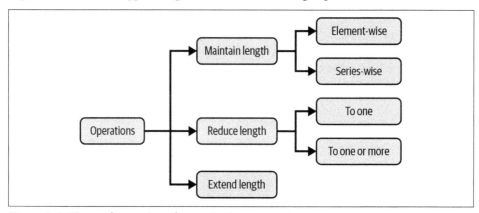

Figure 8-1. Types of operations for continuing expressions

Related Methods, Different Sections

While we trust this organization to be useful, it does cause certain related methods to appear in different sections. For example, both `Expr.unique()` and `Expr.is_unique()` are concerned with unique values, but because the former may reduce the length of the Series while the latter does not, they're in different sections.

Here are four examples to demonstrate what we mean by the various types of operations.

Example A: Element-Wise Operations

In the first example, we'll use two methods to create two additional columns: Expr.sqrt() and Expr.exp(). Both methods operate *element-wise* (that is, they consider one element at a time) and maintain the length of the Series:

```
penguins = pl.read_csv("data/penguins.csv", null_values="NA").select(
    "species",
    "island",
    "sex",
    "year",
    mass=pl.col("body_mass_g") / 1000,
)
penguins.with_columns(
    mass_sqrt=pl.col("mass").sqrt(),     ❶
    mass_exp=pl.col("mass").exp(),
)
```

❶ The Expr.sqrt() method computes the square root of the mass column. Notice how null values remain null.

shape: (344, 7)

species	island	sex	year	mass	mass_sqrt	mass_exp
str	str	str	i64	f64	f64	f64
Adelie	Torgersen	male	2007	3.75	1.936492	42.521082
Adelie	Torgersen	female	2007	3.8	1.949359	44.701184
Adelie	Torgersen	female	2007	3.25	1.802776	25.79034
Adelie	Torgersen	null	2007	null	null	null
Adelie	Torgersen	female	2007	3.45	1.857418	31.500392
…	…	…	…	…	…	…
Chinstrap	Dream	male	2009	4.0	2.0	54.59815
Chinstrap	Dream	female	2009	3.4	1.843909	29.9641
Chinstrap	Dream	male	2009	3.775	1.942936	43.597508
Chinstrap	Dream	male	2009	4.1	2.024846	60.340288
Chinstrap	Dream	female	2009	3.775	1.942936	43.597508

Now let's move on to operations that go from many rows to one.

Example B: Operations That Summarize to One

In the second example, we apply two methods that summarize the Series to a single value:

```
penguins.select(pl.col("mass").mean(), pl.col("island").first())
```

shape: (1, 2)

```
| mass     | island    |
| ---      | ---       |
| f64      | str       |
|==========|===========|
| 4.201754 | Torgersen |
```

Having seen this example, let's take a look at expressions that summarize, but not just to one line, but to one or more.

Example C: Operations That Summarize to One or More

In the third example, we use the `Expr.unique()` method to get the unique values in a Series. This is a type of operation that summarizes to one or more values:

```
penguins.select(pl.col("island").unique())
```

shape: (3, 1)

```
| island    |
| ---       |
| str       |
|===========|
| Torgersen |
| Biscoe    |
| Dream     |
```

Now that we've covered everything that makes the result smaller, let's go big.

Example D: Operations That Extend

In the fourth example, we use the `Expr.extend_constant()` method to append a specific value to the end of the Series. This type of operation is used less often. The example is perhaps a bit contrived, but it does illustrate how powerful expressions can be if you add additional methods:

```
penguins.select(
    pl.col("species")
    .unique()               ❶
    .repeat_by(3000)        ❷
    .explode()              ❸
    .extend_constant("Saiyan", n=1)  ❹
)
```

❶ Get the three unique values of the Series.

❷ Repeat each value three thousand times. This produces a Series of three long lists.

❸ Use the `explode()` method to get one long Series of nine thousand values.

❹ Add one more value at the end of the Series. The result is a Series with a length that's just over nine thousand.

shape: (9_001, 1)

```
| species   |
| ---       |
| str       |
| Adelie    |
| Adelie    |
| Adelie    |
| Adelie    |
| Adelie    |
| …         |
| Chinstrap |
| Chinstrap |
| Chinstrap |
| Chinstrap |
| Saiyan    |
```

With these four examples, you should have an idea of the type of operations we can use to continue expressions.

Element-Wise Operations

This section is about operations that consider one element at a time. Each element is computed independently, and the order in which they appear doesn't matter. Examples include the Expr.sqrt() method for computing the square root of each value and the Expr.round() method for rounding values.

In the next five subsections, we're looking at element-wise operations that perform mathematical transformations, that are related to trigonometry, that round and bin, that are concerned with missing or infinite values, and others.

Operations That Perform Mathematical Transformations

Mathematical transformations, such as computing the log or the square root, form the basis of any data-related task. The methods listed in Table 8-1 all perform some mathematical transformation. Arithmetic between two expressions (such as adding and multiplication) is discussed in Chapter 9 because that's mostly about *combining* expressions.

Table 8-1. Element-wise operations for performing elementary mathematical transformations

Method	Description
Expr.abs()	Compute absolute values.
Expr.cbrt()	Compute the cube root of the elements.
Expr.exp()	Compute the exponential, element-wise.
Expr.log(…)	Compute the logarithm to a given base.
Expr.log10()	Compute the base 10 logarithm of the input array, element-wise.
Expr.log1p()	Compute the natural logarithm of each element plus one.
Expr.sign()	Compute the element-wise indication of the sign.
Expr.sqrt()	Compute the square root of the elements.

The methods Expr.abs(), Expr.exp(), Expr.log(), Expr.log10(), Expr.log1p(), Expr.sign(), and Expr.sqrt() are demonstrated in the following code snippet for a variety of numerical values. The method Expr.cbrt() is similar in usage:

```
(
    pl.DataFrame({"x": [-2.0, 0.0, 0.5, 1.0, math.e, 1000.0]}).with_columns(
        abs=pl.col("x").abs(),
        exp=pl.col("x").exp(),
        log2=pl.col("x").log(2),    ❶
        log10=pl.col("x").log10(),
        log1p=pl.col("x").log1p(),
        sign=pl.col("x").sign(),
        sqrt=pl.col("x").sqrt(),
    )
)
```

❶ The method Expr.log() is the only one here that takes an optimal argument, namely the base of the logarithm. By default it uses the natural log.

```
shape: (6, 8)
```

x	abs	exp	log2	log10	log1p	sign	sqrt
---	---	---	---	---	---	---	---
f64	f64	f64	f64	f64	f64	f64	f64
-2.000	2.000	0.135	NaN	NaN	NaN	-1.000	NaN
0.000	0.000	1.000	-inf	-inf	0.000	0.000	0.000
0.500	0.500	1.649	-1.000	-0.301	0.405	1.000	0.707
1.000	1.000	2.718	0.000	0.000	0.693	1.000	1.000
2.718	2.718	15.154	1.443	0.434	1.313	1.000	1.649
1000.000	1000.000	inf	9.966	3.000	6.909	1.000	31.623

Operations Related to Trigonometry

Trigonometry is the branch of mathematics that studies the relationships between angles and sides of triangles. It plays a crucial role in various aspects of data science, including signal processing, spacial data analysis, and feature engineering. Table 8-2 lists all methods related to trigonometry that Polars supports.

Table 8-2. Element-wise operations related to trigonometry

Method	Description
`Expr.arccos()`	Compute the element-wise value for the inverse cosine.
`Expr.arccosh()`	Compute the element-wise value for the inverse hyperbolic cosine.
`Expr.arcsin()`	Compute the element-wise value for the inverse sine.
`Expr.arcsinh()`	Compute the element-wise value for the inverse hyperbolic sine.
`Expr.arctan()`	Compute the element-wise value for the inverse tangent.
`Expr.arctanh()`	Compute the element-wise value for the inverse hyperbolic tangent.
`Expr.cos()`	Compute the element-wise value for the cosine.
`Expr.cosh()`	Compute the element-wise value for the hyperbolic cosine.
`Expr.degrees()`	Convert from radians to degrees.
`Expr.radians()`	Convert from degrees to radians.
`Expr.sin()`	Compute the element-wise value for the sine.
`Expr.sinh()`	Compute the element-wise value for the hyperbolic sine.
`Expr.tan()`	Compute the element-wise value for the tangent.
`Expr.tanh()`	Compute the element-wise value for the hyperbolic tangent.

In the following code snippet we apply the methods `Expr.arccos()`, `Expr.cos()`, `Expr.degrees()`, `Expr.radians()`, and `Expr.sin()` to a variety of numerical values. The remaining methods, namely `Expr.arccosh()`, `Expr.arcsin()`, `Expr.arcsinh()`, `Expr.arctan()`, `Expr.arctanh()`, `Expr.cosh()`, `Expr.sinh()`, `Expr.tan()`, and `Expr.tanh()`, can be used in a similar way. None of these methods require arguments:

```
(
    pl.DataFrame(
        {"x": [-math.pi, 0.0, 1.0, math.pi, 2 * math.pi, 90.0, 180.0, 360.0]}
    ).with_columns(
        arccos=pl.col("x").arccos(),    ❶
        cos=pl.col("x").cos(),
        degrees=pl.col("x").degrees(),
        radians=pl.col("x").radians(),
        sin=pl.col("x").sin(),
    )
)
```

❶ With element-wise operations, when an operation results in a NaN, the other
values are not affected.

shape: (8, 6)

x	arccos	cos	degrees	radians	sin
f64	f64	f64	f64	f64	f64
-3.141593	NaN	-1.0	-180.0	-0.054831	-1.2246e-16
0.0	1.570796	1.0	0.0	0.0	0.0
1.0	0.0	0.540302	57.29578	0.017453	0.841471
3.141593	NaN	-1.0	180.0	0.054831	1.2246e-16
6.283185	NaN	1.0	360.0	0.109662	-2.4493e-16
90.0	NaN	-0.448074	5156.620156	1.570796	0.893997
180.0	NaN	-0.59846	10313.240312	3.141593	-0.801153
360.0	NaN	-0.283691	20626.480625	6.283185	0.958916

Operations That Round and Categorize

Sometimes your data contains too much precision or too many distinct values. In
those cases it can be useful to round them or to cut them into discrete categories.
Table 8-3 lists the methods that Polars provides for this.[1]

Table 8-3. Element-wise operations for rounding and binning

Method	Description
Expr.ceil()	Round up to the nearest integer value.
Expr.clip(…)	Clip (limit) the values in an array to a min and max boundary.
Expr.cut(…)	Cut continuous values into discrete categories.
Expr.floor()	Round down to the nearest integer value.
Expr.qcut(…)	Cut continuous values into discrete categories based on their quantiles.
Expr.round(…)	Round underlying floating-point data by decimal digits.

Here, we demonstrate these methods (and Expr.round() twice) for a range of
numbers:

```
(
    pl.DataFrame(
        {"x": [-6.0, -0.5, 0.0, 0.5, math.pi, 9.9, 9.99, 9.999]}
    ).with_columns(
        ceil=pl.col("x").ceil(),
```

---

1 Technically, the method Expr.qcut() is not an element-wise operation because quantiles are based on an
entire Series. In this case we thought it best to keep it close to its cousin Expr.cut().

```
            clip=pl.col("x").clip(-1, 1),
            cut=pl.col("x").cut([-1, 1], labels=["bad", "neutral", "good"]),  ❶
            floor=pl.col("x").floor(),
            qcut=pl.col("x").qcut([0.5], labels=["below median", "above median"]),
            round2=pl.col("x").round(2),
            round0=pl.col("x").round(0),  ❷
        )
    )
```

❶ The methods Expr.cut() and Expr.qcut() construct a Categorical Series. If you
   want it to be an Integer, you can add, for instance, Expr.cast(pl.Int64) to the
   expression.

❷ Even when rounding to zero decimals using Expr.round(0) (or by using
   Expr.ceil() or Expr.floor()), the type remains Float.

shape: (8, 8)

x	ceil	clip	cut	floor	qcut	round2	round0
---	---	---	---	---	---	---	---
f64	f64	f64	cat	f64	cat	f64	f64
-6.0	-6.0	-1.0	bad	-6.0	below median	-6.0	-6.0
-0.5	-0.0	-0.5	neutral	-1.0	below median	-0.5	-1.0
0.0	0.0	0.0	neutral	0.0	below median	0.0	0.0
0.5	1.0	0.5	neutral	0.0	below median	0.5	1.0
3.141593	4.0	1.0	good	3.0	above median	3.14	3.0
9.9	10.0	1.0	good	9.0	above median	9.9	10.0
9.99	10.0	1.0	good	9.0	above median	9.99	10.0
9.999	10.0	1.0	good	9.0	above median	10.0	10.0

Operations for Missing or Infinite Values

When your data is based on the real world, you're bound to have some missing
values. NaNs or infinite values are usually the result of some invalid transformation.
If you need to deal with these, Polars offers a couple of convenient methods (see
Table 8-4). Later in this chapter, there are a few more methods for dealing with
missing values in a Series-wise manner.

Table 8-4. Element-wise operations concerned with missing or infinite values

Method	Description
Expr.fill_nan(…)	Fill floating-point NaN value with a fill value.
Expr.fill_null(…)	Fill null values using the specified value or strategy.
Expr.is_finite()	Return a Boolean Series indicating which values are finite.
Expr.is_infinite()	Return a Boolean Series indicating which values are infinite.

Method	Description
Expr.is_nan()	Return a Boolean Series indicating which values are NaN.
Expr.is_not_nan()	Return a Boolean Series indicating which values are not NaN.
Expr.is_not_null()	Return a Boolean Series indicating which values are not null.
Expr.is_null()	Return a Boolean Series indicating which values are null.

The following code snippet applies the methods Expr.fill_nan(), Expr.fill_null(), Expr.is_finite(), Expr.is_infinite(), Expr.is_nan(), and Expr.is_null() to a couple of numerical values, some of which are infinite or missing. The methods Expr.is_not_nan() and Expr.is_not_null() produce the inverse of Expr.is_nan() and Expr.is_null(), respectively.

```
x = [42.0, math.nan, None, math.inf, -math.inf]
(
    pl.DataFrame({"x": x}).with_columns(
        fill_nan=pl.col("x").fill_nan(999),
        fill_null=pl.col("x").fill_null(0),   ❶
        is_finite=pl.col("x").is_finite(),
        is_infinite=pl.col("x").is_infinite(),
        is_nan=pl.col("x").is_nan(),
        is_null=pl.col("x").is_null(),
    )
)
```

❶ The method Expr.fill_null() has a keyword argument strategy that allows for more advanced usage. This can make it depend on other values in the rows around it. We've discussed this earlier in Chapter 4.

shape: (5, 7)

x	fill_nan	fill_null	is_finite	is_infinite	is_nan	is_null
f64	f64	f64	bool	bool	bool	bool
42.0	42.0	42.0	true	false	false	false
NaN	999.0	NaN	false	false	true	false
null	null	0.0	null	null	null	true
inf	inf	inf	false	true	false	false
-inf	-inf	-inf	false	true	false	false

NaN Versus Null

This is a good reminder that NaNs and nulls are not the same type. If you need to fill both types in a Series, you can add `Expr.fill_nan()` and `Expr.fill_null()` to the expression. And if you need to know whether a value is either Nan or null, you can combine `Expr.is_nan()` and `Expr.is_null()` with the Boolean OR operator (`|`):

```
(
    pl.DataFrame({"x": x}).with_columns(
        fill_both=pl.col("x").fill_nan(0).fill_null(0),
        is_either=(pl.col("x").is_nan() |
        pl.col("x").is_null()),
    )
)
```

```
shape: (5, 3)
┌───────┬───────────┬───────────┐
│ x     │ fill_both │ is_either │
│ ---   │ ---       │ ---       │
│ f64   │ f64       │ bool      │
╞═══════╪═══════════╪═══════════╡
│ 42.0  │ 42.0      │ false     │
│ NaN   │ 0.0       │ true      │
│ null  │ 0.0       │ true      │
│ inf   │ inf       │ false     │
│ -inf  │ -inf      │ false     │
└───────┴───────────┴───────────┘
```

You'll learn more about Boolean operators in the next chapter. Whether you actually *want* to treat NaNs and nulls the same way depends on the task at hand.

Other Operations

There are three element-wise operators that don't fall into any of the preceding categories (see Table 8-5).

Table 8-5. Miscellaneous element-wise operations

Method	Description
Expr.hash(…)	Hash the elements in the selection.
Expr.repeat_by(…)	Repeat the elements in this Series as specified in the given expression.
Expr.replace(…)	Replace values in column according to remapping dictionary.

The following code snippet demonstrates these three methods:

```
(
    pl.DataFrame({"x": ["here", "there", "their", "they're"]}).with_columns(
```

```
        hash=pl.col("x").hash(seed=1337),  ❶
        repeat_by=pl.col("x").repeat_by(3),
        replace=pl.col("x").replace(
            {
                "here": "there",
                "they're": "they are",
            }
        ),
    )
)
```

❶ With the method `Expr.hash()`, different computers or computers with different
   versions of Polars will generate different hash values. More information can be
   found on the AHash website (*https://oreil.ly/G6BPD*).

```
shape: (4, 4)
┌─────────┬──────────────────────┬─────────────────────────────┬──────────┐
│ x       │ hash                 │ repeat_by                   │ replace  │
│ ---     │ ---                  │ ---                         │ ---      │
│ str     │ u64                  │ list[str]                   │ str      │
╞═════════╪══════════════════════╪═════════════════════════════╪══════════╡
│ here    │ 12695211751326448172 │ ["here", "here", "here"]    │ there    │
│ there   │ 17329794691236705436 │ ["there", "there", "there"] │ there    │
│ their   │ 2663095961041830581  │ ["their", "their", "their"] │ their    │
│ they're │ 6743063676290245144  │ ["they're", "they're", "they'r… │ they are │
└─────────┴──────────────────────┴─────────────────────────────┴──────────┘
```

Nonreducing Series-Wise Operations

In the remaining sections, we're no longer looking at element-wise operations, but at
Series-wise operations. That means that the Series is transformed as a whole, and the
values themselves (and sometimes also their order) depend on each other. Examples
include the `Expr.cum_sum()` method for computing the cumulative sum and the
`Expr.forward_fill()` method for filling missing values.

In the next six subsections we're looking at operations which do not change the
length of the Series, including operations that accumulate, fill, shift, compute rolling
statistics, sort, and more.

Operations That Accumulate

Cumulative operations progress through a Series and maintain, for instance, the sum
or the maximum. See Table 8-6 for all the cumulative methods that Polars provides.

Table 8-6. Series-wise operations that are cumulative

Method	Description
`Expr.cum_count(…)`	Get an array with the cumulative count computed at every element.
`Expr.cum_max(…)`	Get an array with the cumulative max computed at every element.
`Expr.cum_min(…)`	Get an array with the cumulative min computed at every element.
`Expr.cum_prod(…)`	Get an array with the cumulative product computed at every element.
`Expr.cum_sum(…)`	Get an array with the cumulative sum computed at every element.
`Expr.diff(…)`	Calculate the nth discrete difference.
`Expr.pct_change(…)`	Compute percentage change between values.

All of these methods accept one argument, `reverse`, which indicates whether the Series should be reversed first, i.e., before the operation is applied. The following code snippet applies all methods to a variety of numerical values, including a missing value and a NaN:

```
(
    pl.DataFrame(
        {"x": [0.0, 1.0, 2.0, None, 2.0, np.nan, -1.0, 2.0]}
    ).with_columns(
        cum_count=pl.col("x").cum_count(),        ❶
        cum_max=pl.col("x").cum_max(),
        cum_min=pl.col("x").cum_min(),
        cum_prod=pl.col("x").cum_prod(reverse=True),     ❷
        cum_sum=pl.col("x").cum_sum(),
        diff=pl.col("x").diff(),
        pct_change=pl.col("x").pct_change(),
    )
)
```

❶ The method `Expr.cum_count()` does not count missing values.

❷ If we didn't reverse this operation, the entire column would be filled with zeros.

```
shape: (8, 8)
```

x	cum_count	cum_max	cum_min	cum_prod	cum_sum	diff	pct_change
---	---	---	---	---	---	---	---
f64	u32	f64	f64	f64	f64	f64	f64
0.0	1	0.0	0.0	NaN	0.0	null	null
1.0	2	1.0	0.0	NaN	1.0	1.0	inf
2.0	3	2.0	0.0	NaN	3.0	1.0	1.0
null	3	null	null	null	null	null	0.0
2.0	4	2.0	0.0	NaN	5.0	null	0.0
NaN	5	2.0	0.0	NaN	NaN	NaN	NaN
-1.0	6	2.0	-1.0	-2.0	NaN	NaN	NaN

| 2.0 | 7 | 2.0 | -1.0 | 2.0 | NaN | 3.0 | -3.0 |

 Contagious NaNs

NaNs may affect the output of Series-wise operations. In this example:

- The output of `Expr.cum_count()`, `Expr.cum_max()`, and `Expr.cum_min()` is not affected at all.

- The output of `Expr.cum_prod()` and `Expr.cum_sum()` remains affected once a NaN has been seen.

- The output of `Expr.diff()` and `Expr.pct_change()` is only affected for two values for every NaN.

Operations That Fill and Shift

Sometimes it's useful to process data on rows using data of the rows around it. Examples can be shifting data by an *x* amount of rows or filling empty values based on the rows before or after them. This is where the following expressions come in handy.

Table 8-7 lists the nonreducing Series-wise methods for filling and shifting.

Table 8-7. Series-wise operations for filling and shifting

Method	Description
`Expr.backward_fill(…)`	Fill missing values with the next to-be-seen value.
`Expr.forward_fill(…)`	Fill missing values with the latest seen value.
`Expr.interpolate(…)`	Fill missing values using interpolation.
`Expr.shift(…)`	Shift the values by a given period.

Let's apply the methods `Expr.backward_fill()`, `Expr.forward_fill()`, `Expr.inter` `polate()` (twice), and `Expr.shift()` (twice) to some values, including missing values:

```
(
    pl.DataFrame(
        {"x": [-1.0, 0.0, 1.0, None, None, 3.0, 4.0, math.nan, 6.0]}
    ).with_columns(
        backward_fill=pl.col("x").backward_fill(),          ❶
        forward_fill=pl.col("x").forward_fill(limit=1),
        interp1=pl.col("x").interpolate(method="linear"),    ❷
        interp2=pl.col("x").interpolate(method="nearest"),
        shift1=pl.col("x").shift(1),
        shift2=pl.col("x").shift(-2),
```

```
      )
)
```

❶ NaNs do not get filled or interpolated.

❷ Note the difference between the two interpolation methods linear and nearest. The former interpolates between the previous and next nonmissing values in the Series, while the latter uses the actual closest nonmissing value.

```
shape: (9, 7)
┌───────┬───────────────┬──────────────┬──────────┬────────┬────────┬────────┐
│ x     │ backward_fill │ forward_fill │ interp1  │ interp2│ shift1 │ shift2 │
│ ---   │ ---           │ ---          │ ---      │ ---    │ ---    │ ---    │
│ f64   │ f64           │ f64          │ f64      │ f64    │ f64    │ f64    │
╞═══════╪═══════════════╪══════════════╪══════════╪════════╪════════╪════════╡
│ -1.0  │ -1.0          │ -1.0         │ -1.0     │ -1.0   │ null   │ 1.0    │
│ 0.0   │ 0.0           │ 0.0          │ 0.0      │ 0.0    │ -1.0   │ null   │
│ 1.0   │ 1.0           │ 1.0          │ 1.0      │ 1.0    │ 0.0    │ null   │
│ null  │ 3.0           │ 1.0          │ 1.666667 │ 1.0    │ 1.0    │ 3.0    │
│ null  │ 3.0           │ null         │ 2.333333 │ 3.0    │ null   │ 4.0    │
│ 3.0   │ 3.0           │ 3.0          │ 3.0      │ 3.0    │ null   │ NaN    │
│ 4.0   │ 4.0           │ 4.0          │ 4.0      │ 4.0    │ 3.0    │ 6.0    │
│ NaN   │ NaN           │ NaN          │ NaN      │ NaN    │ 4.0    │ null   │
│ 6.0   │ 6.0           │ 6.0          │ 6.0      │ 6.0    │ NaN    │ null   │
└───────┴───────────────┴──────────────┴──────────┴────────┴────────┴────────┘
```

Operations Related to Duplicate Values

There are four nonreducing Series-wise methods that are concerned with unique and duplicate values (see Table 8-8). There are other methods which are concerned with this, but since they reduce the length of the Series, they are discussed later in the chapter.

Table 8-8. Series-wise operations that return a Boolean Series

Method	Description
Expr.is_duplicated()	Get a Boolean Series that indicates which values are duplicated.
Expr.is_first_distinct()	Get a Boolean Series that indicates which values are first unique.
Expr.is_last_distinct()	Get a Boolean Series that indicates which values are last unique.
Expr.is_unique()	Get a Boolean Series that indicates which values are unique.

Here we apply these four methods to a couple of Strings:

```
(
    pl.DataFrame({"x": ["A", "C", "D", "C"]}).with_columns(  ❶
        is_duplicated=pl.col("x").is_duplicated(),
        is_first_distinct=pl.col("x").is_first_distinct(),
        is_last_distinct=pl.col("x").is_last_distinct(),
```

```
        is_unique=pl.col("x").is_unique(),
    )
)
```

❶ Keep in mind that many of these methods can also be applied to other data types.

```
shape: (4, 5)
┌─────┬───────────────┬──────────────────┬─────────────────┬───────────┐
│ x   │ is_duplicated │ is_first_distinct │ is_last_distinct │ is_unique │
│ --- │ ---           │ ---              │ ---             │ ---       │
│ str │ bool          │ bool             │ bool            │ bool      │
╞═════╪═══════════════╪══════════════════╪═════════════════╪═══════════╡
│ A   │ false         │ true             │ true            │ true      │
│ C   │ true          │ true             │ false           │ false     │
│ D   │ false         │ true             │ true            │ true      │
│ C   │ true          │ false            │ true            │ false     │
└─────┴───────────────┴──────────────────┴─────────────────┴───────────┘
```

Operations That Compute Rolling Statistics

To make your data analyses more robust, rolling statistics can offer an outcome. In the next section we'll go over these and show an example of smoothing stock prices where these come in handy.

Rolling statistics are used to smooth the values of a Series (see Table 8-9).

Table 8-9. Series-wise operations for rolling statistics

Method	Description
Expr.ewm_mean(…)	Exponentially weighted moving average.
Expr.ewm_std(…)	Exponentially weighted moving standard deviation.
Expr.ewm_var(…)	Exponentially weighted moving variance.
Expr.rolling_apply(…)	Apply a custom rolling window function.
Expr.rolling_map(…)	Compute a custom rolling window function.
Expr.rolling_max(…)	Apply a rolling max (moving max) over the values in this array.
Expr.rolling_mean(…)	Apply a rolling mean (moving mean) over the values in this array.
Expr.rolling_median(…)	Compute a rolling median.
Expr.rolling_min(…)	Apply a rolling min (moving min) over the values in this array.
Expr.rolling_quantile(…)	Compute a rolling quantile.
Expr.rolling_skew(…)	Compute a rolling skew.
Expr.rolling_std(…)	Compute a rolling standard deviation.
Expr.rolling_sum(…)	Apply a rolling sum (moving sum) over the values in this array.
Expr.rolling_var(…)	Compute a rolling variance.

The following code snippet applies `Expr.ewm_mean()`, `Expr.rolling_mean()`, and `Expr.rolling_min()` to the `close` column of some stock data. The remaining methods work similarly:

```
stock = (
    pl.read_csv("data/stock/nvda/2023.csv", try_parse_dates=True)
    .select("date", "close")
    .with_columns(
        ewm_mean=pl.col("close").ewm_mean(com=7, ignore_nulls=True),   ❶
        rolling_mean=pl.col("close").rolling_mean(window_size=7),
        rolling_min=pl.col("close").rolling_min(window_size=7),
    )
)

stock
```

❶ `ignore_nulls=True` is used to handle missing stock price data (if any) more smoothly, ensuring that the weighted average is calculated based on the actual available data rather than being influenced by the presence of null values.

shape: (124, 5)

date	close	ewm_mean	rolling_mean	rolling_min
date	f64	f64	f64	f64
2023-01-03	143.149994	143.149994	null	null
2023-01-04	147.490005	145.464667	null	null
2023-01-05	142.649994	144.398755	null	null
2023-01-06	148.589996	145.664782	null	null
2023-01-09	156.279999	148.388917	null	null
…	…	…	…	…
2023-06-26	406.320007	407.54911	425.805716	406.320007
2023-06-27	418.76001	408.950473	424.695718	406.320007
2023-06-28	411.170013	409.227915	422.445718	406.320007
2023-06-29	408.220001	409.101926	418.180006	406.320007
2023-06-30	423.019989	410.841684	417.118574	406.320007

Because it's difficult to see the difference between these methods in a table, let's visualize it using the plotnine package (see Figure 8-2):

```
from plotnine import *

(
    ggplot(stock.unpivot(index="date"), aes("date", "value", color="variable"))
    + geom_line(size=1)
    + labs(x="Date", y="Value", color="Method")
    + theme_tufte(base_family="Guardian Sans", base_size=14)
    + theme(figure_size=(8, 5), dpi=200)
)
```

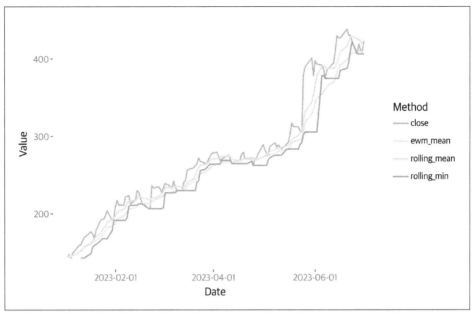

Figure 8-2. Several rolling statistics operations applied to stock data

In Chapter 16 you'll learn more about creating data visualizations with Polars.

Operations That Sort

Is the data sorted wrong within the column itself? Or is the data sorted, but should it be shuffled instead? These expressions come to the rescue!

Table 8-10 lists the methods that Polars provides for sorting expressions.

Table 8-10. Series-wise operations that sort

Method	Description
Expr.arg_sort(…)	Get the index values that would sort this column.
Expr.shuffle(…)	Shuffle the contents of this expression.
Expr.sort(…)	Sort this column.
Expr.sort_by(…)	Sort this column by the ordering of other columns.
Expr.rank(…)	Assign ranks to data, dealing with ties appropriately.
Expr.reverse()	Reverse the selection.

Sorting Single Expressions Is Not That Common

In real-world datasets, a row often represents an observation or event. For that reason, you'll most likely want to sort entire rows so that the measurements of each observation or event stay together. The methods in this section, however, only deal with a single expression or column. DataFrame methods for sorting, such as df.sort(), are covered in Chapter 11.

Let's apply those six methods on a couple of numbers. We've also added a column y to demonstrate the method Expr.sort_by():

```
(
    pl.DataFrame(
        {
            "x": [1, 3, None, 3, 7],
            "y": ["D", "I", "S", "C", "O"],
        }
    ).with_columns(
        arg_sort=pl.col("x").arg_sort(),
        shuffle=pl.col("x").shuffle(seed=7),
        sort=pl.col("x").sort(nulls_last=True),
        sort_by=pl.col("x").sort_by("y"),
        reverse=pl.col("x").reverse(),
        rank=pl.col("x").rank(),
    )
)
```

```
shape: (5, 8)
```

x	y	arg_sort	shuffle	sort	sort_by	reverse	rank
i64	str	u32	i64	i64	i64	i64	f64
1	D	2	1	1	3	7	1.0
3	I	0	null	3	1	3	2.5
null	S	1	3	3	3	null	null
3	C	3	7	7	7	3	2.5
7	O	4	3	null	null	1	4.0

Other Operations

There's one nonreducing Series-wise operator that doesn't fall into any of the preceding categories (see Table 8-11).

Table 8-11. One other Series-wise operation

Method	Description
`Expr.rle_id()`	Get a distinct Integer ID for each run of identical values. The ID starts at 0 and increases by one each time the value of the column changes.

Let's apply `Expr.rle_id()` to a numerical Series:

```
(
    pl.DataFrame({"x": [33, 33, 27, 33, 60, 60, 60, 33, 60]}).with_columns(
        rle_id=pl.col("x").rle_id(),
    )
)
```

```
shape: (9, 2)
┌─────┬────────┐
│ x   │ rle_id │
│ --- │ ---    │
│ i64 │ u32    │
╞═════╪════════╡
│ 33  │ 0      │
│ 33  │ 0      │
│ 27  │ 1      │
│ 33  │ 2      │
│ 60  │ 3      │
│ 60  │ 3      │
│ 60  │ 3      │
│ 33  │ 4      │
│ 60  │ 5      │
└─────┴────────┘
```

Now let's move on to the expressions that summarize to one row.

Series-Wise Operations That Summarize to One

We continue with Series-wise operations, but in this section we're looking at operations which summarize all values in the Series into one value. Examples include the `Expr.mean()` method for computing the mean value and the `Expr.null_count()` method for counting the number of missing values.

In the next four subsections we look at operations that summarize to one using quantifiers, by computing statistics, by counting, and others.

Repeated Values

If you use an operation that summarizes to one value and you keep any of the original columns, the computed value gets repeated to create a column that is as long as the rest (which is required in Polars). For example, here the mean of the Series gets repeated four times:

```
(
    pl.DataFrame({"x": [1, 3, 3, 7]}).with_columns(
        mean=pl.col("x").mean(),
    )
)
```

shape: (4, 2)

x	mean
i64	f64
1	3.5
3	3.5
3	3.5
7	3.5

Because summarizing operations are most often used in an aggregation context, this is not really an issue. For example, see what happens when you compute the mean per group:

```
(
    pl.DataFrame({"cluster": ["a", "a", "b", "b"], "x": [1, 3, 3, 7]})
    .group_by("cluster")
    .agg(
        mean=pl.col("x").mean(),
    )
)
```

shape: (2, 2)

cluster	mean
str	f64
a	2.0
b	5.0

In the remainder of this chapter, we'll use the df.select() method to exclude the original columns and thus avoid repeated values.

Operations That Are Quantifiers

Using quantifiers allows you to summarize multiple Boolean values into one. Polars supports the universal and existential quantifiers via Expr.all() and Expr.any() (see Table 8-12).

Table 8-12. Series-wise operations that summarize to one value using quantifiers

Method	Description
Expr.all(…)	Return whether all values in the column are True.
Expr.any(…)	Return whether any of the values in the column are True.

Both methods accept one argument, ignore_nulls, that indicates whether missing values should be ignored. The following code snippet applies Expr.all() and Expr.any() to three Boolean columns, x, y, and z:

```python
df = pl.DataFrame(
    {
        "x": [True, False, False],
        "y": [True, True, True],
        "z": [False, False, False],
    }
)
print(df)
print(
    df.select(
        pl.all().all().name.suffix("_all"),
        pl.all().any().name.suffix("_any"),
    ),
)
```

```
shape: (3, 3)
┌───────┬──────┬───────┐
│ x     │ y    │ z     │
│ ---   │ ---  │ ---   │
│ bool  │ bool │ bool  │
╞═══════╪══════╪═══════╡
│ true  │ true │ false │
│ false │ true │ false │
│ false │ true │ false │
└───────┴──────┴───────┘

shape: (1, 6)
┌───────┬───────┬───────┬───────┬───────┬───────┐
│ x_all │ y_all │ z_all │ x_any │ y_any │ z_any │
│ ---   │ ---   │ ---   │ ---   │ ---   │ ---   │
│ bool  │ bool  │ bool  │ bool  │ bool  │ bool  │
╞═══════╪═══════╪═══════╪═══════╪═══════╪═══════╡
│ false │ true  │ false │ true  │ true  │ false │
└───────┴───────┴───────┴───────┴───────┴───────┘
```

Operations That Compute Statistics

Polars supports many methods to compute a variety of statistics of a numerical Series (see Table 8-13).

Table 8-13. Series-wise operations that summarize to one element by computing statistics

Method	Description
`Expr.entropy(…)`	Compute the entropy.
`Expr.kurtosis(…)`	Compute the kurtosis (Fisher or Pearson) of a dataset.
`Expr.max()`	Get maximum value.
`Expr.mean()`	Get mean value.
`Expr.median()`	Get median value using linear interpolation.
`Expr.min()`	Get minimum value.
`Expr.nan_max()`	Get maximum value, but propagate/poison encountered NaN values.
`Expr.nan_min()`	Get minimum value, but propagate/poison encountered NaN values.
`Expr.product()`	Compute the product of an expression.
`Expr.quantile(…)`	Get quantile value.
`Expr.skew(…)`	Compute the sample skewness of a dataset.
`Expr.std(…)`	Get standard deviation.
`Expr.sum()`	Get sum value.
`Expr.var(…)`	Get variance.

In the following code snippet, we apply the methods `Expr.max()`, `Expr.mean()`, `Expr.quantile()`, `Expr.skew()`, `Expr.std()`, `Expr.sum()`, and `Expr.var()` to a million values. These values are sampled from a normal distribution with a mean of 5 and a standard deviation of 3:

```
samples = rng.normal(loc=5, scale=3, size=1_000_000)

(
    pl.DataFrame({"x": samples}).select(
        max=pl.col("x").max(),
        mean=pl.col("x").mean(),
        quantile=pl.col("x").quantile(quantile=0.95),
        skew=pl.col("x").skew(),
        std=pl.col("x").std(),
        sum=pl.col("x").sum(),
        var=pl.col("x").var(),
    )
)
shape: (1, 7)
```

max	mean	quantile	skew	std	sum	var
f64	f64	f64	f64	f64	f64	f64
20.752443	4.994978	9.931565	0.003245	2.999926	4.9950e6	8.999558

The other methods, `Expr.entropy()`, `Expr.kurtosis()`, `Expr.median()`, `Expr.min()`, `Expr.nan_max()`, `Expr.nan_min()`, and `Expr.product()` work similarly.

Operations That Count

Polars offers several methods for counting certain things (see Table 8-14).

Table 8-14. Series-wise operations that summarize to one element by counting

Method	Description
`Expr.approx_n_unique()`	Approximate count of unique values.
`Expr.count()`	Count the number of values in this expression.
`Expr.len()`	Count the number of values in this expression.
`Expr.n_unique()`	Count unique values.
`Expr.null_count()`	Count null values.

To demonstrate these methods, let's generate 1,729 random integers between 0 and 10,000, and make one value missing:

```
samples = pl.Series(rng.integers(low=0, high=10_000, size=1_729))
samples[403] = None    ❶
df_ints = pl.DataFrame({"x": samples}).with_row_index()    ❷
df_ints.slice(400, 6)    ❸
```

❶   The 403rd element is made missing.

❷   The DataFrame method `df.with_row_index()` adds a row index as the first column.

❸   We use the DataFrame method `df.slice()` to display a subset of the rows.

```
shape: (6, 2)
┌───────┬──────┐
│ index │ x    │
│ ---   │ ---  │
│ u32   │ i64  │
╞═══════╪══════╡
│ 400   │ 807  │
│ 401   │ 8634 │
│ 402   │ 2109 │
│ 403   │ null │
│ 404   │ 1740 │
│ 405   │ 3333 │
└───────┴──────┘
```

Let's apply these five methods to column x:

```
df_ints.select(
    approx_n_unique=pl.col("x").approx_n_unique(),
    count=pl.col("x").count(),
    len=pl.col("x").len(),
    n_unique=pl.col("x").n_unique(),
    null_count=pl.col("x").null_count(),
)
```

shape: (1, 5)

approx_n_unique	count	len	n_unique	null_count
---	---	---	---	---
u32	u32	u32	u32	u32
1572	1728	1729	1575	1

You can wonder what the use case is for the Expr.approx_n_unique() method when compared side-by-side to Expr.n_unique().

What you can't see here is that this method is a lot quicker than Expr.n_unique(), so in situations where performance is more important than an exact number, this can be the perfect solution. Let's create a large DataFrame to showcase it:

```
large_df_ints = pl.DataFrame(
    {"x": rng.integers(low=0, high=10_000, size=10_000_000)}
)
```

Let's time the runtime for the Expr.n_unique() method:

```
%%time
large_df_ints.select(pl.col("x").n_unique())
```

```
CPU times: user 155 ms, sys: 21.6 ms, total: 177 ms
Wall time: 54.5 ms
shape: (1, 1)
```

x
---
u32
10000

And compare it with Expr.approx_n_unique():

```
%%time
large_df_ints.select(pl.col("x").approx_n_unique())
```

```
CPU times: user 26.8 ms, sys: 50 µs, total: 26.8 ms
Wall time: 26.8 ms
shape: (1, 1)
```

x

```
| u32   |
|=======|
| 10013 |
```

Even though the value is off by approximately 0.1%, it takes 30% less time to get that information.

Other Operations

There are eight Series-wise operators that summarize to one that don't fall into any of the previous categories (see Table 8-15).

Table 8-15. Several miscellaneous Series-wise operations that summarize to one element

Method	Description
Expr.arg_max()	Get the index of the maximal value.
Expr.arg_min()	Get the index of the minimal value.
Expr.first()	Get the first value.
Expr.get(…)	Return a single value by index.
Expr.implode()	Aggregate values into a list.
Expr.last()	Get the last value.
Expr.lower_bound()	Calculate the lower bound.
Expr.upper_bound()	Calculate the upper bound.

Here we apply the methods Expr.arg_min(), Expr.first(), Expr.get(), Expr.implode(), Expr.last(), and Expr.upper_bound() to the same values as the previous section. The method Expr.arg_max() is similar to Expr.arg_min(), and Expr.lower_bound() is similar to Expr.upper_bound():

```
df_ints.select(
    arg_min=pl.col("x").arg_min(),
    first=pl.col("x").first(),
    get=pl.col("x").get(403),      ❶
    implode=pl.col("x").implode(),
    last=pl.col("x").last(),
    upper_bound=pl.col("x").upper_bound(),
)
```

❶ The result is null because, in the previous section, we made the 403rd element missing.

```
shape: (1, 6)
┌─────────┬───────┬─────┬───────────┬──────┬─────────────┐
│ arg_min │ first │ get │ implode   │ last │ upper_bound │
│ ---     │ ---   │ --- │ ---       │ ---  │ ---         │
│ u32     │ i64   │ i64 │ list[i64] │ i64  │ i64         │
```

```
| 0        | 0      | null | [0, 7245, … 3723] | 3723 | 9223372036854775807 |
```

Series-Wise Operations That Summarize to One or More

Besides Series-wise operations that summarize to one, there are also some that summarize to one or more. The actual length of the output Series depends on the values.

In the next four subsections, we cover Series-wise operations that summarize to one
or more based on unique values, by selecting, dropping missing values, and others.

Operations Related to Unique Values

We're all unique in our own way. That goes for data too. The following expressions
help showcase our uniqueness.

Table 8-16 lists four methods related to unique values.

*Table 8-16. Several Series-wise operations that summarize to one or more elements based on
unique values*

Method	Description
Expr.arg_unique()	Get index of first unique value.
Expr.unique(…)	Get unique values of this expression.
Expr.unique_counts()	Return a count of the unique values in the order of appearance.
Expr.value_counts(…)	Count the occurrences of unique values.

Let's apply those four methods to a Series of Strings:

```
(
    pl.DataFrame({"x": ["A", "C", "D", "C"]}).select(
        arg_unique=pl.col("x").arg_unique(),
        unique=pl.col("x").unique(maintain_order=True),      ❶
        unique_counts=pl.col("x").unique_counts(),
        value_counts=pl.col("x").value_counts(sort=True),    ❷
    )
)
```

❶ Maintaining the order of the values is computationally more intensive.

❷ The result of `Expr.value_counts()` is of data type `pl.Struct`: a combination of `Expr.unique()` and `Expr.unique_counts()`, though not necessarily in the same order.[2]

```
shape: (3, 4)
┌────────────┬────────┬───────────────┬──────────────┐
│ arg_unique │ unique │ unique_counts │ value_counts │
│ ---        │ ---    │ ---           │ ---          │
│ u32        │ str    │ u32           │ struct[2]    │
╞════════════╪════════╪═══════════════╪══════════════╡
│ 0          │ A      │ 1             │ {"C",2}      │
│ 1          │ C      │ 2             │ {"A",1}      │
│ 2          │ D      │ 1             │ {"D",1}      │
└────────────┴────────┴───────────────┴──────────────┘
```

Operations That Select

Sometimes you just have to reach out and grab it. These expressions allow you to snatch exactly what you want from your DataFrames.

Table 8-17 lists several methods for selecting specific elements based on their position or value.

Table 8-17. Several Series-wise operations that summarize to one or more elements by selecting

Method	Description
`Expr.bottom_k(…)`	Return the *k* smallest elements.
`Expr.head(…)`	Get the first *n* rows.
`Expr.limit(…)`	Get the first *n* rows (alias for `Expr.head()`).
`Expr.sample(…)`	Sample from this expression.
`Expr.slice(…)`	Get a slice of this expression.
`Expr.tail(…)`	Get the last *n* rows.
`Expr.gather(…)`	Take values by index.
`Expr.gather_every(…)`	Take every *n*th value in the Series and return as a new Series.
`Expr.top_k(…)`	Return the *k* largest elements.

The following code snippet applies the methods `Expr.bottom_k()`, `Expr.head()`, `Expr.sample()`, `Expr.slice()`, `Expr.gather()`, `Expr.gather_every()`, and `Expr.top_k()` to the samples generated earlier.

---

2 Because of Polars' heavily parallelized nature, work that can be done in parallel is not deterministic, because of slight differences in timing on when the work completes.

The method `Expr.limit()` is an alias for `Expr.head()`. The method `Expr.tail()` works just like `Expr.head()`, except it starts at the bottom:

```
df_ints.select(
    bottom_k=pl.col("x").bottom_k(7),  ❶
    head=pl.col("x").head(7),
    sample=pl.col("x").sample(7),
    slice=pl.col("x").slice(400, 7),
    gather=pl.col("x").gather([1, 1, 2, 3, 5, 8, 13]),
    gather_every=pl.col("x").gather_every(247),  ❷
    top_k=pl.col("x").top_k(7),
)
```

❶ Note that nulls are first.

❷ Has to match a height of 7, otherwise you get an error saying that the lengths don't match. In this example, taking every 247th value from a Series of length 1,729 yields 7 values.

```
shape: (7, 7)
┌──────────┬──────┬────────┬───────┬────────┬──────────────┬───────┐
│ bottom_k │ head │ sample │ slice │ gather │ gather_every │ top_k │
│ ---      │ ---  │ ---    │ ---   │ ---    │ ---          │ ---   │
│ i64      │ i64  │ i64    │ i64   │ i64    │ i64          │ i64   │
╞══════════╪══════╪════════╪═══════╪════════╪══════════════╪═══════╡
│ 0        │ 0    │ 6871   │ 807   │ 7245   │ 0            │ 9998  │
│ 1        │ 7245 │ 2202   │ 8634  │ 7245   │ 8680         │ 9988  │
│ 6        │ 5227 │ 7328   │ 2109  │ 5227   │ 8483         │ 9988  │
│ 7        │ 2747 │ 1648   │ null  │ 2747   │ 8358         │ 9986  │
│ 10       │ 9816 │ 5761   │ 1740  │ 2657   │ 1805         │ 9985  │
│ 21       │ 2657 │ 9315   │ 3333  │ 5393   │ 3638         │ 9979  │
│ 29       │ 4578 │ 8370   │ 788   │ 8203   │ 5843         │ 9975  │
└──────────┴──────┴────────┴───────┴────────┴──────────────┴───────┘
```

Operations That Drop Missing Values

Empty values are usually not that relevant to work with. Using these expressions, you can drop them like they're hot.

Table 8-18 lists two methods for dropping missing values: `Expr.drop_nans()` and `Expr.drop_nulls()`.

Table 8-18. Several Series-wise operations that summarize to one or more elements by dropping missing values

Method	Description
`Expr.drop_nans()`	Drop floating-point NaN values.
`Expr.drop_nulls()`	Drop all null values.

Here's how you can apply both methods:

```
x = [None, 1.0, 2.0, 3.0, np.nan]
(
    pl.DataFrame({"x": x}).select(
        drop_nans=pl.col("x").drop_nans(), drop_nulls=pl.col("x").drop_nulls()
    )
)
```

```
shape: (4, 2)
┌───────────┬────────────┐
│ drop_nans │ drop_nulls │
│ ---       │ ---        │
│ f64       │ f64        │
╞═══════════╪════════════╡
│ null      │ 1.0        │
│ 1.0       │ 2.0        │
│ 2.0       │ 3.0        │
│ 3.0       │ NaN        │
└───────────┴────────────┘
```

Other Operations

There are six Series-wise operators that summarize to one or more that don't fall into any of the preceding categories (see Table 8-19).

Table 8-19. Miscellaneous Series-wise operations that summarize to one or more elements

Method	Description
Expr.arg_true()	Return indices where expression evaluates to True.
Expr.flatten()	Flatten a list or String column.
Expr.mode()	Compute the most occurring value(s).
Expr.reshape(…)	Reshape this Expr to a flat Series or a Series of lists.
Expr.rle()	Get the lengths of runs of identical values.
Expr.search_sorted(…)	Find indices where elements should be inserted to maintain order.

Here we apply the methods `Expr.arg_true()`, `Expr.mode()`, `Expr.reshape()`, `Expr.rle()`, and `Expr.search_sorted()` to an unsorted Series of integers. We demonstrate the methods separately, because they construct Series of different lengths.

First, the method `Expr.arg_true()` can be applied as follows:

```
numbers = [33, 33, 27, 33, 60, 60, 60, 33, 60]

(
    pl.DataFrame({"x": numbers}).select(
        arg_true=(pl.col("x") >= 60).arg_true(),   ❶
```

```
        )
)
```

❶ We use the greater than or equal to operator (>=) to get a Boolean Series first. You'll learn more about this and other comparison operators in Chapter 9.

```
shape: (4, 1)
┌──────────┐
│ arg_true │
│ ---      │
│ u32      │
╞══════════╡
│ 4        │
│ 5        │
│ 6        │
│ 8        │
└──────────┘
```

Second, the method Expr.mode() can be applied as follows:

```
(
    pl.DataFrame({"x": numbers}).select(
        mode=pl.col("x").mode().sort(),
    )
)
```

```
shape: (2, 1)
┌──────┐
│ mode │
│ ---  │
│ i64  │
╞══════╡
│ 33   │
│ 60   │
└──────┘
```

Third, the method Expr.reshape() can be applied as follows:

```
(
    pl.DataFrame({"x": numbers}).select(
        reshape=pl.col("x").reshape((3, 3)),   ❶
    )
)
```

❶ The total number of elements must remain the same. For example, it's not possible to reshape this into five rows, where the last row is a pl.List of one element.

```
shape: (3, 1)
┌───────────────┐
│ reshape       │
│ ---           │
│ array[i64, 3] │
```

```
┌─────────────┐
│ [33, 33, 27] │
│ [33, 60, 60] │
│ [60, 33, 60] │
└─────────────┘
```

Fourth, the method Expr.rle() can be applied as follows:

```
(
    pl.DataFrame({"x": numbers}).select(
        rle=pl.col("x").rle(),  ❶
    )
)
```

❶ Compare with Expr.rle_id() discussed earlier in this chapter.

```
shape: (6, 1)
┌───────────┐
│ rle       │
│ ---       │
│ struct[2] │
╞═══════════╡
│ {2,33}    │
│ {1,27}    │
│ {1,33}    │
│ {3,60}    │
│ {1,33}    │
│ {1,60}    │
└───────────┘
```

Finally, the method Expr.search_sorted() can be applied as follows:

```
(
    pl.DataFrame({"x": numbers}).select(
        rle=pl.col("x").sort().search_sorted(42),  ❶
    )
)
```

❶ The method Expr.search_sorted() is probably most useful on a sorted Series.

```
shape: (1, 1)
┌─────┐
│ rle │
│ --- │
│ u32 │
╞═════╡
│ 5   │
└─────┘
```

You'll learn more about Expr.flatten() in Chapter 12, because it's an alias for Expr.list.explode().

Series-Wise Operations That Extend

There are only two operations that can extend the length of a Series (see Table 8-20).

Table 8-20. Two Series-wise operations that extend

Method	Description
Expr.explode()	Explode a list expression.
Expr.extend_constant(…)	Extend the Series with a constant value.

Here we use the method `Expr.explode()` to turn a List Series into a regular, flat Series:

```
(
    pl.DataFrame(
        {
            "x": [["a", "b"], ["c", "d"]],
        }
    ).select(explode=pl.col("x").explode())
)
```

```
shape: (4, 1)
┌─────────┐
│ explode │
│ ---     │
│ str     │
╞═════════╡
│ a       │
│ b       │
│ c       │
│ d       │
└─────────┘
```

We demonstrated the method `Expr.extend_constant()` at the beginning of this chapter.

Takeaways

In this chapter, we have explored the various expressions Polars has available. You have learned that:

- Expressions in Polars can be extended with operations such as mathematical transformations, handling missing values, and applying statistical summaries.
- Different types of operations include element-wise, Series-wise, and those that reduce, extend, or summarize the Series.

- Element-wise operations apply to each value independently, including methods like `Expr.sqrt()`, `Expr.log()`, and `Expr.sin()`, while Series-wise operations consider the entire Series, such as `Expr.cum_sum()` or `Expr.rolling_mean()`.

- Methods like `Expr.unique()`, `Expr.mean()`, and `Expr.is_null()` help summarize Series to single or multiple values.

- Missing values can be handled with methods like `Expr.fill_nan()` and `Expr.fill_null()`, while duplication can be addressed with `Expr.is_duplicated()` and `Expr.is_unique()`.

- Rolling statistics, such as `Expr.rolling_mean()` and `Expr.rolling_sum()`, are useful for smoothing data over a window of values.

- Sorting methods, including `Expr.sort()`, `Expr.reverse()`, and `Expr.rank()`, allow for advanced data manipulation.

- Methods that extend Series, such as `Expr.extend_constant()` or `Expr.explode()`, can increase the length of a Series.

In the next chapter you're going to learn how to combine expressions.

## CHAPTER 9

Combining Expressions

Now that you understand the fundamentals of expressions and know various methods to continue them, it's time to learn how to combine them.

Combining expressions is necessary whenever the Series you want to construct is based on more than one value or column. This happens to be the case more often than you might think: for example, when you want to compute the ratio between two Float columns, filter rows based on multiple conditions, or concatenate multiple String columns into one.

In fact, you've already combined expressions several times in the previous chapters. Let's look at an example from Chapter 7 to refresh your memory:

```
fruit = pl.read_csv("data/fruit.csv")
fruit.filter(pl.col("is_round") & (pl.col("weight") > 1000))
```

```
shape: (2, 5)
```

name	weight	color	is_round	origin
str	i64	str	bool	str
Cantaloupe	2500	orange	true	Africa
Watermelon	5000	green	true	Africa

This code combines, in two steps, two existing columns (is_round and weight), and one value (1000) into one expression. The df.filter() method then uses this expression to filter rows.

Because of how the parentheses are organized, the comparison greater than operator (>) combines the weight column and the value 1000. When the value is larger, it produces the Boolean True. Second, the Boolean AND operator (&) combines the is_round column and the Series constructed in the first step. Only when they're both True is the output True. The df.filter() method interprets True as "keep this row."

Operator Precedence

The operators follow the precedence that is standard in Python. A table that shows their precedence can be found in the Python documentation (*https://oreil.ly/u4V4X*).

That's only the tip of the iceberg when it comes to combining expressions in Polars. In this chapter, you'll learn:

- About the difference between inline operators and method chaining
- How to combine expressions:
  - Through arithmetic, such as adding and multiplying
  - By comparing, such as greater than and equals
  - With Boolean algebra, such as conjunction and negation
  - Via bitwise operations, such as AND and XOR
  - Using a variety of module-level functions

The instructions to get any files you might need are in Chapter 2. We assume that you have the files in the *data* subdirectory.

Inline Operators Versus Methods

In the previous two chapters, you used method chaining to continue expressions. To combine expressions, you can often use inline operators instead of method chaining. Both approaches produce the same result, as illustrated in Figure 9-1.

Not in Line

While every inline operator has a corresponding Expr method, not every method (or function) to combine expressions has a corresponding inline operator. Examples are the method Expr.dot() and the function pl.concat_list().

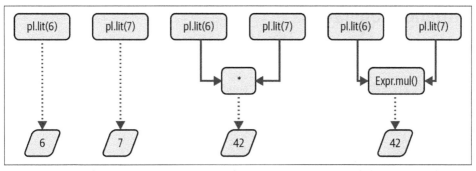

Figure 9-1. Combining expressions using inline operators or method chaining produces the same result

To illustrate this in code, the following snippet multiplies two columns i and j using both approaches:

```
(
    pl.DataFrame({"i": [6.0, 0, 2, 2.5], "j": [7.0, 1, 2, 3]}).with_columns(
        (pl.col("i") * pl.col("j")).alias("*"),
        pl.col("i").mul(pl.col("j")).alias("Expr.mul()"),
    )
)
shape: (4, 4)
```

i	j	*	Expr.mul()
f64	f64	f64	f64
6.0	7.0	42.0	42.0
0.0	1.0	0.0	0.0
2.0	2.0	4.0	4.0
2.5	3.0	7.5	7.5

As expected, both approaches yield the same result. We think that the spaces around the inline operator make it clear that you're combining two expressions into a new one. For this reason, we generally recommend that you use the corresponding inline operator, if one exists. However, note that with the inline-operator approach, you need to wrap the combined expressions in parentheses in order to continue with additional methods, as you can see when we apply Expr.alias() to the new expression.

That's it for multiplying expressions. Now let's look at some other arithmetic operations.

Arithmetic Operations

Arithmetic is the cornerstone of any data-related task. You can perform arithmetic with both expressions and Python values.

Here's a fruity example that divides the `weight` column (an expression) by `1000` (a Python Integer):

```
fruit.select(pl.col("name"), (pl.col("weight") / 1000))
```

```
shape: (10, 2)
┌────────────┬────────┐
│ name       │ weight │
│ ---        │ ---    │
│ str        │ f64    │
╞════════════╪════════╡
│ Avocado    │ 0.2    │
│ Banana     │ 0.12   │
│ Blueberry  │ 0.001  │
│ Cantaloupe │ 2.5    │
│ Cranberry  │ 0.002  │
│ Elderberry │ 0.001  │
│ Orange     │ 0.13   │
│ Papaya     │ 1.0    │
│ Peach      │ 0.15   │
│ Watermelon │ 5.0    │
└────────────┴────────┘
```

Table 9-1 lists all inline operators and methods used to perform arithmetic in Polars.

Table 9-1. Inline operators and their corresponding methods for performing arithmetic

Inline Operator	Method	Description
+	Expr.add(…)	Addition
-	Expr.sub(…)	Subtraction
*	Expr.mul(…)	Multiplication
/	Expr.truediv(…)	Division
//	Expr.floordiv(…)	Floor division
**	Expr.pow(…)	Power
%	Expr.mod(…)	Modulus
N/A	Expr.dot(…)	Dot product

The following code snippet demonstrates how to use these inline operators on two Integer columns (`i` and `j`). Polars automatically creates a Float column when needed. Because the method `Expr.dot()` has no corresponding inline operator, we use the method instead:

```
pl.Config(float_precision=2, tbl_cell_numeric_alignment="RIGHT")  ❶
(
    pl.DataFrame({"i": [0.0, 2, 2, -2, -2], "j": [1, 2, 3, 4, -5]}).with_columns(
        (pl.col("i") + pl.col("j")).alias("i + j"),
        (pl.col("i") - pl.col("j")).alias("i - j"),
        (pl.col("i") * pl.col("j")).alias("i * j"),
        (pl.col("i") / pl.col("j")).alias("i / j"),
        (pl.col("i") // pl.col("j")).alias("i // j"),
        (pl.col("i") ** pl.col("j")).alias("i ** j"),
        (pl.col("j") % 2).alias("j % 2"),  ❷
        pl.col("i").dot(pl.col("j")).alias("i · j"),  ❸
    )
)
```

❶ We're temporarily changing these two display settings to fit this wide DataFrame on the page.

❷ The modulo operator (%) accepts a second expression, just like the other arithmetic operations.

❸ Since there isn't a dedicated inline operator for the dot product, we use the dot character (·) in the column name to represent it. The dot product is a mathematical operation that multiplies corresponding elements from two vectors and then sums the results. In this case, it operates on entire columns of data, rather than individual elements.

shape: (5, 10)

i	j	i + j	i - j	i * j	i / j	i // j	i ** j	j % 2	i · j
f64	i64	f64	f64	f64	f64	f64	f64	i64	f64
0.00	1	1.00	-1.00	0.00	0.00	0.00	0.00	1	12.00
2.00	2	4.00	0.00	4.00	1.00	1.00	4.00	0	12.00
2.00	3	5.00	-1.00	6.00	0.67	0.00	8.00	1	12.00
-2.00	4	2.00	-6.00	-8.00	-0.50	-1.00	16.00	0	12.00
-2.00	-5	-7.00	3.00	10.00	0.40	0.00	-0.03	1	12.00

This is why the last column contains the same value (12.0) repeated five times—the result of applying the dot product to the entire column.

Comparison Operations

- *"Which of these experiments produced a significant result?"*
- *"Which movies released in the '90s have an IMDB score of 8.7 or higher?"*

- *"Are these voltages within the allowed range?"*

These are all data-related questions that involve comparing values.

Comparing values in Polars works pretty much the same as in Python, except that they cannot be chained (explained below):

```
pl.select(pl.lit("a") > pl.lit("b"))

shape: (1, 1)
┌─────────┐
│ literal │
│ ---     │
│ bool    │
╞═════════╡
│ false   │
└─────────┘
```

You'll most likely compare two numeric columns (such as `pl.Int8` and `pl.Float64`). You can also compare Strings and temporal data types (which includes `pl.Date`, `pl.Datetime`, `pl.Duration`, and `pl.Time`).

A comparison always constructs a Boolean Series. This Series can be added as a column to a DataFrame, but it's more often used for filtering rows, using `df.filter()`, or in conditional expressions using `pl.when()`.

Here's an example using the DataFrame `fruit` that compares the column `weight` with the value `1000` using the greater than or equal operator (`>=`). The constructed Boolean Series is used to filter the rows:

```
(
    fruit.select(
        pl.col("name"),
        pl.col("weight"),
    ).filter(pl.col("weight") >= 1000)
)

shape: (3, 2)
┌────────────┬────────┐
│ name       │ weight │
│ ---        │ ---    │
│ str        │ i64    │
╞════════════╪════════╡
│ Cantaloupe │ 2500   │
│ Papaya     │ 1000   │
│ Watermelon │ 5000   │
└────────────┴────────┘
```

Table 9-2 lists all inline operators and methods for performing comparisons in Polars.

Table 9-2. Inline operators and their methods for performing comparisons

Inline Operator	Method	Description
<	Expr.lt(…)	Less than
<=	Expr.le(…)	Less than or equal to
==	Expr.eq(…)	Equal
>=	Expr.ge(…)	Greater than or equal to
>	Expr.gt(…)	Greater than
!=	Expr.ne(…)	Not equal

Chaining Comparisons

In Python itself, you can chain the inline operators listed in Table 9-2. Consider the following example, which uses the less than operator (<) twice to test whether the value of x is between 3 and 5:

```
x = 4
3 < x < 5
```

```
True
```

With Polars, however, if you do this, you get an error:

```
pl.select(pl.lit(3) < pl.lit(x) < pl.lit(5))
```

```
TypeError: the truth value of an Expr is ambiguous
```

```
You probably got here by using a Python standard library function instead of
  the native expressions API.
Here are some things you might want to try:
- instead of `pl.col('a') and pl.col('b')`, use `pl.col('a') & pl.col('b')`
- instead of `pl.col('a') in [y, z]`, use `pl.col('a').is_in([y, z])`
- instead of `max(pl.col('a'), pl.col('b'))`, use `pl.max_horizontal(pl.col(
  'a'), pl.col('b'))`
```

A solution is to perform two separate comparisons and combine them using the AND (&) operator:

```
pl.select((pl.lit(3) < pl.lit(x)) & (pl.lit(x) < pl.lit(5))).item()
```

```
True
```

You'll learn more about the AND (&) operator in the next section, where we discuss combining expressions using Boolean algebra. Another solution is to browse the API documentation (*https://oreil.ly/uCUEE*) to find a suitable Polars expression method for it. In this case, that would be the method Expr.is_between():

```
pl.select(pl.lit(x).is_between(3, 5)).item()
```

```
True
```

Let's apply a couple of comparison operators to two numerical columns a and b:

```
(
    pl.DataFrame(
        {"a": [-273.15, 0, 42, 100], "b": [1.4142, 2.7183, 42, 3.1415]}
    ).with_columns(
        (pl.col("a") == pl.col("b")).alias("a == b"),
        (pl.col("a") <= pl.col("b")).alias("a <= b"),
        (pl.all() > 0).name.suffix(" > 0"),
        ((pl.col("b") - pl.lit(2).sqrt()).abs() < 1e-3).alias("b ≈ √2"),    ❶
        ((1 < pl.col("b")) & (pl.col("b") < 3)).alias("1 < b < 3"),
    )
)
```

❶ Here we use both arithmetic and comparison to combine expressions.

shape: (4, 8)

a	b	a == b	a <= b	a > 0	b > 0	b ≈ √2	1 < b < 3
f64	f64	bool	bool	bool	bool	bool	bool
-273.15	1.4142	false	true	false	true	true	true
0.0	2.7183	false	true	false	true	false	true
42.0	42.0	true	true	true	true	false	false
100.0	3.1415	false	false	true	true	false	false

The following code snippet demonstrates a few more comparisons between different data types. Two of those are not allowed: String with Integer and Datetime with Time.

```
pl.select(
    bool_num=pl.lit(True) > 0,
    time_time=pl.time(23, 58) > pl.time(0, 0),
    datetime_date=pl.datetime(1969, 7, 21, 2, 56) < pl.date(1976, 7, 20),
    str_num=pl.lit("5") < pl.lit(3).cast(pl.String),    ❶
    datetime_time=pl.datetime(1999, 1, 1).dt.time() != pl.time(0, 0),    ❷
).transpose(    ❸
    include_header=True, header_name="comparison", column_names=["allowed"]
)
```

❶ You cannot compare a String and a number. A solution is to first cast the number to String using Expr.cast(pl.String).

❷ You also cannot compare a Datetime and a Time. A solution is to first extract the Time component from the Datetime using the method Expr.dt.time().

❸ We transpose the DataFrame to make it easier to compare the results of the different comparisons.

```
shape: (5, 2)
┌───────────────┬─────────┐
│ comparison    │ allowed │
│ ---           │ ---     │
│ str           │ bool    │
╞═══════════════╪═════════╡
│ bool_num      │ true    │
│ time_time     │ true    │
│ datetime_date │ true    │
│ str_num       │ false   │
│ datetime_time │ false   │
└───────────────┴─────────┘
```

Boolean Algebra Operations

In the previous section, we combined two comparison expressions to check whether the value of x is between two values. Let's use that example again, but set the value of x to 7. We'll also assign the two comparison expressions to two variables, p and q:

```
x = 7
p = pl.lit(3) < pl.lit(x)  # True
q = pl.lit(x) < pl.lit(5)  # False
pl.select(p & q).item()
```

```
False
```

We combine the expressions p and q using the Boolean operator AND (&), which evaluates to True if and only if both p and q are True. Since q is False in this case, the result is False. This Boolean operation is known as *conjunction*.

Conjunction is one of the three basic operations of Boolean algebra: *conjunction* (&), *disjunction* (|), and *negation* (~).[1] With these three basic operations you can create any *secondary* Boolean operation. Polars provides one secondary operation: exclusive or (^). Table 9-3 lists the four Boolean operations with their inline operators and methods.

Table 9-3. Inline operators and their corresponding methods for performing Boolean operations

Operation	Inline Operator	Method	Description
Conjunction	&	Expr.and_(…)	Logical AND
Disjunction	|	Expr.or_(…)	Logical OR
Negation	~	Expr.not_()	Logical NOT
Exclusive OR	^	Expr.xor(…)	Logical XOR

---

1 Because negation (~) operates on a single expression, it's not combining expressions, but we're still discussing it here. It's only logical.

Ugly Underscores

In Python itself, and, or, and not are reserved keywords. This means they are not allowed to be used as method or variable names, and so Polars cannot use them as method names. That's why the first three methods listed in Table 9-3 have underscores (_) at the end. They're ugly, but you'll most likely use the corresponding inline operators (&, |, and ~) anyway.

The conjunction operation results in True only if both expressions are True. The following code snippet applies six Boolean operations to all possible combinations of p and q: the four listed in Table 9-3 and two bonus operations, *NAND* and *NOR*. Here NAND stands for NOT AND, NOR stands for NOT OR. The output is known as a *truth table*:

```
(
    pl.DataFrame(
        {"p": [True, True, False, False], "q": [True, False, True, False]}
    ).with_columns(
        (pl.col("p") & pl.col("q")).alias("p & q"),
        (pl.col("p") | pl.col("q")).alias("p | q"),
        (~pl.col("p")).alias("~p"),
        (pl.col("p") ^ pl.col("q")).alias("p ^ q"),
        (~(pl.col("p") & pl.col("q"))).alias("p ↑ q"),    ❶
        ((pl.col("p").or_(pl.col("q"))).not_()).alias("p ↓ q"),    ❷
    )
)
```

❶ The NAND (NOT AND) operator is not part of Polars, but it can be emulated by combining the NOT (~) and the AND (&) operators.

❷ The same holds for the NOR (NOT OR) operator. Here we use an alternative syntax with methods instead of inline operators.

shape: (4, 8)

p	q	p & q	p	q	~p	p ^ q	p ↑ q	p ↓ q
bool	bool	bool	bool	bool	bool	bool	bool
true	true	true	true	false	false	false	false
true	false	false	true	false	true	true	false
false	true	false	true	true	true	true	false
false	false	false	false	true	false	true	true

Being able to combine Boolean expressions via these Boolean operations allows you to express complex relationships between expressions. In the next section we're going to apply the same methods and inline operations to Integers instead of Booleans.

Bitwise Operations

You can also apply the AND (&), OR (|), XOR (^), and NOT(~) operators to Integers. In this case, these operators perform bitwise operations.[2]

Here's an example that applies the bitwise OR operator (|) to the values 10 and 34, which yields, logically,[3] 42:

```
pl.select(pl.lit(10) | pl.lit(34)).item()

42
```

Under the hood, Polars is applying the OR operator to each pair of bits that makes up the numbers 10 and 34. The output bit is 1 when at least one input bit is 1:

```
   00001010 (decimal 10)
OR 00100010 (decimal 34)
 = 00101010 (decimal 42)
```

So 10 | 34 is 42, because in either 10 or 34, the second, fourth, and sixth bits from the right are all 1. You can think of these bits as a sequence of Booleans—it's the same logic.

Table 9-4 lists the four bitwise operations and their inline operators and methods.

Table 9-4. Inline operators and their methods for performing bitwise operations

Inline Operator	Method	Description
&	Expr.and_(…)	Bitwise AND
|	Expr.or_(…)	Bitwise OR
~	Expr.not_(…)	Bitwise NOT
^	Expr.xor(…)	Bitwise XOR

The following code snippet applies the bitwise operations listed in Table 9-4 to a couple of Integers:

```
bits = pl.DataFrame(
    {"x": [1, 1, 0, 0, 7, 10], "y": [1, 0, 1, 0, 2, 34]},
    schema={"x": pl.UInt8, "y": pl.UInt8},
).with_columns(  ❶
    (pl.col("x") & pl.col("y")).alias("x & y"),
    (pl.col("x") | pl.col("y")).alias("x | y"),
    (~pl.col("x")).alias("~x"),
    (pl.col("x") ^ pl.col("y")).alias("x ^ y"),
```

---

2 Bitwise operations are perhaps a bit niche, but this is *The Definitive Guide*, after all.

3 See Douglas Adams's *The Hitchhiker's Guide to the Galaxy* for a comprehensive explanation.

```
)
bits
```

❶ We're using 8-bit unsigned Integers (pl.UInt8) so that it's easy to reason about the operations on a bit level. You can apply bitwise operators to any Integer type.

```
shape: (6, 6)
┌─────┬─────┬───────┬───────┬─────┬───────┐
│ x   │ y   │ x & y │ x | y │ ~x  │ x ^ y │
│ --- │ --- │ ---   │ ---   │ --- │ ---   │
│ u8  │ u8  │ u8    │ u8    │ u8  │ u8    │
╞═════╪═════╪═══════╪═══════╪═════╪═══════╡
│ 1   │ 1   │ 1     │ 1     │ 254 │ 0     │
│ 1   │ 0   │ 0     │ 1     │ 254 │ 1     │
│ 0   │ 1   │ 0     │ 1     │ 255 │ 1     │
│ 0   │ 0   │ 0     │ 0     │ 255 │ 0     │
│ 7   │ 2   │ 2     │ 7     │ 248 │ 5     │
│ 10  │ 34  │ 2     │ 42    │ 245 │ 40    │
└─────┴─────┴───────┴───────┴─────┴───────┘
```

Let's take a look at the binary String representations of these Integers to understand how each operator works:

```
bits.select(pl.all().map_elements("{0:08b}".format, return_dtype=pl.String))
```

```
shape: (6, 6)
┌──────────┬──────────┬──────────┬──────────┬──────────┬──────────┐
│ x        │ y        │ x & y    │ x | y    │ ~x       │ x ^ y    │
│ ---      │ ---      │ ---      │ ---      │ ---      │ ---      │
│ str      │ str      │ str      │ str      │ str      │ str      │
╞══════════╪══════════╪══════════╪══════════╪══════════╪══════════╡
│ 00000001 │ 00000001 │ 00000001 │ 00000001 │ 11111110 │ 00000000 │
│ 00000001 │ 00000000 │ 00000000 │ 00000001 │ 11111110 │ 00000001 │
│ 00000000 │ 00000001 │ 00000000 │ 00000001 │ 11111111 │ 00000001 │
│ 00000000 │ 00000000 │ 00000000 │ 00000000 │ 11111111 │ 00000000 │
│ 00000111 │ 00000010 │ 00000010 │ 00000111 │ 11111000 │ 00000101 │
│ 00001010 │ 00100010 │ 00000010 │ 00101010 │ 11110101 │ 00101000 │
└──────────┴──────────┴──────────┴──────────┴──────────┴──────────┘
```

Ones and Zeros

When you use ones and zeros to represent Booleans, the result of these operators is the same as if they were Booleans, except for the NOT operator. The inverse of True is False, whereas the inverse of 1 is 254 (and not 0), because the 7 left-most bits add up to 254 (128 + 64 + 32 + 16 + 8 + 4 + 2 = 254).

Additionally, Booleans are more memory efficient than Integers. Booleans take up only 1 bit of memory, whereas Integers take up 8 bits.

We recommend using Booleans whenever an expression or column should be able to take only two values.

Using Functions

Table 9-5 lists all module-level functions that combine existing expressions into a single one.

Table 9-5. Module-level functions to combine expressions

Function	Description
pl.all_horizontal(…)	Compute the bitwise AND horizontally across columns.
pl.any_horizontal(…)	Compute the bitwise OR horizontally across columns.
pl.arctan2(…)	Compute two argument arctan in radians.
pl.arctan2d(…)	Compute two argument arctan in degrees.
pl.arg_sort_by(…)	Return the row indices that would sort the columns.
pl.arg_where(…)	Return indices where condition evaluates True.
pl.coalesce(…)	Fold the columns from left to right, keeping the first non-null value.
pl.concat_list(…)	Horizontally concatenate columns into a single List column.
pl.concat_str(…)	Horizontally concatenate columns into a single String column.
pl.corr(…)	Compute the Pearson's or Spearman's rank correlation between two columns.
pl.cov(…)	Compute the covariance between two columns/expressions.
pl.cum_fold(…)	Cumulatively fold horizontally across columns with a left fold.
pl.cum_reduce(…)	Cumulatively reduce horizontally across columns with a left fold.
pl.cum_sum_horizontal(…)	Cumulatively sum all values horizontally across columns.
pl.fold(…)	Accumulate over multiple columns horizontally/row-wise with a left fold.
pl.format(…)	Format expressions as a String.
pl.map_batches(…)	Map a custom function over multiple columns/expressions.
pl.max_horizontal(…)	Get the maximum value horizontally across columns.
pl.min_horizontal(…)	Get the minimum value horizontally across columns.
pl.reduce(…)	Accumulate over multiple columns horizontally/row wise with a left fold.
pl.rolling_corr(…)	Compute the rolling correlation between two columns/expressions.
pl.rolling_cov(…)	Compute the rolling covariance between two columns/expressions.
pl.struct(…)	Collect columns into a struct column.
pl.sum_horizontal(…)	Sum all values horizontally across columns.
pl.when(…)	Start a when-then-otherwise expression.

We cannot discuss them all in detail, but here are few noteworthy examples.

First is two functions that combine the values of multiple expressions into one structure. The functions pl.concat_list() and pl.struct() create a List and a Struct, respectively. We cover Lists and Structs in more detail in Chapter 12. You can see how to use these methods in the following example:

```
scientists = pl.DataFrame(
    {
        "first_name": ["George", "Grace", "John", "Kurt", "Ada"],
        "last_name": ["Boole", "Hopper", "Tukey", "Gödel", "Lovelace"],
        "country": [
            "England",
            "United States",
            "United States",
            "Austria-Hungary",
            "England",
        ],
    }
)
scientists
```

```
shape: (5, 3)
┌────────────┬───────────┬─────────────────┐
│ first_name │ last_name │ country         │
│ ---        │ ---       │ ---             │
│ str        │ str       │ str             │
╞════════════╪═══════════╪═════════════════╡
│ George     │ Boole     │ England         │
│ Grace      │ Hopper    │ United States   │
│ John       │ Tukey     │ United States   │
│ Kurt       │ Gödel     │ Austria-Hungary │
│ Ada        │ Lovelace  │ England         │
└────────────┴───────────┴─────────────────┘
```

```
scientists.select(
    concat_list=pl.concat_list(pl.col("^*_name$")),
    struct=pl.struct(pl.all()),
)
```

```
shape: (5, 2)
┌─────────────────────┬─────────────────────────────────────┐
│ concat_list         │ struct                              │
│ ---                 │ ---                                 │
│ list[str]           │ struct[3]                           │
╞═════════════════════╪═════════════════════════════════════╡
│ ["George", "Boole"] │ {"George","Boole","England"}        │
│ ["Grace", "Hopper"] │ {"Grace","Hopper","United States"}  │
│ ["John", "Tukey"]   │ {"John","Tukey","United States"}    │
│ ["Kurt", "Gödel"]   │ {"Kurt","Gödel","Austria-Hungary"}  │
│ ["Ada", "Lovelace"] │ {"Ada","Lovelace","England"}        │
└─────────────────────┴─────────────────────────────────────┘
```

Second, the functions pl.concat_str() and pl.format() create one String based on multiple expressions. The latter gives you a bit more flexibility in how the Strings are combined. Here's an example:

```
scientists.select(
    concat_str=pl.concat_str(pl.all(), separator=" "),
    format=pl.format("{}, {} from {}", "last_name", "first_name", "country"),
)
```

shape: (5, 2)

concat_str	format
str	str
George Boole England	Boole, George from England
Grace Hopper United States	Hopper, Grace from United States
John Tukey United States	Tukey, John from United States
Kurt Gödel Austria-Hungary	Gödel, Kurt from Austria-Hungary
Ada Lovelace England	Lovelace, Ada from England

The functions `pl.all_horizontal()` and `pl.any_horizontal()` are analogous to using the AND (&) and OR (|) operators on multiple columns. This is especially useful if you have many columns to combine and you don't want to write them all out. For instance:

```
prefs = pl.DataFrame(
    {
        "id": [1, 7, 42, 101, 999],
        "has_pet": [True, False, True, False, True],
        "likes_travel": [False, False, False, False, True],
        "likes_movies": [True, False, True, False, True],
        "likes_books": [False, False, True, True, True],
    }
).with_columns(
    all=pl.all_horizontal(pl.exclude("id")),
    any=pl.any_horizontal(pl.exclude("id")),
)

prefs
```

shape: (5, 7)

id	has_pet	likes_travel	likes_movies	likes_books	all	any
i64	bool	bool	bool	bool	bool	bool
1	true	false	true	false	false	true
7	false	false	false	false	false	false
42	true	false	true	true	false	true
101	false	false	false	true	false	true
999	true	true	true	true	true	true

Related are the functions `pl.sum_horizontal()`, `pl.max_horizontal()`, and `pl.min_horizontal()`, which compute the sum, maximum, and minimum across columns, respectively. They work on both Boolean and numerical columns:

```
prefs.select(
    sum=pl.sum_horizontal(pl.all()),
    max=pl.max_horizontal(pl.all()),
    min=pl.min_horizontal(pl.all()),
)
```

shape: (5, 3)

sum	max	min
i64	i64	i64
4	1	0
7	7	0
46	42	0
103	101	0
1005	999	1

When, Then, Otherwise

A function that deserves a special mention is `pl.when()`. It creates a conditional expression. Think of it as a vectorized `if` statement. Here's an example:

```
prefs.select(
    pl.col("id"),
    likes_what=pl.when(pl.all_horizontal(pl.col("^likes_.*$")))
    .then(pl.lit("Likes everything"))
    .when(pl.any_horizontal(pl.col("^likes_.*$")))
    .then(pl.lit("Likes something"))
    .otherwise(pl.lit("Likes nothing")),
)
```

shape: (5, 2)

id	likes_what
i64	str
1	Likes something
7	Likes nothing
42	Likes something
101	Likes something
999	Likes everything

The function `pl.when()` can be extremely powerful. It allows you to create complex conditional expressions in a single statement. In this example, we check whether a person likes all, some, or none of the things listed in the columns `likes_travel`, `likes_movies`, and `likes_books`. A single usage of `pl.when()` is enough to combine all these cases.

The way it is evaluated is like a Python `if`, `elif`, `else` block. This means that the first condition that evaluates to `True` will be picked and others after it will not be evaluated anymore. If none of the conditions are `True`, `pl.otherwise()` gets picked if it's added to the chain; otherwise the resulting value is `null`.

What Else?

If there is no `pl.otherwise()` added to the chain, `null` will be returned. In the next example, we construct a small DataFrame with payment data. If an order amount is over 1,000, it needs to be flagged for further verification:

```
orders = pl.DataFrame(
    {
        "order_amount": [500, 750, 1200, 800, 1100],
        "status": [
            "Approved",
            "Processing",
            "Processing",
            "Declined",
            "Processing",
        ],
    }
)
orders.with_columns(
    status=pl.when(pl.col("order_amount") > 1000).then(pl.lit("Flagged"))
)
```

```
shape: (5, 2)
┌──────────────┬─────────┐
│ order_amount │ status  │
│ ---          │ ---     │
│ i64          │ str     │
╞══════════════╪═════════╡
│ 500          │ null    │
│ 750          │ null    │
│ 1200         │ Flagged │
│ 800          │ null    │
│ 1100         │ Flagged │
└──────────────┴─────────┘
```

The problem here is that the original status gets overwritten with `null`. This may be counterintuitive to some, since not adding an `else` statement in Python leaves the state as is. In case you want the original value returned instead of `null`, you can call `pl.otherwise()` with the original column as an argument:

```
orders.with_columns(
    status=pl.when(pl.col("order_amount") > 1000)
    .then(pl.lit("Flagged"))
    .otherwise(pl.col("status"))
)
```

shape: (5, 2)

order_amount	status
i64	str
--------------	------------
500	Approved
750	Processing
1200	Flagged
800	Declined
1100	Flagged

That looks more like it.

For the other functions, we refer you to the online documentation.

Takeaways

In this chapter you've learned that:

- Combining expressions in Polars allows you to create complex data manipulations based on multiple values or columns.

- You can use inline operators (like +, -, *, /, &, |, etc.) or method chaining to combine expressions. Both approaches yield the same result.

- Arithmetic operations can be performed using inline operators or corresponding methods, enabling addition, subtraction, multiplication, division, and more between expressions.

- Comparison operations in Polars cannot be chained as in Python; instead, you combine multiple comparisons using Boolean operators like & (AND) and | (OR).

- Boolean algebra operations—including conjunction (&), disjunction (|), negation (~), and exclusive OR (^)—are available for combining Boolean expressions.

- Bitwise operations can be applied to Integer expressions using the same operators as Boolean operations, operating at the bit level.
- Polars provides a variety of module-level functions to combine expressions, such as `pl.concat_list()`, `pl.concat_str()`, `pl.format()`, `pl.all_horizontal()`, `pl.any_horizontal()`, `pl.sum_horizontal()`, and `pl.when()`, allowing for advanced data manipulation.

This concludes the third and last chapter of Part III, "Express". You're now equipped with the knowledge to begin, continue, and combine expressions in Polars.

## PART IV

Transform

## CHAPTER 10

Selecting and Creating Columns

Now that you have a solid understanding of how expressions work, let's look at how to use them. In this chapter, we cover operations that are related to the columns of a DataFrame.[1] We'll focus on selecting existing columns and creating new ones, which are probably the most common operations when working with data.

First, we'll revisit how to select columns using the df.select() method that we've already seen in Chapter 7. Then we're going to introduce you to a more flexible way of selecting columns: using so-called *column selectors*. Selectors offer various ways to specify columns based on their name, data type, and position. They can also be combined in different ways. We'll continue with how to create new columns and rearrange them. Finally, we'll briefly discuss related column operations, such as renaming and dropping columns and combining the columns of two DataFrames.

You'll be working with a DataFrame about our favorite rebels from the Star Wars universe:

```
starwars = pl.read_parquet("data/starwars.parquet")
rebels = starwars.drop("films").filter(
    pl.col("name").is_in(["Luke Skywalker", "Leia Organa", "Han Solo"])
)

print(rebels[:, :6])  ❶
print(rebels[:, 6:11])
print(rebels[:, 11:])
```

❶ Here we slice the DataFrame into pieces column-wise so we can show it off in this book. Foldable pages are usually reserved for different types of literature.

---

1 The methods covered in this chapter can also be applied to LazyFrames.

shape: (3, 6)

name	height	mass	hair_color	skin_color	eye_color
str	u16	f64	str	str	str
Han Solo	180	80.0	brown	fair	brown
Leia Organa	150	49.0	brown	light	brown
Luke Skywalker	172	77.0	blond	fair	blue

shape: (3, 5)

birth_year	sex	gender	homeworld	species
f64	cat	cat	str	str
29.0	male	masculine	Corellia	Human
19.0	female	feminine	Alderaan	Human
19.0	male	masculine	Tatooine	Human

shape: (3, 4)

vehicles	starships	birth_date	screen_time
list[str]	list[str]	date	duration[µs]
null	["Millennium Falcon"…	1948-06-01	1h 12m 37s
["Imperial Speeder B…	null	1958-05-30	1h 3m 40s
["Snowspeeder", "Imp…	["X-wing", "Imperial…	1958-05-30	1h 58m 44s

The rebels DataFrame has 3 rows and 15 columns with a variety of data types, which is precisely what we need to demonstrate various column operations. This DataFrame comes from the R package dplyr. We've added two columns: birth_date and screen_time.[2]

The instructions to get any files you might need are in Chapter 2. We assume that you have the files in the *data* subdirectory.

---

2 The years in the birth_year column are designated in *before Battle of Yavin* (BBY) in the Galactic Standard Calendar, meaning that Luke and Leia were both 19 years old when the Battle of Yavin took place. The dates in the birth_date column are designated in AD in the Gregorian Calendar, assuming 0 BBY started on May 25, 1977 AD, the date *Star Wars: Episode IV: A New Hope* was released in the US. The time in the screen_time column is the total amount of time the character appears on screen (*https://oreil.ly/xLxjv*) across the three movies of the original trilogy. In other words, we were having way too much fun coming up with additional temporal columns for this DataFrame.

Selecting Columns

The columns of a DataFrame can be selected with the df.select() method. You can select one column, multiple columns, or all columns, in any order. You can select the same column more than once, if you make sure that they don't have the same name. (Column names have to be unique.) You can even, as we'll see later, create new columns with this method. Figure 10-1 illustrates this operation conceptually.

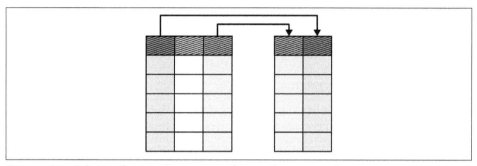

Figure 10-1. Selecting keeps columns according to their name, data type, or position

Selecting columns is especially useful when you have too many of them and you know there are certain columns that you won't need anymore.

To select columns, you specify which columns you want to keep. In Chapter 7 you saw two ways to do this: using the name of the column as a String and using the pl.col() method. The former has the advantage that it's shorter to type. The latter has the advantage that it's an expression, offering the ability to customize the column. Here's a demonstration to refresh your memory:

```
rebels.select(
    "name",
    pl.col("homeworld"),
    pl.col("^.*_color$"),
    (pl.col("height") / 100).alias("height_m"),
)
```

shape: (3, 6)

name	homeworld	hair_color	skin_color	eye_color	height_m
str	str	str	str	str	f64
Han Solo	Corellia	brown	fair	brown	1.8
Leia Organa	Alderaan	brown	light	brown	1.5
Luke Skywalker	Tatooine	blond	fair	blue	1.72

Note that the columns appear in the order you specify them.

In the next section, we'd like to introduce you to a third way of specifying the columns you want: using selectors.

Introducing Selectors

The best way to explain selectors is to demonstrate them. To use selectors, you first need to import the `polars.selectors` submodule:

```
import polars.selectors as cs
```

It is customary to import it as `cs`, which stands for *column selectors*. In this submodule, there are over 30 functions that you can use to specify columns.

Selectors Everywhere

Selectors can be used not only with the `df.select()` method, but anywhere where you can specify columns, including `df.filter()` and `df.group_by()`.

The function that resembles the `pl.col()` function the most is the `cs.by_name()` function. In fact, selectors are expressions under the hood, so you can use them in the same way as expressions. So our previous example can be rewritten as:

```
rebels.select(
    "name",
    cs.by_name("homeworld"),
    cs.by_name("^.*_color$"),
    (cs.by_name("height") / 100).alias("height_m"),
)
```

shape: (3, 6)

name	homeworld	hair_color	skin_color	eye_color	height_m
str	str	str	str	str	f64
Han Solo	Corellia	brown	fair	brown	1.8
Leia Organa	Alderaan	brown	light	brown	1.5
Luke Skywalker	Tatooine	blond	fair	blue	1.72

This function by itself doesn't really do selectors any justice. (It's even longer to type than `pl.col()`.) The flexibility of selectors becomes clear when we use other functions and combine them using set operations.

In the next three sections, we're going to look at three types of selectors: for specifying based on the column name, column data type, and position.

Selecting Based on Name

Besides the `cs.by_name()` function, there are a few other functions that allow you to specify columns based on their name. These are listed in Table 10-1.

Table 10-1. Functions for selecting columns by name

Function	Description
`cs.alpha(…)`	Select all columns with alphabetic names (e.g., only letters).
`cs.alphanumeric(…)`	Select all columns with alphanumeric names (e.g., only letters and the digits 0-9).
`cs.by_name(…)`	Select all columns matching the given names.
`cs.contains(…)`	Select columns whose names contain the given literal substring(s).
`cs.digit(…)`	Select all columns having names consisting only of digits.
`cs.ends_with(…)`	Select columns that end with the given substring(s).
`cs.matches(…)`	Select all columns that match the given regex pattern.
`cs.starts_with(…)`	Select columns that start with the given substring(s).

Here are a few examples. To select all columns whose names start with `birth_`, use the `cs.starts_with()` function:

```
rebels.select(cs.starts_with("birth_"))
```

shape: (3, 2)

birth_year	birth_date
f64	date
29.0	1948-06-01
19.0	1958-05-30
19.0	1958-05-30

To select all columns whose names end with `_color`, use the `cs.ends_with()` function:

```
rebels.select(cs.ends_with("_color"))
```

shape: (3, 3)

hair_color	skin_color	eye_color
str	str	str
brown	fair	brown
brown	light	brown
blond	fair	blue

To match names against a substring, use the `cs.contains()` function:

```
rebels.select(cs.contains("_"))
```

shape: (3, 6)

hair_color	skin_color	eye_color	birth_year	birth_date	screen_time
---	---	---	---	---	---
str	str	str	f64	date	duration[µs]
brown	fair	brown	29.0	1948-06-01	1h 12m 37s
brown	light	brown	19.0	1958-05-30	1h 3m 40s
blond	fair	blue	19.0	1958-05-30	1h 58m 44s

The `cs.matches()` function allows you to specify columns using a regular expression. For example, to select only columns whose names consist of four lowercase characters:

```
rebels.select(cs.matches("^[a-z]{4}$"))
```

shape: (3, 2)

name	mass
---	---
str	f64
Han Solo	80.0
Leia Organa	49.0
Luke Skywalker	77.0

Let's move on to selectors that allow you to specify columns based on their data type.

Selecting Based on Data Type

The second type of selectors employs the data type of the column. There are situations where you care more about a column's data type than the actual name. For example, when you want to summarize all the numerical columns in a DataFrame by calculating their mean:

```
rebels.group_by("hair_color").agg(cs.numeric().mean())
```

shape: (2, 4)

hair_color	height	mass	birth_year
---	---	---	---
str	f64	f64	f64
brown	165.0	64.5	24.0
blond	172.0	77.0	19.0

The function `cs.numeric()` selects all unsigned integers, signed integers, and floats. Likewise, the function `cs.temporal()` selects all date, time, datetime, and duration columns. Very convenient. Table 10-2 lists all selector functions related to data types.

Table 10-2. Functions for selecting columns by type

Function	Description
`cs.binary()`	Select all binary columns.
`cs.boolean()`	Select all Boolean columns.
`cs.by_dtype(…)`	Select all columns matching the given data types.
`cs.categorical()`	Select all categorical columns.
`cs.date()`	Select all date columns.
`cs.datetime(…)`	Select all datetime columns, optionally filtering by time unit/zone.
`cs.decimal()`	Select all decimal columns.
`cs.duration(…)`	Select all duration columns, optionally filtering by time unit.
`cs.float()`	Select all float columns.
`cs.integer()`	Select all integer columns.
`cs.numeric()`	Select all numeric columns.
`cs.signed_integer()`	Select all signed integer columns.
`cs.string(…)`	Select all String (and, optionally, Categorical) columns.
`cs.temporal()`	Select all temporal columns.
`cs.time()`	Select all time columns.
`cs.unsigned_integer()`	Select all unsigned integer columns.

Here are a few more examples:

```
rebels.select(cs.string())
```

shape: (3, 6)

name	hair_color	skin_color	eye_color	homeworld	species
str	str	str	str	str	str
Han Solo	brown	fair	brown	Corellia	Human
Leia Organa	brown	light	brown	Alderaan	Human
Luke Skywalker	blond	fair	blue	Tatooine	Human

```
rebels.select(cs.temporal())
```

shape: (3, 2)

birth_date	screen_time
date	duration[µs]

```
| 1948-06-01 | 1h 12m 37s |
| 1958-05-30 | 1h 3m 40s  |
| 1958-05-30 | 1h 58m 44s |
```

Nested data types are more cumbersome because you also need to specify the inner data type:

```
rebels.select(cs.by_dtype(pl.List(pl.String)))
```

```
shape: (3, 2)
```

vehicles	starships
list[str]	list[str]
null	["Millennium Falcon"…
["Imperial Speeder B…	null
["Snowspeeder", "Imp…	["X-wing", "Imperial…

Selecting Based on Position

The third type of selector employs the position of the column. Table 10-3 lists the three selector functions related to position.

Table 10-3. Functions for selecting columns by position

Function	Description
cs.by_index(…)	Select all columns matching the given indices (or range objects).
cs.first()	Select the first column in the current scope.
cs.last()	Select the last column in the current scope.

There are very few situations where you'll want to use this. One example is where you have a DataFrame with many columns that follow a pattern, and the column names are not specific enough to distinguish. In that case you could, say, select every third column using the cs.by_index() function and a range object. In our rebels DataFrame, there is nothing that ties together every third column, but if we wanted to select every third column, then here's how to do it:

```
rebels.select(cs.by_index(range(0, 999, 3)))  ❶
```

❶ The end value of the range doesn't matter, as long as it's higher than the number of columns.

```
shape: (3, 5)
```

name	hair_color	birth_year	homeworld	starships

str	str	f64	str	list[str]
Han Solo	brown	29.0	Corellia	["Millennium Falcon"…
Leia Organa	brown	19.0	Alderaan	null
Luke Skywalker	blond	19.0	Tatooine	["X-wing", "Imperial…

Another example: say you've just created two new columns using the df.with_col
umns() method (coming up in the next section) and you want to select those along
with the name column. Knowing that these were added the right end of the Data-
Frame, you could do the following:

```
rebels.select("name", cs.by_index(range(-2, 0)))
```

shape: (3, 3)

name	birth_date	screen_time
---	---	---
str	date	duration[µs]
Han Solo	1948-06-01	1h 12m 37s
Leia Organa	1958-05-30	1h 3m 40s
Luke Skywalker	1958-05-30	1h 58m 44s

If it's a single column, you could also use the function cs.last().

Out of Bounds

If you pass an index that's out of bounds to cs.index(), you'll get
an error:

```
rebels.select(cs.by_index(20))

ColumnNotFoundError: nth
```

```
Resolved plan until failure:

        ---> FAILED HERE RESOLVING 'select' <---
DF ["name", "height", "mass", "hair_color"]; PROJECT */15 COLUMNS
```

However, if you pass a range object that is out of bounds (for
instance, range(20, 22)), you won't get an error; you'll just get an
empty DataFrame:

```
rebels.select(cs.by_index(range(20, 22)))
```

shape: (0, 0)

```
┌───┐
│   │
└───┘
```

Combining Selectors

Selectors can be combined to produce complex selections. This is where their flexibility becomes clear: they allow you to specify columns in a way that wasn't previously possible.

For example, in Chapter 7, we demonstrated that it isn't possible to specify columns by name and data type at the same time. With selectors, this is possible. Selecting, say, a column with the name hair_color and all columns with numeric data types would look like this:

```
rebels.select(cs.by_name("hair_color") | cs.numeric())
```

```
shape: (3, 4)
┌────────┬──────┬───────────┬────────────┐
│ height │ mass │ hair_color │ birth_year │
│ ---    │ ---  │ ---       │ ---        │
│ u16    │ f64  │ str       │ f64        │
╞════════╪══════╪═══════════╪════════════╡
│ 180    │ 80.0 │ brown     │ 29.0       │
│ 150    │ 49.0 │ brown     │ 19.0       │
│ 172    │ 77.0 │ blond     │ 19.0       │
└────────┴──────┴───────────┴────────────┘
```

The character | is the OR operator, one of five supported set operators for selectors, listed in Table 10-4 with a description.

Table 10-4. Set operators for combining selectors

Operation	Inline Operator	Description
Union	|	x, or y, or both
Intersection	&	Both x and y
Difference	-	x and not in y
Exclusive OR	^	x, or y, but not both
Negation	~	Not in x

The following code snippet demonstrates these five set operators for two selectors x and y, applied to the DataFrame df:

```
df = pl.DataFrame({"d": 1, "i": True, "s": True, "c": True, "o": 1.0})

print(df)

x = cs.by_name("d", "i", "s")
y = cs.boolean()

print("\nselector => columns")
```

```
for s in ["x", "y", "x | y", "x & y", "x - y", "x ^ y", "~x", "x - x"]:
    print(f"{s:8} => {cs.expand_selector(df, eval(s))}")
```

```
shape: (1, 5)
```

d	i	s	c	o
i64	bool	bool	bool	f64
1	true	true	true	1.0

```
selector => columns
x        => ('d', 'i', 's')
y        => ('i', 's', 'c')
x | y    => ('d', 'i', 's', 'c')
x & y    => ('i', 's')
x - y    => ('d',)
x ^ y    => ('d', 'c')
~x       => ('c', 'o')
x - x    => ()
```

Even though we call them set operators, the results are actually tuples. That's a good thing, because the order of the columns is preserved when you use these operators.

The selector x - x shows that you can end up with no columns, which results in an empty DataFrame if you apply it to a DataFrame:

```
df.select(x - x)
```

```
shape: (0, 0)
```

┌──┐
├──┤
└──┘

Bring Forth the Columns

Here's a nifty snippet to easily bring specific columns to the front, made possible by the walrus operator (*https://oreil.ly/6cCg4*) (:=) introduced in Python 3.8. The walrus operator allows you to assign a selector to a variable first in the first argument, which you can reuse and modify in the second argument. The following example pulls two specific columns to the front, namely c and i:

```
print(df.select(first := cs.by_name("c", "i"), ~first))
print(f"first: {first}, ~first: {~first}")
```

```
shape: (1, 5)
```

c	i	d	s	o
bool	bool	i64	bool	f64

```
| true | true | 1  | true | 1.0 |
```
```
first: cols(["c", "i"]), ~first: selector
```

And the next example pulls the last column (the o) to the front. This is especially useful right after you create a new column, which is the subject of the next section:

```
print(df.select(first := cs.last(), ~first))
print(f"first: {first}, ~first: {~first}")
```

```
shape: (1, 5)
```

o	d	i	s	c
f64	i64	bool	bool	bool
1.0	1	true	true	true

```
first: nth(-1), ~first: selector
```

Creating Columns

You can create one or more new columns using the `df.with_columns()` method. These new columns are added at the right end of the DataFrame. Figure 10-2 illustrates this operation conceptually.

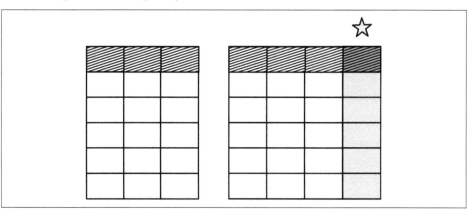

Figure 10-2. Creating a new column, which is added to the right

For example, using the columns mass and height, we can compute the body mass index (BMI) of each rebel:

```
rebels.with_columns(bmi=pl.col("mass") / ((pl.col("height") / 100) ** 2))
```

```
shape: (3, 16)
```

| name | | height | mass | … | birth_date | screen_time | bmi | |
| ---- | | ------ | ---- | - | ---------- | ----------- | --- | |

```
| ---            | ---  | ---  |   | ---        | ---         | ---       |
| str            | u16  | f64  |   | date       | duration[µs]| f64       |
| Han Solo       | 180  | 80.0 | …  | 1948-06-01 | 1h 12m 37s  | 24.691358 |
| Leia Organa    | 150  | 49.0 | …  | 1958-05-30 | 1h 3m 40s   | 21.777778 |
| Luke Skywalker | 172  | 77.0 | …  | 1958-05-30 | 1h 58m 44s  | 26.027582 |
```

Here, all the original columns are included, and the new column is added to the end.

Columns Can Be Overwritten

If you create a new column with the same name as an existing column, the existing column will be overwritten. This is a common pitfall, so be careful when creating new columns:

```
df = pl.DataFrame({"a": [1, 2, 3]})
df.with_columns(pl.col("a") * 2)
```

```
shape: (3, 1)
┌─────┐
│ a   │
│ --- │
│ i64 │
╞═════╡
│ 2   │
│ 4   │
│ 6   │
└─────┘
```

In this example, the original column a is overwritten with the new column a.

If you want to keep the original column, you can rename the new column:

```
df.with_columns(a2=pl.col("a") * 2)
```

```
shape: (3, 2)
┌─────┬─────┐
│ a   │ a2  │
│ --- │ --- │
│ i64 │ i64 │
╞═════╪═════╡
│ 1   │ 2   │
│ 2   │ 4   │
│ 3   │ 6   │
└─────┴─────┘
```

In this example, the new column is named a2, so the original column a is preserved.

You can create more than one new column using a single df.with_columns() call. Let's also calculate how old our rebels were when the Death Star's main reactor was destroyed:[3]

```
rebels.with_columns(
    bmi=pl.col("mass") / ((pl.col("height") / 100) ** 2),
    age_destroy=(
        (pl.date(1983, 5, 25) - pl.col("birth_date")).dt.total_days() / 365
    ).cast(pl.UInt8),
)
```

shape: (3, 17)

name	height	mass	...	screen_time	bmi	age_destroy
---	---	---	...	---	---	---
str	u16	f64		duration[μs]	f64	u8
Han Solo	180	80.0	...	1h 12m 37s	24.691358	35
Leia Organa	150	49.0	...	1h 3m 40s	21.777778	25
Luke Skywalker	172	77.0	...	1h 58m 44s	26.027582	25

Expressions cannot depend on each other because they are executed in parallel. That means if you want to create two new columns, the second one cannot depend on the first. If they do, you would have to do it in separate df.with_columns() calls.

The following snippet, where we want to add the BMI category, yields an error saying it cannot find the bmi column:

```
rebels.with_columns(
    bmi=pl.col("mass") / ((pl.col("height") / 100) ** 2),
    bmi_cat=pl.col("bmi").cut(
        [18.5, 25], labels=["Underweight", "Normal", "Overweight"]
    ),
)
```

ColumnNotFoundError: bmi

Resolved plan until failure:

```
        ---> FAILED HERE RESOLVING 'with_columns' <---
DF ["name", "height", "mass", "hair_color"]; PROJECT */15 COLUMNS
```

The solution is to use the df.with_columns() method multiple times:

```
(
    rebels.with_columns(
        bmi=pl.col("mass") / ((pl.col("height") / 100) ** 2)
    ).with_columns(
        bmi_cat=pl.col("bmi").cut(
```

---

3 The second one, from *Return of the Jedi*, of course.

```
                    [18.5, 25], labels=["Underweight", "Normal", "Overweight"]
                )
        )
)

shape: (3, 17)
```

```
┌─────────────────┬────────┬──────┬─────┬──────────────┬───────────┬────────────┐
│ name            │ height │ mass │ ... │ screen_time  │ bmi       │ bmi_cat    │
│ ---             │ ---    │ ---  │     │ ---          │ ---       │ ---        │
│ str             │ u16    │ f64  │     │ duration[μs] │ f64       │ cat        │
╞═════════════════╪════════╪══════╪═════╪══════════════╪═══════════╪════════════╡
│ Han Solo        │ 180    │ 80.0 │ ... │ 1h 12m 37s   │ 24.691358 │ Normal     │
│ Leia Organa     │ 150    │ 49.0 │ ... │ 1h 3m 40s    │ 21.777778 │ Normal     │
│ Luke Skywalker  │ 172    │ 77.0 │ ... │ 1h 58m 44s   │ 26.027582 │ Overweight │
└─────────────────┴────────┴──────┴─────┴──────────────┴───────────┴────────────┘
```

You can also use the df.select() method to create new columns. This allows you to select a subset of the columns and create new ones at the same time.

In fact, df.with_columns(<new_columns>) does the same thing as df.select(pl.all(), <new_columns>), but it's more clear and concise.

Remember that keyword arguments must appear last in Python, so if you want a new column to appear somewhere in the middle, be sure to use the Expr.alias() method to name it instead of using the keyword method of naming new columns.

If you were to try to add a new column to the middle of the DataFrame using the keyword method, you would get a SyntaxError:

```
starwars.select(
    "name",
    bmi=(pl.col("mass") / ((pl.col("height") / 100) ** 2)),
    "species",
)

SyntaxError: positional argument follows keyword argument (1147293163.py,
line 5)
```

Let's do it the right way and see which Star Wars characters have the highest BMI:

```
(
    starwars.select(
        "name",
        (pl.col("mass") / ((pl.col("height") / 100) ** 2)).alias("bmi"),   ❶
        "species",
    )
    .drop_nulls()
    .top_k(5, by="bmi")   ❷
)
```

❶   Note that the columns mass and height do not need to be selected.

❷ You'll learn more about the `Expr.drop_nulls()` and `Expr.top_k()` methods in Chapter 11.

```
shape: (5, 3)
┌─────────────────────┬────────────┬───────────────┐
│ name                │ bmi        │ species       │
│ ---                 │ ---        │ ---           │
│ str                 │ f64        │ str           │
╞═════════════════════╪════════════╪═══════════════╡
│ Jabba Desilijic Tiure │ 443.428571 │ Hutt          │
│ Dud Bolt            │ 50.928022  │ Vulptereen    │
│ Yoda                │ 39.02663   │ Yoda's species │
│ Owen Lars           │ 37.874006  │ Human         │
│ IG-88               │ 35.0       │ Droid         │
└─────────────────────┴────────────┴───────────────┘
```

Creating New Columns

Effectively, `df.with_columns()` is a convenient method that is syntactic sugar for `df.select()`, which selects all existing columns in addition to the expressions put into the `df.with_columns()` method. To illustrate:

```
df.with_columns(pl.lit(1).alias("ones"))
```

```
shape: (3, 2)
┌─────┬──────┐
│ a   │ ones │
│ --- │ ---  │
│ i64 │ i32  │
╞═════╪══════╡
│ 1   │ 1    │
│ 2   │ 1    │
│ 3   │ 1    │
└─────┴──────┘
```

is the same as:

```
df.select(pl.all(), pl.lit(1).alias("ones"))
```

```
shape: (3, 2)
┌─────┬──────┐
│ a   │ ones │
│ --- │ ---  │
│ i64 │ i32  │
╞═════╪══════╡
│ 1   │ 1    │
│ 2   │ 1    │
│ 3   │ 1    │
└─────┴──────┘
```

Related Column Operations

Besides selecting and creating, there are a few related column operations worth knowing about, namely: dropping, renaming, and stacking.

Dropping

Sometimes it can be more convenient to specify which columns you do *not* want to keep than to specify all the columns that you *do* want to keep. For this, there is the df.drop() method:

```
rebels.drop("name", "films", "screen_time", strict=False)  ❶
```

❶ Setting the keyword argument `strict` to `False` allows you to specify columns that don't exist in the DataFrame without getting an error.

```
shape: (3, 13)
```

height	mass	hair_color	...	vehicles	starships	birth_date
u16	f64	str		list[str]	list[str]	date
180	80.0	brown	...	null	["Millennium Falcon"...	1948-06-01
150	49.0	brown	...	["Imperial Speeder B...	null	1958-05-30
172	77.0	blond	...	["Snowspeeder", "Imp...	["X-wing", "Imperial...	1958-05-30

The df.drop() method is arguably easier and more explicit than using:

```
rebels.select(~cs.by_name("name", "films", "screen_time"))
```

or:

```
rebels.select(cs.exclude("name", "films", "screen_time"))
```

Renaming

Technically, you can rename columns using the df.select() method, but it is not very convenient, because you have to specify all the columns that you would like to rename and keep. It's better to use the df.rename() method, which accepts either a dictionary or a function. The following code snippet demonstrates both:

```
(
    rebels.rename({"homeworld": "planet", "mass": "weight"})
    .rename(lambda s: s.removesuffix("_color"))
    .select("name", "planet", "weight", "hair", "skin", "eye")  ❶
)
```

❶ This `df.select()` is only used here so that the new column names appear next to each other.

```
shape: (3, 6)
```

name	planet	weight	hair	skin	eye
str	str	f64	str	str	str
Han Solo	Corellia	80.0	brown	fair	brown
Leia Organa	Alderaan	49.0	brown	light	brown
Luke Skywalker	Tatooine	77.0	blond	fair	blue

Stacking

If you have a second DataFrame or one or more Series that have the same length as the first DataFrame, then you can combine them by horizontally stacking them, using the `df.hstack()` method. Let's create two small DataFrames and one new Series with quotes, and combine them:

```
rebel_names = rebels.select("name")
rebel_colors = rebels.select(cs.ends_with("_color"))
rebel_quotes = pl.Series(
    "quote",
    [
        "You know, sometimes I amaze myself.",
        "That doesn't sound too hard.",
        "I have a bad feeling about this.",
    ],
)

(rebel_names.hstack(rebel_colors).hstack([rebel_quotes]))  ❶
```

❶ Make sure you pass a list of Series.

```
shape: (3, 5)
```

name	hair_color	skin_color	eye_color	quote
str	str	str	str	str
Han Solo	brown	fair	brown	You know, sometimes I amaze myself.
Leia Organa	brown	light	brown	That doesn't sound too hard.
Luke Skywalker	blond	fair	blue	I have a bad feeling about this.

When combining DataFrames or Series this way, you have to make sure that they are properly aligned; otherwise you'll get bad results. We'll discuss stacking, together with joining, which may sometimes be a better fit, in Chapter 14.

Adding Row Indices

If you want to add a column with increasing integers, you can use the df.with_row_index() method. This method takes two optional arguments, name and offset, with index and 0 as the default values, respectively:

```
rebels.with_row_index(name="rebel_id", offset=1)
```

shape: (3, 16)

rebel_id	name	height	…	birth_date	screen_time
---	---	---		---	---
u32	str	u16		date	duration[µs]
1	Han Solo	180	…	1948-06-01	1h 12m 37s
2	Leia Organa	150	…	1958-05-30	1h 3m 40s
3	Luke Skywalker	172	…	1958-05-30	1h 58m 44s

Takeaways

In this chapter we've looked at selecting and creating columns and a few related operations. The key takeaways are:

- You can select columns in various ways.

- In many cases, using pl.col() is sufficient to specify columns.

- Selectors allow you to specify columns based on their name, data type, and position.

- Selecting based on position is rarely a good idea.

- Selectors offer more flexibility because they can be combined using set operations.

- You can create new columns using either df.select() or df.with_columns().

- When creating multiple new columns that have dependencies on each other, use multiple df.with_columns() calls.

- There are many related column operations, including renaming and stacking.crej

In the next chapter we're going to look at how to filter and sort rows.

## CHAPTER 11

Filtering and Sorting Rows

Whereas the previous chapter was about columns, this chapter is all about the rows in a DataFrame.[1] We'll mainly look at two types of operations you can perform on rows:

- Filtering rows using the df.filter() method
- Sorting rows using the df.sort() method

With filtering, you select a subset of the rows based on their values. With sorting, you reorder the rows based on their values; the number of rows remains the same. Besides that, we'll discuss various other methods that are related to filtering and sorting.

You'll be working with a small DataFrame about power tools that you'd typically find in the garage of an amateur woodworker. For each tool, we have its type, product code, brand, price, revolutions per minute (RPM), and whether it's cordless or not. Here's what the tools DataFrame looks like:

```
tools = pl.read_csv("data/tools.csv")
tools
```

shape: (10, 6)

tool	product	brand	cordless	price	rpm
---	---	---	---	---	---
str	str	str	bool	i64	i64
Rotary Hammer	HR2230	Makita	false	199	1050
Miter Saw	GCM 8 SJL	Bosch	false	391	5500
Plunge Cut Saw	DSP600ZJ	Makita	true	459	6300
Impact Driver	DTD157Z	Makita	true	156	3000
Jigsaw	PST 900 PEL	Bosch	false	79	3100

---

1 The methods covered in this chapter can also be applied to LazyFrames.

```
| Angle Grinder         | DGA504ZJ     | Makita | true  | 229 | 8500  |
| Nail Gun              | DPSB2IN1-XJ  | DeWalt | true  | 129 | null  |
| Router                | POF 1400 ACE | Bosch  | false | 185 | 28000 |
| Random Orbital Sander | DBO180ZJ     | Makita | true  | 199 | 11000 |
| Table Saw             | DWE7485      | DeWalt | false | 516 | 5800  |
```

The instructions to get any files you might need are in Chapter 2. We assume that you have the files in the *data* subdirectory. Let's get filtering.

Filtering Rows

The rows of a DataFrame can be filtered with the `df.filter()` method. Filtering allows us to answer questions that involve phrases such as "is at least" or "is equal to." For example, which tools are by Makita? Or, which tools are cordless? Figure 11-1 illustrates this operation conceptually.

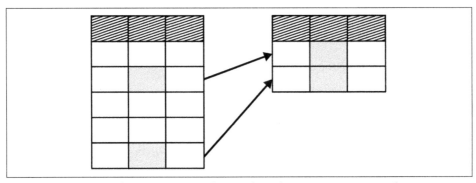

Figure 11-1. Filtering keeps rows according to the values in one or more columns or expressions

To filter rows, you specify which rows you want to keep. This can be done using expressions, column names, and constraints. We'll first discuss expressions, since they're the most flexible of the three.

Filtering Based on Expressions

The first way to filter rows is using expressions. You've already seen them in action in Chapter 7. They're the most flexible way to filter of the three because you can use all types of comparisons (such as equals and greater than) and combine them using Boolean algebra (such as OR and AND). Comparison and Boolean algebra operations are discussed in Chapter 9 if you need a refresher.

Expressions allow you to conjure up all sorts of filters. Just make sure that the expression evaluates to a Boolean Series. A `True` means that the corresponding row will be kept, and a `False` means that it will be discarded.

Let's filter the `tools` DataFrame to keep our favorite tools, which happen to be cordless tools by Makita:

```
tools.filter(pl.col("cordless") & (pl.col("brand") == "Makita"))  ❶
```

❶ You don't need to write `pl.col("cordless") == True` because the data type of column `cordless` is already Boolean.

```
shape: (4, 6)
┌─────────────────────┬──────────┬────────┬──────────┬───────┬───────┐
│ tool                ┆ product  ┆ brand  ┆ cordless ┆ price ┆ rpm   │
│ ---                 ┆ ---      ┆ ---    ┆ ---      ┆ ---   ┆ ---   │
│ str                 ┆ str      ┆ str    ┆ bool     ┆ i64   ┆ i64   │
╞═════════════════════╪══════════╪════════╪══════════╪═══════╪═══════╡
│ Plunge Cut Saw      ┆ DSP600ZJ ┆ Makita ┆ true     ┆ 459   ┆ 6300  │
│ Impact Driver       ┆ DTD157Z  ┆ Makita ┆ true     ┆ 156   ┆ 3000  │
│ Angle Grinder       ┆ DGA504ZJ ┆ Makita ┆ true     ┆ 229   ┆ 8500  │
│ Random Orbital Sander ┆ DBO180ZJ ┆ Makita ┆ true     ┆ 199   ┆ 11000 │
└─────────────────────┴──────────┴────────┴──────────┴───────┴───────┘
```

Commas Instead of Ampersands

If your expression is composed of multiple parts that are combined using the AND operator (&), then you can alternatively pass those parts as separate arguments to the `df.filter()` method. That means that the last code snippet can be rewritten as:

```
tools.filter(pl.col("cordless"), pl.col("brand") == "Makita")
```

Depending on your preference, this might improve the readability of your filter. Keep in mind that this doesn't work for the OR operator (|).

Filtering Based on Column Names

The second way to use `df.filter()` is by specifying column names. If a column is Boolean, such as the column `cordless` in the `tools` DataFrame, you can directly use the column name without having to turn it into an expression yourself. For example, to select all cordless tools (not just those from Makita), you can use:

```
tools.filter("cordless")
```

shape: (5, 6)

tool	product	brand	cordless	price	rpm
str	str	str	bool	i64	i64
Plunge Cut Saw	DSP600ZJ	Makita	true	459	6300
Impact Driver	DTD157Z	Makita	true	156	3000
Angle Grinder	DGA504ZJ	Makita	true	229	8500
Nail Gun	DPSB2IN1-XJ	DeWalt	true	129	null
Random Orbital Sander	DBO180ZJ	Makita	true	199	11000

You can specify multiple column names, but keep in mind that they all need to be Boolean.

Polars Can't Handle the Truthy

In the Python language, there are the concepts of *truthy* and *falsy*. Whether a value is truthy or falsy depends on whether it would become True or False if cast to a Boolean. Falsy values include False itself, the number zero, and empty sequences, collections, and Strings. Everything else is truthy. This means that Python code such as (my_name != "") and (len(my_list) > 0) can be rewritten as my_name and my_list.

Because of this language concept, you might think that Python Polars would allow non-Boolean columns and expressions when filtering. However, Polars is built in Rust and is therefore stricter than Python: only Boolean columns and expressions that construct a Boolean Series can be used for filtering.

You can turn an expression that's not Boolean into a Boolean one by using comparisons. For example, to test for nonempty Strings and nonempty Lists, you can use pl.col("my_name") != "" and pl.col("my_list").list.len() > 0, respectively.

Filtering Based on Constraints

The third way to use df.filter() is by specifying constraints. A *constraint* consists of a column name and a value.[2] Filtering again for cordless Makita tools using constraints looks like this:

---

2 Under the hood, Polars converts these constraints to expressions like pl.col(<column name>).eq(<value>).

```
tools.filter(cordless=True, brand="Makita")
shape: (4, 6)
```

tool	product	brand	cordless	price	rpm
str	str	str	bool	i64	i64
Plunge Cut Saw	DSP600ZJ	Makita	true	459	6300
Impact Driver	DTD157Z	Makita	true	156	3000
Angle Grinder	DGA504ZJ	Makita	true	229	8500
Random Orbital Sander	DBO180ZJ	Makita	true	199	11000

Effectively, the column names are specified as keyword arguments. Due to how the Python language works, this has a couple of limitations:

- The column name can only contain letters (a-z, A-Z), digits (0-9), and underscores (_), cannot start with a digit, and cannot be a reserved keyword in Python (e.g., if, class, global).

- Constraints must appear last if you combine them with the other two ways (expressions and column names).

- The value must always be specified, including True.

- Only equality comparisons are supported and must be written with one equals sign (=) instead of two. On top of that, the Python style guide (*https://oreil.ly/8INhc*) states that there shouldn't be any spaces around the equals sign.

Don't Constrain Yourself

Because of their limitations, we advise against using constraints. Our recommendation is to use expressions for filtering. They're more verbose, but at least you won't be constraining your expressiveness.

Sorting Rows

With sorting, you change the order of the rows based on the values in one or more columns. The number of rows remains the same. Sorting enables us to answer questions that involve phrases such as "the most" or "the lowest." For example, for which brand do we have the most tools? Or, what is the tool with the lowest price? Figure 11-2 illustrates this operation conceptually.

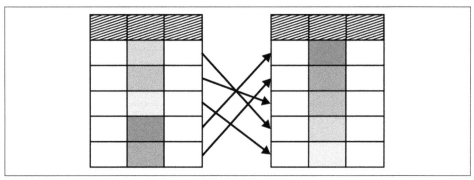

Figure 11-2. Sorting reorders rows according to the values in one or more columns or expressions

Most often you'll be sorting numbers, but you can also sort Strings (alphabetically), Dates (chronologically), and Times (also chronologically). You can also sort container data types such as Structs and Lists, as we'll show you later. In the next few sections we'll look at sorting based on a single column, multiple columns, and expressions.

Sorting Based on a Single Column

To sort, you use the `df.sort()` method. The easiest way to invoke this method is by specifying a column name:

```
tools.sort("price")
```

```
shape: (10, 6)
```

tool	product	brand	cordless	price	rpm
str	str	str	bool	i64	i64
Jigsaw	PST 900 PEL	Bosch	false	79	3100
Nail Gun	DPSB2IN1-XJ	DeWalt	true	129	null
…	…	…	…	…	…
Plunge Cut Saw	DSP600ZJ	Makita	true	459	6300
Table Saw	DWE7485	DeWalt	false	516	5800

As you see, by default the values are sorted in ascending order. Table 11-1 lists all the arguments that the `df.sort()` method accepts.

Table 11-1. Arguments for the method df.sort()

Argument	Description
by and *more_by	Column(s) to sort by. Accepts expression input, including selectors. Strings are parsed as column names.

Argument	Description
descending	Sort in descending order. When sorting by multiple columns, can be specified per column by passing a sequence of Booleans. Default: `False`.
nulls_last	Place null values last. Default: `False`.
multithreaded	Sort using multiple threads. Default: `True`.[a]
maintain_order	Whether the order should be maintained if elements are equal. Default: `False`.

[a] Only set this to `False` when your Polars is code part of an application that's already multithreaded.

Sorting in Reverse

You can change the default order by setting the `descending` keyword to `True`:

```
tools.sort("price", descending=True)
```

shape: (10, 6)

tool	product	brand	cordless	price	rpm
str	str	str	bool	i64	i64
Table Saw	DWE7485	DeWalt	false	516	5800
Plunge Cut Saw	DSP600ZJ	Makita	true	459	6300
…	…	…	…	…	…
Nail Gun	DPSB2IN1-XJ	DeWalt	true	129	null
Jigsaw	PST 900 PEL	Bosch	false	79	3100

Up or Down?

Make sure to use the `descending` keyword instead of `ascending`, otherwise you get an error:

```
tools.sort("price", ascending=False)
```

```
TypeError: DataFrame.sort() got an unexpected keyword
argument 'ascending'
```

It's easy to forget this, especially if you're used to pandas, where you can use `ascending=False` to reverse the order.

Sorting Based on Multiple Columns

To sort based on multiple columns, you specify multiple column names as separate arguments:

```
tools.sort("brand", "price")
```

shape: (10, 6)

tool	product	brand	cordless	price	rpm

str	str	str	bool	i64	i64
Jigsaw	PST 900 PEL	Bosch	false	79	3100
Router	POF 1400 ACE	Bosch	false	185	28000
…	…	…	…	…	…
Angle Grinder	DGA504ZJ	Makita	true	229	8500
Plunge Cut Saw	DSP600ZJ	Makita	true	459	6300

Again, the default order is ascending for all columns that you specify. Setting descend ing to True will apply to all columns. If you want to have different directions per column, you can pass a list of Booleans to descending:

```
tools.sort("brand", "price", descending=[False, True])
```

shape: (10, 6)

tool	product	brand	cordless	price	rpm
---	---	---	---	---	---
str	str	str	bool	i64	i64
Miter Saw	GCM 8 SJL	Bosch	false	391	5500
Router	POF 1400 ACE	Bosch	false	185	28000
…	…	…	…	…	…
Random Orbital Sander	DBO180ZJ	Makita	true	199	11000
Impact Driver	DTD157Z	Makita	true	156	3000

Make sure that the number of Booleans is equal to the number of columns you are sorting on.

Sorting Based on Expressions

The df.sort() method also accepts one or more expressions:

```
tools.sort(pl.col("rpm") / pl.col("price"))
```

shape: (10, 6)

tool	product	brand	cordless	price	rpm
---	---	---	---	---	---
str	str	str	bool	i64	i64
Nail Gun	DPSB2IN1-XJ	DeWalt	true	129	null
Rotary Hammer	HR2230	Makita	false	199	1050
…	…	…	…	…	…
Random Orbital Sander	DBO180ZJ	Makita	true	199	11000
Router	POF 1400 ACE	Bosch	false	185	28000

A temporary Series is created to sort the DataFrame on. Note that this column will not appear in the resulting DataFrame.

Just as with filtering, expressions will give you the most flexibility. However, from our experience, you'll most often sort on columns already present in the DataFrame.

Sorting Nested Data Types

It's possible to sort nested data types, like Structs, Lists, and Arrays. (We'll cover this in more detail in Chapter 12). Polars uses the row encoding to sort the underlying data. Lists and Arrays are sorted element-wise. This means that the first element of each list is compared first, then the second element, and so on:

```
lists = pl.DataFrame({"lists": [[2, 2], [2, 1, 3], [1]]})
lists.sort("lists")
```

```
shape: (3, 1)
┌───────────┐
│ lists     │
│ ---       │
│ list[i64] │
╞═══════════╡
│ [1]       │
│ [2, 1, 3] │
│ [2, 2]    │
└───────────┘
```

Structs do field-wise sorting, which means that the first field is sorted first, then the second field, and so on:

```
structs = pl.DataFrame(
    {
        "structs": [
            {"a": 1, "b": 2, "c": 3},
            {"a": 1, "b": 3, "c": 1},
            {"a": 1, "b": 1, "c": 2},
        ]
    }
)
structs.sort("structs")
```

```
shape: (3, 1)
┌───────────┐
│ structs   │
│ ---       │
│ struct[3] │
╞═══════════╡
│ {1,1,2}   │
│ {1,2,3}   │
│ {1,3,1}   │
└───────────┘
```

Alternatively, you can first extract or create a value that is sortable. To demonstrate this, let's create a new DataFrame tools_collection that groups all the tools, by brand, into a List of Structs:

```
tools_collection = tools.group_by("brand").agg(collection=pl.struct(pl.all()))
tools_collection
```

shape: (3, 2)

brand	collection
str	list[struct[6]]
Makita	[{"Rotary Hammer","HR2230","Makita",false,199,1050}, {"Plung…
Bosch	[{"Miter Saw","GCM 8 SJL","Bosch",false,391,5500}, {"Jigsaw"…
DeWalt	[{"Nail Gun","DPSB2IN1-XJ","DeWalt",true,129,null}, {"Table …

You can then sort the Lists by their length, because that's an Integer which can be
sorted:

```
tools_collection.sort(pl.col("collection").list.len(), descending=True)
```

shape: (3, 2)

brand	collection
str	list[struct[6]]
Makita	[{"Rotary Hammer","HR2230","Makita",false,199,1050}, {"Plung…
Bosch	[{"Miter Saw","GCM 8 SJL","Bosch",false,391,5500}, {"Jigsaw"…
DeWalt	[{"Nail Gun","DPSB2IN1-XJ","DeWalt",true,129,null}, {"Table …

Another example is to sort on the average price for each brand:

```
tools_collection.sort(
    pl.col("collection")
    .list.eval(pl.element().struct.field("price"))
    .list.mean()
)
```

shape: (3, 2)

brand	collection
str	list[struct[6]]
Bosch	[{"Miter Saw","GCM 8 SJL","Bosch",false,391,5500}, {"Jigsaw","PST…
Makita	[{"Rotary Hammer","HR2230","Makita",false,199,1050}, {"Plunge Cut…
DeWalt	[{"Nail Gun","DPSB2IN1-XJ","DeWalt",true,129,null}, {"Table Saw",…

Materialize First, Sort Second

Sometimes, like with the last code snippet, things can get a bit complicated and make you wonder whether you're sorting correctly. In those cases, it can be helpful to first construct a new column using the df.with_columns() method to inspect the values on which you're sorting:

```
tools_collection.with_columns(
    mean_price=pl.col("collection")
    .list.eval(pl.element().struct.field("price"))
    .list.mean()
).sort("mean_price")
```

```
shape: (3, 3)
┌────────┬─────────────────────────────────────┬────────────┐
│ brand  │ collection                          │ mean_price │
│ ---    │ ---                                 │ ---        │
│ str    │ list[struct[6]]                     │ f64        │
╞════════╪═════════════════════════════════════╪════════════╡
│ Bosch  │ [{"Miter Saw","GCM 8 SJL","Bosch",f… │ 218.333333 │
│ Makita │ [{"Rotary Hammer","HR2230","Makita"… │ 248.4      │
│ DeWalt │ [{"Nail Gun","DPSB2IN1-XJ","DeWalt"… │ 322.5      │
└────────┴─────────────────────────────────────┴────────────┘
```

Turns out we were sorting on the correct values. Now we can safely turn that df.with_columns() back into a df.sort().

Related Row Operations

Besides filtering and sorting, there are a few related row operations worth knowing about.

Filtering Missing Values

Sometimes, your analysis or machine learning algorithm cannot handle missing values. The method df.drop_nulls() keeps only rows without missing values. You can specify which columns should be considered. For example:

```
tools.drop_nulls("rpm").height
```

```
9
```

By default, all columns are considered, in which case it's effectively the same as:

```
tools.filter(pl.all_horizontal(pl.all().is_not_null())).height
```

```
9
```

Slicing

Sometimes you want to keep the rows based on their position in the DataFrame, irrespective of the values they contain. This is generally known as *slicing*, and there are several methods for this:

- With df.head() and df.tail() you keep the first or last few rows, respectively. For example, keep the first five rows with df.head(5).
- With df.slice() you keep a range of rows. For example, keep from the third to the seventh row with df.slice(2, 7).
- With df.gather_every() you keep a row every so often. For example, keep every second row with df.gather_every(2).

You can, of course, combine these methods to create complex slices; for example, the first three rows of a DataFrame that takes every other observation:

```
tools.with_row_index().gather_every(2).head(3)
```

```
shape: (3, 7)
```

index	tool	product	...	cordless	price	rpm
u32	str	str		bool	i64	i64
0	Rotary Hammer	HR2230	...	false	199	1050
2	Plunge Cut Saw	DSP600ZJ	...	true	459	6300
4	Jigsaw	PST 900 PEL	...	false	79	3100

The method df.with_row_index() is used here to clarify which row positions are kept.

Order, Order!

Note that with the preceding functions, the order that the rows appear in is important.

Generally, depending on exact locations of data in a DataFrame is considered an antipattern in Polars, because it usually means that you know something about the data that Polars doesn't. It then can't use that information for further optimization, and it will clash with Polars' declarative nature, where you define operations based on data conditions instead of location. Additionally, because of Polars' parallelized nature, exact data locations may shift differently on different runs.

Top and Bottom

With the methods df.top_k() and df.bottom_k(), you keep the *k* rows with the largest or smallest value. For example, to keep the top three most expensive tools:

```
tools.top_k(3, by="price")
```

shape: (3, 6)

tool	product	brand	cordless	price	rpm
str	str	str	bool	i64	i64
Table Saw	DWE7485	DeWalt	false	516	5800
Plunge Cut Saw	DSP600ZJ	Makita	true	459	6300
Miter Saw	GCM 8 SJL	Bosch	false	391	5500

No Guarantees

Note that the resulting values are *not* sorted and can be in any particular order. If you want them sorted, you have to call df.sort() afterwards.

Sampling

The method df.sample() filters the rows based on randomness. For example, to keep only 20% of the rows:

```
tools.sample(fraction=0.2)
```

shape: (2, 6)

tool	product	brand	cordless	price	rpm
str	str	str	bool	i64	i64
Rotary Hammer	HR2230	Makita	false	199	1050
Router	POF 1400 ACE	Bosch	false	185	28000

Note that df.sample() only works on DataFrames, because it needs to know the total amount of data before sampling.

Semi-Joins

Another way to filter is to semi-join with another DataFrame. For example, let's say you have a DataFrame saws which contains all sorts of saws. You can use this to keep only the saws in the tools DataFrame:

```
saws = pl.DataFrame(
    {
        "tool": [
            "Table Saw",
            "Plunge Cut Saw",
            "Miter Saw",
            "Jigsaw",
            "Bandsaw",
            "Chainsaw",
            "Seesaw",
        ]
    }
)
tools.join(saws, how="semi", on="tool")
```

shape: (4, 6)

tool	product	brand	cordless	price	rpm
str	str	str	bool	i64	i64
Miter Saw	GCM 8 SJL	Bosch	false	391	5500
Plunge Cut Saw	DSP600ZJ	Makita	true	459	6300
Jigsaw	PST 900 PEL	Bosch	false	79	3100
Table Saw	DWE7485	DeWalt	false	516	5800

You'll learn more about joining in general in Chapter 14.

Takeaways

In this chapter we've looked at filtering and sorting rows, and a few related operations. The key takeaways are:

- Filtering based on expressions gives you the most flexibility.
- With filtering, expressions must evaluate to a Boolean Series.
- Filtering based on constraints has many limits.
- Expressions, column names, and constraints separated by commas are combined under the hood with the AND operator (&).
- Sorting based on a single column is often sufficient, but sorting on multiple columns is possible as well.
- Use descending=True to reverse the default sort order.

- To sort nested data types, first create or extract a sortable value from them.
- There are many related row operations, including slicing and sampling.

In the next chapter we're going to look at how to work with special data types such as Strings, Categoricals, and temporal data types.

## CHAPTER 12

Working with Textual, Temporal, and Nested Data Types

In Chapter 4, we covered the basic data types that Polars offers and how they are used to store data in Series. Certain data types deserve special attention because they either have special methods or they are optimized for specific use cases.

These data types can be grouped into textual, temporal, and nested data types. The three textual data types are String, Categorical, and Enum. The four temporal data types are Date, Datetime, Time, and Duration. The three nested data types are List, Array, and Struct.

All these data types, except for Enum, have their own *namespace*. A namespace groups multiple methods into one accessor. For example, the `Expr.str` namespace has all the methods for String, and the `Expr.dt` namespaces have all the methods for temporal data types.

In this chapter, you'll learn how to:

- Create Series with textual, temporal, and nested data types
- Work with text using the String data type
- Use Categoricals and Enums for efficiently working with textual data
- Process temporal data using Dates and Datetimes
- Store sequences and nested data using Lists, Arrays, and Structs

The instructions to get any files you might need are in Chapter 2. We assume that you have the files in the *data* subdirectory.

String

A String is a data type for representing text, consisting of a sequence of characters, digits, or symbols. This brings with it a unique set of operations that can be performed on Strings, such as searching for patterns, splitting into parts, and converting to other data types. For this reason, the String data type has its own namespace in Polars, called `Expr.str`.

For more in-depth information on how the String data type is stored in memory, see Chapter 18.

String Methods

The methods for the String data type can be categorized into three groups: conversion, descriptive, and manipulation.

String methods for conversion

The methods listed in Table 12-1 allow you to convert Strings to and from different data types or formats.

Table 12-1. Conversion methods for the String data type

Method	Description
`Expr.str.decode(…)`	Decode values using the provided encoding.
`Expr.str.encode(…)`	Encode values using the provided encoding.
`Expr.str.json_decode(…)`	Parse String values as JSON.
`Expr.str.json_path_match(…)`	Extract the first match of JSON String with the provided JSONPath expression.
`Expr.str.strptime(…)`	Convert a String column into a Date, Datetime, or Time column.
`Expr.str.to_date(…)`	Convert a String column into a Date column.
`Expr.str.to_datetime(…)`	Convert a String column into a Datetime column.
`Expr.str.to_decimal(…)`	Convert a String column into a Decimal column.
`Expr.str.to_integer(…)`	Convert a String column into an Int64 column with base radix.[a]
`Expr.str.to_time(…)`	Convert a String column into a Time column.

[a] *Radix* refers to the base of a number system, specifying how many digits it uses. In the context of converting Strings to integers, the radix determines how to interpret the symbols in the String. Without knowing the radix, the conversion can be ambiguous. For example, "101" could represent different values depending on whether it's in decimal (101), binary (5), or hexadecimal (272). The default radix is decimal (10).

String methods for describing and querying

The methods listed in Table 12-2 can return attributes of Strings or allow you to query for certain patterns.

Table 12-2. Descriptive methods for the String data type

Method	Description
`Expr.str.contains(…)`	Check if the String contains a sub-String that matches a pattern.
`Expr.str.contains_any(…)`	Use the Aho-Corasick[a] algorithm to find matches.
`Expr.str.count_matches(…)`	Count all successive nonoverlapping regex matches.
`Expr.str.ends_with(…)`	Check if String values end with a sub-String.
`Expr.str.find(…)`	Return the index position of the first sub-String matching a pattern.
`Expr.str.len_bytes()`	Return the length of each String as the number of bytes.
`Expr.str.len_chars()`	Return the length of each String as the number of characters.
`Expr.str.starts_with(…)`	Check if String values start with a sub-String.

[a] The Aho-Corasick algorithm finds multiple words in text quickly by organizing them in a tree (trie) and using "failure links" to skip ahead when parts of a word don't match. This lets it check all words in a single pass through the text.

String methods for manipulation

The methods listed in Table 12-3 allow you to manipulate the String values in a Series.

Table 12-3. Manipulation methods for the String data type

Method	Description
`Expr.str.concat(…)`	Vertically concatenate the String values in the column to a single String value.
`Expr.str.escape_regex()`	Return String values with all regular expression metacharacters escaped.
`Expr.str.explode()`	Return a column with a separate row for every String character.
`Expr.str.extract(…)`	Extract the target capture group from provided patterns.
`Expr.str.extract_all(…)`	Extract all matches for the given regex pattern.
`Expr.str.extract_groups(…)`	Extract all capture groups for the given regex pattern.
`Expr.str.extract_many(…)`	Use the Aho-Corasick algorithm to extract many matches.
`Expr.str.head(…)`	Return the first *n* characters of each String in a String Series.
`Expr.str.join(…)`	Vertically concatenate the String values in the column to a single String value.
`Expr.str.pad_end(…)`	Pad the end of the String until it reaches the given length.
`Expr.str.pad_start(…)`	Pad the start of the String until it reaches the given length.
`Expr.str.replace(…)`	Replace first matching regex/literal sub-String with a new String value.
`Expr.str.replace_all(…)`	Replace all matching regex/literal sub-Strings with a new String value.
`Expr.str.replace_many(…)`	Use the Aho-Corasick algorithm to replace many matches.

Method	Description
Expr.str.reverse()	Return String values in reversed order.
Expr.str.slice(…)	Extract a sub-String from each String value.
Expr.str.split(…)	Split the String by a sub-String.
Expr.str.split_exact(…)	Split the String by a sub-String using *n* splits.
Expr.str.splitn(…)	Split the String by a sub-String, restricted to returning at most *n* items.
Expr.str.strip_chars(…)	Remove leading and trailing characters.
Expr.str.strip_chars_end(…)	Remove trailing characters.
Expr.str.strip_chars_start(…)	Remove leading characters.
Expr.str.strip_prefix(…)	Remove prefix.
Expr.str.strip_suffix(…)	Remove suffix.
Expr.str.tail(…)	Return the last *n* characters of each String in a String Series.
Expr.str.to_lowercase()	Modify Strings to their lowercase equivalent.
Expr.str.to_titlecase()	Modify Strings to their title case equivalent.
Expr.str.to_uppercase()	Modify Strings to their uppercase equivalent.
Expr.str.zfill(…)	Pad the start of the String with zeros until it reaches the given length.

String Examples

Let's dive into some examples. First, you'll create a DataFrame with some sample data:

```
corpus = pl.DataFrame(
    {
        "raw_text": [
            "  Data Science is amazing ",
            "Data_analysis > Data entry",
            " Python&Polars; Fast",
        ]
    }
)

corpus
```

```
shape: (3, 1)
┌────────────────────────────┐
│ raw_text                   │
│ ---                        │
│ str                        │
╞════════════════════════════╡
│   Data Science is amazing  │
│ Data_analysis > Data entry │
│  Python&Polars; Fast       │
└────────────────────────────┘
```

This example DataFrame showcases some of the String methods available in Polars. Let's start by cleaning up the Strings:

```
corpus = corpus.with_columns(
    processed_text=pl.col("raw_text")   ❶
    .str.strip_chars()   ❷
    .str.to_lowercase()   ❸
    .str.replace_all("_", " ")   ❹
)
corpus
```

❶ Creates a new column with the processed text and names it appropriately.

❷ The `Expr.str.strip_chars()` method removes leading and trailing characters from the String. Since you haven't provided any characters to strip, it defaults to whitespace.

❸ Converting everything to lowercase can make it easier to work with, as issues around case matching go away.

❹ You may want to replace all underscores with spaces when working with file-names or URLs.

```
shape: (3, 2)
┌───────────────────────────┬───────────────────────────┐
│ raw_text                  │ processed_text            │
│ ---                       │ ---                       │
│ str                       │ str                       │
╞═══════════════════════════╪═══════════════════════════╡
│    Data Science is amazing │ data science is amazing   │
│ Data_analysis > Data entry │ data analysis > data entry │
│   Python&Polars; Fast     │ python&polars; fast       │
└───────────────────────────┴───────────────────────────┘
```

Now that you have clean data to work with, let's get into manipulating and selecting it. Common operations are slicing and splitting Strings:

```
corpus.with_columns(
    first_5_chars=pl.col("processed_text").str.slice(0, 5),   ❶
    first_word=pl.col("processed_text")
    .str.split(" ")   ❷
    .list.get(0),   ❸
    second_word=pl.col("processed_text").str.split(" ").list.get(1),   ❹
)
```

❶ From the String values in the `processed_text` column, you slice the first five characters and save them in the `first_5_chars` column.

❷ You split the String values in the `processed_text` column on spaces. This creates a List of Strings with a length of the amount of spaces in the String + 1. We cover Lists later in this chapter.

❸ You get the first element from that List of Strings, which will be the first word.

❹ You get the second element from that List of Strings.

```
shape: (3, 5)
```

raw_text	processed_tex	first_5_chars	first_word	second_word
---	t	---	---	---
str	---	str	str	str
	str			
Data Science is am…	data science is amaz…	data	data	science
Data_analysis > Data…	data analysis > data…	data	data	analysis
Python&Polars; Fast	python&polars ; fast	pytho	python&polars ;	fast

You can also query the String for some information about it, as follows:

```
corpus.with_columns(
    len_chars=pl.col("processed_text").str.len_chars(),  ❶
    len_bytes=pl.col("processed_text").str.len_bytes(),  ❷
    count_a=pl.col("processed_text").str.count_matches("a"),  ❸
)
```

❶ Calculates the number of characters in the String.

❷ Calculates the number of bytes that the String takes in memory.

❸ Counts how often the letter "a" occurs in the String.

```
shape: (3, 5)
```

raw_text	processed_text	len_chars	len_bytes	count_a
---	---	---	---	---
str	str	u32	u32	u32
Data Science is amazing	data science is amazing	23	23	4
Data_analysis > Data entry	data analysis > data entry	26	26	6
Python&Polars; Fast	python&polars; fast	19	19	2

Length and Performance with Strings Attached

Polars encodes Strings as UTF-8, which is variable in length. This means that it uses different numbers of bytes to represent different characters. UTF-8 can use anywhere from 1 to 4 bytes to encode a single character, depending on the character's Unicode value.

In the preceding example, the numbers returned by both methods are the same because you're using only characters in the ASCII range, which include common English letters, numbers, and basic symbols. When using non-ASCII characters, such as Asian characters or emojis, the length in bytes is not the same as the length in characters. In that case, you may want to use `Expr.str.len_chars()` instead of `Expr.str.len_bytes()`.

Keep in mind that the `Expr.str.len_bytes()` method is much more performant than the `Expr.str.len_chars()` method. The time to execute `Expr.str.len_bytes()` is constant, regardless of the size of the String. On the other hand, the time to execute `Expr.str.len_chars()` is linearly proportional to the size of the String. So, the longer the String, the longer this method takes.

The following sample code uses a regular expression to find all the hashtags in a String:

```
posts = pl.DataFrame(
    {"post": ["Loving #python and #polars!", "A boomer post without a hashtag"]}
)

hashtag_regex = r"#(\w+)"  ❶

posts.with_columns(
    hashtags=pl.col("post").str.extract_all(hashtag_regex)  ❷
)
```

❶ You define a regex pattern that matches a hashtag followed by a word. Here the `\w` matches any word character. A *word character* is a character that is included in the ranges `a-z`, `A-Z`, or `0-9`, or is an underscore (`_`). The plus (`+`) means that the previous character can occur one or more times, capturing the entire word and not just the first character.

❷ You extract all matches of the regex pattern from the `post` column and save them in the `hashtags` column.

```
shape: (2, 2)
┌───────┬───────────┐
│ post  │ hashtags  │
│ ---   │ ---       │
│ str   │ list[str] │
```

```
| Loving #python and #polars!       | ["#python", "#polars"] |
| A boomer post without a hashtag   | []                     |
```

Categorical

The Categorical data type encodes Series of String values efficiently. With the String data type, all the values are stored in physical memory separately, even if they are the same.

The Categorical data type uses a *String Cache*. A String Cache is a dictionary behind the scenes that stores the unique String values and an accompanying integer (the data type UInt32, to be precise) representation for all unique Strings in that Series. Instead of storing the String for all values in the Series, the smaller integer representation is used for efficient storage. The integer is called the *physical representation*, whereas the String is called the *lexical representation*.

If a Series contains many repeated String values, this allows for more efficient storage and faster operations (because String comparisons are expensive). Categoricals are stored in two parts: a dictionary and indices.

Let's explore the Categorical data type and its methods. First, you'll create a DataFrame with a Categorical column. Additionally, you'll create a column with its physical representation:

```
cats = pl.DataFrame(
    {"name": ["Persian cat", "Siamese Cat", "Lynx", "Lynx"]},
    schema={"name": pl.Categorical},
)

cats.with_columns(name_physical=pl.col("name").to_physical())
```

```
shape: (4, 2)
┌─────────────┬───────────────┐
│ name        │ name_physical │
│ ---         │ ---           │
│ cat         │ u32           │
╞═════════════╪═══════════════╡
│ Persian cat │ 0             │
│ Siamese Cat │ 1             │
│ Lynx        │ 2             │
│ Lynx        │ 2             │
└─────────────┴───────────────┘
```

Categorical Methods

The Categorical data type has only one method (see Table 12-4).

Table 12-4. Method for the Categorical data type

Method	Description
Expr.cat.get_categories()	Get the categories stored in this data type.

Categorical Examples

The order of Strings in the column determines what the Categorical and the dictionary will look like. Even if a column of a different DataFrame contains the same unique Strings, the Categorical will be different if the order is not the same. That's because the order of the dictionary, and thus its physical representation (the integer), is different:

```
more_cats = pl.DataFrame(
    {"name": ["Maine Coon Cat", "Lynx", "Lynx", "Siamese Cat"]},
    schema={"name": pl.Categorical},
)

more_cats.with_columns(name_physical=pl.col("name").to_physical())
```

```
shape: (4, 2)
┌────────────────┬───────────────┐
│ name           │ name_physical │
│ ---            │ ---           │
│ cat            │ u32           │
╞════════════════╪═══════════════╡
│ Maine Coon Cat │ 0             │
│ Lynx           │ 1             │
│ Lynx           │ 1             │
│ Siamese Cat    │ 2             │
└────────────────┴───────────────┘
```

For this reason, trying to combine two different Categoricals will cause a `Categori calRemappingWarning`:

```
cats.join(more_cats, on="name")
```

```
CategoricalRemappingWarning: Local categoricals have different encodings, expens
ive re-encoding is done to perform this merge operation. Consider using a String
Cache or an Enum type if the categories are known in advance
  cats.join(more_cats, on="name")
```

```
shape: (5, 1)
┌──────┐
│ name │
│ ---  │
```

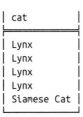

```
| cat         |
|=============|
| Lynx        |
| Lynx        |
| Lynx        |
| Lynx        |
| Siamese Cat |
```

To combine two Categorical Series in a performant way, you can make their String Caches match by creating them under the same String Cache. You can do this with a *Global String Cache*. A Global String Cache is a String Cache that is shared across all Categoricals. This way, all Categoricals tap into the same String Cache, preventing any mismatch. The Global String Cache is turned off by default because using the same String Cache for all Categoricals incurs a performance penalty. Because the String Cache is a global object, it needs to be locked while it's accessed, making threads wait for each other, which results in longer processing times.

The following example shows how to create Categoricals under the same String Cache with a `StringCache` context manager:

```python
with pl.StringCache():
    left = pl.DataFrame(
        {
            "categorical_column": ["value3", "value2", "value1"],
            "other": ["a", "b", "c"],
        },
        schema={"categorical_column": pl.Categorical, "other": pl.String},
    )
    right = pl.DataFrame(
        {
            "categorical_column": ["value2", "value3", "value4"],
            "other": ["d", "e", "f"],
        },
        schema={"categorical_column": pl.Categorical, "other": pl.String},
    )
```

Even outside the context manager, you can now join the two DataFrames containing Categorical columns:

```python
left.join(right, on="categorical_column")
```

```
shape: (2, 3)
```

categorical_column	other	other_right
cat	str	str
value2	b	d
value3	a	e

You can also enable the Global String Cache, using:

```
pl.enable_string_cache()
```

Note, however, that this means the Global String Cache will *always* be used, which can be a suboptimal solution compared to using the context manager.

To retrieve the unique categories that the Categorical column contains, use the `Expr.cat.get_categories()` method:

```
right.select(pl.col("categorical_column").cat.get_categories())
```

```
shape: (3, 1)
┌───────────────────┐
│ categorical_column │
│ ---               │
│ str               │
╞═══════════════════╡
│ value2            │
│ value3            │
│ value4            │
└───────────────────┘
```

The last relevant attribute is the way the column is ordered when sorting it. There are two options:

Physical (default)
　　The physical (Integer) representation is used to sort.

Lexical
　　The String value is used to sort.

You can set these options as soon as you create the Categorical data type. You can swap by casting the Categorical to the other variant.

First, prepare one of the DataFrames:

```
sorting_comparison_df = cats.select(cat_lexical=pl.col("name")).with_columns(
    cat_physical=pl.col("cat_lexical").to_physical()
)
```

```
sorting_comparison_df
```

```
shape: (4, 2)
┌─────────────┬──────────────┐
│ cat_lexical │ cat_physical │
│ ---         │ ---          │
│ cat         │ u32          │
╞═════════════╪══════════════╡
│ Persian cat │ 0            │
│ Siamese Cat │ 1            │
│ Lynx        │ 2            │
│ Lynx        │ 2            │
└─────────────┴──────────────┘
```

Here the cat_lexical column is sorted by physical representation, which can be seen in the cat_physical column:

```
sorting_comparison_df.with_columns(
    pl.col("cat_lexical").cast(pl.Categorical("physical"))
).sort(by="cat_lexical")
```

shape: (4, 2)

cat_lexical	cat_physical
cat	u32
Persian cat	0
Siamese Cat	1
Lynx	2
Lynx	2

Let's Get Lexical

The default ordering of a Categorical is "physical." The other possible value is "lexical."

Here, the DataFrame is sorted by lexical representation, which can be seen in the cat_lexical column:

```
sorting_comparison_df.with_columns(
    pl.col("cat_lexical").cast(pl.Categorical("lexical"))
).sort(by="cat_lexical")
```

shape: (4, 2)

cat_lexical	cat_physical
cat	u32
Lynx	2
Lynx	2
Persian cat	0
Siamese Cat	1

Enum

If you know the categories of a Series in advance, you can use the Enum data type. This data type currently uses the Categorical data type under the hood, but may later get its own implementation. The following example demonstrates how to create a new Enum data type called `bear_enum_dtype` and how to instantiate a Series based on that new Enum:

```
bear_enum_dtype = pl.Enum(["Polar", "Panda", "Brown"])

bear_enum_series = pl.Series(
    ["Polar", "Panda", "Brown", "Brown", "Polar"], dtype=bear_enum_dtype
)

bear_cat_series = pl.Series(
    ["Polar", "Panda", "Brown", "Brown", "Polar"], dtype=pl.Categorical
)
```

Enums are a new data type in Polars and, at the time of writing, don't have their own namespace yet.

Temporal

Temporal data types are specialized formats for working with time-based information, like points and intervals in time. These data types allow for comparison, arithmetic, and other time-specific operations.

Table 12-5 lists the four data types that Polars offers to store temporal data.

Table 12-5. Temporal data types

Data type	Description	Example	Storage
Date	Represents a calendar date without a time of day.	Birthdays	Int32 representing the amount of days since the Unix epoch (1970-01-01).
Datetime	Represents a calendar date and a time of day on that date.	Timestamps in logging	Int64 since the Unix epoch, and can have different units such as ns, us, ms.
Duration	Represents a time interval, the difference between two points in time. It's similar to `timedelta` in Python.	Elapsed time between two events	Int64 created when subtracting Date/Datetime.
Time	Focuses only on a time of day.	Scheduling of daily tasks.	Int64 representing nanoseconds since midnight.

Temporal Methods

The `Expr.dt` namespace has a variety of methods for converting, describing, and manipulating temporal data types.

Temporal methods for conversion

The methods in Table 12-6 allow you to convert temporal data to and from other data types or formats.

Table 12-6. Methods for converting temporal data types

Method	Description
`Expr.dt.cast_time_unit(…)`	Cast the underlying data to another time unit.
`Expr.dt.strftime(…)`	Convert a Date/Time/Datetime column into a String column with the given format.
`Expr.dt.to_string(…)`	Convert a Date/Time/Datetime column into a String column with the given format.

Temporal methods for describing and querying

The methods in Table 12-7 return attributes of the temporal data.

Table 12-7. Methods for describing temporal data types

Method	Description
`Expr.dt.base_utc_offset()`	Base offset from UTC.
`Expr.dt.century()`	Extract the century from underlying Date representation.
`Expr.dt.date()`	Extract date from Datetime.
`Expr.dt.datetime()`	Return Datetime.
`Expr.dt.day()`	Extract day from underlying Date representation.
`Expr.dt.dst_offset()`	Additional offset currently in effect (typically due to daylight saving time).
`Expr.dt.epoch(…)`	Get the time passed since the Unix epoch in the given time unit.
`Expr.dt.hour()`	Extract the hour from underlying Datetime representation.
`Expr.dt.is_leap_year()`	Determine whether the year of the underlying Date is a leap year.
`Expr.dt.iso_year()`	Extract ISO year from underlying Date representation.
`Expr.dt.microsecond()`	Extract microseconds from underlying Datetime representation.
`Expr.dt.millennium()`	Extract the millennium from underlying Date representation.
`Expr.dt.millisecond()`	Extract milliseconds from underlying Datetime representation.
`Expr.dt.minute()`	Extract minutes from underlying Datetime representation.
`Expr.dt.month()`	Extract the month from underlying Date representation.
`Expr.dt.nanosecond()`	Extract nanoseconds from underlying Datetime representation.
`Expr.dt.ordinal_day()`	Extract ordinal day from underlying Date representation.
`Expr.dt.quarter()`	Extract quarter from underlying Date representation.
`Expr.dt.second(…)`	Extract seconds from underlying Datetime representation.
`Expr.dt.time()`	Extract time.
`Expr.dt.timestamp(…)`	Return a timestamp in the given time unit.
`Expr.dt.total_days()`	Extract the total days from a Duration data type.
`Expr.dt.total_hours()`	Extract the total hours from a Duration data type.
`Expr.dt.total_microseconds()`	Extract the total microseconds from a Duration data type.

Method	Description
`Expr.dt.total_milliseconds()`	Extract the total milliseconds from a Duration data type.
`Expr.dt.total_minutes()`	Extract the total minutes from a Duration data type.
`Expr.dt.total_nanoseconds()`	Extract the total nanoseconds from a Duration data type.
`Expr.dt.total_seconds()`	Extract the total seconds from a Duration data type.
`Expr.dt.year()`	Extract year from underlying Date representation.

Temporal methods for manipulation

The methods in Table 12-8 allow you to manipulate temporal data.

Table 12-8. Methods for manipulating temporal data types

Method	Description
`Expr.dt.add_business_days(…)`	Offset by *n* business days.
`Expr.dt.combine(…)`	Create a naive Datetime from an existing Date/Datetime expression and a Time.
`Expr.dt.convert_time_zone(…)`	Convert to given time zone for an expression of data type Datetime.
`Expr.dt.month_start()`	Roll backward to the first day of the month.
`Expr.dt.month_end()`	Roll forward to the last day of the month.
`Expr.dt.offset_by(…)`	Offset this date by a relative time offset.
`Expr.dt.replace_time_zone(…)`	Replace time zone for an expression of data type Datetime.
`Expr.dt.round(…)`	Divide the Date/Datetime range into buckets.
`Expr.dt.truncate(…)`	Divide the Date/Datetime range into buckets.
`Expr.dt.week()`	Extract the week from the underlying Date representation.
`Expr.dt.weekday()`	Extract the week day from the underlying Date representation.
`Expr.dt.with_time_unit(…)`	Set time unit of an expression of data type Datetime or Duration.

Temporal Examples

The field of time-series analysis is grand, and we can't cover it all. However, we can cover some of the more common operations used in time-series analysis and illustrate how they are handled in Polars. In the upcoming example you'll mostly work with Dates, but the methods we're about to show you should work for other temporal data types as well.

Loading from a CSV file

To get started with temporal data in Polars, you first need to load some. You can load temporal data from a CSV file. Use the `pl.read_csv()` function and set the `try_parse_dates` argument to `True`:

```
pl.read_csv("data/all_stocks.csv", try_parse_dates=True)
```

shape: (18_476, 8)

symbol	date	open	...	close	adj close	volume
---	---	---		---	---	---
str	date	f64		f64	f64	i64
ASML	1999-01-04	11.765625	...	12.140625	7.522523	1801867
ASML	1999-01-05	11.859375	...	13.96875	8.655257	8241600
ASML	1999-01-06	14.25	...	16.875	10.456018	16400267
ASML	1999-01-07	14.742188	...	16.851563	10.441495	17722133
ASML	1999-01-08	16.078125	...	15.796875	9.787995	10696000
...	...	...	...	...	...	...
TSM	2023-06-26	102.019997	...	100.110001	99.125954	8560000
TSM	2023-06-27	101.150002	...	102.080002	101.076591	9732000
TSM	2023-06-28	100.5	...	100.919998	99.927986	8160900
TSM	2023-06-29	101.339996	...	100.639999	99.650742	7383900
TSM	2023-06-30	101.400002	...	100.919998	99.927986	11701700

Here, you can see by the data type in the column header that the `date` column has been read in the correct format.

Converting to and from a String

Alternatively, to parse a date from a String, you can do the following:

```
dates = pl.DataFrame({"date_str": ["2023-12-31", "2024-02-29"]}).with_columns(
    date=pl.col("date_str").str.to_date("%Y-%m-%d")
)
```

```
dates
```

shape: (2, 2)

date_str	date
str	date
2023-12-31	2023-12-31
2024-02-29	2024-02-29

If you want to write a date to a String in a certain format, you can do the following:

```
dates.with_columns(formatted_date=pl.col("date").dt.to_string("%d-%m-%Y"))
```

shape: (2, 3)

date_str	date	formatted_date
str	date	str
2023-12-31	2023-12-31	31-12-2023

| 2024-02-29 | 2024-02-29 | 29-02-2024 | |

Here, the formatting you provide to the `Expr.dt.to_string()` method is `%d-%m-%Y`, which means that the day, month, and year are separated by hyphens. The options for formatting are defined in the chrono strftime documentation (*https://oreil.ly/m_lwV*), which Polars uses.

Generating date ranges

Instead of loading data from other sources, it's also possible to generate date ranges and Datetime ranges directly in Polars:

```
pl.DataFrame(
    {
        "monday": pl.date_range(
            start=pl.date(2024, 10, 28),
            end=pl.date(2024, 12, 1),
            interval="1w",      ❶
            eager=True,         ❷
        ),
    }
)
```

❶ The `interval` argument can be set to a String that represents the interval: for example, `1w` for one week, `1d` for one day, `1h` for one hour, and so on.

❷ Set the `eager` argument to `True` to return the range as a Series object, or `False` to return an expression instead. Since you're working with a DataFrame constructor here, you can't use an expression because it would lead to a `TypeError: passing Expr objects to the DataFrame constructor is not supported`.

```
shape: (5, 1)
┌────────────┐
│ monday     │
│ ---        │
│ date       │
╞════════════╡
│ 2024-10-28 │
│ 2024-11-04 │
│ 2024-11-11 │
│ 2024-11-18 │
│ 2024-11-25 │
└────────────┘
```

Time zones

One of the most unpleasant things about working with temporal data is time zones. Daylight saving time in particular can be a real pain. For this reason, Coordinated Universal Time (UTC) is often used in time-series analysis because it's a universal fixed time zone. From there you can convert to any time zone you want.

In this example, you've got a dataset that's in UTC, and you want to convert it to the time zone of Amsterdam: Central European Time (CEST):

```
pl.DataFrame(  ❶
    {
        "utc_mixed_offset": [
            "2021-03-27T00:00:00+0100",
            "2021-03-28T00:00:00+0100",
            "2021-03-29T00:00:00+0200",
            "2021-03-30T00:00:00+0200",
        ]
    }
).with_columns(
    parsed=pl.col("utc_mixed_offset").str.to_datetime(
        "%Y-%m-%dT%H:%M:%S%z"
    )  ❷
).with_columns(
    converted=pl.col("parsed").dt.convert_time_zone("Europe/Amsterdam")  ❸
)
```

❶ You create a DataFrame with a column that contains dates with mixed offsets from Strings.

❷ You parse the Strings to a Datetime with the `Expr.str.to_datetime()` method. The `%z` in the format String is used to parse the time zone offset.

❸ You convert the parsed Datetime to the time zone of Amsterdam with the `Expr.dt.convert_time_zone()` method.

```
shape: (4, 3)
┌──────────────────────────┬─────────────────────────┬─────────────────────────┐
│ utc_mixed_offset         │ parsed                  │ converted               │
│ ---                      │ ---                     │ ---                     │
│ str                      │ datetime[μs, UTC]       │ datetime[μs,            │
│                          │                         │ Europe/Amsterdam]       │
╞══════════════════════════╪═════════════════════════╪═════════════════════════╡
│ 2021-03-27T00:00:00+0100 │ 2021-03-26 23:00:00 UTC │ 2021-03-27 00:00:00 CET │
│ 2021-03-28T00:00:00+0100 │ 2021-03-27 23:00:00 UTC │ 2021-03-28 00:00:00 CET │
│ 2021-03-29T00:00:00+0200 │ 2021-03-28 22:00:00 UTC │ 2021-03-29 00:00:00 CEST│
│ 2021-03-30T00:00:00+0200 │ 2021-03-29 22:00:00 UTC │ 2021-03-30 00:00:00 CEST│
└──────────────────────────┴─────────────────────────┴─────────────────────────┘
```

In the resulting DataFrame, you can see that the dates have been converted to the time zone of Amsterdam. The offset has been parsed according to Central Eastern Time (CET) and Central European Summer Time (CEST).

In Chapter 13 we'll show you how to summarize and aggregate temporal data using window functions, dynamic group by operations, and more.

List

There are three ways to store a collection of data points in a single column: using an Array, a List, or a Struct.

The List data type can contain lists of varying lengths with values of the same data type.

A Tale of Two Lists

The Polars List, which holds only values of the *same* data type, is different from the Python built-in List type, which can contain values of *different* data types.

It is possible to achieve the same in Polars by using the Object type to store a Python List, but this is not recommended, because the contents will be binary objects of serialized Python data. When using Objects, there are no special list manipulations, there's no room for the optimizations that can normally be applied to Polars data types, and all operations performed on it have to be done in Python, which is slower than running them in Rust.

The List data type is implemented in memory as Arrow's *Variable-Size List Layout*. We provide more information on the Arrow memory layout in Chapter 18. Similar to the String data type, it has a contiguous data buffer and an offset buffer pointing to the memory locations of the values in the data buffer.

List Methods

The methods listed in Table 12-9 allow you to work with the List data type.

Table 12-9. Methods for the List data type

Method	Description
Expr.list.all()	Evaluate whether all Boolean values in a List are true.
Expr.list.any()	Evaluate whether any Boolean value in a List is true.
Expr.list.arg_max()	Retrieve the index of the maximum value in every sub-List.
Expr.list.arg_min()	Retrieve the index of the minimal value in every sub-List.

Method	Description
`Expr.list.concat(…)`	Concat the Arrays in a List Series in linear time.
`Expr.list.contains(…)`	Check if sub-Lists contain the given item.
`Expr.list.count_matches(…)`	Count how often the value produced by element occurs.
`Expr.list.diff(…)`	Calculate the first discrete difference between shifted items of every sub-List.
`Expr.list.drop_nulls()`	Drop all null values in the List.
`Expr.list.eval(…)`	Run any Polars expression against the Lists' elements.
`Expr.list.explode()`	Returns a column with a separate row for every List element.
`Expr.list.first()`	Get the first value of the sub-Lists.
`Expr.list.gather(…)`	Take sub-Lists by multiple indices.
`Expr.list.gather_every(…)`	Take every *n*th value start from offset in sub-Lists.
`Expr.list.get(…)`	Get the value by index in the sub-Lists.
`Expr.list.head(…)`	Slice the first *n* values of every sub-List.
`Expr.list.join(…)`	Join all String items in a sub-List and place a separator between them.
`Expr.list.last()`	Get the last value of the sub-Lists.
`Expr.list.len()`	Return the number of elements in each List.
`Expr.list.max()`	Compute the max value of the Lists in the Array.
`Expr.list.mean()`	Compute the mean value of the Lists in the Array.
`Expr.list.median()`	Compute the median value of the Lists in the Array.
`Expr.list.min()`	Compute the min value of the Lists in the Array.
`Expr.list.n_unique()`	Count the number of unique values in every sub-List.
`Expr.list.reverse()`	Reverse the Arrays in the List.
`Expr.list.sample(…)`	Sample from this List.
`Expr.list.set_difference(…)`	Compute the SET DIFFERENCE between the elements in this List and the elements of another.
`Expr.list.set_intersection(…)`	Compute the SET INTERSECTION between the elements in this List and the elements of another.
`Expr.list.set_symmetric_difference(…)`	Compute the SET SYMMETRIC DIFFERENCE between the elements in this List and the elements of another.
`Expr.list.set_union(…)`	Compute the SET UNION between the elements in this List and the elements of another.
`Expr.list.shift(…)`	Shift List values by the given number of indices.
`Expr.list.slice(…)`	Slice every sub-List.
`Expr.list.sort(…)`	Sort the Lists in this column.
`Expr.list.std(…)`	Compute the std value of the Lists in the Array.
`Expr.list.sum()`	Sum all the Lists in the Array.

Method	Description
Expr.list.tail(…)	Slice the last *n* values of every sub-List.
Expr.list.to_array(…)	Convert a List column into an Array column with the same inner data type.
Expr.list.to_struct(…)	Convert the Series of data type List to a Series of data type Struct.
Expr.list.unique(…)	Get the unique/distinct values in the List.
Expr.list.var(…)	Compute the var value of the Lists in the Array.

List Examples

Let's show you some of the methods you can use with the List data type.

You can use the Expr.list.all() and Exprl.list.any() methods to evaluate whether all or any Boolean values in a List are true:

```
bools = pl.DataFrame({"values": [[True, True], [False, False, True], [False]]})

bools.with_columns(
    all_true=pl.col("values").list.all(),
    any_true=pl.col("values").list.any(),
)
```

```
shape: (3, 3)
┌─────────────────────┬──────────┬──────────┐
│ values              │ all_true │ any_true │
│ ---                 │ ---      │ ---      │
│ list[bool]          │ bool     │ bool     │
╞═════════════════════╪══════════╪══════════╡
│ [true, true]        │ true     │ true     │
│ [false, false, true]│ false    │ true     │
│ [false]             │ false    │ false    │
└─────────────────────┴──────────┴──────────┘
```

A powerful method that combines well with Expr.list.any() and Expr.list.all() is the Expr.list.eval() method. This method allows you to run any Polars expression against the List's elements. In the following example, you'll use the Expr.list.eval() method to check whether the ages in the List elements are greater than 40:

```
groups = pl.DataFrame({"ages": [[18, 21], [30, 40, 50], [42, 69]]})

groups.with_columns(
    over_forty=pl.col("ages").list.eval(
        pl.element() > 40,    ❶
        parallel=True,        ❷
    )
).with_columns(               ❸
    all_over_forty=pl.col("over_forty").list.all()    ❹
)
```

❶ The `pl.element()` function is used to access the elements of the List.

❷ Because the `parallel` argument is set to `True`, the `eval()` method will run the expression in parallel. This is off by default, but can seriously speed up your calculations if the expression you run allows for parallelism.

❸ To ensure parallel processing within `df.with_columns()`, any further modifications to a newly created column require a separate subsequent `df.with_columns()` call.

❹ The `Expr.list.all()` method is used to evaluate whether all Boolean values in a List are true.

```
shape: (3, 3)
```

ages	over_forty	all_over_forty
list[i64]	list[bool]	bool
[18, 21]	[false, false]	false
[30, 40, 50]	[false, false, true]	false
[42, 69]	[true, true]	true

You can sort the Lists in a column using the `Expr.list.sort()` method:

```
groups.with_columns(
    ages_sorted_descending=pl.col("ages").list.sort(descending=True)
)
```

```
shape: (3, 2)
```

ages	ages_sorted_descending
list[i64]	list[i64]
[18, 21]	[21, 18]
[30, 40, 50]	[50, 40, 30]
[42, 69]	[69, 42]

You can unpack a List to separate rows by using the `df.explode()` method:

```
groups.explode("ages")
```

```
shape: (7, 1)
```

ages
i64

```
| 18 |
| 21 |
| 30 |
| 40 |
| 50 |
| 42 |
| 69 |
```

Alternatively, you can use `Expr.list.explode()`, or its alias `Expr.flatten()`, which can be applied through an expression:

```
groups.select(ages=pl.col("ages").list.explode())
```

```
shape: (7, 1)
┌──────┐
│ ages │
│ ---  │
│ i64  │
╞══════╡
│ 18   │
│ 21   │
│ 30   │
│ 40   │
│ 50   │
│ 42   │
│ 69   │
└──────┘
```

We will further discuss `df.explode()` in Chapter 15.

Array

The Array data type can hold sequences of fixed lengths with values of the same data type. It is analogous to NumPy's `ndarray` data type.

Array Is More Performant Than List

The Array data type is implemented in memory by Arrow's *Fixed Size List Layout*. For this data type, the data buffer is also contiguous, just like List, but the offset buffer isn't needed because the length is constant. This makes the Array data type more memory efficient and more performant because fewer lookups are required to load the relevant data.

Array Methods

The Array data type has a variety of methods for converting, describing, and manipulating data Table 12-10.

Table 12-10. Methods for the Array data type

Method	Description
Expr.arr.all()	Evaluate whether all Boolean values are true for every sub-Array.
Expr.arr.any()	Evaluate whether any Boolean value is true for every sub-Array.
Expr.arr.arg_max()	Retrieve the index of the maximum value in every sub-Array.
Expr.arr.arg_min()	Retrieve the index of the minimal value in every sub-Array.
Expr.arr.contains(…)	Check if sub-Arrays contain the given item.
Expr.arr.count_matches(…)	Count how often the value produced by element occurs.
Expr.arr.explode()	Returns a column with a separate row for every Array element.
Expr.arr.first()	Get the first value of the sub-Arrays.
Expr.arr.get(…)	Get the value by index in the sub-Arrays.
Expr.arr.join(…)	Join all String items in a sub-Array and place a separator between them.
Expr.arr.last()	Get the last value of the sub-Arrays.
Expr.arr.max()	Compute the max values of the sub-Arrays.
Expr.arr.median()	Compute the median of the values of the sub-Arrays.
Expr.arr.min()	Compute the min values of the sub-Arrays.
Expr.arr.n_unique()	Count the number of unique values in every sub-Array.
Expr.arr.reverse()	Reverse the Arrays in this column.
Expr.arr.shift(…)	Shift Array values by the given number of indices.
Expr.arr.sort(…)	Sort the Arrays in this column.
Expr.arr.std(…)	Compute the std of the values of the sub-Arrays.
Expr.arr.sum()	Compute the sum values of the sub-Arrays.
Expr.arr.to_list()	Convert an Array column into a List column with the same inner data type.
Expr.arr.to_struct(…)	Convert the Series of data type Array to a Series of data type Struct.
Expr.arr.unique(…)	Get the unique/distinct values in the Array.
Expr.arr.var(…)	Compute the variance of the values of the sub-Arrays.

Array Examples

To showcase the Array data type, create a DataFrame with an Array column. In the following example, you'll create a DataFrame with an Array column that contains sequences of integers that represent temperatures in different locations:

```
events = pl.DataFrame(
    [
        pl.Series(
            "location", ["Paris", "Amsterdam", "Barcelona"], dtype=pl.String
        ),
        pl.Series(
```

```
            "temperatures",
            [
                [23, 27, 21, 22, 24, 23, 22],
                [17, 19, 15, 22, 18, 20, 21],
                [30, 32, 28, 29, 34, 33, 31],
            ],
            dtype=pl.Array(pl.Int64, shape=7),
        ),
    ]
)

events
```

shape: (3, 2)

location	temperatures
str	array[i64, 7]
-----------	----------------
Paris	[23, 27, … 22]
Amsterdam	[17, 19, … 21]
Barcelona	[30, 32, … 31]

Some methods that are available for the Array data type are `Expr.arr.median()`, `Expr.arr.max()`, and `Exp.arr.arg_max()`:

```
events.with_columns(
    median=pl.col("temperatures").arr.median(),
    max=pl.col("temperatures").arr.max(),
    warmest_dow=pl.col("temperatures").arr.arg_max(),
)
```

shape: (3, 5)

location	temperatures	median	max	warmest_dow
str	array[i64, 7]	f64	i64	u32
-----------	----------------	--------	-----	-------------
Paris	[23, 27, … 22]	23.0	27	1
Amsterdam	[17, 19, … 21]	19.0	22	3
Barcelona	[30, 32, … 31]	31.0	34	4

In the resulting DataFrame, you can see that the median column contains the median temperature for each location, the max column contains the maximum temperature for each location, and the warmest_dow column contains the index of the warmest weekday for each location.

Struct

A *Struct* is a nested data type for storing multiple Series in a single Series. On the row level, this can be interpreted as a Python dictionary with keys and values. The keys are the Series names, which are called *fields*, and the values are the values of the field for that row. A field also has a certain data type associated with it, which dictates the data type of the value. The Struct data type is an idiomatic way of working with multiple Series in Polars. An illustration of what it looks like can be found in Figure 12-1.

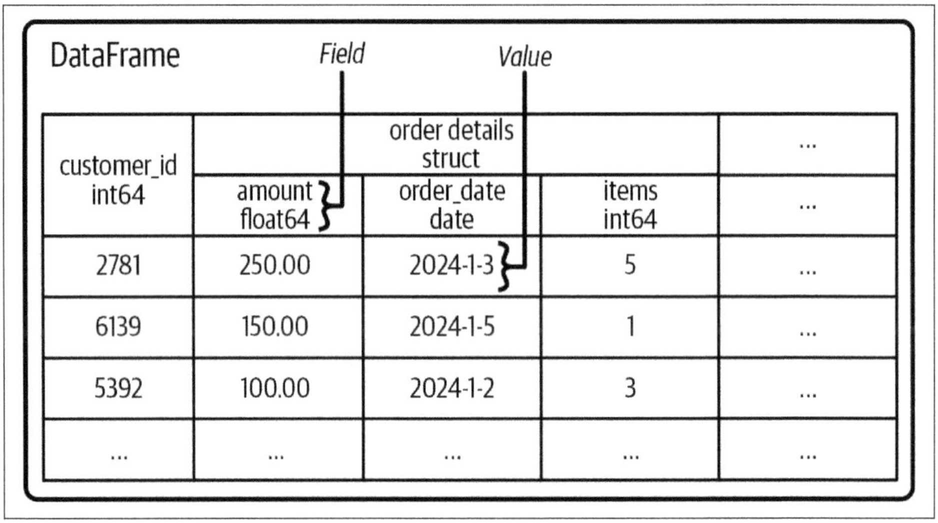

Figure 12-1. The way a Struct is represented in a DataFrame

By encapsulating multiple Series within a Struct, you can still do multicolumn operations, while keeping the expression paradigm intact. Generally, an expression maps a Series to a new Series, so Structs were created to allow working on multiple Series at once. Turning multiple Series into a Struct does not duplicate data, but allows the new Struct data type to point to existing data buffers in memory, ensuring efficient memory usage.

Struct Methods

The Struct data type has the methods listed in Table 12-11:

Table 12-11. Methods for the Struct data type

Method	Description
`Expr.struct.field(…)`	Retrieve a Struct field as a new Series.
`Expr.struct.json_encode()`	Convert this Struct to a String column with JSON values.

Method	Description
Expr.struct.rename_fields(…)	Rename the fields of the Struct.
Expr.struct.unnest()	Expand the Struct into its individual fields.
Expr.struct.with_fields(…)	Add or overwrite fields of this Struct.

Struct Examples

To play around with Structs, you have to make them first. There are a number of methods that return Structs, or you can create them by constructing a DataFrame using a dictionary:

```
from datetime import date

orders = pl.DataFrame(
    {
        "customer_id": [2781, 6139, 5392],
        "order_details": [
            {"amount": 250.00, "date": date(2024, 1, 3), "items": 5},
            {"amount": 150.00, "date": date(2024, 1, 5), "items": 1},
            {"amount": 100.00, "date": date(2024, 1, 2), "items": 3},
        ],
    },
)

orders
```

```
shape: (3, 2)
┌─────────────┬──────────────────────┐
│ customer_id │ order_details        │
│ ---         │ ---                  │
│ i64         │ struct[3]            │
╞═════════════╪══════════════════════╡
│ 2781        │ {250.0,2024-01-03,5} │
│ 6139        │ {150.0,2024-01-05,1} │
│ 5392        │ {100.0,2024-01-02,3} │
└─────────────┴──────────────────────┘
```

One Struct to Store Them All

As you can see in the preceding example, the Struct is created by providing a list of Python dictionaries. However, because of Polars' columnar storage, Structs are stored as a dictionary of lists. (Figure 12-1 also illustrates this.)

You can retrieve values from a Struct using the `Expr.struct.field()` method:

```
orders.select(pl.col("order_details").struct.field("amount"))
```

```
shape: (3, 1)
┌────────┐
│ amount │
│ ---    │
│ f64    │
╞════════╡
│ 250.0  │
│ 150.0  │
│ 100.0  │
└────────┘
```

To return multiple columns, you can use the `df.unnest()` method on the DataFrame, or `Expr.struct.unnest()` on the column of an expression:

```
order_details_df = orders.unnest("order_details")
```

```
order_details_df
```

```
shape: (3, 4)
┌─────────────┬────────┬────────────┬───────┐
│ customer_id │ amount │ date       │ items │
│ ---         │ ---    │ ---        │ ---   │
│ i64         │ f64    │ date       │ i64   │
╞═════════════╪════════╪════════════╪═══════╡
│ 2781        │ 250.0  │ 2024-01-03 │ 5     │
│ 6139        │ 150.0  │ 2024-01-05 │ 1     │
│ 5392        │ 100.0  │ 2024-01-02 │ 3     │
└─────────────┴────────┴────────────┴───────┘
```

> **Unnest and Fields**
>
> `Expr.struct.unnest()` is effectively the same as `Expr.struct.field("*")`.

If you want to do the opposite and combine multiple columns, turn them into a Struct:

```
order_details_df.select(
    "amount",
    "date",
    "items",
    order_details=pl.struct(pl.col("amount"), pl.col("date"), pl.col("items")),
)
```

```
shape: (3, 4)
┌────────┬──────┬───────┬───────────────┐
│ amount │ date │ items │ order_details │
│ ---    │ ---  │ ---   │ ---           │
```

```
| f64   | date       | i64 | struct[3]                |
|=======|============|=====|==========================|
| 250.0 | 2024-01-03 | 5   | {250.0,2024-01-03,5}     |
| 150.0 | 2024-01-05 | 1   | {150.0,2024-01-05,1}     |
| 100.0 | 2024-01-02 | 3   | {100.0,2024-01-02,3}     |
```

One common method that returns a Struct is `Expr.value_counts()`. This method is used to count the occurrences of unique values in a Series. The `Expr.value_counts()` method returns a Struct column with two fields: the original column name being counted and `count`.

First, create a DataFrame with a Struct column:

```
basket = pl.DataFrame(
    {
        "fruit": ["cherry", "apple", "banana", "banana", "apple", "banana"],
    }
)

basket
```

```
shape: (6, 1)
┌────────┐
│ fruit  │
│ ---    │
│ str    │
╞════════╡
│ cherry │
│ apple  │
│ banana │
│ banana │
│ apple  │
│ banana │
└────────┘
```

You can count the number of occurrences per unique element in the `fruit` column using the `Expr.value_counts()` method:

```
basket.select(pl.col("fruit").value_counts(sort=True))
```

```
shape: (3, 1)
┌──────────────┐
│ fruit        │
│ ---          │
│ struct[2]    │
╞══════════════╡
│ {"banana",3} │
│ {"apple",2}  │
│ {"cherry",1} │
└──────────────┘
```

In the resulting DataFrame, you can see that the `Expr.value_counts()` method is called with the `sort` argument set to `True`. This means that the values are sorted in descending order by their counts.

You can then unnest this Struct directly by applying `Expr.struct.unnest()`:

```
basket.select(pl.col("fruit").value_counts(sort=True).struct.unnest())
```

```
shape: (3, 2)
┌────────┬───────┐
│ fruit  │ count │
│ ---    │ ---   │
│ str    │ u32   │
╞════════╪═══════╡
│ banana │ 3     │
│ apple  │ 2     │
│ cherry │ 1     │
└────────┴───────┘
```

In the resulting DataFrame, you can see that the Series returned by the `Expr.value_counts()` method has been unnested into separate columns.

Takeaways

This chapter covered data types in Polars that have their own namespaces and how to work with them. You learned about:

- Strings, with a focus on optimizing for variable length using an optimized memory layout
- Categoricals' and Enums' memory-efficient way of working with repeated Strings
- How temporal data types Date, Datetime, Time, and Duration address the challenges of working with time-based information
- How nested data types List, Array, and Struct allow you to store sequences and nested data in a single column

With these data types, you can work with a wide variety of data using the rich set of methods Polars provides to work with them. In the next chapter, you'll learn how to summarize and aggregate data.

## CHAPTER 13

Summarizing and Aggregating

Summarizing and aggregating data is a crucial step to transforming raw datasets into meaningful insights. Whether you're working with sales data, customer information, or sensor readings, the ability to group and aggregate your data allows you to answer important questions and identify trends that might otherwise be hidden.

You'll often find yourself asking questions like:

- "What is the average sales revenue per store?"
- "How many unique products did each customer purchase?"
- "What is the total expenditure by product category each month?"

These are exactly the types of questions that aggregation helps you answer. By grouping your data based on one or more columns and then performing calculations—such as sums, averages, or counts—you can gain a clearer understanding of the underlying patterns in your dataset.

Polars makes this process simple and efficient with the `df.group_by()` method, which allows you to group your DataFrame by one or more columns and expressions. Once you've grouped the data, you can apply a variety of aggregation functions to summarize the results. For example, you can calculate the sum, mean, or median for each group, or count the number of rows in each group.

In this chapter, you'll learn about:

- The GroupBy context and its available methods, and how to use them to analyze your data
- Working with grouping data based on temporal values using the methods `df.group_by_dynamic()`, `df.rolling()`, and `Expr.over()`

- Optimizations you can use to improve performance

The instructions to get any files you might need are in Chapter 2. We assume that you have the files in the *data* subdirectory.

Split, Apply, and Combine

At the heart of grouping and aggregation is a concept known as *split, apply, and combine*. This is a powerful strategy for performing operations on groups of data. Here's how it works:

Split
First, you split your data into groups based on the column or columns you want to group by.

Apply
Then, you apply an aggregation function (like sum, mean, or count) to each group.

Combine
Finally, the results of the aggregation are combined into a new DataFrame.

This process allows you to efficiently perform operations on large datasets and obtain meaningful summaries from them.

In the next section, we'll dive into how to use the `df.group_by()` method to perform these operations in Polars, providing practical examples along the way.

GroupBy Context

The `df.group_by()` method determines how the DataFrame is split into groups. Consider the following example:

```
fruit = pl.read_csv("data/fruit.csv")
fruit_grouped = fruit.group_by("is_round")
fruit_grouped

<polars.dataframe.group_by.GroupBy at 0x129732240>
```

As you can see, the DataFrame isn't actually split just yet. The object `fruit_grouped` is a so-called *GroupBy context*. It's essentially a description of how to split the DataFrame, and it accepts one of the methods listed in Table 13-1. When calling one of these methods, the calculation is applied per group, and the groups are combined into a DataFrame. For example, to count the number of round and nonround fruit:

```
fruit_grouped.len()

shape: (2, 2)
┌─────────┬─────────┐
```

```
| is_round | len |
| ---      | --- |
| bool     | u32 |
| false    | 6   |
| true     | 4   |
```

The result is a DataFrame with two rows, because there were two unique values in the
is_round column. Table 13-1 lists the available methods for the GroupBy context.

Table 13-1. The available methods in the GroupBy context

Method	Description
GroupBy.__iter__()	Allows iteration over the groups (sub-DataFrames) of the group_by operation.
GroupBy.agg(…)	Compute aggregations for each group (sub-DataFrame) of a group_by operation.
GroupBy.all()	Aggregate the groups into a Series.
GroupBy.count()	Return the number of rows in each group.
GroupBy.first()	Aggregate the first values in the group.
GroupBy.head(…)	Get the first *n* rows of each group.
GroupBy.last()	Aggregate the last values in the group.
GroupBy.len(…)	Return the number of rows in each group.
GroupBy.map_groups(…)	Apply a custom/user-defined function (UDF) over the groups as a sub-DataFrame.
GroupBy.max()	Reduce the groups to the maximal value.
GroupBy.mean()	Reduce the groups to the mean values.
GroupBy.median()	Return the median per group.
GroupBy.min()	Reduce the groups to the minimal value.
GroupBy.n_unique()	Count the unique values per group.
GroupBy.quantile(…)	Compute the quantile per group.
GroupBy.sum()	Reduce the groups to the sum.
GroupBy.tail(…)	Get the last *n* rows of each group.

To further showcase the df.group_by() method, let's start by loading the Top2000
dataset you previously encountered in Chapter 6. Just to refresh your memory, this
dataset contains information about the top two thousand songs of all times as chosen
by the Dutch in 2023, including their position in the Top2000, the artist, song title,
and year of release.

```
top2000 = pl.read_excel(
    "data/top2000-2023.xlsx", read_options={"skip_rows": 1}
).set_sorted("positie")
```

All Right Then, Don't Keep Your Secrets

Here we use the `df.set_sorted()` method to let Polars know that the `positie` column is already sorted. This is information we know, but Polars doesn't. By telling Polars this, it can make use of some *fast path optimizations* that are only possible when it knows the data is sorted. A fast path optimization is a way to make a program run faster by taking advantage of some special knowledge about the data.

It's important to know that if this is set wrong, Polars may make false assumptions about the data and deliver incorrect results.

You can show the values the `df.group_by()` aggregation methods are applied to by turning the groups into Lists, which you can do by running the following code:

```
(
    top2000.group_by("jaar")
    .agg(  ❶
        songs=pl.concat_str(
            pl.col("artiest"), pl.lit(" - "), pl.col("titel")
        ),  ❷
    )
    .sort("jaar", descending=True)
)
```

❶ The `GroupBy.agg()` method allows you to list the aggregations you want to apply to the group data. We will come back to this after going over the standard `df.group_by()` aggregations.

❷ You create a list of song titles by concatenating the strings of the artist, a separating dash, and then the title.

```
shape: (67, 2)
┌──────┬─────────────────────────────────────────┐
│ jaar │ songs                                   │
│ ---  │ ---                                     │
│ i64  │ list[str]                               │
╞══════╪═════════════════════════════════════════╡
│ 2022 │ ["Son Mieux - Multicolor", "Bankzitters - Je Blik …  │
│ 2021 │ ["Goldband - Noodgeval", "Bankzitters - Stapelgek"…  │
│ 2020 │ ["DI-RECT - Soldier On", "Miss Montreal - Door De …  │
│ 2019 │ ["Danny Vera - Roller Coaster", "Floor Jansen & He…  │
│ 2018 │ ["Lady Gaga & Bradley Cooper - Shallow", "White Li… │
│ …    │ …                                       │
│ 1960 │ ["Etta James - At Last", "Shadows - Apache"]         │
│ 1959 │ ["Jacques Brel - Ne Me Quitte Pas", "Elvis Presley…  │
│ 1958 │ ["Chuck Berry - Johnny B. Goode", "Ella Fitzgerald… │
│ 1957 │ ["Johnny Cash - I Walk The Line", "Elvis Presley -… │
└──────┴─────────────────────────────────────────┘
```

```
| 1956 | ["Elvis Presley - Love Me Tender", "Elvis Presley … |
```

Here, using `df.group_by()` we can group the songs into a List per year of release.

The Descriptives

In the following example, you'll get the top three songs per year of release for the three most recent years of release, using the `GroupBy.head()` method:

```
(
    top2000.group_by("jaar", maintain_order=True)  ❶
    .head(3)  ❷
    .sort("jaar", descending=True)
    .head(9)  ❸
)
```

❶ The Top2000 dataset is sorted by position, and since you are using this sort order, you want to maintain it. By setting the `maintain_order` argument to `True`, you make sure to preserve that order. When set to `False`, its default value, this order can be lost because of the parallel processing of groups.

❷ You want to get the top three songs per year of release, so use the `GroupBy.head()` method. This `GroupBy.head(3)` method is applied to the GroupBy context, which means it will return the first three songs per group.

❸ You use the `df.head(9)` method again, but this time to get the top three songs per year of release for the three most recent years of release, because it's a DataFrame method, instead of a GroupBy context method.

```
shape: (9, 4)
```

jaar	positie	titel	artiest
i64	i64	str	str
2022	179	Multicolor	Son Mieux
2022	370	Je Blik Richting Mij	Bankzitters
2022	395	L'enfer	Stromae
2021	55	Noodgeval	Goldband
2021	149	Stapelgek	Bankzitters
2021	210	Dat Heb Jij Gedaan	Meau
2020	19	Soldier On	DI-RECT
2020	38	Door De Wind	Miss Montreal
2020	77	Impossible (Orchestr…	Nothing But Thieves

In the same vein, you can get the lowest three positions per year of release for the three most recent years of release, using the `GroupBy.tail()` method.

```
(
    top2000.group_by("jaar", maintain_order=True)
    .tail(3)
    .sort("jaar", descending=True)
    .head(9)
)
```

shape: (9, 4)

jaar	positie	titel	artiest
i64	i64	str	str
2022	1391	De Diepte	S10
2022	1688	Zeit	Rammstein
2022	1716	THE LONELIEST	Måneskin
2021	1865	Bon Gepakt	Donnie & Rene Froger
2021	1978	Hold On	Armin van Buuren ft.…
2021	2000	Drivers License	Olivia Rodrigo
2020	1824	Smoorverliefd	Snelle
2020	1879	The Business	Tiësto
2020	1902	Levitating	Dua Lipa ft. DaBaby

Heads or Tails

The GroupBy.first() method is the same as the GroupBy.head(1) method, but it's more explicit and easier to read. The GroupBy.last() method is also the same as the GroupBy.tail(1) method.

Now, say you want to know the top 10 artists based on the number of songs in the Top2000. You can accomplish this by grouping the data by artist and then getting the length of the groups using the GroupBy.len() method:

```
(top2000.group_by("artiest").len().sort("len", descending=True).head(10))
```

shape: (10, 2)

artiest	len
str	u32
Queen	34
The Beatles	31
ABBA	25
Bruce Springsteen	22
The Rolling Stones	22
Coldplay	20
Fleetwood Mac	20
Michael Jackson	20

```
| David Bowie         | 18 |
| U2                  | 18 |
```

Looks like Dutch people really like Queen, The Beatles, and ABBA.

The next methods are better explained with a different dataset. This dataset contains sales data which allows us to showcase all kinds of analyses:

```
sales = pl.read_csv("data/sales.csv")
sales.columns

['Date',
 'Day',
 'Month',
 'Year',
 'Customer_Age',
 'Age_Group',
 'Customer_Gender',
 'Country',
 'State',
 'Product_Category',
 'Sub_Category',
 'Product',
 'Order_Quantity',
 'Unit_Cost',
 'Unit_Price',
 'Profit',
 'Cost',
 'Revenue']
```

Let's kick it off by demonstrating the GroupBy.min() and GroupBy.max() methods. Say you want to know the most expensive category and subcategory. You can accomplish this by grouping the data by product category and subcategory, and then getting the maximum unit price using the GroupBy.max() method:

```
(
    sales.select("Product_Category", "Sub_Category", "Unit_Price")  ❶
    .group_by("Product_Category", "Sub_Category")  ❷
    .max()
    .sort("Unit_Price", descending=True)  ❸
    .head(10)
)
```

❶ You select the relevant columns so you can focus on the data you need.

❷ You group the data by the product category and subcategory. Unlike the previous examples, you group by two columns. This means that the GroupBy.max() method will return the maximum unit price for each combination of product category and subcategory.

❸ You sort the data by unit price in descending order and get the top 10 most expensive subcategories.

shape: (10, 3)

Product_Category	Sub_Category	Unit_Price
str	str	i64
Bikes	Road Bikes	3578
Bikes	Mountain Bikes	3400
Bikes	Touring Bikes	2384
Clothing	Vests	2384
Accessories	Bike Stands	159
Accessories	Bike Racks	120
Clothing	Shorts	70
Clothing	Socks	70
Accessories	Hydration Packs	55
Clothing	Jerseys	54

Now, let's say you want to know the total profit per country. You can accomplish this by grouping the data by country, then getting the sum of the profit using the GroupBy.sum() method:

```
(
    sales.select("Country", "Profit")
    .group_by("Country")
    .sum()
    .sort("Profit", descending=True)
)
```

shape: (6, 2)

Country	Profit
str	i64
United States	11073644
Australia	6776030
United Kingdom	4413853
Canada	3717296
Germany	3359995
France	2880282

How about the subcategories with the most unique products? You can accomplish this by grouping the data by subcategory and then getting the number of unique products using the GroupBy.n_unique() method:

```
(
    sales.select("Sub_Category", "Product")
```

```
    .group_by("Sub_Category")
    .n_unique()
    .sort("Product", descending=True)
    .head(10)
)
```

shape: (10, 2)

Sub_Category	Product
str	u32
Road Bikes	38
Mountain Bikes	28
Touring Bikes	22
Tires and Tubes	11
Jerseys	8
Gloves	4
Vests	4
Bottles and Cages	3
Helmets	3
Shorts	3

Say you want to know the average order quantity per age group. You can accomplish this by grouping the data by age group and then getting the mean of the order quantity using the GroupBy.mean() method:

```
(
    sales.select("Age_Group", "Order_Quantity")
    .group_by("Age_Group")
    .mean()
    .sort("Order_Quantity", descending=True)
)
```

shape: (4, 2)

Age_Group	Order_Quantity
str	f64
Seniors (64+)	13.530137
Youth (<25)	12.124018
Adults (35-64)	12.045303
Young Adults (25-34)	11.560899

Additionally, you can use the GroupBy.quantile() method to get specific percentiles of the order quantity per age group:

```
(
    sales.select("Age_Group", "Revenue")
    .group_by("Age_Group")
    .quantile(0.9)
```

```
    .sort("Revenue", descending=True)
)

shape: (4, 2)
┌─────────────────────┬─────────┐
│ Age_Group           │ Revenue │
│ ---                 │ ---     │
│ str                 │ f64     │
╞═════════════════════╪═════════╡
│ Young Adults (25-34)│ 2227.0  │
│ Adults (35-64)      │ 2217.0  │
│ Youth (<25)         │ 1997.0  │
│ Seniors (64+)       │ 943.0   │
└─────────────────────┴─────────┘
```

It seems like the young urban professionals are at it again. In the Netherlands, the young urban professionals, known as *Yuppies*, are often associated with high income and high spending. Apparently, Yuppies are spending a lot on orders, with the 90th percentile of their order quantity being 2,227.

Another method is the GroupBy.median() method, which is an alias to GroupBy.quantile(0.5).

Now that we've seen the basic aggregations available in the GroupBy context, it's time to get weird with it and move on to the advanced stuff.

Advanced Methods

All the methods we've discussed so far are great for simple aggregations. However, sometimes you want to do more complex aggregations, do multiple aggregations at the same time, or even apply your own custom aggregation functions. This is where the multifunctional GroupBy.agg() method comes in, which allows you to:

- Aggregate column elements into a List per group
- Control what the resulting column names will be
- Use expressions to apply multiple aggregation functions at the same time, and to multiple columns
- Apply your own custom aggregation functions through expressions

Let's go through these one by one.

Aggregate values to a List

First, GroupBy.agg() allows you to aggregate column elements into a List per group. This is done by passing a column selector to the GroupBy.agg() method. Let's see how by aggregating the profit and revenue per country:

```
(
    sales.select("Country", "Profit", "Revenue")
    .group_by("Country")
    .agg(
        pl.col("Profit"),
        pl.col("Revenue"),
    )
)
```

shape: (6, 3)

Country	Profit	Revenue
str	list[i64]	list[i64]
Canada	[590, 590, … 630]	[950, 950, … 1014]
Australia	[1366, 1188, … 655]	[2401, 2088, … 1183]
United States	[524, 407, … 542]	[929, 722, … 878]
Germany	[160, 53, … 746]	[295, 98, … 1250]
France	[427, 427, … 655]	[787, 787, … 1207]
United Kingdom	[1053, 1053, … 112]	[1728, 1728, … 184]

Gathering results like this is the first step of the aggregation process and is normally followed by applying a function to these values.

Rename aggregated columns

The second thing you can do with the GroupBy.agg() method is name the resulting columns. This can be done using the Expr.alias() method, using the keyword syntax, or through the name namespace. You can refer to Table 7-2 in Chapter 7 for more information on the name namespace.

```
(
    sales.group_by("Country").agg(
        pl.col("Profit").alias("All Profits Per Transactions"),
        pl.col("Revenue").name.prefix("All "),
        Cost=pl.col("Revenue") - pl.col("Profit"),
    )
)
```

shape: (6, 4)

Country	All Profits Per Tran…	All Revenue	Cost
str	list[i64]	list[i64]	list[i64]
Canada	[590, 590, … 630]	[950, 950, … 1014]	[360, 360, … 384]
Australia	[1366, 1188, … 655]	[2401, 2088, … 1183]	[1035, 900, … 528]
United States	[524, 407, … 542]	[929, 722, … 878]	[405, 315, … 336]

Germany	[160, 53, … 746]	[295, 98, … 1250]	[135, 45, … 504]
France	[427, 427, … 655]	[787, 787, … 1207]	[360, 360, … 552]
United Kingdom	[1053, 1053, … 112]	[1728, 1728, … 184]	[675, 675, … 72]

Apply multiple aggregations at once

Third, GroupBy.agg() allows you to apply multiple aggregation functions at the same time, including multiple columns. You can do this by passing a list of expressions to the GroupBy.agg() method:

```
(
    sales.select("Country", "Profit", "Revenue")
    .group_by("Country")
    .agg(
        pl.col("Profit").sum().name.prefix("Total "),
        pl.col("Profit").mean().alias("Average Profit per Transaction"),
        pl.col("Revenue").sum().name.prefix("Total "),
        pl.col("Revenue").mean().alias("Average Revenue per Transaction"),
    )
)
```

shape: (6, 5)

Country	Total Profit	Average Profit per T…	Total Revenue	Average Revenue per …
---	---	---	---	---
str	i64	---	i64	---
		f64		f64
Canada	3717296	262.187615	7935738	559.721964
Australia	6776030	283.089489	21302059	889.959016
United States	11073644	282.447687	27975547	713.552696
Germany	3359995	302.756803	8978596	809.028293
France	2880282	261.891435	8432872	766.764139
United Kingdom	4413853	324.071439	10646196	781.659031

Alternatively, you can use column selectors in combination with these expressions to apply an aggregation function to multiple columns at the same time in a single expression:

```
(
    sales.select("Country", "Profit", "Revenue")
    .group_by("Country")
    .agg(
        pl.all().sum().name.prefix("Total "),
        pl.all().mean().name.prefix("Average "),
    )
)
```

```
shape: (6, 5)
```

Country	Total Profit	Total Revenue	Average Profit	Average Revenue
str	i64	i64	f64	f64
Canada	3717296	7935738	262.187615	559.721964
Australia	6776030	21302059	283.089489	889.959016
United States	11073644	27975547	282.447687	713.552696
Germany	3359995	8978596	302.756803	809.028293
France	2880282	8432872	261.891435	766.764139
United Kingdom	4413853	10646196	324.071439	781.659031

When you're using expressions, it's even possible to work with comparisons. The comparison returns a Boolean Series, marking the rows for which the comparison holds with True and the rows that don't with False. A common trick is to use the GroupBy.sum() method to sum the Boolean Series. This is possible because True is interpreted as a 1, and False as a 0. Essentially, you are counting the number of rows for which the comparison holds.

For example, we can find the number of transactions with a large profit, grouped by country, by running the following example. To show what the Boolean Series of the expression looks like, you can only aggregate using the expression. This creates a list of Boolean values:

```
(
    sales.select("Country", "Profit")
    .group_by("Country")
    .agg(
        (pl.col("Profit") > 1000).alias("Profit > 1000"),
        (pl.col("Profit") > 1000)
        .sum()
        .alias("Transactions with Profit > 1000"),
    )
)
```

```
shape: (6, 3)
```

Country	Profit > 1000	Transactions with Profit > 1000
str	list[bool]	u32
Canada	[false, false, … false]	868
Australia	[true, true, … false]	1233
United States	[false, false, … false]	2623
Germany	[false, false, … false]	659
France	[false, false, … false]	482
United Kingdom	[true, true, … false]	788

Because you can use expressions in the `GroupBy.agg()` method, you can also put in Python functions that return expressions. While you should normally only combine Polars and Python when absolutely necessary, this is one of the exceptions. This is because the Python function runs before Polars does and returns a Polars expression, which Polars then runs in Rust.

In the following example, you define a Python function that creates an expression resulting in two expressions. It creates one expression that shows the condition that is built from the input: a specified column and a threshold that the column is evaluated on. After that, it creates another expression where it sums the transactions of the sales where the condition is `True`:

```python
def sum_transactions_above_threshold(
    col: pl.Expr, threshold: float
) -> tuple[pl.Expr, pl.Expr]:
    """Sums transactions where the column col exceeds specified threshold"""
    original_column_name = col.meta.root_names()[0]  ❶
    condition_column = (col > threshold).alias(
        f"{original_column_name} > {threshold}"
    )
    new_column = (
        (col > threshold)
        .sum()
        .alias(f"Transactions with {original_column_name} > {threshold}")
    )
    return condition_column, new_column


sales.select("Country", "Profit").group_by("Country").agg(
    sum_transactions_above_threshold(pl.col("Profit"), 999)
)
```

❶ The `meta.root_names()` method returns the names of the columns from which the expression originates.

```
shape: (6, 3)
```

Country	Profit > 999	Transactions with Profit > 999
str	list[bool]	u32
Canada	[false, false, … false]	868
Australia	[true, true, … false]	1233
United States	[false, false, … false]	2623
Germany	[false, false, … false]	659
France	[false, false, … false]	482
United Kingdom	[true, true, … false]	788

Allowing custom expressions like this shows the versatility of the `GroupBy.agg()` method, and it is something that truly sets Polars apart from other packages.

There are also ways to apply Python functions to your data. Since this is a more advanced feature, we'll dive into that in Chapter 17.

Row-Wise Aggregations

Polars provides a lot of standard horizontal aggregations out of the box. These expressions are shown in Table 9-5. Two methods that allow you to build more complex horizontal aggregations are `pl.reduce()` and `pl.fold()`. These methods operate on a whole Series at the same time, often in a vectorized manner, keeping it performant.

Here's how `pl.reduce()` and `pl.fold()` work. First, they create a new column called the *accumulator*. This accumulator is a new column with initial values to which the aggregation is applied. The other input is the value resulting from the expression that is being aggregated over. This accumulator is updated with the result of a function that gets as input the accumulator and that value.

Both `pl.reduce()` and `pl.fold()` accept the arguments listed in Table 13-2.

Table 13-2. Arguments for the functions pl.reduce() and pl.fold()

Argument	Description
function	The function to apply over the accumulator and the value that gets folded.
exprs	The expressions to aggregate over.

In addition, the `pl.fold()` function allows you to set an initial value for the accumulator with the `acc` argument, whereas `pl.reduce()` uses the first value it comes across as the accumulator. Let's look at an example to understand how `pl.fold()` works:

```
fold_example = pl.DataFrame({"col1": [2], "col2": [3], "col3": [4]})

fold_example.with_columns(
    sum=pl.fold(
        acc=pl.lit(0),  ❶
        function=lambda acc, x: acc + x,  ❷
        exprs=pl.col("*"),  ❸
    )
)
```

❶ Because you are summing the values of the columns, you set the initial value of the accumulator to 0. Using the `pl.reduce()` method would have set the accumulator to the first value in the column.

❷ This lambda function sums. The value in the accumulator column is added to the value in the next column you are aggregating over.

❸ Since `pl.col("*")` functions as a wildcard representing any column, you are aggregating over all columns in the DataFrame without changing them in any way.

```
shape: (1, 4)
```

col1	col2	col3	sum
i64	i64	i64	i64
2	3	4	9

The execution would look like Figure 13-1:

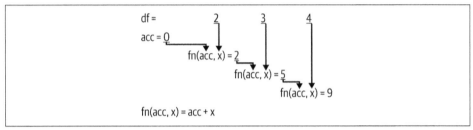

Figure 13-1. How a fold function is executed

One possible use case for `pl.fold()` is when you want to sum with weights per column. For example, you have a DataFrame with sales data for different products, and you want to calculate the weighted sum of the sales:

```python
products = pl.DataFrame(
    {
        "product_A": [10, 20, 30],
        "product_B": [20, 30, 40],
        "product_C": [30, 40, 50],
    }
)

weights = {"product_A": 0.5, "product_B": 1.5, "product_C": 2.0}  ❶

weighted_exprs = [  ❷
    (pl.col(product) * weight).alias(product)
    for product, weight in weights.items()
]

products_with_weighted_sum = products.with_columns(
    weighted_sum=pl.fold(  ❸
        acc=pl.lit(0),  ❹
```

```
            function=lambda acc, x: acc + x,  ❺
            exprs=weighted_exprs,  ❻
        )
    )

    products_with_weighted_sum
```

❶ Define weights for each product.

❷ Create a Polars expression that multiplies each column by its respective weight.

❸ Apply the fold function to calculate the weighted sum.

❹ Start with an initial value of 0 for the accumulator.

❺ Once again, use a summing function.

❻ Apply the weighted expressions to the fold function.

```
shape: (3, 4)
┌───────────┬───────────┬───────────┬──────────────┐
│ product_A │ product_B │ product_C │ weighted_sum │
│ ---       │ ---       │ ---       │ ---          │
│ i64       │ i64       │ i64       │ f64          │
╞═══════════╪═══════════╪═══════════╪══════════════╡
│ 10        │ 20        │ 30        │ 95.0         │
│ 20        │ 30        │ 40        │ 135.0        │
│ 30        │ 40        │ 50        │ 175.0        │
└───────────┴───────────┴───────────┴──────────────┘
```

Window Functions in Selection Context

Sometimes, instead of aggregating data into groups, you want to add information to the DataFrame. This is where Expr.over() comes in. The Expr.over() method allows you to perform aggregations on groups in the select context. Additionally, it allows you to map the results back to the original DataFrame, keeping its original dimensions. This is practical when you need the context of individual rows and want to enrich it with information from the group. The Expr.over() method has the following arguments:

Table 13-3. Arguments for the method Expr.over()

Argument	Description
partition_by	Column(s) to group by. Accepts expression input. Strings are parsed as column names.
*more_exprs	Additional columns to group by, specified as positional arguments.

Argument	Description
order_by	Order the window functions/aggregations with the partitioned groups by the result of the expression passed to order_by.
mapping_strategy	• group_to_rows: If the aggregation results in multiple values, assign them back to their position in the DataFrame. This can only be done if the group yields the same elements before aggregation as after. • join: Join the groups as *List<group_dtype>* to the row positions. Warning: this can be memory intensive. • explode: Explodes the grouped data into new rows, similar to the results of df.group_by(), df.agg(), and df.explode(). Sorting of the given groups is required if the groups are not part of the window operation for the operation, otherwise the result would not make sense. This operation changes the number of rows.

Let's return to the Top2000 dataset from the beginning of this chapter. If you want to add information to the DataFrame instead of aggregating results for an analysis, you can use the Expr.over() method. For example, let's try calculating the position of a song for its release year:

```
(
    top2000.select(
        "jaar",
        "artiest",
        "titel",
        "positie",
        year_rank=pl.col("positie").rank().over("jaar"),
    ).sample(10, seed=42)
)
```

shape: (10, 5)

jaar	artiest	titel	positie	year_rank
i64	str	str	i64	f64
2013	Stromae	Papaoutai	318	6.0
1969	John Denver	Leaving On A Jet Pla…	607	16.0
1971	Led Zeppelin	Immigrant Song	590	19.0
2009	Anouk	For Bitter Or Worse	1453	23.0
2015	Snollebollekes	Links Rechts	1076	14.0
1984	Alphaville	Forever Young	302	11.0
1977	ABBA	Take A Chance On Me	636	23.0
1975	Rod Stewart	Sailing	918	20.0
1986	Metallica	Master Of Puppets	29	1.0
2005	Alderliefste & Ramse…	Laat Me/Vivre	463	5.0

Here we can see that Stromae's "Papaoutai" was ranked 6th best song in 2013 according to Top2000 voters, while it was ranked 318th overall.

Dynamic Grouping

When you're working with temporal data, it can be practical to create groups based on a time window. This is where the df.group_by_dynamic() method comes in. This method calculates a time window of a fixed step size and length, to which it assigns the rows in your DataFrame. This is different from a normal df.group_by(), because rows can occur in multiple time windows, depending on the window steps' size and length. This is useful for calculating yearly or quarterly sales data, where you want to divide data into specific time periods. Table 13-4 lists the arguments for the df.group_by_dynamic() method.

Table 13-4. Arguments for the method df.group_by_dynamic()

Argument	Description
every	The interval at which the windows start.
offset	Used to shift the start of the window. For example, if you want to start our time window at 9 a.m. every day to align with business hours, you can set every=1d, and offset=9h.
period	The length of the time window. It matches every if not specified, resulting in adjacent, nonoverlapping groups. However, if you want to create overlapping windows, you can set period to a value larger than every.
start_by	Sets the strategy for determining the start of the first window, allowing you to align the start with the earliest data point, with a specific day of the week, or by adjusting to the earliest timestamp and then applying an offset based on your specified every interval.

The every, period, and offset arguments can be specified using the Strings listed in Table 13-5:

Table 13-5. Duration Strings and their meaning

Duration string	Description
1ns	1 nanosecond
1us	1 microsecond
1ms	1 millisecond
1s	1 second
1m	1 minute
1h	1 hour
1d	1 calendar day
1w	1 calendar week
1mo	1 calendar month
1q	1 calendar quarter
1y	1 calendar year
1i	1 index count

These can also be combined. For example: "1y6m1w5d" would be 1 year, 6 months, 1 week, and 5 days. With these settings you can create regular time windows and group your data into them. There are three types of window configurations you can create, as shown in Figure 13-2.

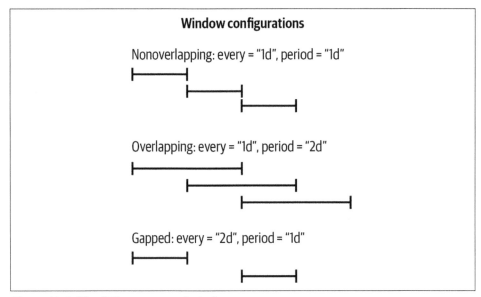

Figure 13-2. The different types of windows

Additionally, the closed argument determines whether values that are exactly the lower or upper bound are included or excluded. The options provided are shown in Table 13-6.

Table 13-6. Possible values for the closed argument of the method df.group_by_dynamic()

Argument	Description	Interval	Contains a	Contains b
left	The lower bound is inclusive, the upper bound is exclusive.	[a, b)	✓	✗
right	The lower bound is exclusive, the upper bound is inclusive.	(a, b]	✗	✓
both	Both the lower and upper bounds are inclusive.	[a, b]	✓	✓
none	Both the lower and upper bounds are exclusive.	(a, b)	✗	✗

Rolling Aggregations

Where df.group_by_dynamic() creates time windows of fixed size and length, the df.rolling() method creates windows tailored around values in the DataFrame itself. This is useful when you want to calculate rolling aggregations, such as moving averages or cumulative sums. The df.rolling() method accepts the arguments listed in Table 13-7.

Table 13-7. Arguments for the method `df.rolling()`

Argument	Description
index_column	The column that contains values that will be used as the anchor point of the window.
period	The size of the window.
offset	Shifts the window backward or forward.
closed	Defines how boundary values are handled. Works exactly like explained earlier for `df.group_by_dynamic()`.
group_by	Groups the data by the specified columns before applying the rolling aggregation.

For a DataFrame with timestamps, the rolling operation will create a window for each timestamp that extends backwards by the specified `period`. If `offset` is set, it shifts the entire window forward or backward, offering a way to adjust the focus of the analysis. This is illustrated in Figure 13-3.

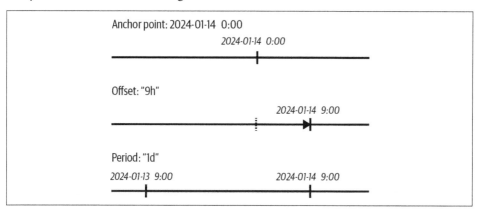

Figure 13-3. How a time window is determined using the `df.rolling()` method

The `group_by` argument allows you to perform rolling aggregation within groups of data.

Imagine you're analyzing a dataset from a chain of retail stores. You have sales data from multiple locations and want to understand the rolling average sales over a seven-day period for each store. This will help us identify trends, such as which stores are consistently performing well and which might be experiencing declines or variability in sales.

Let's create a small DataFrame with some random sales numbers. The DataFrame will contain two weeks of sales data for two stores that are only open on weekdays. You'll calculate the rolling sum of the last week of sales for each store:

```
dates = pl.date_range(   ❶
    start=pl.date(2024, 4, 1),
```

```
        end=pl.date(2024, 4, 26),
        interval="2d",
        eager=True,  ❷
    )
    dates = dates.filter(dates.dt.weekday() < 6)  ❸
    dates_repeated = pl.concat([dates, dates]).sort()  ❹

    small_sales_df = (
        pl.DataFrame(
            {
                "date": dates_repeated,
                "store": ["Store A", "Store B"] * dates.len(),
                "sales": [
                    200, 150, 220, 160, 250, 180, 270, 190, 280, 210,
                    210, 170, 220, 180, 240, 190, 250, 200, 260, 210,
                ],
            }
        )
        .set_sorted("date")  ❺
        .set_sorted("store")
    )
```

❶ Create a date range from April 1st to April 25th.

❷ The eager argument is set to True to create the date range immediately.

❸ Filter out weekend days.

❹ Repeat the dates for the two weeks and sort them.

❺ Indicate that the date and store columns are sorted.

Now that you have a nice dataset, you can calculate the rolling sum of the last seven days of sales for each store:

```
    result = small_sales_df.rolling(  ❶
        index_column="date",
        period="7d",
        group_by="store",
    ).agg(  ❷
        sum_of_last_7_days_sales=pl.sum("sales")
    )

    final_df = small_sales_df.join(result, on=["date", "store"])  ❸

    final_df
```

❶ The df.rolling() method creates windows that contain the current row and rows that are within seven days before the current row.

❷ Calculate the sum of the created time windows with the `df.rolling()` method.

❸ Join rolling results back to the original DataFrame.

```
shape: (20, 4)
┌────────────┬─────────┬───────┬─────────────────────────┐
│ date       │ store   │ sales │ sum_of_last_7_days_sales │
│ ---        │ ---     │ ---   │ ---                      │
│ date       │ str     │ i64   │ i64                      │
╞════════════╪═════════╪═══════╪═════════════════════════╡
│ 2024-04-01 │ Store A │ 200   │ 200                      │
│ 2024-04-03 │ Store A │ 220   │ 420                      │
│ 2024-04-05 │ Store A │ 250   │ 670                      │
│ 2024-04-09 │ Store A │ 270   │ 740                      │
│ 2024-04-11 │ Store A │ 280   │ 800                      │
│ 2024-04-15 │ Store A │ 210   │ 760                      │
│ 2024-04-17 │ Store A │ 220   │ 710                      │
│ 2024-04-19 │ Store A │ 240   │ 670                      │
│ 2024-04-23 │ Store A │ 250   │ 710                      │
│ 2024-04-25 │ Store A │ 260   │ 750                      │
│ 2024-04-01 │ Store B │ 150   │ 150                      │
│ 2024-04-03 │ Store B │ 160   │ 310                      │
│ 2024-04-05 │ Store B │ 180   │ 490                      │
│ 2024-04-09 │ Store B │ 190   │ 530                      │
│ 2024-04-11 │ Store B │ 210   │ 580                      │
│ 2024-04-15 │ Store B │ 170   │ 570                      │
│ 2024-04-17 │ Store B │ 180   │ 560                      │
│ 2024-04-19 │ Store B │ 190   │ 540                      │
│ 2024-04-23 │ Store B │ 200   │ 570                      │
│ 2024-04-25 │ Store B │ 210   │ 600                      │
└────────────┴─────────┴───────┴─────────────────────────┘
```

Here you see the rolling sum of the last seven days is calculated for each store. The first seven days have a rolling sum of only the days available before them in the dataset, because there are no more days to include in the window. This rolling aggregation allows you to see how the sales of each store are developing over time.

Upsampling

The opposite of an aggregation on temporal data is `df.upsample()`. In case the temporal resolution of your data is too coarse, you can use it to create more entries. Table 13-8 lists the arguments that the `df.upsample()` method accepts.

Table 13-8. Arguments for the method df.upsample()

Argument	Description
time_column	Time column will be used to determine a date_range. Note that this column has to be sorted for the output to make sense.
every	Interval will start every duration.

Argument	Description
group_by	First group by these columns and then upsample for every group.
maintain_order	Keep the ordering predictable. This is slower.

Our `small_sales_df` DataFrame from before only has data every other day. We can upsample it to daily as follows:

```
upsampled_small_sales_df = small_sales_df.upsample(
    time_column="date", every="1d", group_by="store", maintain_order=True
)
```

```
upsampled_small_sales_df
```

shape: (50, 3)

```
| date       | store   | sales |
| ---        | ---     | ---   |
| date       | str     | i64   |
| 2024-04-01 | Store A | 200   |
| 2024-04-02 | null    | null  |
| 2024-04-03 | Store A | 220   |
| 2024-04-04 | null    | null  |
| 2024-04-05 | Store A | 250   |
| 2024-04-06 | null    | null  |
| 2024-04-07 | null    | null  |
| 2024-04-08 | null    | null  |
| 2024-04-09 | Store A | 270   |
| 2024-04-10 | null    | null  |
| …          | …       | …     |
| 2024-04-16 | null    | null  |
| 2024-04-17 | Store B | 180   |
| 2024-04-18 | null    | null  |
| 2024-04-19 | Store B | 190   |
| 2024-04-20 | null    | null  |
| 2024-04-21 | null    | null  |
| 2024-04-22 | null    | null  |
| 2024-04-23 | Store B | 200   |
| 2024-04-24 | null    | null  |
| 2024-04-25 | Store B | 210   |
```

This creates new rows, but they still have missing values. These will have to be filled up by imputing the data. We go into detail on how to do this in Chapter 8. For this example, we will forward fill the stores and interpolate the sales:

```
upsampled_small_sales_df.select(
    "date", pl.col("store").forward_fill(), pl.col("sales").interpolate()
)
```

shape: (50, 3)

```
| date       | store   | sales |
| ---        | ---     | ---   |
| date       | str     | f64   |
|============|=========|=======|
| 2024-04-01 | Store A | 200.0 |
| 2024-04-02 | Store A | 210.0 |
| 2024-04-03 | Store A | 220.0 |
| 2024-04-04 | Store A | 235.0 |
| 2024-04-05 | Store A | 250.0 |
| 2024-04-06 | Store A | 255.0 |
| 2024-04-07 | Store A | 260.0 |
| 2024-04-08 | Store A | 265.0 |
| 2024-04-09 | Store A | 270.0 |
| 2024-04-10 | Store A | 275.0 |
| …          | …       | …     |
| 2024-04-16 | Store B | 175.0 |
| 2024-04-17 | Store B | 180.0 |
| 2024-04-18 | Store B | 185.0 |
| 2024-04-19 | Store B | 190.0 |
| 2024-04-20 | Store B | 192.5 |
| 2024-04-21 | Store B | 195.0 |
| 2024-04-22 | Store B | 197.5 |
| 2024-04-23 | Store B | 200.0 |
| 2024-04-24 | Store B | 205.0 |
| 2024-04-25 | Store B | 210.0 |
```

Like this, you can effectively upsample your temporal data and fill in missing values to create a more granular dataset.

Takeaways

In this chapter you learned how to perform aggregations on your data. You learned about:

- The basic aggregations available in the GroupBy context, such as sum(), mean(), quantile(), and median()

- The advanced aggregations available in the GroupBy.agg() method, which allow you to aggregate column elements into a list per group, control the resulting column names, and apply multiple aggregation functions at the same time

- Performing aggregations on groups in the select context using the Expr.over() method

- Creating groups based on a time window using the df.group_by_dynamic() method

- Creating rolling aggregations around the values in your DataFrame using the df.rolling() method

- How you can let Polars know if the data is already sorted using the `df.set_sorted()` method

- How to upsample your data using the `df.upsample()` method

In the next chapter you'll look at how you can combine multiple DataFrames using joins and unions.

## CHAPTER 14

Joining and Concatenating

Data often comes from multiple sources that you will have to connect and combine in a meaningful way. There are multiple ways to combine DataFrames, which we'll go over in this chapter.

Funnily enough, this is where Polars once started. Faced with combining two CSV files in Rust, Ritchie Vink started his journey which ultimately led to where we are now. This gives a special sentiment to the operations in this chapter.

In this chapter, you'll learn:

- That you can use `df.join()` to combine DataFrames based on the values in the DataFrames and the strategies outlined here

- That `df.join_asof()` is a special join that joins DataFrames based on the nearest value in the other DataFrame

- How to combine DataFrames using `pl.concat()`, `df.vstack()`, `df.hstack()`, and `df.extend()`

- How to combine Series with `series.append()`

- The differences between all these methods and when to use them

The instructions to get any files you might need are in Chapter 2. We assume that you have the files in the *data* subdirectory.

Joining

To combine different DataFrames, Polars offers the `df.join()` method. It takes the arguments listed in Table 14-1.

Table 14-1. Arguments for the method df.join()

Argument	Description
other	The DataFrame to join with.
on	The column to join on when the name is the same in the left and right DataFrames.
left_on and right_on	The columns to join if they have different names in the left and right DataFrames.
how	The join strategy to use.
suffix	The suffix which will be appended to the column that appears in both DataFrames.
validate	Validates that the join is of a certain type.
join_nulls	Joins null values. By default, null values are not joined.

Join Strategies

Joining can be done according to different strategies. Depending on your situation, you need to combine the two datasets in a different way. The strategies that the df.join() method supports are:

inner *(default)*
> Only keep rows that have a match in both DataFrames.

left
> Keep all rows from the left DataFrame and only the rows from the right DataFrame that have a match.

right
> Keep all rows from the right DataFrame and only the rows from the left DataFrame that have a match.

full
> Keep all rows from both DataFrames.

cross
> Create a *Cartesian product* of both DataFrames. The Cartesian product comes from set theory and represents the set of all possible combinations of the elements of two sets. You'll see an example of this later in this section.

semi
> Keep all rows from the left DataFrame that have a match in the right DataFrame.

anti
> Keep all rows from the left DataFrame that do not have a match in the right DataFrame.

Throughout this section you'll use the following DataFrames to demonstrate the different join strategies:

```
df_left = pl.DataFrame({"key": ["A", "B", "C", "D"], "value": [1, 2, 3, 4]})

df_right = pl.DataFrame({"key": ["B", "C", "D", "E"], "value": [5, 6, 7, 8]})
```

Inner

The default join strategy in Polars is the inner join. This join strategy only keeps rows
that have a match in both DataFrames, discarding any rows that do not. You'll see in
the following example that the row of the left DataFrame with the key A is not present
in the resulting DataFrame, as is the row of the right DataFrame with the key E. All
the other rows are there, as they have a match in both DataFrames:

```
df_left.join(df_right, on="key", how="inner")
```

shape: (3, 3)

key	value	value_right
str	i64	i64
B	2	5
C	3	6
D	4	7

Full

The full join strategy keeps all rows from both DataFrames, filling the missing
values with nulls. Additionally, you can change the default suffixes for columns with
duplicate names in the right DataFrame. In the following example, we'll change the
suffix to _other:

```
df_left.join(df_right, on="key", how="full", suffix="_other")
```

shape: (5, 4)

key	value	key_other	value_other
str	i64	str	i64
B	2	B	5
C	3	C	6
D	4	D	7
null	null	E	8
A	1	null	null

Left

The left join strategy keeps all rows from the left DataFrame and only the rows from
the right DataFrame that have a match, filling the missing values with nulls:

```
df_left.join(df_right, on="key", how="left")
```

shape: (4, 3)

key	value	value_right
str	i64	i64
A	1	null
B	2	5
C	3	6
D	4	7

Left Joins Preserve the Order

A left join preserves the row order of the left DataFrame.

Right

The right join strategy is the reverse of a left join. It keeps all the rows in the right DataFrame and matches the ones in the left DataFrame with it:

```
df_left.join(df_right, on="key", how="right")
```

shape: (4, 3)

value	key	value_right
i64	str	i64
2	B	5
3	C	6
4	D	7
null	E	8

Cross

The cross join strategy creates a Cartesian product of both DataFrames. This means that the resulting DataFrame will have a length equal to the length of the left DataFrame multiplied by the length of the right DataFrame, resulting in potentially huge DataFrames. The on argument is not needed for this join, as all rows will be joined with each other:

```
df_left.join(df_right, how="cross")
```

shape: (16, 4)

| key | value | key_right | value_right |

```
| --- | --- | --- | --- |
| str | i64 | str | i64 |

| A | 1 | B | 5 |
| A | 1 | C | 6 |
| A | 1 | D | 7 |
| A | 1 | E | 8 |
| B | 2 | B | 5 |
| ... | ... | ... | ... |
| C | 3 | E | 8 |
| D | 4 | B | 5 |
| D | 4 | C | 6 |
| D | 4 | D | 7 |
| D | 4 | E | 8 |
```

Semi

A `semi` join is a special join that doesn't add any data from the right DataFrame to the resulting DataFrame. Instead, it only keeps the rows from the left DataFrame that have a match in the right DataFrame. This makes the `semi` join one of the additional ways to filter the left DataFrame:

```
df_left.join(df_right, on="key", how="semi")
```

shape: (3, 2)

```
| key | value |
| --- | ---   |
| str | i64   |

| B   | 2     |
| C   | 3     |
| D   | 4     |
```

Anti

The `anti` join strategy is the opposite of the `semi` join. It only keeps the rows from the left DataFrame that do not have a match in the right DataFrame:

```
df_left.join(df_right, on="key", how="anti")
```

shape: (1, 2)

```
| key | value |
| --- | ---   |
| str | i64   |

| A   | 1     |
```

Joining on Multiple Columns

You can join DataFrames on multiple columns by passing a list of column names to the on argument. This will join the DataFrames on all the columns in the list.

To try this, you'll need two DataFrames with more columns. For this example, you'll use the following example DataFrames. In these DataFrames, you'll join on the name and city columns:

```
residences_left = pl.DataFrame(
    {
        "name": ["Alice", "Bob", "Charlie", "Dave"],
        "city": ["NY", "LA", "NY", "SF"],
        "age": [25, 30, 35, 40],
    }
)

departments_right = pl.DataFrame(
    {
        "name": ["Alice", "Bob", "Charlie", "Dave"],
        "city": ["NY", "LA", "NY", "Chicago"],
        "department": ["Finance", "Marketing", "Engineering", "Operations"],
    }
)

residences_left.join(departments_right, on=["name", "city"], how="inner")
```

shape: (3, 4)

name	city	age	department
---	---	---	---
str	str	i64	str
Alice	NY	25	Finance
Bob	LA	30	Marketing
Charlie	NY	35	Engineering

Validation

After joining data, you can validate whether the join was of a certain *cardinality*. This involves checking the nature of the relationships between the joined tables to make sure that they joined according to the expected relationships. The following relationships can be validated.

Many-to-many

A *many-to-many join* (m:m) is when multiple rows in the left DataFrame match multiple rows in the right DataFrame. An example of this would be joining a table of employees to a table of projects. Each employee can be involved in multiple projects, and projects usually have multiple employees working on them. In Polars this is the default option, and it doesn't result in checks.

One-to-many

A *one-to-many join* (1:m) is when a single row in the left DataFrame matches multiple rows in the right DataFrame. An example of this relationship would be joining a list of departments with a list of employees. Each department has multiple employees, but each employee only belongs to one department. Polars validates whether the join values are unique in the left DataFrame.

Many-to-one

A *many-to-one join* (m:1) is when multiple rows in the left DataFrame match a single row in the right DataFrame. An example of this would be joining a table of employees with a table of cities they live in. Each employee can only live in one city, but a city can contain multiple employees. Polars validates whether the join values are unique in the right DataFrame.

One-to-one

A *one-to-one join* (1:1) is when a single row in the left DataFrame has a match with a single row in the right DataFrame. An example of this would be joining a table of employees with a table of employee IDs. Polars validates whether the join values are unique in both DataFrames.

To validate the join, you can pass the `validate` argument to the `join` method. This argument takes a string with the relationship you want to validate.

In the following example, you'll make two DataFrames containing a set of employees and a set of departments which you will join in a many-to-one fashion. Each employee only belongs to one department, but each department can have multiple employees:

```
employees = pl.DataFrame(
    {
        "employee_id": [1, 2, 3, 4],
        "name": ["Alice", "Bob", "Charlie", "Dave"],
        "department_id": [10, 10, 30, 10],
    }
)

departments = pl.DataFrame(
    {
        "department_id": [10, 20, 30],
        "department_name": [
            "Information Technology",
            "Finance",
```

```
                "Human Resources",
        ],
    }
)

employees.join(departments, on="department_id", how="left", validate="m:1")

shape: (4, 4)
```

employee_id	name	department_id	department_name
i64	str	i64	str
1	Alice	10	Information Technolo…
2	Bob	10	Information Technolo…
3	Charlie	30	Human Resources
4	Dave	10	Information Technolo…

The moment there are multiple departments sharing the same ID, the validation will fail:

```
departments = pl.DataFrame(
    {
        "department_id": [10, 20, 10],
        "department_name": [
            "Information Technology",
            "Finance",
            "Human Resources",
        ],
    }
)

employees.join(departments, on="department_id", how="left", validate="m:1")

ComputeError: join keys did not fulfill m:1 validation
```

Inexact Joining

When joining DataFrames, you might want to connect two datasets based on values that are close to each other but not exactly the same. An example of this would be joining datasets of sales from different sources where one system timestamps it on writing the sale into a database, while the other system timestamps it on the time of payment. This creates an inconsistent discrepancy in the timestamps, which can be solved by joining the DataFrames on the closest value. You can do this with Polars by using the df.join_asof() method. Table 14-2 lists the arguments that df.join_asof() accepts.

Table 14-2. Arguments for the method df.join_asof()

Argument	Description
other	The DataFrame to join with.
on	The columns to join on when the name is the same in the left and right DataFrames.
left_on and right_on	The columns to join on when there are different names in the left and right DataFrames.
by	Columns to join on before doing the df.join_asof().
by_left and by_right	Columns to join on before doing the df.join_asof() in case they have different names in the left and right DataFrames.
strategy	The strategy to use when joining.
suffix	The suffix to use for columns appearing in both DataFrames with the same name.
tolerance	The maximum difference between the values to consider them a match.
allow_parallel	Allow Polars to calculate the DataFrames up to the join in parallel. True by default.
force_parallel	Force parallel DataFrame computation before the join. False by default.

Before we dive into some examples, you'll need to know that df.join_asof() only works if both DataFrames are sorted on the columns you want to join on.

Let's create two DataFrames to demonstrate this:

```
df_left = pl.DataFrame({"int_id": [10, 5], "value": ["b", "a"]})

df_right = pl.DataFrame({"int_id": [4, 7, 12], "value": [1, 2, 3]})
```

If the DataFrames are not sorted, you'll get an error:

```
df_left.join_asof(df_right, on="int_id", tolerance=3)

InvalidOperationError: argument in operation 'asof_join' is not sorted, please
sort the 'expr/series/column' first
```

In this case, you can sort the DataFrames by calling the sort("int_id") method to make it run:

```
df_left = df_left.sort("int_id")
df_right = df_right

df_left.join_asof(df_right, on="int_id")
```

```
shape: (2, 3)
┌────────┬───────┬─────────────┐
│ int_id │ value │ value_right │
│ ---    │ ---   │ ---         │
│ i64    │ str   │ i64         │
╞════════╪═══════╪═════════════╡
│ 5      │ a     │ 1           │
│ 10     │ b     │ 2           │
└────────┴───────┴─────────────┘
```

Note that this also drops the right join columns if they have the same name. If this is not what you want, you can set coalesce to False:

```
df_left.join_asof(
    df_right,
    on="int_id",
    coalesce=False,
)
```

shape: (2, 4)

int_id	value	int_id_right	value_right
i64	str	i64	i64
5	a	4	1
10	b	7	2

In case the columns didn't have the same name in the first place, you can use left_on and right_on to select the columns you want to join on in both DataFrames:

```
df_left.join_asof(
    df_right.rename({"int_id": "int_id_right"}),
    left_on="int_id",
    right_on="int_id_right",
)
```

shape: (2, 4)

int_id	value	int_id_right	value_right
i64	str	i64	i64
5	a	4	1
10	b	7	2

Inexact Join Strategies

The df.join_asof() method has three strategies to join DataFrames:

backward *(default)*
> Join with the last row that has an equal or smaller value.

forward
> Join with the first row that has an equal or larger value.

nearest
> Join with the row that has the closest value.

Let's review our DataFrames so we can easily see the behavior of these strategies:

```
print(df_left)
print(df_right)
```

```
shape: (2, 2)
┌────────┬───────┐
│ int_id │ value │
│ ---    │ ---   │
│ i64    │ str   │
╞════════╪═══════╡
│ 5      │ a     │
│ 10     │ b     │
└────────┴───────┘
```

```
shape: (3, 2)
┌────────┬───────┐
│ int_id │ value │
│ ---    │ ---   │
│ i64    │ i64   │
╞════════╪═══════╡
│ 4      │ 1     │
│ 7      │ 2     │
│ 12     │ 3     │
└────────┴───────┘
```

The default strategy is the backward strategy. This strategy joins the row on the first value in the other DataFrame's join column that is equal to or smaller than the value in the left DataFrame, while still falling in the range defined in tolerance:

```
df_left.join_asof(
    df_right,
    on="int_id",
    tolerance=3,
    strategy="backward",
)
```

```
shape: (2, 3)
┌────────┬───────┬─────────────┐
│ int_id │ value │ value_right │
│ ---    │ ---   │ ---         │
│ i64    │ str   │ i64         │
╞════════╪═══════╪═════════════╡
│ 5      │ a     │ 1           │
│ 10     │ b     │ 2           │
└────────┴───────┴─────────────┘
```

The forward strategy looks for the first value in the other DataFrame's join column that is equal to or larger than the value in the left DataFrame:

```
df_left.join_asof(
    df_right,
    on="int_id",
    tolerance=3,
    strategy="forward",
)
```

```
shape: (2, 3)
┌────────┬───────┬─────────────┐
│ int_id │ value │ value_right │
│ ---    │ ---   │ ---         │
│ i64    │ str   │ i64         │
╞════════╪═══════╪═════════════╡
│ 5      │ a     │ 2           │
│ 10     │ b     │ 3           │
└────────┴───────┴─────────────┘
```

Finally, the `nearest` strategy joins the row on the closest value:

```
df_left.join_asof(
    df_right,
    on="int_id",
    tolerance=3,
    strategy="nearest",
)
```

```
shape: (2, 3)
┌────────┬───────┬─────────────┐
│ int_id │ value │ value_right │
│ ---    │ ---   │ ---         │
│ i64    │ str   │ i64         │
╞════════╪═══════╪═════════════╡
│ 5      │ a     │ 1           │
│ 10     │ b     │ 3           │
└────────┴───────┴─────────────┘
```

Additional Fine-Tuning

When you set the `tolerance` argument, rows are only joined if the nearest matching value falls within a certain range. You can set the tolerance for numeric and temporal data types. For temporal data types, use a `datetime.timedelta` or the duration Strings (as we previously talked about in Table 13-5), such as `"7d12h30m"`.

If you want to ensure that rows are first joined only with exact matches in the other DataFrame, instead of just joining with any nearest match, you can use the `by` keyword. And again, if the names of the columns don't match, use the combination of `by_left` and `by_right`.

Now let's put these arguments to good use in a use case.

Use Case: Marketing Campaign Attribution

Imagine that you're tasked with finding out the efficacy of your company's marketing campaigns. You've gathered two datasets, one containing the sales data, the other containing the marketing campaigns for the past year:

```
campaigns = pl.scan_csv("data/campaigns.csv")
campaigns.head(1).collect()
```

```
shape: (1, 3)
```

Campaign Name	Campaign Date	Product Type
str	str	str
Launch	2023-01-01 20:00:00	Electronics

```
campaigns.select(pl.col("Product Type").unique()).collect()
```

```
shape: (4, 1)
```

Product Type
str
Electronics
Furniture
Clothing
Books

```
transactions = pl.scan_csv("data/transactions.csv")
transactions.head(1).collect()
```

```
shape: (1, 3)
```

Sale Date	Product Type	Quantity
str	str	i64
2023-01-01 02:00:00.…	Books	7

You can see that the timestamps are still a String data type. To work with this data, you first need to format it to a matching temporal data type. Also, since the dates don't match exactly, use the df.join_asof() method to join the two DataFrames. Additionally, match the campaigns with the sales data of the same product category, which you can do by setting the by argument accordingly. And last, campaigns don't work forever. You can assume in this instance that a campaign is in effect for two months, so set the tolerance to two months:

```
transactions = transactions.with_columns(
    pl.col("Sale Date")
    .str.to_datetime("%Y-%m-%d %H:%M:%S%.f")
    .cast(pl.Datetime("us")),
)
campaigns = campaigns.with_columns(
    pl.col("Campaign Date").str.to_datetime("%Y-%m-%d %H:%M:%S"),
)

sales_with_campaign_df = (
```

```
transactions.sort("Sale Date")
.join_asof(
    campaigns.sort("Campaign Date"),
    left_on="Sale Date",
    right_on="Campaign Date",
    by="Product Type",
    strategy="backward",
    tolerance="60d",
)
.collect()
)
sales_with_campaign_df
```

shape: (20_000, 5)

Sale Date	Product Type	Quantity	Campaign Name	Campaign Date
datetime[μs]	str	i64	str	datetime[μs]
2023-01-01 01:26:12.…	Electronics	2	null	null
2023-01-01 02:00:00	Books	7	null	null
2023-01-01 06:14:30.…	Toys	9	null	null
2023-01-01 06:52:25.…	Clothing	9	null	null
2023-01-01 07:44:50.…	Books	7	null	null
…	…	…	…	…
2023-12-31 15:45:29.…	Clothing	10	null	null
2023-12-31 18:15:09.…	Toys	4	null	null
2023-12-31 18:33:47.…	Electronics	7	null	null
2023-12-31 18:37:54.…	Books	6	null	null
2023-12-31 19:41:22.…	Furniture	4	null	null

Now, if you want to find out whether the campaigns led to a higher average sales quantity, you can group the data by Product Type and Campaign Name. This lets you compare the products sold with versus without the campaign and calculate the average quantity, as discussed in Chapter 13:

```
(
    sales_with_campaign_df.group_by("Product Type", "Campaign Name")
    .agg(pl.col("Quantity").mean())
    .sort("Product Type", "Campaign Name")
)
```

```
shape: (9, 3)
```

Product Type	Campaign Name	Quantity
---	---	---
str	str	f64
Books	null	5.527716
Clothing	null	5.433385
Clothing	New Arrivals	8.200581
Electronics	null	5.486832
Electronics	Launch	8.080775
Electronics	Seasonal Sale	8.471406
Furniture	null	5.430222
Furniture	Discount	8.191888
Toys	null	5.50318

From this result we can see that campaigns generally lead to a higher sales quantity, with the exception of the Books and Toys categories. The Toys category never ran a campaign, which explains it, but what about the Books category? Let's tkae a look:

```
campaigns.filter(pl.col("Product Type") == "Books").collect()
```

```
shape: (1, 3)
```

Campaign Name	Campaign Date	Product Type
---	---	---
str	datetime[µs]	str
Clearance	2023-12-31 21:00:00	Books

It seems that the Books category only ran one campaign: a New Year's Eve clearance sale. Let's see if there are any sales after that moment:

```
(
    transactions.filter(
        (pl.col("Product Type") == "Books")
        & (
            pl.col("Sale Date")
            > pl.lit("2023-12-31 21:00:00").str.to_datetime()
        )
    ).collect()
)
```

```
shape: (0, 3)
```

Sale Date	Product Type	Quantity
---	---	---
datetime[µs]	str	i64

It seems that after the clearance started, no more books were sold. Since our `df.join_asof()` strategy was `backward`, this campaign wasn't joined to any of the values, which explains why it's missing in the results. This means that the sales it might have caused are not in the dataset, making it look ineffective.

Unstable Non-Equi Joins

At the time of writing, Polars supports what are called *non-equi joins*. These joins are used to join DataFrames based on conditions other than equality, and can be accessed by using `df.join_where()`. Since these joins are still in an experimental phase, they will not be covered in this book, but it's good to know they exist.

Vertical and Horizontal Concatenation

The `df.join()` method combines DataFrames based on the values in a DataFrame, but sometimes you just want to add DataFrames together without regard to their values. Usually DataFrames are stored in different locations in memory. When you want to combine them, you can do three things:

- Combine the data in a new DataFrame by copying it to a new location.
- Point the new DataFrame to the locations where the data is stored.
- Copy the second DataFrame's data behind the data of the first DataFrame.

The first way is to copy data to a new location. This is the default behavior of `pl.concat()`. This function takes a list of DataFrames, LazyFrames, or Series and can concatenate them vertically, horizontally, or diagonally. After combining the DataFrames, it rechunks the resulting DataFrame, copying the data to a new location into a single chunk. This guarantees optimal querying performance afterwards.

As explained in Chapter 18, *rechunking* copies data to a new location in memory to make it contiguous again. This improves the performance of queries and is especially helpful when the resulting DataFrame is queried multiple times.

Table 14-3 lists the arguments that the `pl.concat()` function accepts.

Table 14-3. Arguments for the function pl.concat()

Argument	Description
`items`	The list of DataFrames, LazyFrames, or Series to concatenate.
`how`	The strategy to combine these items.
`rechunk`	Whether to rechunk the resulting DataFrame. `True` by default.
`parallel`	Determines if LazyFrames should be computed in parallel. `True` by default.

For the how argument, you can choose from the following concatenation strategies: vertical, vertical_relaxed, horizontal, diagonal, diagonal_relaxed, and align.

Vertical

The first strategy is *vertical* concatenation. This is the default strategy of pl.con cat(). It combines the DataFrames vertically, meaning that the rows of the Data-Frames are stacked on top of each other. How this works is shown in Figure 14-1.

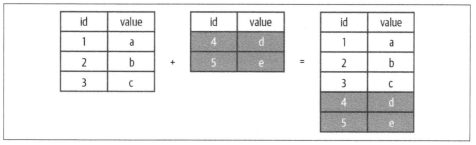

Figure 14-1. Vertical concatenation

Here's the corresponding code:

```
df1 = pl.DataFrame(
    {
        "id": [1, 2, 3],
        "value": ["a", "b", "c"],
    }
)
df2 = pl.DataFrame(
    {
        "id": [4, 5],
        "value": ["d", "e"],
    }
)
pl.concat([df1, df2], how="vertical")
```

```
shape: (5, 2)
┌─────┬───────┐
│ id  │ value │
│ --- │ ---   │
│ i64 │ str   │
╞═════╪═══════╡
│ 1   │ a     │
│ 2   │ b     │
│ 3   │ c     │
│ 4   │ d     │
│ 5   │ e     │
└─────┴───────┘
```

Horizontal

The second strategy is *horizontal* concatenation. This strategy combines the DataFrames horizontally, meaning that the columns of the DataFrames are stacked next to each other. When the lengths of the DataFrames don't match, the resulting DataFrame will be filled with null values. Columns cannot have the same name, and if they do, the operation will fail. You can circumvent this by renaming the columns before concatenating. How this works is shown in Figure 14-2.

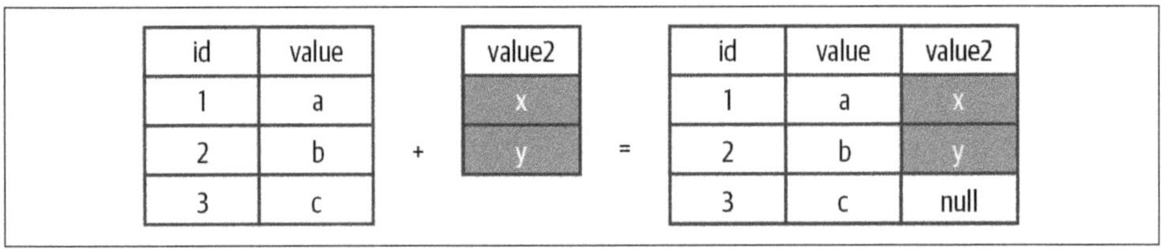

Figure 14-2. Horizontal concatenation

Here's the corresponding code:

```
df1 = pl.DataFrame(
    {
        "id": [1, 2, 3],
        "value": ["a", "b", "c"],
    }
)
df2 = pl.DataFrame(
    {
        "value2": ["x", "y"],
    }
)
pl.concat([df1, df2], how="horizontal")
```

```
shape: (3, 3)
┌─────┬───────┬────────┐
│ id  ┆ value ┆ value2 │
│ --- ┆ ---   ┆ ---    │
│ i64 ┆ str   ┆ str    │
╞═════╪═══════╪════════╡
│ 1   ┆ a     ┆ x      │
│ 2   ┆ b     ┆ y      │
│ 3   ┆ c     ┆ null   │
└─────┴───────┴────────┘
```

Diagonal

The third strategy is *diagonal* concatenation. This strategy combines the DataFrames by creating a union of their columns. Any values that are missing in the DataFrames will be filled with null values. How this works is shown in Figure 14-3.

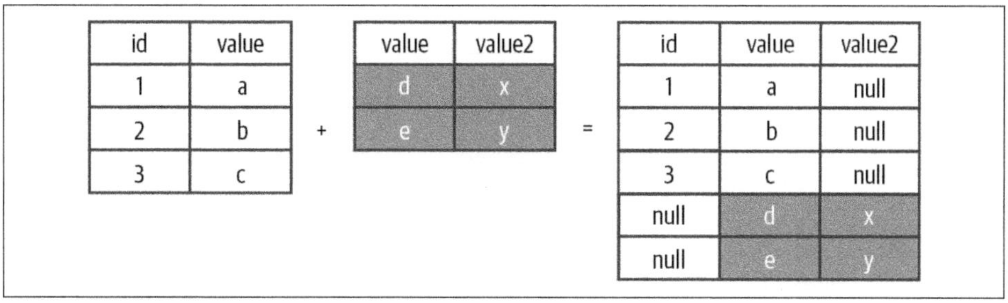

Figure 14-3. Diagonal concatenation

Here's the corresponding code:

```
df1 = pl.DataFrame(
    {
        "id": [1, 2, 3],
        "value": ["a", "b", "c"],
    }
)
df2 = pl.DataFrame(
    {
        "value": ["d", "e"],
        "value2": ["x", "y"],
    }
)
pl.concat([df1, df2], how="diagonal")

shape: (5, 3)
```

```
┌──────┬───────┬────────┐
│ id   │ value │ value2 │
│ ---  │ ---   │ ---    │
│ i64  │ str   │ str    │
╞══════╪═══════╪════════╡
│ 1    │ a     │ null   │
│ 2    │ b     │ null   │
│ 3    │ c     │ null   │
│ null │ d     │ x      │
│ null │ e     │ y      │
└──────┴───────┴────────┘
```

Align

The fourth and last strategy is *align* concatenation. This strategy doesn't simply tape rows or columns together. Instead it finds matching values in columns that are available in both DataFrames, and aligns the rows based on these values, as shown in Figure 14-4.

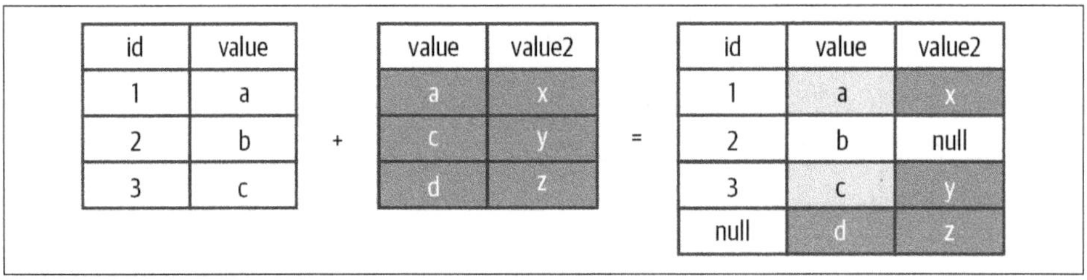

Figure 14-4. Aligned concatenation

The following snippet demonstrates the `pl.concat()` function:

```
df1 = pl.DataFrame(
    {
        "id": [1, 2, 3],
        "value": ["a", "b", "c"],
    }
)
df2 = pl.DataFrame(
    {
        "value": ["a", "c", "d"],
        "value2": ["x", "y", "z"],
    }
)
pl.concat([df1, df2], how="align")

shape: (4, 3)
┌──────┬───────┬────────┐
│ id   │ value │ value2 │
│ ---  │ ---   │ ---    │
│ i64  │ str   │ str    │
╞══════╪═══════╪════════╡
│ 1    │ a     │ x      │
│ 2    │ b     │ null   │
│ 3    │ c     │ y      │
│ null │ d     │ z      │
└──────┴───────┴────────┘
```

The align strategy is based on the `pl.align_frames()` function. This function lets you pick a column and aligns the rows of a set of DataFrames according to the values in that column. If a value is missing in one of the DataFrames, the resulting DataFrame will have a null value in that row. If values appear multiple times, the Cartesian product of the rows will be created. The function returns the same DataFrames, but with their rows aligned to each other. Table 14-4 lists the arguments that `pl.align_frames()` accepts.

Table 14-4. Arguments for the function pl.align_frames()

Argument	Description
*frames	The DataFrames you want to align to each other.

Argument	Description
*on	The column to align the DataFrames on.
how	The join strategy used to determine the resulting values. The default is `full`.
select	Columns and their order to select from the resulting DataFrames.
descending	Whether to sort the resulting DataFrame in descending order. This can also be a List of Booleans with a matching length of the columns provided in on.

The following snippet demonstrates the `pl.align_frames()` function:

```
df1 = pl.DataFrame(
    {
        "id": [1, 2, 2],
        "value": ["a", "c", "b"],
    }
)
df2 = pl.DataFrame(
    {
        "id": [2, 2],
        "value": ["x", "y"],
    }
)
pl.align_frames(df1, df2, on="id")

[shape: (5, 2)
┌─────┬───────┐
│ id  │ value │
│ --- │ ---   │
│ i64 │ str   │
╞═════╪═══════╡
│ 1   │ a     │
│ 2   │ c     │
│ 2   │ b     │
│ 2   │ c     │
│ 2   │ b     │
└─────┴───────┘,
shape: (5, 2)
┌─────┬───────┐
│ id  │ value │
│ --- │ ---   │
│ i64 │ str   │
╞═════╪═══════╡
│ 1   │ null  │
│ 2   │ x     │
│ 2   │ x     │
│ 2   │ y     │
│ 2   │ y     │
└─────┴───────┘]
```

Note that in the second DataFrame, which is missing the id with the value 1, the value is filled with null. Additionally, because both DataFrames have the id with the value 2 twice, the resulting DataFrame will contain the Cartesian product of the rows with that value.

Relaxed

In addition, the vertical, horizontal, and diagonal strategies each have a relaxed version. This means that if the types of columns with the same names in both DataFrames don't match, the columns will be coerced to become a *supertype*. For example, a column with Integers and Floats will be coerced to a Float column, and a column with Integers and Strings will be coerced to a String column. This is useful when you want to concatenate DataFrames that have the same columns but different data types.

The following example shows what happens when you try to concatenate two Data-Frames with the same columns but different data types:

```
df1 = pl.DataFrame(
    {
        "id": [1, 2, 3],
        "value": ["a", "b", "c"],
    }
)
df2 = pl.DataFrame(
    {
        "id": [4.0, 5.0],
        "value": [1, 2],
    }
)
pl.concat([df1, df2], how="vertical")
```

```
SchemaError: type Float64 is incompatible with expected type Int64
```

That's right, you get an error. When you use the vertical_relaxed strategy, the concatenation will succeed:

```
pl.concat([df1, df2], how="vertical_relaxed")
```

```
shape: (5, 2)
┌─────┬───────┐
│ id  │ value │
│ --- │ ---   │
│ f64 │ str   │
╞═════╪═══════╡
│ 1.0 │ a     │
│ 2.0 │ b     │
│ 3.0 │ c     │
│ 4.0 │ 1     │
│ 5.0 │ 2     │
└─────┴───────┘
```

Stacking

The `df.vstack()` and `df.hstack()` functions use the second way of combining DataFrames. (A comparable function exists for Series, called `Series.append()`.) They combine two DataFrames without moving the data in memory. Instead they create a new DataFrame or Series containing multiple chunks that can be located in different parts of memory. This makes stack operations quick, with the drawback that querying could be slower because data has to be read from multiple locations in memory. The `pl.concat()` vertical strategy uses the `df.vstack()` operation, but this can also be called by itself. `pl.concat()` allows you to rechunk the resulting DataFrame to prevent this performance hit, while `df.vstack()` does not.

These are the preferred methods when you append multiple DataFrames one after the other. Note that stack operations only work on DataFrames, not LazyFrames, since they need to combine existing chunks.

`df.vstack()` requires the width, column names, and their data types to match:

```
df1 = pl.DataFrame(
    {
        "id": [1, 2],
        "value": ["a", "b"],
    }
)
df2 = pl.DataFrame(
    {
        "id": [3, 4],
        "value": ["c", "d"],
    }
)
df1.vstack(df2)

shape: (4, 2)
┌─────┬───────┐
│ id  ┆ value │
│ --- ┆ ---   │
│ i64 ┆ str   │
╞═════╪═══════╡
│ 1   ┆ a     │
│ 2   ┆ b     │
│ 3   ┆ c     │
│ 4   ┆ d     │
└─────┴───────┘
```

Exactly like `df.vstack()`, `df.hstack()` combines DataFrames horizontally. This operation requires the height of the DataFrames to match:

```
df1 = pl.DataFrame(
    {
        "id": [1, 2],
        "value": ["a", "b"],
```

```
        }
    )
    df2 = pl.DataFrame(
        {
            "value2": ["x", "y"],
        }
    )
    df1.hstack(df2)

    shape: (2, 3)
    ┌─────┬───────┬────────┐
    │ id  │ value │ value2 │
    │ --- │ ---   │ ---    │
    │ i64 │ str   │ str    │
    ╞═════╪═══════╪════════╡
    │ 1   │ a     │ x      │
    │ 2   │ b     │ y      │
    └─────┴───────┴────────┘
```

Appending

To append one Series with another, you can use the `series.append()` method. This keeps the name of the original Series:

```
    series_a = pl.Series("a", [1, 2])
    series_b = pl.Series("b", [3, 4])
    series_a.append(series_b)

    shape: (4,)
    Series: 'a' [i64]
    [
            1
            2
            3
            4
    ]
```

Extending

The third way to combine DataFrames is `df.extend()`. When there's enough space available in memory behind the original DataFrame, `df.extend()` copies the data of the second DataFrame behind the first one. This eliminates the need to copy the data to a new location, which can be faster, and still keeps the data contiguous in memory. This works best when you want to add a smaller DataFrame to a larger one:

```
    df1 = pl.DataFrame(
        {
            "id": [1, 2],
            "value": ["a", "b"],
        }
    )
    df2 = pl.DataFrame(
```

```
    {
        "id": [3, 4],
        "value": ["c", "d"],
    }
)
df1.extend(df2)

shape: (4, 2)
┌─────┬───────┐
│ id  │ value │
│ --- │ ---   │
│ i64 │ str   │
╞═════╪═══════╡
│ 1   │ a     │
│ 2   │ b     │
│ 3   │ c     │
│ 4   │ d     │
└─────┴───────┘
```

 In Place is Out of Place

The df.extend() method is one of the few operations in Polars that works *in place*. That means the DataFrame df itself is modified. It does return the resulting DataFrame as well, but just as a convenience.

Takeaways

In this chapter you learned how to combine DataFrames. You've learned how to:

- Combine DataFrames with exact matches in their join columns using df.join(). You can fine-tune the join with the tolerance and by arguments and by selecting the appropriate strategy.
- Combine numerical or temporal columns in DataFrames on their nearest values using df.join_asof().
- Append DataFrames vertically if they have matching columns using pl.concat() or df.vstack().
- Combine DataFrames with matching row counts using pl.concat() and df.hstack().
- Append rows of a DataFrame in place efficiently with df.extend().
- Append Series using series.append().

In the next chapter we'll look into reshaping DataFrames, which is useful when you want to change the structure of your data.

## CHAPTER 15

Reshaping

In the last chapter we focused on aggregating data to create informative summaries. However, what should you do if the data is not in the right shape to perform these aggregations? Reshaping data is a crucial step in the data analysis process.

In this chapter, you'll learn how to:

- Reshape data to make it more suitable for analysis
- Change the dimensions of the data to make it more suitable for analysis, improve computational performance, or prepare it for visualization
- Use the various methods Polars offers, such as `df.pivot()`, `df.unpivot()`, `df.transpose()`, `df.explode()`, and `df.partition_by()`

The instructions to get any files you might need are in Chapter 2. We assume that you have the files in the *data* subdirectory.

Wide Versus Long DataFrames

Wide DataFrames have many columns and few rows. The idea is that every row contains a column with an identifier, and the data is spread over many columns. This format is often used when there are multiple measurements per observation. An example of wide data would be the following:

```
grades_wide = pl.DataFrame(
    {
        "student": ["Jeroen", "Thijs", "Ritchie"],
        "math": [85, 78, 92],
        "science": [90, 82, 85],
        "history": [88, 80, 87],
    }
)
```

```
grades_wide

shape: (3, 4)
┌─────────┬──────┬─────────┬─────────┐
│ student │ math │ science │ history │
│ ---     │ ---  │ ---     │ ---     │
│ str     │ i64  │ i64     │ i64     │
╞═════════╪══════╪═════════╪═════════╡
│ Jeroen  │ 85   │ 90      │ 88      │
│ Thijs   │ 78   │ 82      │ 80      │
│ Ritchie │ 92   │ 85      │ 87      │
└─────────┴──────┴─────────┴─────────┘
```

This DataFrame has three columns, with the subjects as the column names.

Where wide DataFrames have many columns, long DataFrames have few columns and many rows. Instead of having multiple values and variables per row, long Data-Frames have multiple rows, each with one variable and corresponding value. The prececding example in long format would look like the following:

```python
grades_long = pl.DataFrame(
    {
        "student": [
            "Jeroen",
            "Jeroen",
            "Jeroen",
            "Thijs",
            "Thijs",
            "Thijs",
            "Ritchie",
            "Ritchie",
            "Ritchie",
        ],
        "subject": [
            "Math",
            "Science",
            "History",
            "Math",
            "Science",
            "History",
            "Math",
            "Science",
            "History",
        ],
        "grade": [85, 90, 88, 78, 82, 80, 92, 85, 87],
    }
)

grades_long
```

```
shape: (9, 3)
┌──────────┬─────────┬──────┐
```

```
| student | subject | grade |
| ---     | ---     | ---   |
| str     | str     | i64   |

| Jeroen  | Math    | 85    |
| Jeroen  | Science | 90    |
| Jeroen  | History | 88    |
| Thijs   | Math    | 78    |
| Thijs   | Science | 82    |
| Thijs   | History | 80    |
| Ritchie | Math    | 92    |
| Ritchie | Science | 85    |
| Ritchie | History | 87    |
```

This formats the DataFrame so that every row contains only one observation.

The implications of the used format on memory usage and computational performance are significant. Since Polars uses a columnar storage format, long DataFrames tend to be more efficient in terms of memory usage and computational performance.

Tidy Data

In his 2014 paper "Tidy Data," Hadley Wickham described the different formats of data. He is a statistician known for, among other things, his work on the R programming language and the "tidyverse," which is a popular suite of packages to process and visualize data in R. The "Tidy Data" paper introduced the concept of wide and long DataFrames. These concepts are to this day widely used in the data science community to describe the shape of DataFrames, and we use it in this chapter as well.

In addition to the shapes of data, Wickham introduced the term *tidy data*.

Three interrelated rules make a dataset tidy:

1. Each variable must have its own column.

2. Each observation must have its own row.

3. Each value must have its own cell.

Figure 15-1 shows the rules visually.

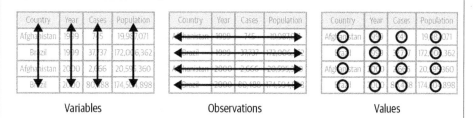

Figure 15-1. An example of a dataset following the three rules, making it tidy data

In the examples about grades, the wide example is considered untidy because each subject has its own column, while in reality, science, history, and math are the values of the variable "subject." This is what the longer example does differently, making it comply with the first rule. That's why the longer example is considered "tidy."

Pivot to a Wider DataFrame

If you want to go from a long format to a wide DataFrame, you can use the df.pivot() method. The df.pivot() method takes the arguments shown in Table 15-1.

Table 15-1. Arguments for the df.pivot() method

Argument	Description
index	Columns to use as identifiers for the rows.
columns	Columns containing what will be the column names.
values	Columns containing the values that will end up in the cells.
aggregate_function	The function used to aggregate the values if there are multiple values for a single cell. If left empty, the function will throw an error if there are multiple values for a single cell.
maintain_order	Sort the grouped keys to make the outcome predictable.
sort_columns	Sort the transposed values of columns, also the transposed columns, by name. The default is to sort by the order of appearance in the DataFrame.
separator	The string used as separator in generated column names.

Let's break it down with an example. You've got to store the grades of a group of students. As the grades come in one by one, you store them in a long DataFrame:

```
grades = pl.DataFrame(
    {
        "student": [
            "Jeroen",
            "Jeroen",
            "Jeroen",
            "Thijs",
            "Thijs",
            "Thijs",
            "Ritchie",
            "Ritchie",
            "Ritchie",
        ],
        "subject": [
            "Math",
            "Science",
            "History",
```

```
            "Math",
            "Science",
            "History",
            "Math",
            "Science",
            "History",
        ],
        "grade": [85, 90, 88, 78, 82, 80, 92, 85, 87],
    }
)

grades

shape: (9, 3)
┌─────────┬─────────┬───────┐
│ student │ subject │ grade │
│ ---     │ ---     │ ---   │
│ str     │ str     │ i64   │
╞═════════╪═════════╪═══════╡
│ Jeroen  │ Math    │ 85    │
│ Jeroen  │ Science │ 90    │
│ Jeroen  │ History │ 88    │
│ Thijs   │ Math    │ 78    │
│ Thijs   │ Science │ 82    │
│ Thijs   │ History │ 80    │
│ Ritchie │ Math    │ 92    │
│ Ritchie │ Science │ 85    │
│ Ritchie │ History │ 87    │
└─────────┴─────────┴───────┘
```

Tidy. Now, when students' report cards are being handed out, you want to create one row per student. You can do this by pivoting on the `subject` column:

```
grades.pivot(index="student", on="subject", values="grade")
```

```
shape: (3, 4)
┌─────────┬──────┬─────────┬─────────┐
│ student │ Math │ Science │ History │
│ ---     │ ---  │ ---     │ ---     │
│ str     │ i64  │ i64     │ i64     │
╞═════════╪══════╪═════════╪═════════╡
│ Jeroen  │ 85   │ 90      │ 88      │
│ Thijs   │ 78   │ 82      │ 80      │
│ Ritchie │ 92   │ 85      │ 87      │
└─────────┴──────┴─────────┴─────────┘
```

You can see how you went to a wide DataFrame with the student names as the index and the subjects as the columns.

In reality, students don't just get one grade, but multiple grades. This means you'll have to aggregate the grades. Luckily, the df.pivot() method can handle this for us.[1]

By default, the df.pivot() method will not aggregate and throw an error if there are multiple values. In our example this didn't happen, because all the values are unique. You can change this behavior by passing the aggregate_function argument with the desired aggregation function's name as a String. You can select from the following aggregation functions: min, max, first, last, sum, mean, median, and len. In our example to calculate the average grade, you can use the mean aggregation function. First, let's create a DataFrame with multiple grades per student:

```
multiple_grades = pl.DataFrame(
    {
        "student": [
            "Jeroen",
            "Jeroen",
            "Jeroen",
            "Jeroen",
            "Jeroen",
            "Jeroen",
            "Thijs",
            "Thijs",
            "Thijs",
            "Thijs",
            "Thijs",
            "Thijs",
        ],
        "subject": [
            "Math",
            "Math",
            "Math",
            "Science",
            "Science",
            "Science",
            "Math",
            "Math",
            "Math",
            "Science",
            "Science",
            "Science",
        ],
        "grade": [85, 88, 85, 60, 66, 63, 51, 79, 62, 82, 85, 82],
    }
)

multiple_grades
```

---

[1] As made famous by Ross in the TV show *Friends*, "Pivot!" is a lot easier to perform on a DataFrame than a couch that has to be moved upstairs.

```
shape: (12, 3)
┌─────────┬─────────┬───────┐
│ student │ subject │ grade │
│ ---     │ ---     │ ---   │
│ str     │ str     │ i64   │
╞═════════╪═════════╪═══════╡
│ Jeroen  │ Math    │ 85    │
│ Jeroen  │ Math    │ 88    │
│ Jeroen  │ Math    │ 85    │
│ Jeroen  │ Science │ 60    │
│ Jeroen  │ Science │ 66    │
│ …       │ …       │ …     │
│ Thijs   │ Math    │ 79    │
│ Thijs   │ Math    │ 62    │
│ Thijs   │ Science │ 82    │
│ Thijs   │ Science │ 85    │
│ Thijs   │ Science │ 82    │
└─────────┴─────────┴───────┘
```

Now you can pivot the DataFrame to calculate the average grade per student:

```
multiple_grades.pivot(
    index="student", on="subject", values="grade", aggregate_function="mean"
)
```

```
shape: (2, 3)
┌─────────┬──────┬─────────┐
│ student │ Math │ Science │
│ ---     │ ---  │ ---     │
│ str     │ f64  │ f64     │
╞═════════╪══════╪═════════╡
│ Jeroen  │ 86.0 │ 63.0    │
│ Thijs   │ 64.0 │ 83.0    │
└─────────┴──────┴─────────┘
```

In addition to this list of standard aggregation functions, you can also pass a custom aggregation function through an expression. By creating an expression that can be run against a List's elements, like pl.col(…).list.eval(<your_expression>), you can make use of extended flexibility. For example, you can calculate the difference between the maximum and minimum grade to show the stability of the students' grades:

```
multiple_grades.pivot(
    index="student",
    on="subject",
    values="grade",
    aggregate_function=pl.element().max() - pl.element().min(),
)
```

```
shape: (2, 3)
┌─────────┬──────┬─────────┐
│ student │ Math │ Science │
│ ---     │ ---  │ ---     │
```

str	i64	i64
Jeroen	3	6
Thijs	28	3

Here you can see Thijs has a much larger difference between his maximum and minimum grade than Jeroen in Math. In our use case, you could use this to approach Thijs's mentor to make sure Thijs is OK, because he seems to have slipped up on one of his tests.

Lazy Pivot

When executing the pivot operation, Polars needs to know what values are in a DataFrame in order to pivot them into columns. This means that in a LazyFrame, where data is not yet loaded, you can't use the pivot operation.

There is, however, a workaround. If you know the columns that will exist in the LazyFrame in advance, you can pivot a LazyFrame like so:

```
lf = pl.LazyFrame(
    {
        "col1": ["a", "a", "a", "b", "b", "b"],
        "col2": ["x", "x", "x", "x", "y", "y"],
        "col3": [6, 7, 3, 2, 5, 7],
    }
)

index = pl.col("col1")
on = pl.col("col2")
values = pl.col("col3")
unique_column_values = ["x", "y"]
aggregate_function = lambda col: col.tanh().mean()

lf.group_by(index).agg(
    aggregate_function(values.filter(on == value)).alias(value)
    for value in unique_column_values
).collect()
```

```
shape: (2, 3)
```

col1	x	y
---	---	---
str	f64	f64
a	0.998347	null
b	0.964028	0.999954

Unpivot to a Longer DataFrame

If instead you want to go from a wide format to a long DataFrame, you can use the df.unpivot() method. The df.unpivot() method takes the arguments shown in Table 15-2.

Table 15-2. Arguments for the df.unpivot() method

Argument	Description
id_vars	Columns to use as identifiers for the rows. These will remain columns in the resulting DataFrame.
value_vars	Columns to unpivot. If not specified, uses all columns not set in id_vars.
variable_name	Name of the resulting column that will contain the names of the columns that were unpivoted.
value_name	Name of the resulting column that contains the values of the columns that were unpivoted.

Columns that aren't in either id_vars or value_vars, when they're both provided, will be dropped from the result.

Let's illustrate this with an example. Let's take the wide report card setup of the examples from the previous section. Every student has a row with their grades for math, science, and history:

```
grades_wide = pl.DataFrame(
    {
        "student": ["Jeroen", "Thijs", "Ritchie"],
        "math": [85, 78, 92],
        "science": [90, 82, 85],
        "history": [88, 80, 87],
    }
)

grades_wide
```

```
shape: (3, 4)
┌─────────┬──────┬─────────┬─────────┐
│ student │ math │ science │ history │
│ ---     │ ---  │ ---     │ ---     │
│ str     │ i64  │ i64     │ i64     │
╞═════════╪══════╪═════════╪═════════╡
│ Jeroen  │ 85   │ 90      │ 88      │
│ Thijs   │ 78   │ 82      │ 80      │
│ Ritchie │ 92   │ 85      │ 87      │
└─────────┴──────┴─────────┴─────────┘
```

You can unpivot this DataFrame to get a long DataFrame with one row per student per subject:

```
grades_wide.unpivot(
    index=["student"],
    on=["math", "science", "history"],
    variable_name="subject",
    value_name="grade",
)
```

shape: (9, 3)

student	subject	grade
str	str	i64
Jeroen	math	85
Thijs	math	78
Ritchie	math	92
Jeroen	science	90
Thijs	science	82
Ritchie	science	85
Jeroen	history	88
Thijs	history	80
Ritchie	history	87

Here we identify the rows in the resulting DataFrame by the student column, containing the name of the student. All the columns that contain what will be the values in the returning DataFrame are the columns with subjects (Math, Science, and History). We'll call the columns that contain these subjects by the variable_name column we'll call subject, and the value_name will be stored in the grade column:

```
df = pl.DataFrame(
    {
        "student": ["Jeroen", "Thijs", "Ritchie", "Jeroen", "Thijs", "Ritchie"],
        "class": [
            "Math101",
            "Math101",
            "Math101",
            "Math102",
            "Math102",
            "Math102",
        ],
        "age": [20, 21, 22, 20, 21, 22],
        "semester": ["Fall", "Fall", "Fall", "Spring", "Spring", "Spring"],
        "math": [85, 78, 92, 88, 79, 95],
        "science": [90, 82, 85, 92, 81, 87],
        "history": [88, 80, 87, 85, 82, 89],
    }
)
df
```

shape: (6, 7)

student	class	age	semester	math	science	history

```
| ---     | ---     | --- | ---    | ---   | ---   | ---   |
| str     | str     | i64 | str    | i64   | i64   | i64   |
╞═════════╪═════════╪═════╪════════╪═══════╪═══════╪═══════╡
| Jeroen  | Math101 | 20  | Fall   | 85    | 90    | 88    |
| Thijs   | Math101 | 21  | Fall   | 78    | 82    | 80    |
| Ritchie | Math101 | 22  | Fall   | 92    | 85    | 87    |
| Jeroen  | Math102 | 20  | Spring | 88    | 92    | 85    |
| Thijs   | Math102 | 21  | Spring | 79    | 81    | 82    |
| Ritchie | Math102 | 22  | Spring | 95    | 87    | 89    |
```

```
df.unpivot(
    index=["student", "class", "age", "semester"],
    on=["math", "science", "history"],
    variable_name="subject",
    value_name="grade",
)
```

shape: (18, 6)

student	class	age	semester	subject	grade
str	str	i64	str	str	i64
Jeroen	Math101	20	Fall	math	85
Thijs	Math101	21	Fall	math	78
Ritchie	Math101	22	Fall	math	92
Jeroen	Math102	20	Spring	math	88
Thijs	Math102	21	Spring	math	79
Ritchie	Math102	22	Spring	math	95
Jeroen	Math101	20	Fall	science	90
Thijs	Math101	21	Fall	science	82
Ritchie	Math101	22	Fall	science	85
Jeroen	Math102	20	Spring	science	92
Thijs	Math102	21	Spring	science	81
Ritchie	Math102	22	Spring	science	87
Jeroen	Math101	20	Fall	history	88
Thijs	Math101	21	Fall	history	80
Ritchie	Math101	22	Fall	history	87
Jeroen	Math102	20	Spring	history	85
Thijs	Math102	21	Spring	history	82
Ritchie	Math102	22	Spring	history	89

Transposing

If you want to flip all the columns into rows diagonally, without keeping some columns as identifiers, you can use the df.transpose() method. The df.transpose() method only works on DataFrames, and takes the arguments shown in Table 15-3.

Table 15-3. Arguments for the df.transpose() method

Argument	Description
include_header	Whether to set the column names to the first column in the resulting DataFrame.
header_name	If include_header is set to True, this will be the name of the column containing the original column names. It defaults to column.
column_names	You can pass a list of column names (or another iterable) that will be used as the column names in the resulting DataFrame.

Time for an example. Let's take the wide DataFrame from the previous section:

```
grades_wide = pl.DataFrame(
    {
        "student": ["Jeroen", "Thijs", "Ritchie"],
        "math": [85, 78, 92],
        "science": [90, 82, 85],
        "history": [88, 80, 87],
    }
)

grades_wide
```

```
shape: (3, 4)
┌─────────┬──────┬─────────┬─────────┐
│ student │ math │ science │ history │
│ ---     │ ---  │ ---     │ ---     │
│ str     │ i64  │ i64     │ i64     │
╞═════════╪══════╪═════════╪═════════╡
│ Jeroen  │ 85   │ 90      │ 88      │
│ Thijs   │ 78   │ 82      │ 80      │
│ Ritchie │ 92   │ 85      │ 87      │
└─────────┴──────┴─────────┴─────────┘
```

Now let's flip this DataFrame diagonally:

```
report_columns = (f"report_{i + 1}" for i, _ in enumerate(df.columns))   ❶

grades_wide.transpose(
    include_header=True,
    header_name="original_headers",
    column_names=report_columns,
)
```

❶ Since columns cannot have identical names, we're generating a list of column names with an index number as the suffix.

```
shape: (4, 4)
┌──────────────────┬──────────┬──────────┬──────────┐
│ original_headers │ report_1 │ report_2 │ report_3 │
│ ---              │ ---      │ ---      │ ---      │
│ str              │ str      │ str      │ str      │
╞══════════════════╪══════════╪══════════╪══════════╡
```

```
| student   | Jeroen  | Thijs   | Ritchie  |
| math      | 85      | 78      | 92       |
| science   | 90      | 82      | 85       |
| history   | 88      | 80      | 87       |
```

All the columns are now rows, and the original column names are stored in the original_headers column.

Exploding

When you have a List or Array in your columns, it isn't quite the wide format we talked about earlier, but it's also not a long format. In case you want to unpack these nested values into a long format, you can use the df.explode() method. Instead of blowing stuff up, this method safely creates a row for every value in the nested column, copying the values from the other columns. The only arguments df.explode() takes are the columns it is supposed to unpack to separate rows. Sticking to the student example, let's list the scores for one subject:

```
grades_nested = pl.DataFrame(
    {
        "student": ["Jeroen", "Thijs", "Ritchie"],
        "math": [[85, 90, 88], [78, 82, 80], [92, 85, 87]],
    }
)

grades_nested
```

shape: (3, 2)

```
┌─────────┬──────────────┐
│ student │ math         │
│ ---     │ ---          │
│ str     │ list[i64]    │
╞═════════╪══════════════╡
│ Jeroen  │ [85, 90, 88] │
│ Thijs   │ [78, 82, 80] │
│ Ritchie │ [92, 85, 87] │
└─────────┴──────────────┘
```

To turn this DataFrame into a long format, we can apply df.explode() to the math column:

```
grades_nested.explode("math")
```

shape: (9, 2)

```
┌─────────┬──────┐
│ student │ math │
│ ---     │ ---  │
│ str     │ i64  │
╞═════════╪══════╡
│ Jeroen  │ 85   │
```

```
| Jeroen  | 90 |
| Jeroen  | 88 |
| Thijs   | 78 |
| Thijs   | 82 |
| Thijs   | 80 |
| Ritchie | 92 |
| Ritchie | 85 |
| Ritchie | 87 |
```

And in the case of multiple columns:

```
grades_nested = pl.DataFrame(
    {
        "student": ["Jeroen", "Thijs", "Ritchie"],
        "math": [[85, 90, 88], [78, 82, 80], [92, 85, 87]],
        "science": [[85, 90, 88], [78, 82], [92, 85, 87]],
        "history": [[85, 90, 88], [78, 82], [92, 85, 87]],
    }
)

grades_nested
```

shape: (3, 4)

student	math	science	history
str	list[i64]	list[i64]	list[i64]
Jeroen	[85, 90, 88]	[85, 90, 88]	[85, 90, 88]
Thijs	[78, 82, 80]	[78, 82]	[78, 82]
Ritchie	[92, 85, 87]	[92, 85, 87]	[92, 85, 87]

Again, to turn this DataFrame into a long format, we can apply df.explode() to the math column. But because Thijs didn't take all his tests (classic Thijs), we can't do it at once. The exploded columns must all yield the same number of resulting rows, otherwise you'll get an error:

```
grades_nested.explode("math", "science", "history")
```

```
ShapeError: exploded columns must have matching element counts
```

So first, we need to reshape this DataFrame to a long format using df.unpivot():

```
grades_nested_long = grades_nested.unpivot(
    index="student", variable_name="subject", value_name="grade"
)

grades_nested_long
```

shape: (9, 3)

student	subject	grade

```
|   ---     |   ---     |   ---         |
| str       | str       | list[i64]     |
╞═══════════╪═══════════╪═══════════════╡
| Jeroen    | math      | [85, 90, 88]  |
| Thijs     | math      | [78, 82, 80]  |
| Ritchie   | math      | [92, 85, 87]  |
| Jeroen    | science   | [85, 90, 88]  |
| Thijs     | science   | [78, 82]      |
| Ritchie   | science   | [92, 85, 87]  |
| Jeroen    | history   | [85, 90, 88]  |
| Thijs     | history   | [78, 82]      |
| Ritchie   | history   | [92, 85, 87]  |
```

After that, we can finally unpack all the lists using df.explode():

```
grades_nested_long.explode("grade")
```

shape: (25, 3)

```
| student   | subject   | grade |
|   ---     |   ---     |  ---  |
| str       | str       |  i64  |
╞═══════════╪═══════════╪═══════╡
| Jeroen    | math      |  85   |
| Jeroen    | math      |  90   |
| Jeroen    | math      |  88   |
| Thijs     | math      |  78   |
| Thijs     | math      |  82   |
| …         | …         |  …    |
| Thijs     | history   |  78   |
| Thijs     | history   |  82   |
| Ritchie   | history   |  92   |
| Ritchie   | history   |  85   |
| Ritchie   | history   |  87   |
```

Please note in the case of exploding multiple columns at the same time, the order of values in the lists is important. The items that are lined up end up on the same row in the results. We've discussed the sorting of lists in Chapter 12.

df.explode() can even deal with nested lists:

```
nested_lists = pl.DataFrame(
    {
        "id": [1, 2],
        "nested_value": [[["a", "b"]], [["c"], ["d", "e"]]],
    },
    strict=False,
)
nested_lists
```

shape: (2, 2)

```
| id   | nested_value         |
| ---  | ---                  |
| i64  | list[list[str]]      |
|======|======================|
| 1    | [["a", "b"]]         |
| 2    | [["c"], ["d", "e"]]  |
```

Note that with a nested structure, it will only explode one layer[2] at a time:

```
nested_lists.explode("nested_value")
```

shape: (3, 2)

```
| id   | nested_value |
| ---  | ---          |
| i64  | list[str]    |
|======|==============|
| 1    | ["a", "b"]   |
| 2    | ["c"]        |
| 2    | ["d", "e"]   |
```

If you want to get the String values, you'll have to call it two times:

```
nested_lists.explode("nested_value").explode("nested_value")
```

shape: (5, 2)

```
| id   | nested_value |
| ---  | ---          |
| i64  | str          |
|======|==============|
| 1    | a            |
| 1    | b            |
| 2    | c            |
| 2    | d            |
| 2    | e            |
```

Partition into Multiple DataFrames

Previously, we discussed the `df.group_by()` operation in Chapter 13. You can use a comparable function to split the DataFrame into multiple partitions. By using `df.partition_by()`, you group a DataFrame by some given columns and return the groups as separate DataFrames. Table 15-4 lists the arguments that the `df.partition_by()` method accepts.

---

2 Nested lists are much like onions; they have layers.

Table 15-4. Arguments for the df.partition_by() method

Argument	Description
by and *more_by	The column(s) to group by
maintain_order	Ensure that the order of the groups is deterministic.
include_key	Instead of a list of DataFrames, return a list of tuples with the group key and the DataFrame.
as_dict	Return the group by key(s) as a dictionary.

Let's create an example with some fictional sales data for different regions:

```
sales = pl.DataFrame(
    {
        "OrderID": [1, 2, 3, 4, 5, 6],
        "Product": ["A", "B", "A", "C", "B", "A"],
        "Quantity": [10, 5, 8, 7, 3, 12],
        "Region": ["North", "South", "North", "West", "South", "West"],
    }
)
```

Now you can partition the DataFrame by the Region column:

```
sales.partition_by("Region")
```

```
[shape: (2, 4)
┌─────────┬─────────┬──────────┬────────┐
│ OrderID │ Product │ Quantity │ Region │
│ ---     │ ---     │ ---      │ ---    │
│ i64     │ str     │ i64      │ str    │
╞═════════╪═════════╪══════════╪════════╡
│ 1       │ A       │ 10       │ North  │
│ 3       │ A       │ 8        │ North  │
└─────────┴─────────┴──────────┴────────┘,
shape: (2, 4)
┌─────────┬─────────┬──────────┬────────┐
│ OrderID │ Product │ Quantity │ Region │
│ ---     │ ---     │ ---      │ ---    │
│ i64     │ str     │ i64      │ str    │
╞═════════╪═════════╪══════════╪════════╡
│ 2       │ B       │ 5        │ South  │
│ 5       │ B       │ 3        │ South  │
└─────────┴─────────┴──────────┴────────┘,
shape: (2, 4)
┌─────────┬─────────┬──────────┬────────┐
│ OrderID │ Product │ Quantity │ Region │
│ ---     │ ---     │ ---      │ ---    │
│ i64     │ str     │ i64      │ str    │
╞═════════╪═════════╪══════════╪════════╡
│ 4       │ C       │ 7        │ West   │
│ 6       │ A       │ 12       │ West   │
└─────────┴─────────┴──────────┴────────┘]
```

If you want to drop the column you're partitioning by, you can set the include_key to
False:

```
sales.partition_by("Region", include_key=False)
```

```
[shape: (2, 3)
```

OrderID	Product	Quantity
i64	str	i64
1	A	10
3	A	8

```
shape: (2, 3)
```

OrderID	Product	Quantity
i64	str	i64
2	B	5
5	B	3

```
shape: (2, 3)
```

OrderID	Product	Quantity
i64	str	i64
4	C	7
6	A	12

And finally, if you want to get the results as a dictionary using a tuple with the group
keys as key, and the DataFrames as value, you can set the as_dict argument to True:

```
sales_dict = sales.partition_by(["Region"], as_dict=True)
```

```
sales_dict
```

```
{('North',): shape: (2, 4)
```

OrderID	Product	Quantity	Region
i64	str	i64	str
1	A	10	North
3	A	8	North

```
('South',): shape: (2, 4)
```

OrderID	Product	Quantity	Region

i64	str	i64	str
2	B	5	South
5	B	3	South

`('West',): shape: (2, 4)`

OrderID	Product	Quantity	Region
i64	str	i64	str
4	C	7	West
6	A	12	West

You can then get the DataFrames by accessing the dictionary with the key you want:

```
sales_dict[("North",)]
```

`shape: (2, 4)`

OrderID	Product	Quantity	Region
i64	str	i64	str
1	A	10	North
3	A	8	North

And that's how you can partition your DataFrame into multiple DataFrames.

Takeaways

In this chapter, we covered how to reshape your data. You have learned the following:

- About the wide and long formats of data
- To reshape your data from a long to wide format, use `df.pivot()`
- To reshape your data from wide to long instead, use `df.unpivot()`
- To flip your DataFrame diagonally, use `df.transpose()`
- To unpack nested values into a long format, one layer at a time, use `df.explode()`
- To chop up your DataFrame into (a dictionary of) multiple DataFrames, use `df.partition_by()`

Now that you're ready to reshape your data like a pro, you can prepare your data for visualization, which we'll discuss in the next chapter.

## PART V

Advance

## CHAPTER 16

Visualizing Data

The previous chapters have given you all the tools you need to transform raw data into a polished DataFrame. But how do you turn such a DataFrame into something insightful?

One way is through data visualization, and Python provides a plethora of packages for that. Packages include Matplotlib for low-level plotting, hvPlot for quick visualizations, Bokeh for interactive graphs, plotnine for leveraging the grammar of graphics in Python, and Altair for using the built-in plotting capabilities of Polars. Figure 16-1 gives an impression of Python's elaborate data visualization landscape.

This is both a blessing and a curse, because it's likely there's a package that fits your needs, but it's challenging to choose the right package. Moreover, each package comes with its own set of features, assumptions, and pitfalls.

Data visualization isn't just about making pretty pictures; it's a fundamental part of data science. By transforming a DataFrame into graphical form, you improve your ability to understand trends, spot outliers, and tell stories that can influence decision making. Effective data visualizations clarify the obscure and simplify the complicated, making your data more accessible.

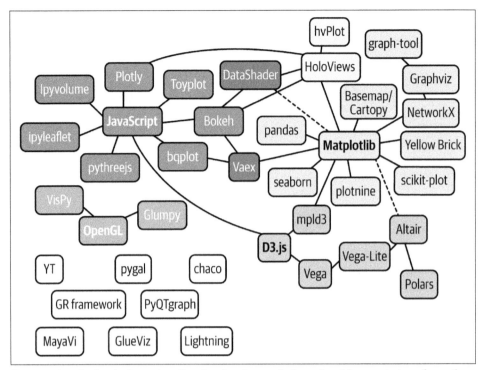

Figure 16-1. Python's data visualization landscape (adapted, with permission, from the original by Jake VanderPlas)

A Couple of Disclaimers

Data visualization is an extensive and multifaceted field, and here we're dedicating just one chapter to cover the essentials you need when working with Polars. Given the sheer variety of visualization packages available, we've chosen to focus on a few packages to keep the material clear and practical. We cannot provide exhaustive coverage of every package, and we won't be comparing them.

While we aim to equip you with the basics for visualizing data in Polars, visualizing data effectively often involves understanding which type of chart best communicates your data's story. For a more comprehensive exploration of chart types and their uses, we recommend *Fundamentals of Data Visualization* by Claus Wilke (O'Reilly), particularly Chapter 5, "Directory of Visualizations."

In this chapter you'll learn how to:

- Quickly create bar charts, scatter plots, density plots, and histograms using the built-in plotting functionality of Polars based on Altair

- Compose and layer multiple plots
- Create interactive visualizations
- Plot millions of points on a map
- Use alternative visualization packages such as hvPlot and plotnine
- Create beautiful tables with nanoplots using the Great Tables package

By the end of this chapter, you'll have a good idea of what the Altair, hvPlot, plotnine, and Great Tables packages have to offer, when to use which, and how to use them in combination with Polars. But first, we need to revisit the dataset that we'll be using.

The instructions to get any files you might need are in Chapter 2. We assume that you have the files in the *data* subdirectory.

NYC Bike Trips

Throughout the chapter we're going to use one dataset, namely the bike trips dataset that we prepared in Chapter 1. To refresh your memory, here's what the data looks like:[1]

```
trips = pl.read_parquet("data/citibike/*.parquet")

print(trips[:, :4])
print(trips[:, 4:7])
print(trips[:, 7:11])
print(trips[:, 11:])
```

```
shape: (2_638_971, 4)
```

bike_type	rider_type	datetime_start	datetime_end
cat	cat	datetime[μs]	datetime[μs]
electric	member	2024-03-01 00:00:02.490	2024-03-01 00:27:39.295
electric	member	2024-03-01 00:00:04.120	2024-03-01 00:09:29.384
…	…	…	…
electric	member	2024-03-31 23:55:41.173	2024-03-31 23:57:25.079
electric	member	2024-03-31 23:57:16.025	2024-03-31 23:59:22.134

```
shape: (2_638_971, 3)
```

duration	station_start	station_end
duration[μs]	str	str

---

1 We're printing the DataFrame in parts because it has 16 columns, which is too wide. If you open up the notebook of this chapter from our public repository (*https://oreil.ly/sEIUh*), you'll be able to see the DataFrame in full when you execute `trips`.

```
| 27m 36s 805ms | W 30 St & 8 Ave             | Maiden Ln & Pearl St     |
| 9m 25s 264ms  | Longwood Ave & Southern Blvd | Lincoln Ave & E 138 St  |
| …             | …                          | …                        |
| 1m 43s 906ms  | S 4 St & Wythe Ave         | S 3 St & Bedford Ave     |
| 2m 6s 109ms   | Montrose Ave & Bushwick Ave | Humboldt St & Varet St  |
```

shape: (2_638_971, 4)

```
| neighborhood_start | neighborhood_end   | borough_start | borough_end |
| ---                | ---                | ---           | ---         |
| str                | str                | str           | str         |
|                    |                    |               |             |
| Chelsea            | Financial District | Manhattan     | Manhattan   |
| Longwood           | Mott Haven         | Bronx         | Bronx       |
| …                  | …                  | …             | …           |
| Williamsburg       | Williamsburg       | Brooklyn      | Brooklyn    |
| Williamsburg       | Williamsburg       | Brooklyn      | Brooklyn    |
```

shape: (2_638_971, 5)

```
| lat_start | lon_start  | lat_end   | lon_end    | distance |
| ---       | ---        | ---       | ---        | ---      |
| f64       | f64        | f64       | f64        | f64      |
|           |            |           |            |          |
| 40.749614 | -73.995071 | 40.707065 | -74.007319 | 4.842569 |
| 40.816459 | -73.896576 | 40.810893 | -73.927311 | 2.659582 |
| …         | …          | …         | …          | …        |
| 40.712996 | -73.965971 | 40.712605 | -73.962644 | 0.283781 |
| 40.707678 | -73.940297 | 40.703172 | -73.940636 | 0.501835 |
```

In March 2024, over 2.6 million Citi Bike rides were made across four boroughs of New York City: the Bronx, Brooklyn, Manhattan, and Queens. (Staten Island, the fifth borough, doesn't have any Citi Bike stations.) Each borough has many neighborhoods.

The bike_type is either "electric" or "classic" and the rider_type is either "member" or "casual." The duration is the difference between datetime_start and datetime_end.

The four columns lat_start, lon_start, lat_end, and lon_end are the start and end GPS coordinates, respectively. The distance is in kilometers as the crow flies between these two coordinates, not the actual distance traveled.

The DataFrame trips has a variety of columns, including timestamps, categories, names, and coordinates. This will allow us to produce plenty of interesting data visualizations.

Alright, let's figure out when people rode, how far they went, and which stations were most popular by making some data visualizations.

Built-In Plotting with Altair

The quickest way to turn a DataFrame into a data visualization is to use the built-in methods that Polars provides. These methods are available through the df.plot namespace and the series.plot namespace: for example, df.plot.scatter() and series.plot.kde(). Under the hood, these methods are being forwarded to another package called Altair.

Plot Twist

As of this writing, the built-in plotting methods in Polars are marked as unstable, meaning they may change at any time. In fact, when plotting capabilities were first introduced, Polars used hvPlot as the backend. A few months later, this shifted to Altair. If the backend changes again in the future, you can always rely on Altair directly for your data visualizations. Keep in mind, the built-in plotting functions are provided solely for convenience and don't offer any unique functionality beyond what Altair provides.

Introducing Altair

Altair (*https://altair-viz.github.io*) is a declarative statistical visualization package for Python, designed to create interactive visualizations with minimal code. It was created by Jake VanderPlas and builds on top of Vega-Lite, a high-level grammar of interactive graphics. Altair aims to provide an easy-to-use yet powerful interface for creating a wide variety of visualizations, enabling you to focus on the data rather than the intricacies of the visualization process.

If you've installed Polars with additional dependencies using either the keywords all or plot, then you already have Altair installed (see Chapter 2 for instructions on how to do so). Alternatively, you can install Altair as follows:

```
$ uv pip install altair
```

If you use the built-in methods, then you usually don't need to explicitly import the Altair package. However, when you do, it can be imported as follows:

```
import altair as alt
```

The design philosophy of Altair revolves around the principles of declarative visualization. This means that you describe *what* you want to visualize rather than *how* to visualize it. Key concepts include:

Data-driven
Altair focuses on the data, allowing you to specify data transformations and encodings directly.

Declarative syntax
> You specify the visual properties (like color, shape, and size) and how they relate to the data without needing to manage rendering details.

Interactivity
> Altair supports interactive features such as tool tips, selections, and dynamic updates, enhancing engagement with visualizations.

Integration with Polars
> Altair works seamlessly with Polars DataFrames, without depending on pandas, thanks to the Narwhals package.

Methods in the Plot Namespaces

To see which methods are available in the two plot namespaces, you can use tab completion (that is, press the Tab key after `df.plot.`):

```
trips.plot.<TAB>
```

Available methods in the `df.plot` namespace are:

`df.plot.bar()`
> Plots a bar chart that can be stacked or grouped

`df.plot.line()`
> Plots a line chart (such as for a time series)

`df.plot.point()`
> Plots a scatter chart comparing two variables

`df.plot.scatter()`
> An alias to `df.plot.point()`

Tab completion may only work properly when you assign the Series to a new variable:

```
bike_type = trips.get_column("bike_type")
bike_type.plot<TAB>
```

Available methods in the `series.plot` namespace are:

`series.plot.hist()`
> Plots the distribution of one or more histograms as a set of bins

`series.plot.density()`
> Plots the kernel density estimate of one or more variables

`series.plot.line()`
> Plots a line chart (such as for a time series)

Let's try out some of these methods.

Plotting DataFrames

Let's start with a scatter plot that shows to what extent trip distance and trip duration are related for both the classic bikes and the electrical bikes:

```
trips_speed = trips.select(
    pl.col("distance"),
    pl.col("duration").dt.total_seconds() / 3600,  ❶
    pl.col("bike_type"),
).with_columns(speed=pl.col("distance") / pl.col("duration"))

trips_speed
```

❶ The unit of the duration column is hours. There is, indeed, the Expr.dt.total_hours() method, but this only returns whole hours.

shape: (2_638_971, 4)

distance	duration	bike_type	speed
f64	f64	cat	f64
4.842569	0.46	electric	10.527324
2.659582	0.156944	electric	16.94601
...	...	...	...
0.283781	0.028611	electric	9.918543
0.501835	0.035	electric	14.338131

You can create an Altair scatter plot using the df.plot.scatter() method:

```
trips_speed.plot.scatter(
    x="distance",
    y="duration",
    color="bike_type:N",
)
```

```
MaxRowsError: The number of rows in your dataset is greater than the maximum all
owed (5000).

Try enabling the VegaFusion data transformer which raises this limit by pre-eval
uating data transformations in Python.
    >> import altair as alt
    >> alt.data_transformers.enable("vegafusion")

Or, see https://altair-viz.github.io/user_guide/large_datasets.html for addition
al information
on how to plot large datasets.
alt.Chart(...)
```

Oops, that's right, Altair doesn't like DataFrames that are too big. In the next section we share some strategies on how to deal with this limitation. For now, let's prepare a smaller DataFrame by filtering on bike trips that started at one particular station:

```
trips_speed = (
    trips.filter(pl.col("station_start") == "W 70 St & Amsterdam Ave")
    .select(
        pl.col("distance"),
        pl.col("duration").dt.total_seconds() / 3600,
        pl.col("bike_type"),
    )
    .with_columns(speed=pl.col("distance") / pl.col("duration"))
)

trips_speed
```

```
shape: (4_963, 4)
```

distance	duration	bike_type	speed
f64	f64	cat	f64
0.596344	0.039167	electric	15.225797
1.134568	0.153611	classic	7.385977
…	…	…	…
6.784337	0.358611	electric	18.918368
2.077397	0.1375	electric	15.108345

Now we have fewer than five thousand rows. Let's try to create a scatter plot again:

```
trips_speed.plot.scatter(
    x="distance",
    y="duration",
    color="bike_type:N",   ❶
)
```

❶ The :N part after the column name bike_type lets Altair interpret this as a nominal value, which ensures that the two groups are colored appropriately (see Figure 16-2).

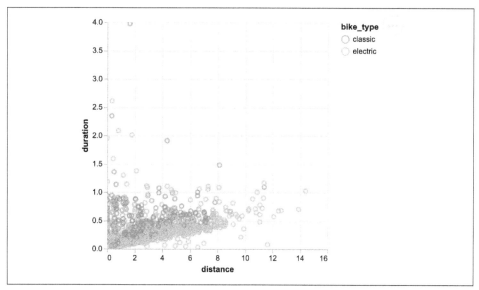

Figure 16-2. A scatter plot made with Altair

Too Large to Handle

Altair has a default limit of five thousand rows, which is a safeguard to prevent performance issues when working with large datasets in the browser. This limit is imposed by the underlying Vega-Lite renderer, not by Altair itself. However, you can override this limit if needed. To increase the row limit, you can adjust the `max_rows` setting like this:

```
import altair as alt

alt.data_transformers.disable_max_rows()
```

This command disables the restriction, allowing Altair to handle larger datasets. Be cautious when doing this, as rendering very large datasets can affect performance, particularly in a browser environment.

A better strategy to address this issue is to use VegaFusion. VegaFusion is an external project that uses efficient Rust implementations to perform data transformations, such as binning and aggregation, which significantly reduces the size of the DataFrame. It also automatically removes unused columns, further optimizing the DataFrame. When enabled, VegaFusion pre-evaluates transformations during chart display, saving, or conversion to dictionaries or JSON.

You can install VegaFusion as follows:

```
$ uv pip install "vegafusion[embed]"
```

And activate it with:

```
alt.data_transformers.enable("vegafusion")
```

Once the VegaFusion data transformer is activated, charts can handle datasets with up to 100,000 rows. The row limit is applied after all supported data transformations are processed, so charts like histograms are unlikely to reach it.

Another strategy of dealing with too many rows is to aggregate the data yourself. For example, when you want to create a (stacked) bar chart, you only need a handful of rows, not all the individual rows:

```
trips_type_counts = trips.group_by("rider_type", "bike_type").len()
trips_type_counts
```

```
shape: (4, 3)
┌───────────┬───────────┬─────────┐
│ rider_type │ bike_type │ len     │
│ ---       │ ---       │ ---     │
│ cat       │ cat       │ u32     │
╞═══════════╪═══════════╪═════════╡
│ member    │ electric  │ 1412598 │
│ casual    │ electric  │ 294679  │
│ member    │ classic   │ 811168  │
│ casual    │ classic   │ 120526  │
└───────────┴───────────┴─────────┘
```

This way, Altair can produce a stacked bar chart with no problem (see Figure 16-3):

```
trips_type_counts.plot.bar(
    x="rider_type", y="len", fill="bike_type:N"
).properties(
    width=300,
)
```

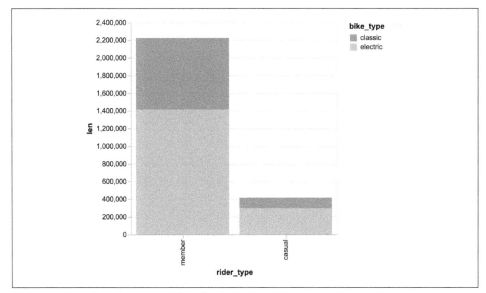

Figure 16-3. A bar chart created with Altair

If none of these strategies work for your situation, you could try a different data visualization package, such as hvPlot or plotnine.

Plotting Series

As mentioned, certain types of data visualizations are only available from the `series.plot` namespace. Here's an example of a density plot based on the `distance` column (see Figure 16-4):

```
trips_speed["distance"].plot.kde()
```

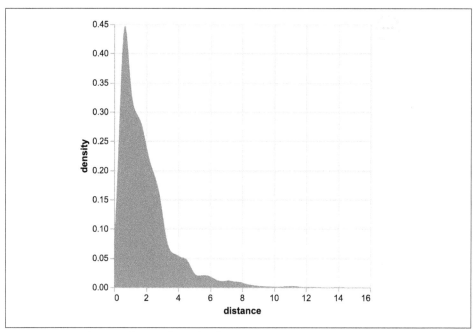

Figure 16-4. A density plot made with Altair

A histogram is created just as easily (see Figure 16-5):

```
trips_speed["distance"].plot.hist()
```

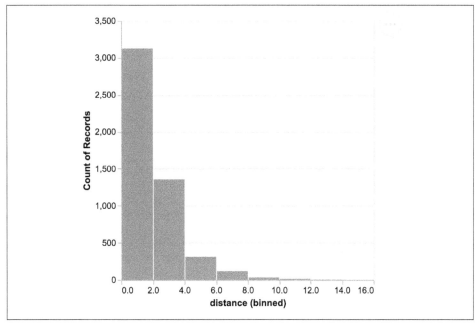

Figure 16-5. A histogram made with Altair

Let's also create a line plot for good measure. The following code snippet prepares a DataFrame with the number of trips and the average speed for each hour in March:

```
trips_hour_num_speed = (
    trips.sort("datetime_start")
    .group_by_dynamic("datetime_start", every="1h")
    .agg(
        num_trips=pl.len(),
        speed=(
            pl.col("distance") / (pl.col("duration").dt.total_seconds() / 3600)
        ).median(),
    )
    .filter(pl.col("datetime_start") > pl.date(2024, 3, 26))
)

trips_hour_num_speed
```

```
shape: (143, 3)
```

datetime_start	num_trips	speed
datetime[μs]	u32	f64
2024-03-26 01:00:00	295	13.813106
2024-03-26 02:00:00	181	14.317642
2024-03-26 03:00:00	119	13.150871
2024-03-26 04:00:00	222	14.239003

```
| 2024-03-26 05:00:00 | 878   | 13.966456 |
| ...                 | ...   | ...       |
| 2024-03-31 19:00:00 | 5170  | 10.692934 |
| 2024-03-31 20:00:00 | 3640  | 11.057322 |
| 2024-03-31 21:00:00 | 2813  | 11.429875 |
| 2024-03-31 22:00:00 | 2333  | 11.432521 |
| 2024-03-31 23:00:00 | 1333  | 12.046345 |
```

Then, using Altair, we can easily create a line plot using the method df.plot.line() (see Figure 16-6):

```
trips_hour_num_speed.plot.line(x="datetime_start", y="num_trips")
```

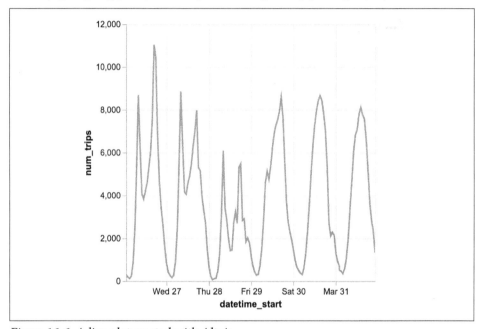

Figure 16-6. A line plot created with Altair

These examples demonstrate how the plotting methods built into Polars can be used to produce data visualizations based on Altair. These built-in methods are especially useful for quick, ad hoc data visualizations. Altair has some more features up its sleeve. For example, you can:

- Create charts with multiple layers
- Concatenate and link charts
- Add tool tips and other types of interactivity

These features are beyond the scope of this chapter. Please refer to Altair's documentation (*https://oreil.ly/PTQ91*) to learn more.

pandas-Like Plotting with hvPlot

hvPlot is unlike most data visualization packages in that it doesn't do any visualization by itself. Instead, it offers a unified interface to three other data visualization packages (Bokeh, Matplotlib, and Plotly), without locking you in. The API is inspired by the pandas API for plotting.

Introducing hvPlot

Figure 16-7 shows an overview of hvPlot's architecture. Let's go over this architecture step by step.

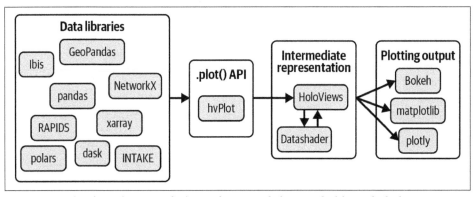

Figure 16-7. hvPlot offers a unified interface to Bokeh, Matplotlib, and Plotly

First, hvPlot's plotting methods accept Polars, pandas, and many other data structures of the PyData ecosystem. Second, hvPlot constructs an intermediate, package-agnostic representation of the visualization using the HoloViews package. Think of this representation as a description of how to create a plot.

It optionally uses the Datashader package when needed, for example, to plot millions of points on a map, which we'll do later. Third, hvPlot translates the intermediate representation into a specification for Bokeh, Matplotlib, or Plotly. At this point, you have the opportunity to customize the plot using the package-specific syntax. Finally, the output package renders the plot, meaning that it turns the raw data into pixels.

You can install hvPlot as follows:

```
$ uv pip install hvplot
```

And import it as follows:

```
import hvplot.polars
```

Upon importing, hvPlot adds the `df.hvplot` namespace so that all plotting methods are directly available from the DataFrame itself.

A First Plot

Let's start with a scatter plot, which is a good way to visualize the relationship between two continuous values. We'll reuse some of the DataFrames created in the previous section.

The following snippet constructs a scatter plot using the method `df.plot.scatter()`:

```
trips_speed.hvplot.scatter(
    x="distance",
    y="duration",
    color="bike_type",    ❶
    xlabel="distance (km)",
    ylabel="duration (h)",    ❷
    ylim=(0, 2),    ❸
)
```

❶ These three arguments are the most important, as they determine which columns are used for the position and color of each point.

❷ Adding or changing labels isn't necessary, but can clarify what the axes represent.

❸ We manually limit the range of the y-axis, because there are some much longer trips that would impact the visualization, making it more difficult to see smaller values. You can also fix these kinds of issues by applying a filter to the DataFrame.

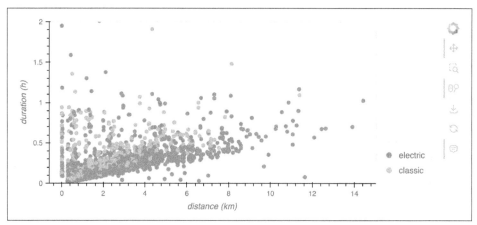

Figure 16-8. The relationship between distance and duration per bike type

Figure 16-8 shows that, generally speaking, electric bikes are faster and travel a greater distance than classic ones.

Methods in the hvPlot Namespace

The method `df.hvplot.scatter()` is just one of the many methods available in the `df.hvplot` namespace. To see which methods are available, you can use Tab completion:

```
trips.hvplot.<TAB>
```

Available methods include:

`df.hvplot.area()`
Plots an area chart similar to a line chart except for filling the area under the curve and optionally stacking

`df.hvplot.bar()`
Plots a bar chart that can be stacked or grouped

`df.hvplot.bivariate()`
Plots 2D density of a set of points

`df.hvplot.box()`
Plots a box-and-whisker chart comparing the distribution of one or more variables

`df.hvplot.density()`
Plots the kernel density estimate of one or more variables

`df.hvplot.heatmap()`
Plots a heatmap for visualizing a variable across two independent dimensions

`df.hvplot.hexbins()`
Plots hex bins

`df.hvplot.hist()`
Plots the distribution of one or more histograms as a set of bins

`df.hvplot.line()`
Plots a line chart (such as for a time series)

`df.hvplot.scatter()`
Plots a scatter chart comparing two variables

`df.hvplot.violin()`
Plots a violin plot comparing the distribution of one or more variables using the kernel density estimate

pandas as Backup

Under the hood, hvPlot first converts the Polars DataFrame to a pandas DataFrame. It only copies the columns that are needed for the plot. This works well most of the time, but not always.

Here's an example where we want to create a heatmap (see Figure 16-9). We first group the DataFrame by the hour of the day and the day of the month, and then count the number of trips per hour:

```
trips_per_day_hour = (
    trips.sort("datetime_start")
    .group_by_dynamic("datetime_start", every="1h")
    .agg(pl.len())
)
```

hvPlot's documentation mentions the special `.hour` and `.day` modifiers to extract the hour and day of a Datetime, respectively. Unfortunately, this is not (yet) supported for Polars DataFrames, so the following yields an error:

```
trips_per_day_hour.hvplot.heatmap(
    x="datetime_start.hour", y="datetime_start.day", C="len", cmap="reds"
)

ValueError: 'datetime_start.day' is not in list
```

We get an error because hvPlot attempts to copy the column `datetime_start.day`, which doesn't exist in our DataFrame. Fret not; we can always fall back to pandas by using the `df.to_pandas()` method:

```
import hvplot.pandas

trips_per_day_hour.to_pandas().hvplot.heatmap(
    x="datetime_start.hour", y="datetime_start.day", C="len", cmap="reds"
)
```

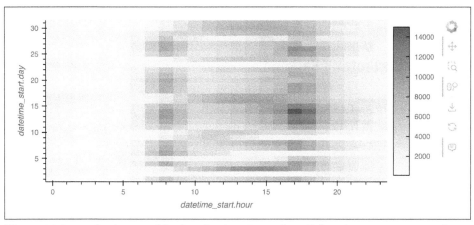

Figure 16-9. pandas is a good backup in situations where Polars is not yet supported

Manual Transformations

Let's try another plot: the bar chart. The bar chart is particularly useful for showing counts for different groups. hvPlot expects the DataFrame you provide to contain the actual values to be used; it doesn't do any transformation for you.

We can reuse the `trips_type_count` DataFrame we created earlier to produce a stacked bar chart, as follows:

```
trips_type_counts.hvplot.bar(
    x="rider_type",
    y="len",
    by="bike_type",
    ylabel="count",
    stacked=True,
    color=["orange", "green"],
)
```

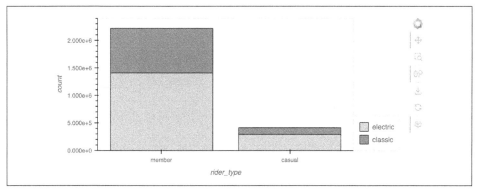

Figure 16-10. A stacked bar chart made with hvPlot showing the number of trips per bike type and rider type

Figure 16-10 shows that most bike trips are performed by Citi Bike members and that the majority use an electric bike.

Changing the Plotting Backend

The default plotting backend in hvPlot is Bokeh. In most cases this suffices, but there are situations where changing the backend to Plotly or Matplotlib is useful. For example, Matplotlib is useful when there's no need for an interactive visualization. Or maybe you need to match the style of other visualizations in a report.

The backend can be changed by using the `hvplot.extension()` method and passing either `"matplotlib"` or `"plotly"`. For this, you first need to explicitly import the `hvplot` package:

```
import hvplot

hvplot.extension("matplotlib")
```

Let's create the same bar chart as in the previous section, but now with Matplotlib as the backend:

```
trips_type_counts.hvplot.bar(
    x="rider_type",
    y="len",
    by="bike_type",
    ylabel="count",
    stacked=True,
    color=["orange", "green"],
)
```

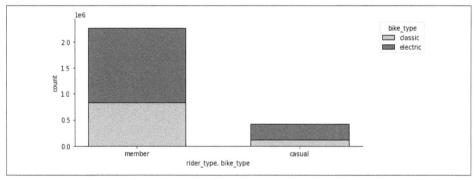

Figure 16-11. The same bar chart as before, but now created by the Matplotlib backend

Figure 16-11 shows that, apart from some minor visual differences, the same unchanged code can produce a Matplotlib image.

Let's reset the plotting backend to Bokeh for the purpose of this chapter:

```
hvplot.extension("bokeh")
```

Plotting Points on a Map

We haven't really used the coordinates in our DataFrame. Let's change that by creating a map. To visualize coordinates we use the df.hvplot.points() method, with the geo argument set to True. This ensures that the coordinates are properly projected onto a proper map:

```
trips.hvplot.points(
    x="lon_start",
    y="lat_start",
    datashade=True,
    geo=True,
    tiles="CartoLight",
    width=800,
    height=600,
)
```

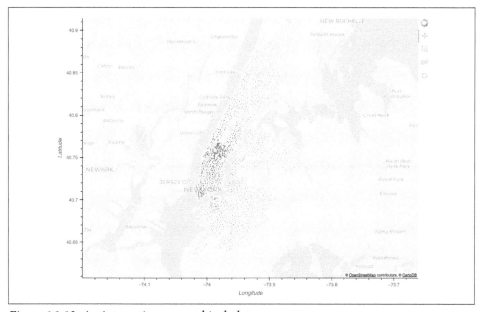

Figure 16-12. An interactive geographical plot

It's difficult to convey in a book, but the map shown statically in Figure 16-12 is actually an interactive visualization. You can pan and zoom. Because we've set the datashade argument to True, only the necessary data is used, maximizing efficiency.

Composing Plots

Sometimes a single plot is not sufficient. Using hvPlot, you can compose multiple plots into one. There are two types of composition: stacking and layering.

We'll use the `trips_hour_num_speed` DataFrame to draw a line plot.

In the first code snippet, we combine two plots using the plus (+) operator, which places two plots next to each other (see Figure 16-13):

```
(
    trips_hour_num_speed.hvplot.line(x="datetime_start", y="num_trips")
    + trips_hour_num_speed.hvplot.line(x="datetime_start", y="speed")
).cols(   ❶
    1
)
```

❶ With the `.cols()` method, we ensure that the two plots are placed beneath each other.

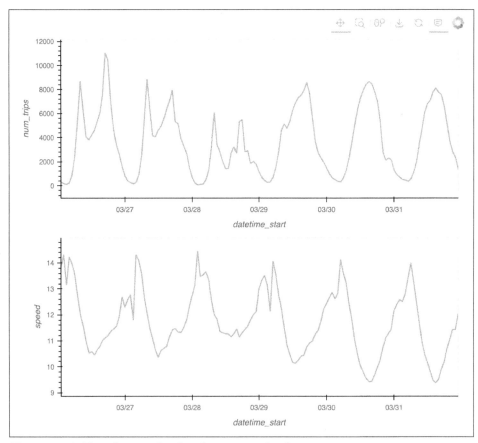

Figure 16-13. Two plots can be placed next to each other

In the second code snippet, we combine two plots into one using the multiply (*) operator (see Figure 16-14):

```
(
    trips_hour_num_speed.hvplot.line(x="datetime_start", y="num_trips")
    * trips_hour_num_speed.filter(pl.col("num_trips") > 9000).hvplot.scatter(
        x="datetime_start", y="num_trips", c="red", s=50
    )
)
```

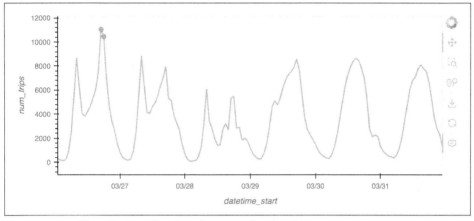

Figure 16-14. Two plots can be placed on top of each other

Notice that we're using two different DataFrames (the second is a subset of the first) and two different plot types (a line plot and a scatter plot).

Adding Interactive Widgets

The Bokeh backend already offers interactivity: you can zoom in and out, pan to move to different parts of the plot, and hover over elements to get more information.

Using the groupby keyword argument, you can add one or more widgets. The column name (or names) passed to this argument slices the data into multiple subsets. With the widgets, you can select which subset of the data is used for the plot.

Here's an example where we group by date. The widget type is based on the type of the column. As you can see in Figure 16-15, the widget for selecting the date is a slider:

```
trips_per_hour = (
    trips.sort("datetime_start")
    .group_by_dynamic("datetime_start", group_by="borough_start", every="1h")
    .agg(pl.len())
    .with_columns(date=pl.col("datetime_start").dt.date())
)
trips_per_hour
```
```
shape: (2_972, 4)
```

borough_start	datetime_start	len	date
str	datetime[µs]	u32	date
Manhattan	2024-03-01 00:00:00	480	2024-03-01
Manhattan	2024-03-01 01:00:00	294	2024-03-01
…	…	…	…
Queens	2024-03-31 22:00:00	173	2024-03-31
Queens	2024-03-31 23:00:00	126	2024-03-31

```
trips_per_hour.hvplot.line(
    x="datetime_start",
    by="borough_start",
    groupby="date",
    widget_location="left_top",
)
```

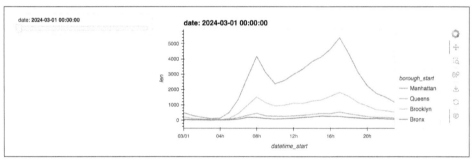

Figure 16-15. Interactive widgets are easily added with the groupby keyword argument

You can also pass a list of column names to the groupby keyword argument to create multiple widgets.

Publication-Quality Graphics with plotnine

plotnine (*https://plotnine.org*) is a data visualization package created by Hassan Kibirige. Its API is similar to ggplot2, a widely successful R package by Hadley Wickham and others.

plotnine is a personal favorite of ours. In fact, we used plotnine to create the data visualizations in the book, most notably in Chapter 1 and the Appendix.

Introducing plotnine

plotnine is based on the layered grammar of graphics.[2] The grammar is accompanied by a consistent API that allows you to quickly and iteratively create different types of beautiful data visualisations while rarely having to consult the documentation.

You can install plotnine as follows:

```
$ uv pip install 'plotnine[all]'
```

And import it as follows:

```
from plotnine import *
```

Import All the Things

While it's generally considered to be bad practice to import everything into the global namespace, we think it's fine to do this in an ad hoc environment such as a notebook, as it makes using plotnine's many functions more convenient.

If you'd rather not clutter your global namespace, we advise you to use `import plotnine as p9` and prefix every function with p9.

Plots for Exploration

plotnine allows you to create ad hoc data visualizations with relatively little code. Let's start with a scatter plot:

```
(
    ggplot(trips_speed, aes(x="distance", y="duration", color="bike_type"))
    + geom_point()  ❶
)
```

❶ In plotnine, the functions needed to create a data visualization are combined using the plus (+) operator (see Figure 16-16).

---

2 See "A Layered Grammar of Graphics" (*https://oreil.ly/Ivj95*) by Hadley Wickham.

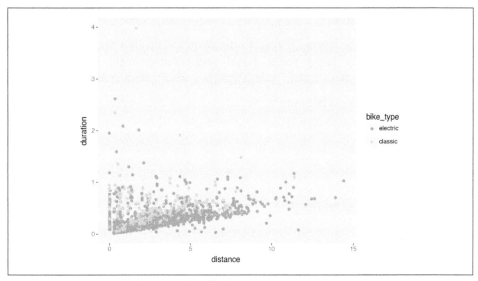

Figure 16-16. A scatter plot created with plotnine

This example captures what we consider the essence of plotnine. The aes() function maps columns in the DataFrame to aesthetics in the visualization. Aesthetics represent properties of the plotted geometry, such as points in this case, thanks to the geom_point() function.

Some geometries first perform a statistical transformation. For example, the geom_hist() function in the following code snippet creates a number of buckets for the range of distance values and then counts the number of trips that fall in each bucket (see Figure 16-17). These counts are used for the y aesthetic:

```
ggplot(trips_speed, aes(x="distance")) + geom_histogram()
```

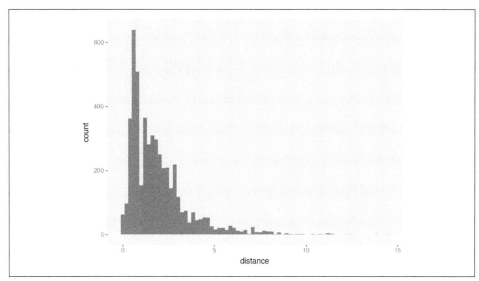

Figure 16-17. A histogram created with plotnine

The geom_bar() function, which is used to create bar charts, also performs a statistical transformation. Because we specify a fill color, Plotine automatically produces a *stacked* bar chart (see Figure 16-18):

```
ggplot(trips, aes(x="rider_type", fill="bike_type")) + geom_bar()
```

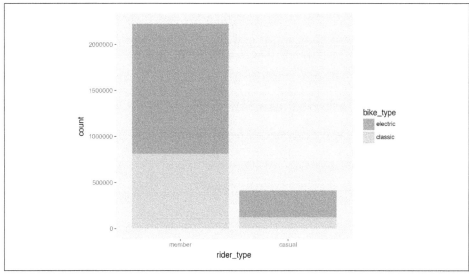

Figure 16-18. A bar chart created with plotnine

Aesthetics can also be a static value. In that case, the argument should not be inside the `aes()` function (see Figure 16-19):

```
ggplot(trips_speed, aes(x="distance", fill="bike_type")) + geom_density(
    alpha=0.7, color="none"
)
```

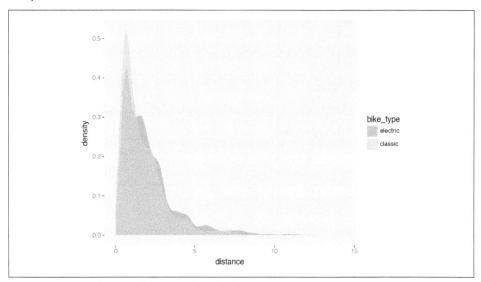

Figure 16-19. A density plot created with plotnine

Every geometry function adds a new layer, and plotnine supports multiple layers—it is based on the *layered* grammar of graphics, after all. Now, let's recreate the line graph we previously created with hvPlot (see Figure 16-20):

```
(
    ggplot(trips_hour_num_speed, aes(x="datetime_start", y="num_trips"))
    + geom_line(size=1, color="steelblue")
    + geom_point(
        data=trips_hour_num_speed.filter(pl.col("num_trips") > 9000),
        color="red",
        size=4,
    )
)
```

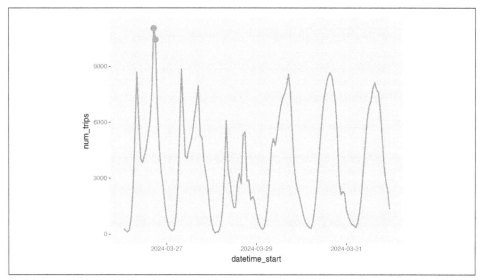

Figure 16-20. A multilayered line plot created with plotnine

Notice that we only needed to specify the aesthetic mapping once, and all layers use this default mapping. It's worth noting that both the mapping and the DataFrame can be adjusted for each layer.

Plots for Communication

The data visualizations in the previous section were created with minimal code, which is typical for exploratory data analysis. While they may not look polished, that's fine for initial exploration. Next, we'll improve them for communication by refining elements like colors, adding titles and labels, and adjusting fonts.

We're going to use plotnine to create scatter plots with a twist. First, we'll add an additional layer. Then, we'll turn the scatter plot into a plot with four panels.

The following code snippet prepares a DataFrame to explore the relationship between distance and duration. This time, we'll analyze bike stations, using the median distance and duration per station. The goal is to determine the correlation between distance and duration, focusing only on bike trips within the same borough:

```
trips_speed = (
    trips.group_by("neighborhood_start", "neighborhood_end")
    .agg(
        pl.col("duration").dt.total_seconds().median() / 60,
        pl.col("distance").median(),
        pl.col("borough_start").first(),
        pl.col("borough_end").first(),
        pl.len(),
    )
```

```
    .filter(
        (pl.col("len") > 30)
        & (pl.col("distance") > 0.2)
        & (pl.col("neighborhood_start") != pl.col("neighborhood_end")),
    )
    .with_columns(speed=pl.col("distance") / pl.col("duration"))
    .sort("borough_start")
)
trips_speed
```

shape: (2_962, 8)

neighborhood_ start	neighborhood _end	duration	...	borough_end	len	speed
---	---	f64		str	u32	f64
str	str					
Longwood	Mott Haven	6.35	...	Bronx	1317	0.17757
Highbridge	Claremont Village	8.483333	...	Bronx	163	0.155674
...	...	...	...	...	...	...
Astoria	Corona	21.233333	...	Queens	51	0.233306
Elmhurst	Williamsburg	27.133333	...	Brooklyn	42	0.24442

Here's the plotnine code needed to create the first scatter plot. Each row (and in Figure 16-21, each point) is a pair of start and end stations within the same borough (see Figure 16-21):

```
(
    ggplot(
        data=trips_speed.filter(
            pl.col("borough_start") == pl.col("borough_end")
        ),
        mapping=aes(x="distance", y="duration", color="borough_end"),
    )
    + geom_point(size=0.25, alpha=0.5)
    + geom_smooth(method="lowess", size=2, se=False, alpha=0.8)   ❶
    + xlim(0, 15)
    + ylim(0, 60)
    + scale_color_brewer(type="qualitative", palette="Set1")   ❷
    + labs(
        title="Trip distance and duration within each borough",
        x="Distance (km)",
        y="Duration (min)",
        color="Borough",
    )
    + theme_tufte(base_family="Guardian Sans", base_size=14)   ❸
    + theme(
        figure_size=(8, 6),
        dpi=300,
        plot_background=element_rect(color="#ffffff"),
```

```
    )
)
```

❶ Adds a regression line.

❷ Changes the color palette for both the points and lines.

❸ Uses a theme inspired by Edward Tufte's best practices for data visualization.

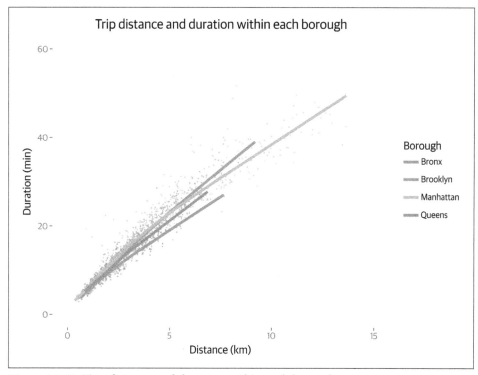

Figure 16-21. Trip distance and duration within each borough

As you can see, this code snippet is quite a bit longer than the examples in the previous section. That's because we're changing many of the (sensible) defaults that plotnine uses. As a rule of thumb, the more you want to adjust, the more code you need.

By negating the filter, we can investigate the relationship between trip distance and duration for trips across boroughs. Because we have four different starting boroughs, it makes sense to create four scatter plots. We use the `facet_wrap()` function to create four panels, one for each borough:

```
(
    ggplot(
```

```
    data=trips_speed.filter(
        pl.col("borough_start") != pl.col("borough_end")
    ).with_columns(
        ("From " + pl.col("borough_start")).alias("borough_start")
    ),
    mapping=aes(x="distance", y="duration", color="borough_end"),
)
+ geom_point(size=0.25, alpha=0.5)
+ geom_smooth(method="lowess", size=2, se=False, alpha=0.8)
+ xlim(0, 15)
+ ylim(0, 60)
+ scale_color_brewer(type="qualitative", palette="Set1")
+ facet_wrap("borough_start")
+ labs(
    title="Trip distance and duration cross borough",
    x="Distance (km)",
    y="Duration (min)",
    color="To Borough",
)
+ theme_linedraw(base_family="Guardian Sans", base_size=14)
+ theme(figure_size=(8, 6), dpi=300)
)
```

The result is shown in Figure 16-22.

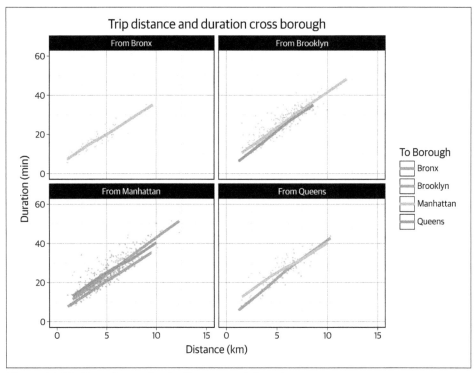

Figure 16-22. Cross-borough trip distance and duration

If you compare the two previous code snippets, you'll find that they share a lot of code. We only changed the `data` argument of the `ggplot()` function, added `facet_wrap` in the second snippet to create the four panels, and updated some of the labels. This is possible thanks to plotnine's composable API. It creates a plot by chaining methods, rather than adding keyword arguments to one method.

For more information about plotnine, refer to its website (*https://plotnine.org*) or Jeroen's blog post "plotnine: Grammar of Graphics for Python" (*https://oreil.ly/ky63Q*).

Styling DataFrames With Great Tables

So far, we've seen two ways of representing data. On the one hand, there's the DataFrame, which shows the raw data. On the other hand, there's a data visualization, which shows colorful pixels.

There's a third way to represent data that sits halfway between these two extremes. We're talking about tables. The Great Tables (*https://oreil.ly/tPxn0*) package by Rich Iannone and Michael Chow enables you to create, well, *great* tables.

A table is great when it presents data in a clear and structured way. That may include:

- Readable column names
- Numerical values with proper formatting
- Row grouping
- Styling to draw attention to important values
- Annotations such as titles, labels, and footnotes

Great Tables' underlying philosophy is based on a cohesive set of table components (see Figure 16-23). Starting with a DataFrame as input, you can iteratively chain methods to add elements and apply formatting.

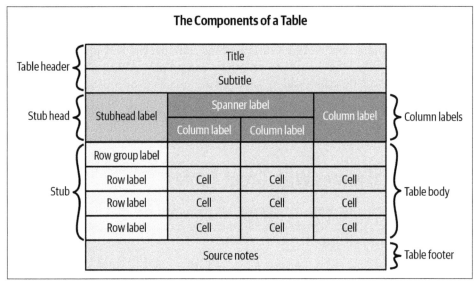

The Components of a Table

Title				
Subtitle				
Stubhead label	**Spanner label**		**Column label**	
	Column label	Column label		
Row group label				
Row label	Cell	Cell	Cell	
Row label	Cell	Cell	Cell	
Row label	Cell	Cell	Cell	
Source notes				

Table header · Stub head · Stub · Column labels · Table body · Table footer

Figure 16-23. Components of a Great Table (reproduced with permission from the Great Tables authors)

The Great Tables package can be installed as follows:

```
$ uv pip install great_tables
```

Let's prepare a DataFrame for a great-looking table. The following code snippet calculates the three busiest stations per borough:

```
import polars.selectors as cs

busiest_stations = (
    trips.group_by( ❶
        station=pl.col("station_start"), date=pl.col("datetime_start").dt.date()
    )
    .agg(
        borough=pl.col("borough_start").first(),
        neighborhood=pl.col("neighborhood_start").first(),
        num_rides=pl.len(),
        percent_member=(pl.col("rider_type") == "member").mean(),
        percent_electric=(pl.col("bike_type") == "electric").mean(),
    )
    .sort("date")
    .group_by("station")
    .agg(
        cs.string().first(),
        cs.numeric().mean(),
        pl.col("num_rides").alias("rides_per_day"), ❷
    )
    .sort("num_rides", descending=True)
    .group_by("borough", maintain_order=True)
```

```
    .head(3)
)

busiest_stations
```

❶ This first aggregation is needed because we want to display counts per station per day using nanoplots (we'll get to these later).

❷ The values in this column will make sense once we use them to create a nanoplot.

```
shape: (12, 7)
```

borough	station	neighbor hood	num_ride s	percent_ member	percent_ electric	rides_pe r_day
---	---	---	---	---	---	---
str	str	---	---	---	---	---
		str	f64	f64	f64	list[u32]
Manhattan	W 21 St & 6 Ave	Chelsea	354.1612 9	0.913765	0.583606	[325, 88, … 306]
…	…	…	…	…	…	…
Bronx	Plaza Dr & W 170 St	Mount Eden	31.70967 7	0.837427	0.948925	[30, 19, … 33]

There are two ways to start styling a DataFrame as a Great Table. The first is using the df.style attribute built in to Polars:

```
df.style
```

The second is using the GT() function from the Great Tables package. For this it's necessary to import the function first:

```
from great_tables import GT
```

```
GT(df)
```

Both ways return a GT object, which you can then use to refine the looks of your table. At the time of writing, the df.style is marked as unstable by the Polars developers, so we'll apply the second way to our busiest_stations DataFrame. The result is shown in Figure 16-24.

```
GT(busiest_stations)
```

Figure 16-24. A table created by Great Tables

Granted, this DataFrame doesn't look too great out of the box, mostly because of the last column, which is very wide. But, we now have something on which we can iterate. The following code snippet adds additional structure and styling via various methods:

```python
from great_tables import style, md

(
    GT(busiest_stations)
    .tab_stub(rowname_col="station", groupname_col="borough")    ❶
    .cols_label(    ❷
        neighborhood="Neighborhood",
        num_rides="Mean Daily Rides",
        percent_member="Members",
        percent_electric="E-Bikes",
        rides_per_day="Rides Per Day",
    )
    .tab_header(
        title="Busiest Bike Stations in NYC",
        subtitle="In March 2024, Per Borough",
    )
    .tab_stubhead(label="Station")
    .fmt_number(columns="num_rides", decimals=1)
    .fmt_percent(columns=cs.starts_with("percent_"), decimals=0)    ❸
    .fmt_nanoplot(columns="rides_per_day", reference_line="mean")
    .data_color(columns="num_rides", palette="Blues")
    .tab_options(row_group_font_weight="bold")
    .tab_source_note(
        source_note=md(
            "Source: [NYC Citi Bike](https://citibikenyc.com/system-data)"
        )
    )
)
```

❶   Stations are grouped by borough to add structure.

❷ We can give table columns proper names without needing to change the underlying DataFrame.

❸ Great Tables accepts column selectors, making our code more compact.

		Busiest Bike Stations in NYC				
		In March 2024, Per Borough				
Station	Neighborhood	Mean Daily Rides	Members	E-Bikes	Rides Per Day	
Manhattan						
W 21 St & 6 Ave	Chelsea	354.2	91%	58%		
Broadway & W 58 St	Midtown	307.5	80%	71%		
8 Ave & W 31 St	Chelsea	288.3	87%	64%		
Brooklyn						
Metropolitan Ave & Bedford Ave	Williamsburg	184.9	85%	68%		
N 7 St & Driggs Ave	Williamsburg	145.7	86%	66%		
Hanson Pl & Ashland Pl	Fort Greene	143.8	84%	61%		
Queens						
Queens Plaza North & Crescent St	Long Island City	126.7	85%	57%		
Vernon Blvd & 50 Ave	Long Island City	95.2	89%	66%		
31 St & Newtown Ave	Astoria	78.2	88%	60%		
Bronx						
Melrose Ave & E 150 St	Melrose	41.6	83%	89%		
E 161 St & River Ave	Concourse	35.5	74%	88%		
Plaza Dr & W 170 St	Mount Eden	31.7	84%	95%		
Source: NYC Citi Bike						

Figure 16-25. A table showing information about the three busiest stations per borough

The output table is shown in Figure 16-25. The line plots in the rightmost column are known as *nanoplots*. They visualize the daily number of rides per station.

A nice property of having these methods as building blocks is that you can quickly create a first table, then iteratively improve on it.

Takeaways

In this chapter we've looked at several ways to turn DataFrames into graphs and tables. The key takeaways are:

- There are many data visualization packages.
- Polars has built-in plotting capabilities that use Altair under the hood.
- hvPlot uses Bokeh, Matplotlib, or Plotly to produce plots.
- You can always use pandas if a certain data visualization package doesn't fully support Polars yet.
- plotnine is a beautiful data visualization package based on the grammar of graphics that allows you create both ad hoc data visualizations for exploration and high-quality graphics for communication.
- A table can be a valuable alternative to a plot, and Great Tables helps you produce one that looks great.

In the next chapter we're going to look at extending Polars.

## CHAPTER 17

Extending Polars

As you've seen in previous chapters, Polars' API is already quite extensive and covers a wide range of functionality. However, there might be cases where you want to extend Polars with your own custom functionality. This could be because you have a specific use case that isn't covered by the built-in functions, or because you want to optimize the performance of your code.

In this chapter, you'll learn how to:

- Apply a custom Python function to Polars data
- Register a Polars namespace
- Write Rust plugins and run them on the Polars engine for maximum performance
- Use Rust crates in those plugins

The instructions to get any files you might need are in Chapter 2. We assume that you have the files in the *data* subdirectory.

User-Defined Functions in Python

Polars has an extensive set of expressions that allow you to perform a wide range of operations. However, sometimes you need to perform an operation that isn't covered by the available expressions, or is performed by an external package. To leave you this option, Polars allows for *user-defined functions* (UDFs). The Polars methods that allow you to do this are:

`Expr.map_elements()`
   Apply a Python function to each element of a Series

```
Expr.map_batches()
```
Apply a Python function to a Series or sequence of Series

```
Expr.map_groups()
```
Apply a Python function to each group in the GroupBy context

```
Expr.pipe()
```
Apply a Python function to an Expression

```
df.pipe()
```
Apply a Python function to an entire DataFrame (and LazyFrame)

Let's dive into how you can use these methods to apply your own custom Python functions to your data.

Applying a Function to Elements

The `Expr.map_elements()` method allows you to apply a Python function to each element in a Series in case you don't need to know anything about the other elements in the Series.

This example performs sentiment analysis on a DataFrame text with reviews:

```
from textblob import TextBlob


def analyze_sentiment(review):
    return TextBlob(review).sentiment.polarity


reviews = pl.DataFrame(
    {
        "reviews": [
            "This product is great!",
            "Terrible service.",
            "Okay, but not what I expected.",
            "Excellent! I love it.",
        ]
    }
)

reviews.with_columns(
    sentiment_score=pl.col("reviews").map_elements(
        analyze_sentiment, return_dtype=pl.Float64
    )
)
shape: (4, 2)
```

reviews	sentiment_score

```
| str                           | f64   |
|===============================|=======|
| This product is great!        | 1.0   |
| Terrible service.             | -1.0  |
| Okay, but not what I expected.| 0.2   |
| Excellent! I love it.         | 0.75  |
```

In this example, we use the `Expr.map_elements()` method to apply the `analyze_sen` `timent()` function to each element in the `reviews` Series. The resulting values range from -1.0 (very negative) to 1.0 (very positive), with 0.0 being neutral.

Warning for Inefficient Mappings

When you use a Python function in Polars, it's important to know that it won't be as fast as the native Polars functions. Polars normally runs its operations in Rust. However, when it has to apply a custom Python function, two things happen:

- The function executes slower Python bytecode instead of faster Rust bytecode.
- The Python function is constrained by the *global interpreter lock* (GIL),[1] which means it can't run in parallel. This is especially detrimental to speed in `df.group_by()` operations, where the aggregation function is normally called in parallel for each group.

Mapping Python lambdas or custom functions to Polars data should be treated as a last resort. When Polars raises a `PolarsInefficientMapWarning`, it's a sign that there are probably alternative ways to use a native Polars expression instead. Only if you've gone through the Polars documentation and found that there's no native expression or combination of expressions that does what you want should you consider using a Python function.

In the following example, you'll see the `PolarsInefficientMapWarning` by mapping a trivial function to a Series:

```
ints = pl.DataFrame({"x": [1, 2, 3, 4]})


def add_one(x):
    return x + 1


ints.with_columns(
    pl.col("x")
    .map_elements(
```

---

1 Newer versions of Python will have a GIL-free interpreter, but this doesn't mean that Python will automatically take advantage of multiple cores.

```
            add_one,
            return_dtype=pl.Int64,
        )
        .alias("x + 1")
)

PolarsInefficientMapWarning:
Expr.map_elements is significantly slower than the native expressions API.
Only use if you absolutely CANNOT implement your logic otherwise.
Replace this expression...
  - pl.col("x").map_elements(add_one)
with this one instead:
  + pl.col("x") + 1

  .map_elements(

shape: (4, 2)
┌─────┬───────┐
│ x   │ x + 1 │
│ --- │ ---   │
│ i64 │ i64   │
╞═════╪═══════╡
│ 1   │ 2     │
│ 2   │ 3     │
│ 3   │ 4     │
│ 4   │ 5     │
└─────┴───────┘
```

These suggestions are usually a good starting point to find a more efficient way to implement your logic.

Applying a Function to a Series

The `Expr.map_batches()` method allows you to apply a Python function to a Series or sequence of Series. This is useful when you need to know something about the other elements in the Series, or when you need to apply a function to multiple Series at the same time. Table 17-1 lists the arguments that the `Expr.map_batches()` method accepts.

Table 17-1. Arguments for the method `Expr.map_batches()`

Argument	Description
function	Function to apply to the Series.
return_dtype	The data type of the Series that is returned by the function.
is_elementwise	Whether the function can be applied elementwise or not. (If it is, it can run in the streaming engine, but it might return incorrect results in the GroupBy context.)
agg_list	Aggregate the values of the expression into a list before applying the function in a GroupBy context. The function will be invoked only once on a list of groups, rather than once per group.

In the following example, we'll demonstrate the `Expr.map_batches()` method by applying a `softmax` normalization function from the NumPy package to the Series `feature1` and `feature2`. The `softmax` normalization function turns a list of numbers into probabilities that sum to 1:

```
import polars.selectors as cs
from scipy.special import softmax

ml_dataset = pl.DataFrame(
    {
        "feature1": [0.3, 0.2, 0.4, 0.1, 0.2, 0.3, 0.5],
        "feature2": [32, 50, 70, 65, 0, 10, 15],
        "label": [1, 0, 1, 0, 1, 0, 0],
    }
)

ml_dataset.select(
    "label",
    cs.starts_with("feature").map_batches(
        lambda x: softmax(x.to_numpy()),
    ),
)
```

```
shape: (7, 3)
```

label	feature1	feature2
i64	f64	f64
1	0.143782	3.1181e-17
0	0.130099	2.0474e-9
1	0.158904	0.993307
0	0.117719	0.006693
1	0.130099	3.9488e-31
0	0.143782	8.6979e-27
0	0.175616	1.2909e-24

Applying a Function to Groups

The `Expr.map_groups()` methods allows you to apply a Python function to each group in the GroupBy context.

Say you have a DataFrame with temperatures measured in different locations, where the temperatures of the American locations are in Fahrenheit and those of the European locations are in Celsius. If only the variation in temperature is relevant for your analysis, you can scale the features within each group to make them comparable. To do so, we can use the scikit-learn StandardScaler on each group:

```
from sklearn.preprocessing import StandardScaler
```

```
def scale_temperature(group):
    scaler = StandardScaler()
    scaled_values = scaler.fit_transform(group[["temperature"]].to_numpy())
    return group.with_columns(
        pl.Series(values=scaled_values.flatten(), name="scaled_feature")
    )


temperatures = pl.DataFrame(
    {
        "country": ["USA", "USA", "USA", "USA", "NL", "NL", "NL"],
        "temperature": [32, 50, 70, 65, 0, 10, 15],
    }
)

temperatures.group_by("country").map_groups(scale_temperature)
```

```
shape: (7, 3)
```

country	temperature	scaled_feature
str	i64	f64
USA	32	-1.502872
USA	50	-0.287066
USA	70	1.063831
USA	65	0.726107
NL	0	-1.336306
NL	10	0.267261
NL	15	1.069045

Lastly, if you need fine-grained control over the individual groups in the GroupBy context, you can also iterate over them. This can be useful when you need to apply a different custom function per group, or when you want to inspect the groups individually. Iterating over the groups returns a tuple containing the group identifiers (or a single identifier if there's only one) and the DataFrame for that group:

```
temperatures = pl.DataFrame(
    {
        "country": ["USA", "USA", "USA", "USA", "NL", "NL", "NL"],
        "temperature": [32, 50, 70, 65, 0, 10, 15],
    }
)

for group, df in temperatures.group_by("country"):
    print(f"{group[0]}:\n{df}\n")
```

```
USA:
shape: (4, 2)
```

| country | temperature |

```
| ---       | ---       |
| str       | i64       |
╞═══════════╪═══════════╡
| USA       | 32        |
| USA       | 50        |
| USA       | 70        |
| USA       | 65        |
└───────────┴───────────┘
```

NL:
shape: (3, 2)
```
| country   | temperature |
| ---       | ---         |
| str       | i64         |
╞═══════════╪═════════════╡
| NL        | 0           |
| NL        | 10          |
| NL        | 15          |
└───────────┴─────────────┘
```

Cache Rules Everything Around Me

The @lru_cache decorator from the functools module in Python is a handy tool for optimizing functions that are computationally intensive. By caching the results of function calls, it can significantly reduce execution time, especially when the function is repeatedly called with the same arguments. This is particularly useful in scenarios where you map a function over a DataFrame column containing repeated values. @lru_cache stores the outcomes of your function calls. When the function is invoked again with the same arguments, it retrieves the result from the cache instead of computing it again.

You can give the @lru_cache decorator a maxsize argument, which determines the number of results that are cached. By default this is set to 128 cache entries, but you can set it higher to prevent cache misses depending on your data size at the cost of used memory. @lru_cache discards the least recently used entries when it fills up. You can set maxsize to None if you want to store all results, but note that RAM can fill up quickly this way. You can clear the cache using the cache_clear() function when it's no longer needed.

This is what it looks like applied to the sentiment analysis you did earlier:

```python
from functools import lru_cache

from textblob import TextBlob


@lru_cache(maxsize=256)
def analyze_sentiment(review):
```

```
        return TextBlob(review).sentiment.polarity


reviews = pl.DataFrame(
    {
        "reviews": [
            "This product is great!",
            "Terrible service.",
            "Okay, but not what I expected.",
            "Excellent! I love it.",
        ]
    }
)

reviews.with_columns(
    sentiment_score=pl.col("reviews").map_elements(
        analyze_sentiment, return_dtype=pl.Float64
    )
)
shape: (4, 2)
```

```
┌───────────────────────┬─────────────────┐
│ reviews               │ sentiment_score │
│ ---                   │ ---             │
│ str                   │ f64             │
╞═══════════════════════╪═════════════════╡
│ This product is grea… │ 1.0             │
│ Terrible service.     │ -1.0            │
│ Okay, but not what I… │ 0.2             │
│ Excellent! I love it… │ 0.75            │
└───────────────────────┴─────────────────┘
```

Note that in this minimal example it doesn't speed up the execution, because there are only unique inputs.

Applying a Function to an Expression

Expr.pipe() offers a structured way to apply Python UDFs to an expression. The first argument the Python function receives is the expression on which it is applied, and it is expected to return another expression.

A small example would be:

```
addresses = pl.DataFrame(
    {
        "address": [
            "Nieuwezijds Voorburgwal 147",
            "Museumstraat 1",
            "Oosterdok 2",
        ]
    }
```

```
)

def extract_house_number(input_expr: pl.Expr) -> pl.Expr:
    """Extract the house number from an address String"""
    return input_expr.str.extract(r"\d+", 0).cast(pl.Int64)


addresses.with_columns(
    house_numbers=pl.col("address").pipe(extract_house_number)
)
```

shape: (3, 2)

address	house_numbers
---	---
str	i64
Nieuwezijds Voorburg…	147
Museumstraat 1	1
Oosterdok 2	2

Applying a Function to a DataFrame or LazyFrame

df.pipe() provides a structured way to apply Python functions to an entire Data-Frame or LazyFrame. Out of the two, LazyFrames are the recommended way of working because optimizations can be applied. The function that is provided receives the DataFrame as the first argument:

```
small_numbers = pl.DataFrame({"ints": [2, 4, 6], "floats": [10.0, 20.0, 30.0]})


def scale_the_input(
    df: pl.DataFrame | pl.LazyFrame, scale_factor: int
) -> pl.DataFrame | pl.LazyFrame:
    """Scales the input by the input factor"""
    return df * scale_factor


small_numbers.pipe(scale_the_input, 5)
```

shape: (3, 2)

ints	floats
---	---
f64	f64
10.0	50.0
20.0	100.0
30.0	150.0

In summary, Polars offers functions to apply custom Python functions to your data through `Expr.map_elements()`, `Expr.map_batches()`, `Expr.map_groups()`, `Expr.pipe()`, and `df.pipe()`. While these user-defined functions allow for extensive customization, it's important to think about performance drawbacks compared to native Polars expressions. If you still need to work with Python functions, but the input is often the same, the `@lru_cache` decorator can help optimize repeated computations. By understanding and leveraging these tools, you can tailor your data transformations to meet specific needs while maintaining optimal performance.

Registering Your Own Namespace

Polars already has a number of built-in namespaces, such as the `str` expression namespace in `pl.col(…).str.…()`, but you can also register your own custom namespaces. You can then register your own custom functions and expressions to that new namespace. This allows you to create a more intuitive and user-friendly API for your users.

To create a custom namespace, you need to create a Python class that is decorated with the decorator for the level at which you want to register the namespace. These levels are shown in Table 17-2:

Table 17-2. The corresponding decorators for creating a namespace per context

Context	Decorator	Usage example
Expression	`@pl.api.register_expr_namespace("…")`	`pl.col(…).<namespace>.<function>`
DataFrame	`@pl.api.register_dataframe_name space("…")`	`df.<namespace>.<function>`
LazyFrame	`@pl.api.register_lazy_frame_name space("…")`	`lf.<namespace>.<function>`
Series	`@pl.api.register_series_namespace("…")`	`col.<namespace>.<function>`

The way you register a custom namespace is the same for all levels. You create a class that is decorated with the corresponding decorator, and you define the functions that you want to register in that class.

Take, for example, the following code snippet that registers a custom namespace `celsius` for the `pl.col(…).celsius.…()` expression:

```
@pl.api.register_expr_namespace("celsius")  ❶
class Celsius:
    def __init__(self, expr: pl.Expr):  ❷
        self._expr = expr

    def to_fahrenheit(self) -> pl.Expr:  ❸
        return (self._expr * 9 / 5) + 32
```

```
def to_kelvin(self) -> pl.Expr:
    return self._expr + 273.15
```

❶ This line registers the custom expression namespace with the name celsius.

❷ The constructor of the class takes an expression as input. This allows you to use the expression that is passed to the custom namespace in the custom functions.

❸ The Celsius.to_fahrenheit() method takes the expression that is passed to the custom namespace and returns a new expression that converts the temperature to Fahrenheit.

You can then use this custom namespace in your code, like this:

```
temperatures = pl.DataFrame({"celsius": [0, 10, 20, 30, 40]})

temperatures.with_columns(fahrenheit=pl.col("celsius").celsius.to_fahrenheit())

shape: (5, 2)
```

celsius	fahrenheit
i64	f64
0	32.0
10	50.0
20	68.0
30	86.0
40	104.0

This code snippet creates a DataFrame with a column celsius and converts the values in that column to Fahrenheit using the custom namespace celsius.

Ghosted by Autocomplete

Because custom namespaces are not part of the Polars package and are created at runtime, they are not recognized by type hinting and autocomplete. This means that you won't get any suggestions or type hints in notebooks and IDEs when using custom namespaces.

Polars Plugins in Rust

If you want to squeeze the maximum performance out of Polars, you can write custom plugins in Rust. This allows the Polars engine to *dynamically link* your custom functions and expressions at runtime. Dynamically linking allows Polars to seamlessly integrate external code into its package without having to recompile the main package. This way, the plugin can use the optimizations, parallelism, and performance that Rust brings; it runs as fast as Polars' own native functions and expressions, with just minimal overhead. This makes it our preferred way of extending Polars with new functionality.

To explore how this works, we'll create a basic custom function that replaces all values in a Series with "Hello, world!"

Prerequisites

Because you'll write the expression in Rust, you'll have to install Rust first. You can install Rust by following the instructions on the Rust website (*https://oreil.ly/hMgl6*). To check whether it has installed correctly, you can run the following:

```
! rustc --version
```

If you see a version number, you're good to go.

The Anatomy of a Plugin Project

A custom expression consists of a separate project folder containing a few key files:

```
/
├── src
│   ├── expressions.rs
│   └── lib.rs
├── hello_world_func
│   └── __init__.py
├── Cargo.toml
```

- *src/expressions.rs* contains the Rust code for the custom expression.
- *src/lib.rs* contains the Rust code that defines the custom expression as a package.
- *hello_world_func/init.py* contains Python code that registers the function with the Polars engine.
- *Cargo.toml* contains the metadata of the Rust project, such as the name, version, and dependencies.

The Plugin

Let's walk through what these files would look like for a function that returns a Series with all values replaced by "Hello, world!" The first file contains the Rust code for the custom expression:

src/expressions.rs
```
    use polars::prelude::*;   ❶
    use pyo3_polars::derive::polars_expr;

    #[polars_expr(output_type=String)]   ❷
    fn hello_world(inputs: &[Series]) -> PolarsResult<Series> {   ❸
```

```
// This function takes a Series as input, and returns a new Series of the
// same length with all values set as "Hello, world!"
let length = inputs[0].len();  ❹
let result: Vec<String> = vec!["Hello, world!".to_string(); length];  ❺
Ok(Series::new("hello_world".into(), result))  ❻
}
```

❶ These lines import the Polars and PyO3 Polars Rust packages.

❷ This line works like a Python decorator and allows the Rust function to be registered as a Polars function that returns a String data type, allowing the Polars engine to optimize for this output.

❸ The input of this function is a slice of Series and it returns a `PolarsResult` of a Series. A `PolarsResult` is a type that can either have a value or an error.

❹ This takes the length of the incoming Series.

❺ This creates a vector of the provided length, with each element set to "Hello, world!"

❻ This returns a new Series with the name `hello_world` and that vector of Strings.

Next is the file that defines the custom expression as a package:

src/lib.rs

```
mod expressions;  ❶

use pyo3::types::PyAnyMethods;  ❷
use pyo3::types::PyModule;
use pyo3::{pymodule, Bound, PyResult};

#[pymodule]  ❸
fn hello_world_func(m: &Bound<'_, PyModule>) -> PyResult<()> {  ❹
    m.setattr("__version__", env!("CARGO_PKG_VERSION"))?;  ❺
    Ok(())  ❻
}
```

❶ This line tells Rust to include the *expressions.rs* file in the module.

❷ Imports that allow PyO3 to build an interface between Python and Rust.

❸ A Rust macro that marks the following function as a Python initialization function. This code is called to initialize the module.

❹ Function that serves as the initializer.

❺ Adds a version tag to the module, based off of the Cargo package version.

❻ Signals successful completion of the function.

The init file runs the moment the plugin is loaded:

`hello_world_func/__init__.py`
```python
from pathlib import Path

import polars as pl
from polars.plugins import register_plugin_function
from polars.type_aliases import IntoExpr


PLUGIN_PATH = Path(__file__).parent


def hello_world(expr: IntoExpr) -> pl.Expr:     ❶
    return register_plugin_function(            ❷
        plugin_path=PLUGIN_PATH,                ❸
        function_name="hello_world",            ❹
        args=expr,                              ❺
        is_elementwise=True,                    ❻
    )
```

❶ Takes a variable of the type `IntoExpr` that is passed to the Rust plugin and returns the expression that is registered with Polars. `IntoExpr` represents a type that is, or can be converted into, a Polars expression. An example of something that can be converted into a Polars expression is a String value that can be converted into a `pl.col("column_name")` expression.

❷ Registers the plugin as a function with Polars.

❸ The filepath where the Rust plugin is situated.

❹ The name of the Rust function to register.

❺ Passes the expression to the Rust plugin. It also allows you to pass multiple arguments to the Rust plugin.

❻ Specifies that the function is *element-wise*, meaning that it operates on each element of the Series independently. This knowledge allows Polars to trigger fast path algorithms and optimizations.

And last is the file containing the metadata of the Rust project:

```
Cargo.toml
        [package]
        name = "hello_world_plugin"
        version = "1.0.0"
        edition = "2021"

        [lib]
        name = "hello_world_func"
        crate-type = ["cdylib"]

        [dependencies]
        polars = { version = "*" }
        pyo3 = { version = "*", features = ["extension-module"] }
        pyo3-polars = { version = "*", features = ["derive"] }
        serde = { version = "*", features = ["derive"] }
```

This file contains the metadata of the Rust project. It specifies the name, version, edition, and dependencies of the project. It also specifies the name and type of the package. The `name` field in the [lib] section should match the name of the Rust project folder (which is `hello_world_func` in this case).

Compiling the Plugin

To make this basic plugin available in your Python code, compile the Rust code by running the following line:

```
! cd plugins/hello_world_plugin && uv run maturin develop --release
```

The --release Flag

The `--release` flag optimizes the compiled code for performance, but makes it take longer to compile. When you are benchmarking the plugin, always use the `--release` flag. If you are developing and want to compile the code quickly, you can omit the flag.

Performance Benchmark

Now that the code is compiled, you can crudely benchmark the performance of the custom expression to get a feeling for how much of a difference this makes by running the following Python code:

```
import polars as pl
from hello_world_func import hello_world  ❶
import time

lots_of_strings = pl.DataFrame(
    {
        "a": ["1", "2", "3", "4"] * 100_000,
    }
```

```
)

times = []
for i in range(10):
    t0 = time.time()
    out = lots_of_strings.with_columns(
        pl.col("a").str.replace_all(r".*", "Hello, world!")
    )
    t1 = time.time()
    times.append(t1 - t0)
print(
    f"Polars native string replace:        {sum(times) / len(times):.5f}"
) ❷


times = []
for i in range(10):
    t0 = time.time()
    out = lots_of_strings.with_columns(hello_world("a"))  ❸
    t1 = time.time()
    times.append(t1 - t0)
print(f"Our custom made Hello world replace: {sum(times) / len(times):.5f}")
```

❶ This line imports the custom function. The module from which the function is imported should be the same, the name of the Rust [lib].

❷ We use a format specifier to limit the amount of digits after the decimal separator for the resulting double in the f-string.

❸ This line uses the custom function to replace all values in the a column with "Hello, world!"

```
Polars native string replace:        0.04523
Our custom made Hello world replace: 0.01301
```

As you can see, the custom expression is faster than the native Polars expression.

Register Arguments

Now that you have a basic understanding of how to create custom expressions, let's dive into the different ways you can use them.

Working with multiple arguments as input

You can pass multiple arguments to the Rust plugin to create custom functions that operate on multiple Series at once. You can do this by passing a list in the args argument of the register_plugin_function() function:

```
def args_func(arg1: IntoExpr, arg2: IntoExpr) -> pl.Expr:
    return register_plugin_function(
```

```
        plugin_path=PLUGIN_PATH,
        function_name="args_func",
        args=[arg1, arg2],
    )
```

Additionally, you can pass keyword arguments to the Rust plugin by passing a dictionary in the kwargs argument of the register_plugin_function() function, as follows:

```
def kwargs_func(
    expr: IntoExpr,
    float_arg: float,
    integer_arg: int,
    string_arg: str,
    boolean_arg: bool,
) -> pl.Expr:
    return register_plugin_function(
        plugin_path=PLUGIN_PATH,
        function_name="kwargs_func",
        args=expr,
        kwargs={
            "float_arg": float_arg,
            "integer_arg": integer_arg,
            "string_arg": string_arg,
            "boolean_arg": boolean_arg,
        },
    )
```

Make sure to mark what arguments are expected on the Rust side. There, you have to define a Rust struct containing the expected arguments, and add the Rust decorator derive to it with the Deserialize trait from the serde crate. A *crate* is a package in Rust, similar to a package in Python.

```
// Provide your own kwargs struct with the proper schema and accept that type
// in your plugin expression.
#[derive(Deserialize)]
pub struct MyKwargs {
    float_arg: f64,
    integer_arg: i64,
    string_arg: String,
    boolean_arg: bool,
}

// If you want to accept `kwargs`, define a `kwargs` argument
// on the second position in your plugin. You can provide any custom struct that
// is deserializable with the pickle protocol (on the Rust side). ❶
#[polars_expr(output_type=String)]
fn append_kwargs(input: &[Series], kwargs: MyKwargs) -> PolarsResult<Series> {
    let input = &input[0];
    let input = input.cast(&DataType::String)?;
    let ca = input.str().unwrap();
```

```
Ok(ca
    .apply_into_string_amortized(|val, buf| {
        write!(
            buf,
            "{}-{}-{}-{}-{}",
            val,
            kwargs.float_arg,
            kwargs.integer_arg,
            kwargs.string_arg,
            kwargs.boolean_arg
        )
            .unwrap()
    })
    .into_series())
}
```

❶ The *pickle protocol* describes the binary protocols for serializing and deserializing a Python object structure. This means that the Rust side can deserialize the Python object structure and use it in the Rust code. *Deserializing* means
converting the serialized data back into a usable format.

Other register arguments

You can give additional information that allows Polars to optimize for the way the
plugin runs. For example:

is_elementwise

    The most basic way of using a custom expression is to apply it element-wise to
a Series. This allows for a high degree of parallelism and fast path algorithms,
and it is the most efficient way of using custom expressions. The is_element
wise=True flag in the Python code specifies that the function is element-wise.

> **Flag Appropriately**
>
> When you don't use the is_elementwise flag correctly, Polars
> won't raise any errors, but the function behavior will be unpredict-
> able. This shows in the case of GroupBy and window operations.
> If the function is not element-wise, but is marked as such, the func-
> tion can ignore the grouping and windowing and return incorrect
> results. Vice versa, if the function is element-wise but not marked
> as such, it will also be incorrect.

changes_length

    Indicate whether the plugin changes the length of the Series. For example,
when applying operations like df.unique(), df.filter(), and df.explode(),
the length of the result differs from the input. If the function changes the length
of the Series, you should set changes_length=True. By default it's set to False.

returns_scalar

If the function returns a list with a single element, setting `returns_scalar=True` will *explode*, or unpack, the list and return the single element. For example, if you have a `sum()` function that sums the elements in a list `[1,2,3]`, normally it would return `[6]`. If you set `returns_scalar=True`, it will return 6 without the list.

cast_to_supertype

If your plugin takes multiple input arguments that can be of mixed types, you can set `cast_to_supertype=True` to cast all inputs to the same type. This helps prevent type errors and ensures that your function runs correctly. For example, if the function takes an Int64 and a Float64 as input, setting `cast_to_supertype=True` will cast the Int64 to a Float64 before running the function.

input_wildcard_expansion

Some expressions represent multiple Series (e.g., `pl.col(*)`). If you set `input_wildcard_expansion=True`, the expressions will be expanded into a list of input Series instead.

pass_name_to_apply

If set to `True`, the Series passed to the function in a `GroupBy` operation will have its name set. If your custom plugin requires the Series name, you can set `pass_name_to_apply=True`. This is turned off by default because it requires an extra heap allocation per group.

Using a Rust Crate

One of the powers of Rust plugins is that you can use any Rust crate in your custom expression. This allows you to use any Rust package in your custom expression, as long as it is compatible with the Polars engine. To showcase this, you'll create the `geo` namespace to calculate whether one point falls within a polygon that's constructed from a list of points in the following use case.

Use Case: geo

To wrap all of this knowledge up, you're going to create the custom `geo` namespace that contains two functions: one that allows you to calculate whether a point falls within a polygon using a Rust plugin and one that calculates the Haversine distance between two points. These are common use cases in geospatial analysis and showcase how you can use the geo Rust crate in your custom expressions. First, you will add the geo crate to the *Cargo.toml* file. After that, you can start writing the Rust code that calculates whether a point falls within a polygon, and the Haversine distance between two points. Then you can make this code available to Python and create a custom namespace to place this functionality.

Adding the geo crate

To add the geo crate to the Rust project, add it to the [dependencies] section in the *Cargo.toml* file:

```
[package]
name = "polars_geo"
version = "1.0.0"
edition = "2021"

[lib]
name = "polars_geo"
crate-type = ["cdylib"]

[dependencies]
geo = "*"
polars = { version = "*" }
pyo3 = { version = "*", features = ["extension-module", "abi3-py38"] }
pyo3-polars = { version = "*", features = ["derive"] }
```

Here you create a new package called polars_geo and add the geo crate to the dependencies. It points to the polars_geo package and specifies that it is a cdylib package. Because you've added the geo crate to the dependencies, it will be downloaded and compiled when building the code. Now you can work with this added crate in your Rust code.

The Rust code

The Rust code needs to do a few things: take the inputs and parse them as a point and a polygon, check whether the point falls within the polygon, and return a Boolean. Hold on to your hat, because if you haven't worked with Rust before, it might look a bit daunting. Don't worry, we'll walk you through it step by step. Let's start with showing off the *expressions.rs* file:

```
use geo::{coord, Contains, Distance, Haversine, Point, Polygon};
use polars::prelude::*;
use polars::series::amortized_iter::AmortSeries;
use pyo3_polars::derive::polars_expr;

fn extract_point(point_opt: Option<AmortSeries>) -> Option<Point> {
    point_opt.and_then(|point| {
        let ca = point.as_ref().f64().ok()?;
        Some(Point::new(ca.get(0)?, ca.get(1)?))
    })
}

fn extract_polygon(polygon_opt: Option<AmortSeries>) -> Option<Polygon> {
    polygon_opt.and_then(|polygon| {
        let lst = polygon.as_ref().list().ok()?;
        let coords: Option<Vec<_>> = lst
            .amortized_iter()
```

```
            .map(|coord| {
                let coord_binding = coord?;
                let ca = coord_binding.as_ref().f64().ok()?;
                Some(coord! { x: ca.get(0)?, y: ca.get(1)? })
            })
            .collect();
        coords.map(|c| Polygon::new(c.into(), vec![]))
    })
}

fn geo_point_in_polygon(
    point_opt: Option<AmortSeries>,
    polygon_opt: Option<AmortSeries>,
) -> Option<bool> {
    let point = extract_point(point_opt);
    let polygon = extract_polygon(polygon_opt);
    match (point, polygon) {
        (Some(p), Some(poly)) => Some(poly.contains(&p)),
        _ => None, // Return None if point or polygon extraction fails
    }
}

#[polars_expr(output_type=Boolean)]
fn point_in_polygon(inputs: &[Series]) -> PolarsResult<Series> {
    let point_series = inputs[0].list()?;
    let polygon_series = inputs[1].list()?;

    let out: BooleanChunked = point_series
        .amortized_iter()
        .zip(polygon_series.amortized_iter())
        .map(|(point_opt, polygon_opt)| match (point_opt, polygon_opt) {
            (Some(point), Some(polygon)) => {
                geo_point_in_polygon(Some(point), Some(polygon))
            }
            _ => None,
        })
        .collect();

    Ok(out.into_series())
}

fn geo_haversine_distance(
    from_opt: Option<AmortSeries>,
    to_opt: Option<AmortSeries>,
) -> Option<f64> {
    let from_point = extract_point(from_opt);
    let to_point = extract_point(to_opt);
    match (from_point, to_point) {
        (Some(from_point), Some(to_point)) => {
            Some(Haversine::distance(from_point, to_point))
        }
        _ => None, // Return None if point extraction fails
```

```
        }
    }

    #[polars_expr(output_type=Float64)]
    fn haversine_distance(inputs: &[Series]) -> PolarsResult<Series> {
        let from_series = inputs[0].list()?;
        let to_series = inputs[1].list()?;

        let out: Float64Chunked = from_series
            .amortized_iter()
            .zip(to_series.amortized_iter())
            .map(|(from_opt, to_opt)| match (from_opt, to_opt) {
                (Some(from_point), Some(to_point)) => {
                    geo_haversine_distance(Some(from_point), Some(to_point))
                }
                _ => None,
            })
            .collect();

        Ok(out.into_series())
    }
```

Here, the `point_in_polygon()` function is available to Polars to use as a plugin. It makes use of three helper functions to extract the values from the input and then uses the geo method `contains()` to see if the point falls into the polygon.

Let's go through this code step by step:

```
use geo::{coord, Contains, Distance, Haversine, Point, Polygon}; ❶
use polars::prelude::*; ❷
use polars::series::amortized_iter::AmortSeries; ❸
use pyo3_polars::derive::polars_expr; ❹
```

These are the imports, or *use declarations* as they're called in Rust.

❶ Imports the necessary components from the geo crate to calculate whether a point is within a polygon.

❷ Imports common items from the Polars package, such as `Series` and `Polars Result`.

❸ Imports the `AmortSeries` Struct from the Polars package to iterate over Series in a more efficient way.

❹ Imports the `polars_expr` macro from the PyO3 Polars package to define a custom expression with Python bindings.

The next snippet of code defines the helper function that extracts a point from a Series:

```
fn extract_point(point_opt: Option<AmortSeries>) -> Option<Point> { ❶
    point_opt.and_then(|point| { ❷
        let ca = point.as_ref().f64().ok()?; ❸
        Some(Point::new(ca.get(0)?, ca.get(1)?)) ❹
    })
}
```

❶ This function takes a Series as input, which might contain a point. It returns the point as a Point Struct, as defined in the geo crate.

❷ The function uses the and_then() method to unwrap the Option and apply a closure to the value. A *closure* is a function that can capture variables from the environment in which it is defined. You can think of it as a lambda function in Python. An Option is a type that can either have a value or not, in which case it is None.

❸ The function tries to cast the Series to a f64 type and returns an Option of the f64 type. If the cast fails, it returns None.

❹ The function creates a new point Struct with the *x* and *y* coordinates from the Series if they can successfully be retrieved.

The next snippet of code defines the helper function that extracts a polygon from a Series:

```
fn extract_polygon(polygon_opt: Option<AmortSeries>) -> Option<Polygon> {
    polygon_opt.and_then(|polygon| {
        let lst = polygon.as_ref().list().ok()?; ❶
        let coords: Option<Vec<_>> = lst
            .amortized_iter() ❷
            .map(|coord| {
                let coord_binding = coord?;
                let ca = coord_binding.as_ref().f64().ok()?; ❸
                Some(coord! { x: ca.get(0)?, y: ca.get(1)? })
            })
            .collect();
        coords.map(|c| Polygon::new(c.into(), vec![])) ❹
    })
}
```

❶ Instead of parsing the input of the list to floats, the function parses it as a list because this input is a list of coordinates (list[list[f64]]).

❷ The amortized_iter() method is used to iterate over the list in an efficient way.

❸ Reads the coordinates and converts it to a Series of Float64.

❹ When all the coordinates are successfully parsed, a new polygon Struct is created
with the coordinates.

Now that you can create both point and polygon, it's time to check whether the point
falls within the polygon. This is done by the following helper function:

```
fn geo_point_in_polygon(
    point_opt: Option<AmortSeries>,
    polygon_opt: Option<AmortSeries>,
) -> Option<bool> {
    let point = extract_point(point_opt); ❶
    let polygon = extract_polygon(polygon_opt); ❷
    match (point, polygon) { ❸
        (Some(p), Some(poly)) => Some(poly.contains(&p)), ❹
        _ => None, ❺
    }
}
```

❶ Extracts the point from the input.

❷ Extracts the polygon from the input.

❸ A match statement is a control flow construct that compares a value against a
Series of patterns and then executes code based on which pattern matches. In this
case, it checks whether both the point and polygon are successfully extracted.

❹ If that's the case, it returns whether the point falls within the polygon.

❺ If not, it returns None.

The final step is to create the custom expression that uses these helper functions to
check whether a point falls within a polygon:

```
#[polars_expr(output_type=Boolean)] ❶
fn point_in_polygon(inputs: &[Series]) -> PolarsResult<Series> { ❷
    let point_series = inputs[0].list()?; ❸
    let polygon_series = inputs[1].list()?;

    let out: BooleanChunked = point_series ❹
        .amortized_iter() ❺
        .zip(polygon_series.amortized_iter()) ❻

        .map(|(point_opt, polygon_opt)| match (point_opt, polygon_opt) {
            (Some(point), Some(polygon)) => {
                geo_point_in_polygon(Some(point), Some(polygon)) ❼
            }
            _ => None, ❽
        })
        .collect();
```

```
    Ok(out.into_series())  ❾
}
```

❶ The `polars_expr` macro is used to define a custom expression with Python bindings. It specifies that the output type of the expression is a Boolean.

❷ The function takes a slice of Series as input and returns a `PolarsResult` of a Series.

❸ Try to cast the input to a list.

❹ Create a new `BooleanChunked` to store the results.

❺ Iterate over the point Series efficiently.

❻ Zip the point and polygon Series together so you can apply the `geo_point_in_polygon()` function to each pair.

❼ Apply the `geo_point_in_polygon()` function to each pair of points and polygons in case they have been successfully extracted.

❽ Return None if the point or polygon extraction failed.

❾ Return the results with the Ok type, indicating the operation was successful.

With the point in polygon check done, we can move to the Haversine distance. The Haversine formula computes the great-circle distance between two points on a sphere, given their longitudes and latitudes. The geo crate also supports this distance metric, so we'll use that implementation.

```
fn geo_haversine_distance(
    from_opt: Option<AmortSeries>,
    to_opt: Option<AmortSeries>,
) -> Option<f64> {
    let from_point = extract_point(from_opt);  ❶
    let to_point = extract_point(to_opt);
    match (from_point, to_point) {  ❷
        (Some(from_point), Some(to_point)) => {
            Some(Haversine::distance(from_point, to_point))  ❸
        }
        _ => None, // Return None if point extraction fails
    }
}
```

❶ Extracts the "from" point as a Point<f64> using the `extract_point` helper function.

❷ Matches the tuple of optional points to handle cases where extraction might fail.

❸ If both points are successfully extracted, calculates the Haversine distance between them using the haversine_distance method from the geo crate, returning the result wrapped in Some(f64).

Now that we've implemented the helper function to calculate the Haversine distance, we'll write a function that uses it to process our data:

```
#[polars_expr(output_type=Float64)]  ❶
fn haversine_distance(inputs: &[Series]) -> PolarsResult<Series> {  ❷
    let from_series = inputs[0].list()?;  ❸
    let to_series = inputs[1].list()?;

    let out: Float64Chunked = from_series
        .amortized_iter()  ❹
        .zip(to_series.amortized_iter())  ❺
        .map(|(from_opt, to_opt)| match (from_opt, to_opt) {  ❻
            (Some(from_point), Some(to_point)) => {
                geo_haversine_distance(Some(from_point), Some(to_point))  ❼
            }
            _ => None,  ❽
        })
        .collect();

    Ok(out.into_series())  ❾
}
```

❶ Decorator indicating that the function is a Polars expression and that its output type is Float64.

❷ Defines the main function that will be registered as a Polars expression.

❸ Retrieves the input Series and ensures it is of list type.

❹ Iterates over the point Series efficiently.

❺ Zips the "from" and "to" iterators to process corresponding elements together.

❻ Maps over each pair of optional points, matching their options.

❼ If both points are Some, calls the geo_haversine_distance function to compute the distance.

❽ If either point is None, returns None for that element.

❾ Converts the resulting `Float64Chunked` into a Series and wraps it in a `Polars Result`.

This Rust code is now ready to be compiled and used in Python.

When you run `maturin develop` in the Rust project folder, the code is compiled and made available to Python. If you want to optimize performance, you can run `maturin develop --release` to enable all optimizations, at the cost of a longer build time. Since we'll be using the plugin in the next section, we'll build a release for optimized speed:

```
! cd plugins/polars_geo && uv run maturin develop --release
```

The Python code

Now that the Rust code is ready, you can create a Python file that registers the custom expression with Polars. For this you need to place a file in the *polars_geo* folder and call it *init.py*:

```python
from pathlib import Path

import polars as pl
from polars.plugins import register_plugin_function
from polars.type_aliases import IntoExpr


PLUGIN_PATH = Path(__file__).parent


def point_in_polygon(point: IntoExpr, polygon: IntoExpr) -> pl.Expr:
    return register_plugin_function(
        plugin_path=PLUGIN_PATH,
        args=[point, polygon],
        function_name="point_in_polygon",
        is_elementwise=True,
    )


def haversine_distance(from_point: IntoExpr, to_point: IntoExpr) -> pl.Expr:
    return register_plugin_function(
        plugin_path=PLUGIN_PATH,
        args=[from_point, to_point],
        function_name="haversine_distance",
        is_elementwise=True,
    )
```

Just like the "Hello, world" example earlier, this file registers the custom expressions with Polars. The difference here is that they both take two arguments, which is why the function takes two `IntoExpr` arguments. The `args` keyword is a list of these arguments, which are passed to the Rust plugin. The file, however, contains more than what's shown here. It also contains code that registers it to a custom namespace. This is not specific to plugins and can be used for any code. Let's show you how.

Making the custom namespace

Now that you have the Rust plugin available, you can wrap it in a custom namespace. This way, you can organize and group relevant methods just as Polars does internally, like `pl.col(…).str.<method>` for Strings. In this case, you will create the `geo` space, which will contain a function that uses your Rust plugin. First, register this custom namespace:

```python
import polars as pl
import coordinates_plugin_py as coord


@pl.api.register_expr_namespace("geo")  ❶
class Geo:
    def __init__(self, input_expression: pl.Expr):  ❷
        self._input_expression = input_expression

    def point_in_polygon(
        self, polygon: list[list[pl.Float64]]
    ) -> pl.Expr:  ❸
        return point_in_polygon(self._input_expression, polygon)

    def haversine_distance(self, to_point: list[pl.Float64]) -> pl.Expr:  ❹
        return haversine_distance(self._input_expression, to_point)
```

❶ Registers the class as a namespace with the `geo` keyword.

❷ The `__init__` stores what the expression will get as input. In this case, the function is intended to be called on the Series containing the point. This means that the expressions with the points will be received as input and that the expression resulting in the polygons will be the input of the later function.

❸ This function in your `geo` namespace will call your Rust code to check if it is within a polygon constructed from the function input.

❹ And this function will call the Rust code to calculate the Haversine distance between two points.

With a small test script, you can check whether the plugin functions as intended. Let's start with a DataFrame that contains one case that should be `true`, a case that should be `false`, and an invalid case that should be `null`:

```python
points_and_polygons = pl.DataFrame(
    {
        "point": [[5.0, 5.0], [20.0, 20.0], [20.0, 20.0]],
```

```
        "polygon": [
            [[0.0, 0.0], [10.0, 0.0], [10.0, 10.0], [0.0, 10.0]],
            [
                [0.0, 0.0],
                [10.0, 0.0],
                [10.0, 10.0],
            ],
            [[0.0, None], [10.0, 0.0], [10.0, 10.0], [0.0, 10.0], [0.0, 0.0]],
        ],
    }
)
```

Now the only thing left to do is call the function in your namespace. Cue the drumroll…

```
from plugins.polars_geo import polars_geo

# Apply the point_in_polygon function
points_and_polygons.with_columns(
    pl.col("point").geo.point_in_polygon(pl.col("polygon")).alias("in_polygon")
)
```

```
shape: (3, 3)
┌──────────────┬─────────────────────────┬────────────┐
│ point        │ polygon                 │ in_polygon │
│ ---          │ ---                     │ ---        │
│ list[f64]    │ list[list[f64]]         │ bool       │
╞══════════════╪═════════════════════════╪════════════╡
│ [5.0, 5.0]   │ [[0.0, 0.0], [10.0, …   │ true       │
│ [20.0, 20.0] │ [[0.0, 0.0], [10.0, …   │ false      │
│ [20.0, 20.0] │ [[0.0, null], [10.0,…   │ null       │
└──────────────┴─────────────────────────┴────────────┘
```

If everything works correctly, this output should roll out of the function call. That's how you can extend Polars with exotic functionality without incurring a performance hit. It can be an adventure, but it is definitely worth it.

We use the Haversine distance in the showcase in Chapter 1.

If you want to dive deeper into creating this kind of custom functionality, we recommend Marco Gorelli's tutorial on plugins (*https://oreil.ly/VGUPO*).

String Tips for Pros

If you want to start working on plugins that work with Strings, `apply_to_buffer()` is a helper method that creates a buffer that is reused to write Strings, which saves heap allocations and boosts performance significantly.

Takeaways

In this chapter you learned how to extend the standard functionality of Polars with your own. The key takeaways are:

- You can apply custom Python functions to your data through `Expr.map_elements()`, `Expr.map_batches()`, `Expr.map_groups()`, `Expr.pipe()`, and `df.pipe()`.
- It's possible to register a custom Polars namespace in Python.
- To get the best performance, you can create Rust plugins and make them available in Python.
- It's even possible to use Rust crates in your custom plugins.
- There are some tips to optimize your custom plugins for performance.

The next chapter will dive into the internals of Polars and explain how it works under the hood so you can write code that never slows you down.

## CHAPTER 18

Polars Internals

In this chapter, we dive deep into the inner workings of Polars, uncovering the mechanisms that make it such a powerful and efficient data manipulation package. Throughout the book, you've encountered references to this chapter for a more comprehensive understanding of Polars' functionality.

In this chapter, you'll learn about:

- The architecture of Polars
- Some technologies under the hood
- Some optimizations that enable Polars' performance
- Tools to profile and test your code, ensuring that you can optimize your data processing tasks to the fullest

The instructions to get any files you might need are in Chapter 2. We assume that you have the files in the *data* subdirectory.

By the end of this chapter, you'll have a deeper appreciation for the engineering that goes into making Polars fast and efficient, as well as practical knowledge on how to leverage these internals for your own data processing tasks.

Polars' Architecture

Everything starts with your code. The code you type is in Polars' *domain-specific language* (DSL). This DSL allows you to define what should be done in a declarative manner.

The DSL is then transformed into an *intermediate representation* (IR) that is a more abstract representation of the work that needs to be done. You can view this IR by calling `lf.explain()` to get its String representation, or you can visualize it with `lf.show_graph()`. The IR is represented as a *directed acyclic graph* (DAG) where each node represents a computation and the edges represent the data flow. Besides defining the computations, the IR is enriched with information about the data types and shapes of the data to support the optimizer. This also allows Polars to determine if operations would lead to errors and return an error message before executing the code, reducing the time spent debugging.

The IR is then passed to the *optimizer*. The optimizer applies a set of rules to the IR to simplify the computations. It can remove unnecessary computations, reorder them, and even replace them with more efficient ones. For more information on what kind of optimizations are applied, see "Query Optimization" on page 424.

After the optimizer has done its work, the optimized IR is passed to the *engine*. The engine is responsible for *how* the computations are done. Polars has several engines to choose from. Currently available are the full-batch in-memory engine and the streaming engine on the CPU, and the GPU full-batch engine. The CPU in-memory engine is the default engine and is used when no other engine is specified. The streaming engine can be used when the data is too large to fit into memory. The GPU engine is used when the data is small enough to fit into the GPU's VRAM and the operations are suitable for GPU acceleration. We will talk more about the GPU engine in the Appendix.

The engine then executes the computations and returns the result. This result is kept in RAM by default, but can also be written to disk.

You can see a diagram that shows these layers and their connection to each other in Figure 18-1.

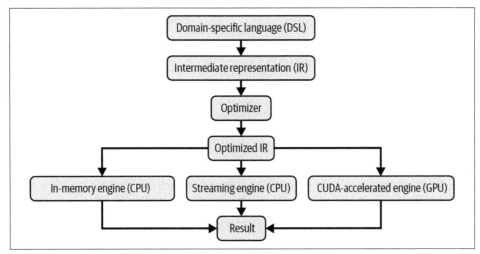

Figure 18-1. The conceptual layers of Polars' architecture

This architecture allows Polars to perform queries as quickly as it can. This is complementary to the way data is stored in memory.

Arrow

At the core of Polars' efficiency is its memory management system, which is built on top of the Apache Arrow project.

Arrow describes itself (*https://oreil.ly/upmyX*) as "a cross-language development platform for in-memory analytics." It defines a "language-independent columnar memory format for flat and hierarchical data, organized for efficient analytic operations on modern hardware like CPUs and GPUs." Arrow brings a few advantages out of the box.

First, it uses a columnar format. The columnar format enables data adjacency for sequential access or scans, which optimizes the process of reading large quantities of data in a contiguous block. This way, you can store the data and read it in large, sequential chunks.

On top of that, this contiguous columnar layout is vectorization friendly. It also lets you use modern Single Instruction, Multiple Data (SIMD) operations, which perform the same operations on multiple data points simultaneously.

To elaborate on these advantages, we'll introduce the metaphor of a filing cabinet, illustrated in Figure 18-2.

Imagine a filing cabinet where you store your sales dossiers. In a row-based format, each drawer of the cabinet contains all the data you need on a single sale: the person it was sold to, what items were sold, the price of the sale, and when the sale happened. If you always want to dig up all the information about each sale you make, it's practical to keep all that information bundled together.

In analytical queries, however, it's more common to look for specific parts of the sales dossier. For example, you might want a report on your five biggest customers. This way you'll know what customers to put some extra effort into and pamper. If you ordered your cabinet in the row-based manner, where every drawer contains the file of one customer, you'd have to open up every single drawer to look at the customer and total price of each sale.

When you order your cabinet in a way that is column based, each drawer contains a single data category. That means one of the drawers would contain all of the customers, and another would contain all of the sale prices.

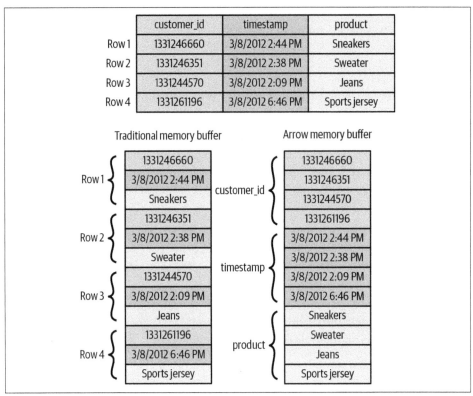

Figure 18-2. The Arrow memory buffer and its advantages for computation

With sequential reading, you can just start at the first file in the drawer and keep going to the next one until you reach the end of the drawer. This speeds things up because you don't have to close the drawer, go to another one, open it, and look for the relevant file. From the price drawer, you can then determine the dossier IDs of the biggest customers. In order to know who the customers are, you go to the name drawer and go over the files until you find the five names matching the dossier IDs. This means you'll only have to open two drawers instead of all of them, saving you a lot of hassle and time.

Because of this columnar format, Arrow provides O(1), or *constant-time*, random access. This means that no matter how large the dataset becomes, the time it takes to access any single piece of data remains constant. In our filing cabinet analogy, this would look like we know exactly where every piece of information is stored: not only which drawer, but also exactly where in the drawer. This means you don't have to go searching through drawers until you come to the relevant piece of data. For operations that need to access specific data points in a large dataset, this is a significant performance benefit.

Arrow supports implementations in many popular languages. At the time of writing, these include C/GLib, C++, C#, Go, Java, JavaScript, Julia, MATLAB, Python, R, Ruby, and Rust. The degree of implementation might differ between languages; for example, the Float16 data type is not implemented in every language.

Implementations in many languages let you use a shared mutable dataset without serialization or deserialization. Normally, different languages represent data differently in the bits in memory. This means that in order to match data across two languages, you first have to deserialize the data from one format, then serialize it to the format of the other language. This translation step takes time. Arrow prevents this by allowing all supported implementations and languages to talk in a unified way to the same dataset. Sharing a mutable dataset is called *inter-process communication* (IPC). Arrow enables zero-copy reads of data within the same process, without serialization/deserialization overhead. You can read a file in Polars and pass it to other packages that support Arrow, such as Great Tables, hvPlot, or Altair, without having to convert it to a different format.

Multithreaded Computations and SIMD Operations

Polars was designed from the ground up to take advantage of modern-day hardware, like CPUs with multiple cores that can run multiple threads and GPUs that can run thousands of basic tasks in parallel. This opens up the possibility of running multiple computations at the same time.

Python has a *global interpreter lock* (GIL) that prevents multiple threads from executing Python code simultaneously.[1] This simplifies the implementation and makes the single thread faster. However, it prevents Python from taking full advantage of multiple cores. If you have a Python program that is doing a lot of computation, it will only use one core of your CPU. To get around this, the core of Polars is written in Rust, which doesn't have this issue (on top of other performance advantages, such as faster bytecode). Polars can run multiple computations in parallel, so you can take advantage of all the cores available to you.

One way Polars takes advantage of multiple cores is by using SIMD operations. By lining up your data in memory, or *vectorizing* it, a computer with multiple computation cores can process the same instruction on multiple data points at the same time. Its origins lie in the early days of graphics processing, which often involved doing the same operation on a lot of pixels at the same time. An example would be a flash on the screen, causing all pictures to increase in brightness at the same time. These days,

---

1 Newer versions of Python will have a GIL-free interpreter, but this doesn't mean that Python will automatically take advantage of multiple cores.

SIMD operations can be performed on data as well, and Polars uses this to speed up its computations.

The String Data Type in Memory

In Chapter 4 we introduced the String data type. One of the challenges of Strings is their variable length. For example, Integers are a fixed length: you can calculate the memory address of the next Integer by adding the size of the Integer to the current memory address. This is not the case for Strings. The length of a String is not known in advance, so the memory address of the next String cannot be predicted purely from the data buffer. This means that Strings have to be stored differently than Integers: contiguously, in a data buffer. *Contiguous memory* is one long memory block where all the values are stored in a row.

The view layout stores several attributes of a String value:

- Bytes 0 to 3 store the length of the String.
- Bytes 4 to 7 store a copy of the first four bytes of a String. This allows for "fast paths," or optimizations, since these four bytes frequently contain the information needed to make a quick comparison.
- Bytes 8 to 11 store the index of the data buffer where the String resides.
- Bytes 12 to 15 store the *offset*: the location within that data buffer where the String starts.

With all this information, you can retrieve the String from the data buffer without having to seek through memory.

Polars has another optimization for Strings shorter than 12 bytes long. In this case, the String is stored in the view layout itself, instead of in the data buffer. This is called *inlining*. When its length is at most 12 bytes, the String can be stored in the 12 bytes that follow the length. This prevents Polars from having to allocate memory and seek in the data buffer, which are both costly operations.

Figure 18-3 illustrates how this storage works, using bands the Polars developers like. "Aerosmith" fits inline and thus is not in the data buffer. "Toots and the Maytals" is stored in the data buffer starting on the 22nd position after "The Velvet Under-Ground" (where the first position is 0).

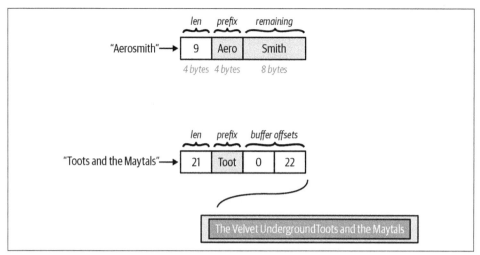

Figure 18-3. How short and long Strings are stored in memory

ChunkedArrays in Series

In Chapter 4 we introduced the Series data structure. That, however, is not yet the lowest level of data structure in Polars. Every Series (and so every column in a DataFrame) is internally represented as a *ChunkedArray*.

A ChunkedArray is a container class for a sequence of arrays of data. Using ChunkedArrays instead of a single array with all the data allows for several optimizations, including optimized memory management. When you add data to a ChunkedArray, the data is added to the existing object. This way, Polars doesn't have to copy over data to a new one or garbage collect the old one, saving time. On top of that, Polars allows for splitting data into chunks that can be operated on individually and in parallel to maximize performance. Each chunk can be processed by a different CPU core, speeding up calculations dramatically.

Chunky Data

Managing chunks optimizes the way Polars works with data. *Rechunking* is the process of changing the chunk size of a Chunked-Array. In Polars, rechunking generally refers to putting all the data into a single chunk. Within every chunk, the data is kept contiguous in memory. In the eager case, after reads, the data is automatically rechunked. Polars assumes that in eager mode, the user wants to perform analysis on the data. Often, the same DataFrame will be queried multiple times, which makes the additional time it takes to rechunk worth the effort. When using a lazy evaluation, the optimizer decides when to rechunk.

Generally, this is something you won't have to take into account, except when benchmarking. In that case it's good to know that when you set the `rechunk` argument to `True` in an operation, there are actually two operations happening.

Query Optimization

In Chapter 5, we talked about how the lazy API optimizes queries, but we didn't go into detail about how this works.

At the time of writing, Table 18-1 gives a general overview of most optimizations that Polars applies.

Table 18-1. Some of the optimizations in Polars

Optimization	Explanation
Predicate pushdown	Applies filters as early as possible, at the scan level.
Projection pushdown	Select only the columns that are needed at the scan level.
Slice pushdown	Only load the required slice from the scan level. Don't materialize sliced outputs (e.g., `lf.head(10)`).
Common subplan elimination	Cache subtrees or file scans that are used by multiple subtrees in the query plan.
Simplify expressions	Various optimizations, such as constant folding and replacing expensive operations with faster alternatives.
Join ordering	Estimate the branches of joins that should be executed first in order to reduce memory pressure.
Type coercion	Coerce types such that operations succeed and run on minimal required memory.
Cardinality estimation	Estimate cardinality to determine optimal group by strategy.

Let's go over some of these optimizations in more detail.

LazyFrame Scan-Level Optimizations

The first group of optimizations considers data loading at the scan level. The *scan level* is the layer of execution where Polars reads data from its source. These optimizations are focused on completely avoiding reading data that won't be used.

Projection pushdown means optimizing a query by moving column selection as far upstream as possible. This prevents unused columns from being read into memory.

In this example, we'll explore the taxi dataset that we used earlier in the book. We will still try to find out the top three vendors by revenue per distance traveled. However, this time we'll use the lazy API instead:

```
taxis = pl.scan_parquet("data/taxi/yellow_tripdata_*.parquet")  ❶
taxis.select(pl.col("trip_distance")).show_graph()  ❷
```

❶ `pl.scan_parquet()` does not immediately read the file from disk. Instead, it returns a LazyFrame for which only relevant metadata is scanned, such as the schema and the number of rows and columns. The LazyFrame exposes the Polars lazy API. The methods available are practically the same, with the difference that it's only executed when you call `lf.collect()`.

❷ This selects only the `trip_distance` column, then prints the query plan with `lf.show_graph()`, so you can see what happens in the query engine. You can see behind π that only 1 in 19 columns will be read into memory at all (see Figure 18-4).

Parquet SCAN [data/taxi/yellow_tripdata_2022-01.parquet, ... 11 other sources]
π 1/19;

Figure 18-4. The resulting query plan when you scan the taxi dataset and select a single column

This image shows the *query plan*. The query plan is a tree structure that shows the steps that will be executed to get the result. It requires some explanation:

- The first step executed is the one at the bottom, so read the query plan from bottom to top.
- Every box corresponds to a stage in the query plan. In this case we have only one step, which is the scan of the Parquet file. In later examples you'll see more steps.
- The σ stands for *selection* and indicates any row filter conditions.
- The π stands for *projection* and indicates choosing a subset of columns.

In Figure 18-4 you can see that π contains a selection of 1 out of the 19 available columns. In Figure 18-5 you can see that the σ contains a filter on the `trip_distance` column.

Moving on to the next optimization, *predicate pushdown* is like projection pushdown, but it focuses on filtering rows instead of selecting columns. This helps avoid reading rows that aren't needed:

```
taxis.filter(pl.col("trip_distance") > 10).show_graph()
```

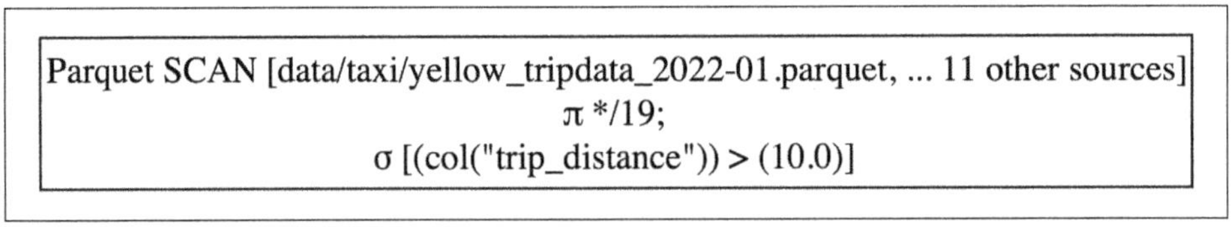

Parquet SCAN [data/taxi/yellow_tripdata_2022-01.parquet, ... 11 other sources]
π */19;
σ [(col("trip_distance")) > (10.0)]

Figure 18-5. The resulting query plan when filtering values in the column trip_distance

The code filters the `trip_distance` column for values larger than 10. In Figure 18-5 you can see the filter behind the σ. This filter will be applied row-wise.

The last optimization is *slice pushdown*, which loads only the required data slice from the scan level (where the data is read into memory). Like predicate pushdown, it prevents reading unused rows, but instead of reading rows based on a filter, it reads rows based on whether they belong to a certain chunk of data, using this command:

```
taxis.head(2).collect()
```

shape: (2, 19)

VendorID	tpep_picku p_datetime	tpep_dropo ff_datetim	...	total_amou nt	congestion _surcharge	airport_f ee
---	---	...		---	---	---
i64	datetime[n s]	--- datetime[n s]		f64	f64	f64
1	2022-01-01 00:35:40	2022-01-01 00:53:29	...	21.95	2.5	0.0
1	2022-01-01 00:33:43	2022-01-01 00:42:07	...	13.3	0.0	0.0

This operation takes only the first two rows of the data at the scan level and returns the result as a DataFrame.

These pushdowns completely prevent the execution of later applied transformations on data that is not necessary to achieve the end result.

Other Optimizations

Other optimizations are more focused on efficient computing. One such optimization is *common subplan elimination*. A *subplan*, or *subtree*, is a group of steps in the query plan. When certain operations or file scans are used by multiple subtrees in the query plan, Polars caches the results for easy reuse. Let's start with a query that makes use of the same underlying LazyFrame. Without optimization it would calculate that same set for every tree of operations separately (see Figure 18-6):

```
values = pl.LazyFrame({"value": [10, 20, 30, 40, 50, 60]})

common_subplan = values.with_columns(pl.col("value") * 2)

branch1 = common_subplan.select(value2=pl.col("value") * 4)
branch2 = common_subplan.select(value3=pl.col("value") * 2)

combined = pl.concat([branch1, branch2])

combined.show_graph(optimized=False)
```

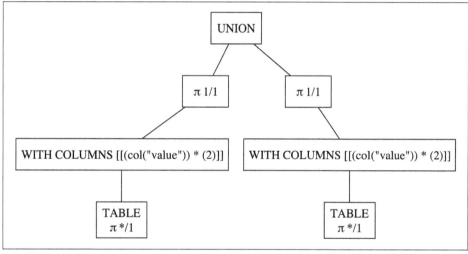

Figure 18-6. Unoptimized query plan

But when we turn on the optimizations, Polars only calculates duplicate trees one time and caches the result for the different subsequent operations to reuse existing results, as shown in Figure 18-7:

```
combined.show_graph()
```

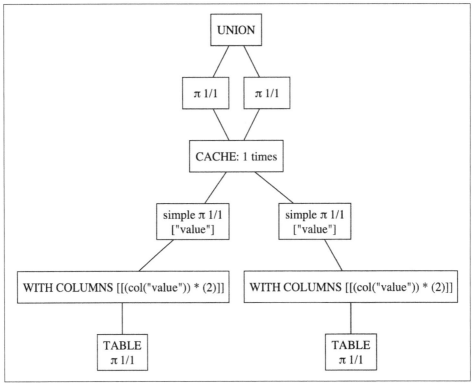

Figure 18-7. Optimized query plan

This saves time reading from disk and can prevent double work.

Secretly Lazy

In many cases, the eager API is actually calling the lazy API under the hood and immediately collecting the result. This has the benefit that the optimizer can still make optimizations within the query itself. On top of that, it's easier for the maintainers because the method of the eager API is a thin wrapper around the lazy API, deduplicating the code.

Another optimization is *clustering* `with_columns`. When you use multiple `lf.with_columns()` calls in a row, Polars will attempt to reduce the number of calls and remove those that are never used. Every separate `lf.with_columns()` call has to happen sequentially, which can be a performance bottleneck if they could've been done in parallel.

Let's create a small example DataFrame with some BMI data:

```
bmi = pl.LazyFrame(
    {"weight_kg": [70, 80, 60, 90], "length_cm": [175, 180, 160, 190]}
)
```

We can start applying a couple of statements in `lf.with_columns()`, like so:

```
bmi = (
    bmi.with_columns(weight_per_cm=pl.col("weight_kg") / pl.col("length_cm"))
    .with_columns(weight_kg_average=pl.lit(0))
    .with_columns(length_m=pl.col("length_cm") / 100)
    .with_columns(weight_kg_average=pl.col("weight_kg").mean())
)
```

The query is optimized and reduced to the following:

```
bmi = bmi.with_columns(
    weight_per_cm=pl.col("weight_kg") / pl.col("length_cm"),
    weight_kg_average=pl.col("weight_kg").mean(),
    length_m=pl.col("length_cm") / 100,
)
```

Notice that the `weight_kg_average` column is no longer added twice, and the `lf.with_columns()` calls are combined into one, which can be parallelized. Like this, Polars optimizes performance for you without you having to optimize your code.

Checking Your Expressions

To up your expressions to the next level, you can use one of Polars' advanced features: the `Expr.meta` namespace. You can use it within expressions, to provide introspection and manipulation capabilities for Polars expressions. Let's start with an overview of this namespace.

meta Namespace Overview

Table 18-2 lists all the methods available under the `Expr.meta` namespace, along with brief descriptions.

Table 18-2. Methods in the `Expr.meta` namespace

Method	Description
`Expr.meta.eq(…)`	Indicate if this expression is the same as another expression.
`Expr.meta.has_multiple_outputs()`	Indicate if this expression expands into multiple expressions.
`Expr.meta.is_column()`	Indicate if this expression is a basic (nonregex) unaliased column.
`Expr.meta.is_column_selection(…)`	Indicate if this expression only selects columns (optionally with aliasing).
`Expr.meta.is_literal(…)`	Indicate if this expression is a literal value (optionally aliased).

Method	Description
`Expr.meta.is_regex_projection()`	Indicate if this expression expands to columns that match a regex pattern.
`Expr.meta.ne(…)`	Indicate if this expression is *not* the same as another expression.
`Expr.meta.output_name(…)`	Get the column name that this expression would produce.
`Expr.meta.pop()`	Pop the latest expression and return the input(s) of the popped expression.
`Expr.meta.root_names()`	Get a list with the root column name.
`Expr.meta.serialize(…)`	Serialize this expression to a file or String in JSON format.
`Expr.meta.show_graph(…)`	Format the expression as a Graphviz graph.
`Expr.meta.tree_format(…)`	Format the expression as a tree.
`Expr.meta.undo_aliases()`	Undo any renaming operation like `alias` or `name.keep`.
`Expr.meta.write_json(…)`	Write expression to JSON.

meta Namespace Examples

Let's explore some of the most useful methods within the `Expr.meta` namespace, illustrating how they can be applied in real-world scenarios.

The `Expr.meta.is_column()` method checks whether an expression represents a basic, unaliased column. This is particularly useful when you want to filter or validate expressions within a larger computation:

```
expr1 = pl.col("name")
expr2 = pl.lit("constant")

print(f"Is {expr1} a column: {expr1.meta.is_column()}")
print(f"Is {expr2} a column: {expr2.meta.is_column()}")

Is col("name") a column: True
Is String(constant) a column: False
```

Use `Expr.meta.is_literal()` to determine if an expression is a literal value. This can help in distinguishing between dynamic column references and static values within your expressions:

```
print(f"Is {expr1} a literal: {expr1.meta.is_literal()}")
print(f"Is {expr2} a literal: {expr2.meta.is_literal()}")

Is col("name") a literal: False
Is String(constant) a literal: True
```

The `Expr.meta.output_name()` method retrieves the name of the column that an expression will produce. This is useful for dynamically handling column names, especially after applying transformations or aliases:

```
expr1 = pl.col("age") * 2
expr2 = pl.col("name").alias("username")
```

```
# Get output names
print(f"{expr1} output name: {expr1.meta.output_name()}")
print(f"{expr2} output name: {expr2.meta.output_name()}")

[(col("age")) * (dyn int: 2)] output name: age
col("name").alias("username") output name: username
```

You can visualize the structure of an expression using Graphviz. The
Expr.meta.show_graph() method generates a graphical representation, which is
invaluable for understanding complex expression trees:

```
expr = (pl.col("age") * 2).alias("double_age")
```

```
expr.meta.show_graph()
```

This code creates the figure shown in Figure 18-8.

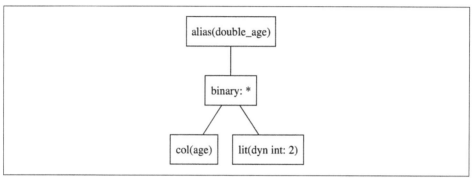

Figure 18-8. Graph showing the tree of operations that the expression represents

If you've aliased columns and need to revert to their original names,
Expr.meta.undo_aliases() is the method to use. This is helpful when prepar-
ing expressions for operations that require original column names. We can use
Expr.meta.output_name() again to verify:

```
expr = pl.col("original_name").alias("new_name")
```

```
original_expr = expr.meta.undo_aliases()
```

```
original_expr.meta.output_name()
```

```
'original_name'
```

The last example we'll go through is the method Expr.meta.root_names() which
shows the origin of an expression:

```
expr = pl.col("origin").alias("destination")
```

```
expr.meta.root_names()
```

```
['origin']
```

The `Expr.meta` namespace in Polars expressions provides a suite of powerful tools for introspecting and manipulating expressions. These methods give you more control of the plane of expressions and allow for better metaprogramming.

Profiling Polars

Polars' lazy API has a built-in utility for profiling. When optimizing performance of a Polars query, while you can time how long every query step takes in the eager API, you can't do this in the lazy API. This is because the lazy API doesn't actually execute the query until you call `lf.collect()` on the LazyFrame, and then every step is executed at once. To compare the performance of the different operations that make up a query on the lazy API, you can use the `lf.profile()` method.

Let's put this method to the test and apply some transformations to a big dataset to create a query plan with several nodes. For this, you can use the yellow taxi trip data from New York City:

```
long_distance_taxis_per_vendor_sorted = (
    pl.scan_parquet("data/taxi/yellow_tripdata_*.parquet")
    .filter(pl.col("trip_distance") > 10)
    .select(pl.col("VendorID"), pl.col("trip_distance"), pl.col("total_amount"))
    .group_by("VendorID")
    .agg(
        total_distance=pl.col("trip_distance").sum(),
        total_amount=pl.col("total_amount").sum(),
    )
    .sort("total_distance", descending=True)
)

long_distance_taxis_per_vendor_sorted.show_graph()
```

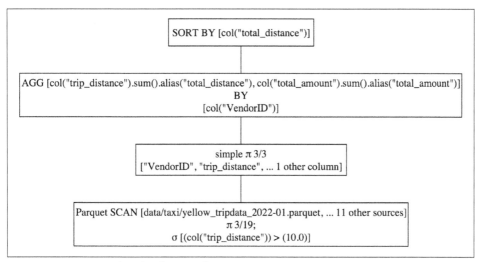

Figure 18-9. Query plan for the taxi dataset

Now that you have a query plan, shown in Figure 18-9, you can profile it:

```
result, profiling_info = long_distance_taxis_per_vendor_sorted.profile()
```

Using `lf.profile()` will return a tuple with the result, like `lf.collect()` would provide:

```
result
```

```
shape: (4, 3)
```

VendorID	total_distance	total_amount
i64	f64	f64
2	1.3752e8	1.6152e8
1	1.3095e7	5.2274e7
6	347579.41	1.3881e6
5	1956.44	8702.21

The second element in the tuple is an additional DataFrame with the profiling information:

```
profiling_info
```

```
shape: (5, 3)
```

node	start	end
str	u64	u64
optimization	0	7

```
| parquet(data/taxi/yellow_tripdata_2022-01.parquet, predic… | 7      | 325779 |
| simple-projection(VendorID, trip_distance, total_amount)   | 325787 | 325793 |
| group_by_partitioned(VendorID)                             | 325796 | 337054 |
| sort(total_distance)                                       | 337059 | 337157 |
```

This DataFrame contains the start and end times of every node in the query plan, in microseconds. This way you can see which nodes take the most time and which ones are the bottlenecks in your query. In this example you can see that the `parquet()` node takes the most time, which is to be expected since this is where Polars reads the data from disk.

To make it even easier to see which nodes take the most time, use the built-in functionality to turn this into a graph by setting the argument `show_plot` to `True`:

```
long_distance_taxis_per_vendor_sorted.profile(show_plot=True, figsize=(15, 5))
```

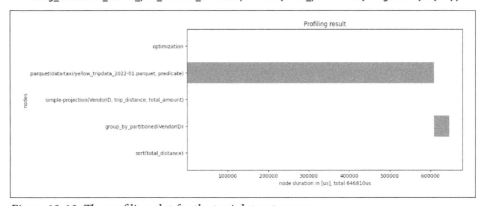

Figure 18-10. The profiling plot for the taxi dataset query

This will show a plot, like in Figure 18-10, with the nodes in the query plan on the *x*-axis, and the time it took to execute them on the *y*-axis, with execution going from top to bottom. You can adjust the size of the figure by providing a `figsize` argument, which uses a `tuple[int, int]` representing the width and height of the figure in inches.

Tests in Polars

Polars has built-in testing functions that you can use to test your codebase. They are somewhat tucked away, since they are not imported by default to keep the performance of the package high.

Comparing DataFrames and Series

You can import the four basic functions, like so:

```
from polars.testing import (
    assert_series_equal,
    assert_frame_equal,
    assert_series_not_equal,
    assert_frame_not_equal,
)
```

These functions compare two Series or DataFrames and will raise errors if they are equal (or aren't, depending on the function).

Let's make two DataFrames with floats that we can then compare:

```
floats = pl.DataFrame({"a": [1.0, 2.0, 3.0, 4.0]})

different_floats = pl.DataFrame({"a": [1.001, 2.0, 3.0, 4.0]})
```

We can compare these two DataFrames, like so:

```
assert_frame_equal(floats, different_floats)

AssertionError: DataFrames are different (value mismatch for column 'a')
[left]:  [1.0, 2.0, 3.0, 4.0]
[right]: [1.001, 2.0, 3.0, 4.0]
```

Exact checks like this aren't always what you need. Sometimes, results that are close enough are good enough. For this there are a number of arguments you can tweak in these methods, as outlined in Table 18-3.

Table 18-3. Arguments for the testing functions

Argument	Description
check_row_order	Requires row order to match exactly.
check_column_order	Requires column order to match exactly.
check_dtypes	Requires data types to match exactly.
check_exact	Requires Float values to match exactly. If set to False, values are considered equal when within tolerance of each other (see rtol and atol). This only affects columns with a Float data type.
rtol	Relative tolerance for inexact checking. Only applied when check_exact is False.
atol	Absolute tolerance for inexact checking. Only applied when check_exact is False.
categorical_as_str	Casts Categorical columns to String before comparing. Enabling this helps compare columns that do not share the same String cache since the physical encoding will likely mismatch.

While the `check_*` arguments explain themselves, the tolerance thresholds require further explanation. The `rtol` and `atol` argument are used to determine how close two floating-point numbers must be to be considered equal.

The `rtol` argument is the *relative tolerance*, meaning it depends on the magnitude of the values being compared and represents the maximum allowed difference between the two values as a fraction of the second value. When broken down to a formula, it looks like this:

$$abs(a - b) \leq rtol * abs(b)$$

The `atol` argument is the *absolute tolerance*, a fixed value setting the difference between the two values. When broken down to a formula, it looks like this:

$$abs(a - b) \leq atol$$

Now let's see how this works on the DataFrames we used in the start of this section, which had a slight inequality of 0.001:

```
assert_frame_equal(floats, different_floats, rtol=0.01)
print("The DataFrames are equal.")

The DataFrames are equal.
```

This will not raise an error, because the values are within the relative tolerance of 0.01 of each other. This is especially useful when you're working with floating-point numbers, where small rounding errors can occur because of their approximate nature.

Repr's Delight

To make the DataFrame initialization in unit tests more readable, you can use the `pl.from_repr()` function, which stands for "from (String) representation." This method takes a String representation of a DataFrame and turns it into a DataFrame. This lets you save your expected DataFrame in your code in a more readable way, making it easier to see what you're testing for.

You can paste the String representation (optionally without the `shape(x, y)` line), and the `pl.from_repr()` function will turn it into a DataFrame, like so:

```
result = pl.DataFrame({"a": [1, 3], "b": [2, 4]}).cast(
    pl.Schema({"a": pl.Int8, "b": pl.Int8})
)

expected = pl.from_repr(
    """
    ┌─────┬─────┐
    │ a   ┆ b   │
    │ --- ┆ --- │
    │ i8  ┆ i8  │
    └─────┴─────┘
```

```
| 1     | 2     |
| 3     | 4     |
└───────┴───────┘
    """
)

assert_frame_equal(result, expected)
print("DataFrames are equal")

DataFrames are equal
```

For bigger DataFrames this is not recommended, as it will reduce the readability of
your code, but for small ones it can be a great help.

Common Antipatterns

Polars is designed to take care of *how* things are executed, so you can focus on *what*
you want to do. This means it tries to run the optimal query plan for you, and
you don't have to worry about implementation details like memory management or
parallelization. However, there are still some things you can do that will slow down
your queries or make them less efficient. In this section we'll go over some of the
common antipatterns you should avoid when working with Polars.

Using Brackets for Column Selection

Although Polars supports bracket notation for slicing and indexing (df[…]), this
is mostly for compatibility with other packages. We do not recommend using this
syntax, as it is less efficient than using the pl.col() method. If you use pl.col() and
turn it into an expression, the Polars optimizer can process, parallelize, and optimize
it (especially when you're using the lazy API). Please refer to Chapter 10 for details on
how to replace the bracket notation with other methods.

Generally, you're on the wrong track if you're thinking about the position of a column
in the DataFrame instead of using the API to define what column you want to
work on.

Misusing Collect

The lazy API is designed to be as efficient as possible: it gathers all the operations
you want to perform, optimizes the query plan with as much knowledge about the
data as possible, and then executes the query. The moment you call lf.collect(), it
executes the query plan and reads the data from disk. However, if you reuse the same
LazyFrame multiple times, you can save a lot of time by not calling lf.collect()
every time you want to use the data, since it will be read and executed from scratch
every time. You might do this if you want to get two different subsets of the data,

like the training and test sets in a machine learning model, or in the following case, splitting it into two different vendors:

```
%%time
taxis = pl.scan_parquet("data/taxi/yellow_tripdata_*.parquet")
vendor0 = taxis.filter(pl.col("VendorID") == 0).collect()
vendor1 = taxis.filter(pl.col("VendorID") == 1).collect()

CPU times: user 5.54 s, sys: 5.3 s, total: 10.8 s
Wall time: 3.62 s
```

This code will read the data from disk twice: once for the first subset, another time for the second. However, it's more effective to materialize the data once and then filter it twice:

```
%%time
taxis = pl.scan_parquet("data/taxi/yellow_tripdata_*.parquet")
vendors = taxis.filter(pl.col("VendorID").is_in([0, 1])).collect()
vendor0 = vendors.filter(pl.col("VendorID") == 0)
vendor1 = vendors.filter(pl.col("VendorID") == 1)

CPU times: user 5.82 s, sys: 4.5 s, total: 10.3 s
Wall time: 3.18 s
```

This leads to a runtime decrease. This example is mostly I/O-bound, but in more complex problems this optimization could lead to even bigger speedups.

However, the other extreme is overusing lf.collect(). When you keep calling lf.collect() on a LazyFrame, you're losing all the benefits of the lazy API: it is performing too much work because the optimizations can't be applied. In that case, you might as well use the eager API instead.

Be mindful of when you call lf.collect(), and only do it when you actually need the data in memory.

Using Python Code in your Polars Queries

Polars is designed to run as much as possible in Rust, which is a compiled language built to safely run in parallel and therefore much faster than Python. When you use Python code in your Polars queries, you're forcing Polars to switch to Python, slowing down the query.

Although the GroupBy.agg() and GroupBy.map_*() methods are designed to be used with Python code, you should still be careful with them. Always scan through the API documentation to see if there are methods you can string together to achieve the same result without using Python code. Additionally, you can always ask the Polars community for help on the Polars Discord server. If you can't find what you need in the API, you can write your own UDF in Rust, which will be much faster than Python code. If there are no ways around it (for example if you're using Python functions from other packages), you can still use Python code, but it should be a last resort.

Takeaways

In this final chapter, you've learned the following key takeaways:

- Polars consists of different layers: the domain-specific language in which you specify your queries, the intermittent representation that contains the query plan with metadata, the optimizer that tunes the plan, and the engines that execute that plan.
- Polars is built on top of Apache Arrow, which provides a columnar memory format optimized for analytics on modern hardware.
- Multithreaded computations and SIMD operations allow Polars to take full advantage of modern hardware.
- String data types in Polars are optimized for performance, using a view layout and inlining for short Strings.
- Polars employs various query optimization techniques, including projection pushdown, predicate pushdown, and slice pushdown.
- Polars provides built-in profiling tools to help identify performance bottlenecks in queries.
- The package includes testing functions for comparing DataFrames and Series, with options for exact and approximate comparisons.
- You should avoid common antipatterns, including using brackets for column selection, misusing `lf.collect()`, and overusing Python code in Polars queries.

Congratulations! You're now equipped with the knowledge to use Polars to its full potential for all your data-processing needs. But this isn't an ending; it's a launchpad. Polars evolves daily and so will you.

Stay connected with the vibrant community of developers and data enthusiasts on the Discord server (*https://oreil.ly/87r6N*), Stack Overflow (*https://oreil.ly/hcMNj*), or the Polars Github repository (*https://oreil.ly/52zgW*). Share your breakthroughs, ask questions, and collaborate—your contributions will shape the future of this ecosystem.

For updates, advanced techniques, and additional resources, visit *polarsguide.com*. As Polars grows, so will this website, ensuring you'll always stay on the cutting edge.

With Polars, your data's potential is limited only by what you're willing to build. So go forth and build the next generation of data solutions.

Accelerating Polars with the GPU

One of Polars' core philosophies is to make full use of *all* available processing power on your machine. This includes utilizing all the cores of the CPU, but there's another type of core we've been overlooking: the cores in your graphics card.

NVIDIA graphics cards, for example, use *Compute Unified Device Architecture* (CUDA) cores. CUDA is a proprietary parallel computing platform that leverages the graphics processing unit (GPU) for accelerated general-purpose computation. Unlike CPUs, which typically have between 2 and 20 cores, a modern GPU can feature over 15,000 cores.

While each individual GPU core is less powerful than a CPU core and is designed for simpler computations, the real advantage comes from its ability to process tasks in parallel. If you can break down complex data processing steps into simpler instructions that can be executed concurrently, the GPU can provide a substantial performance boost.

In this Appendix, we discuss accelerating Polars using the GPU. Specifically, we cover:

- How to install and use the GPU engine
- Supported and unsupported features
- Benchmarks conducted with the GPU engine
- Recommendations for situations where the GPU engine offers the most benefit
- The future of Polars on the GPU

NVIDIA RAPIDS

NVIDIA describes the RAPIDS project (*https://oreil.ly/pChlr*) as a collection of open source software packages and APIs that give you the ability to execute end-to-end data science and analytics pipelines entirely on NVIDIA GPUs using familiar PyData APIs. One such package is cuDF, a Python GPU DataFrame package with an API similar to pandas. pandas users can accelerate their pandas operations by importing cuDF, and the same code is executed on the GPU instead of the CPU.[1]

Here's the exciting news: something similar is now also possible with Polars.

As you've learned, Polars is fast not only because it's implemented in Rust, but also due to its query engine. The optimizer determines which operations need to be executed, in which order, and—more importantly—which operations can be skipped entirely.

However, unlike pandas, swapping out the Polars import for another package isn't feasible due to the role of the query engine. To overcome this, the Polars and NVIDIA teams partnered to develop a GPU engine that integrates seamlessly into the Polars package, offering the best of both worlds.

Here's how it works. The GPU engine is built by the Polars and RAPIDS teams and is based on the libcudf package, the same foundation used by cuDF. Since it's integrated directly into Polars, the GPU engine receives the optimized query plan from the Polars optimizer (see Chapter 18) and can execute it on the GPU. This allows Polars to benefit from both the power of the GPU, through libcudf, and the efficiency of the query engine.

When certain operations aren't supported by the GPU engine, it will automatically fall back to the CPU engine, ensuring that valid results are still returned. (You can change this behavior; we'll cover this configuration option and others later in this chapter, once everything is set up.) The only change you need to make to your code is selecting the engine when collecting results from a LazyFrame. For example, if you have a LazyFrame called lf, change:

```
lf.collect()
```

to:

```
lf.collect(engine="gpu")
```

---

1 See the RAPIDS documentation (*https://oreil.ly/MKDG3*) for instructions to enable cuDF for pandas.

Installing the GPU Engine

To run Polars with GPU acceleration, your system must meet the following requirements:

- An NVIDIA graphics card based on the Volta architecture or later
- CUDA version 11 or 12
- Linux or Windows Subsystem for Linux version 2 (WSL2)

In addition to these hardware and software prerequisites, you'll need to install the necessary dependencies. This section outlines the installation process in six steps.

Steps 1 and 2 are only necessary if you're using Windows. So, if you're running Linux, you can skip to step 3. Unfortunately, GPU acceleration for Polars is not supported on macOS.

The instructions assume Ubuntu 24.04 and CUDA version 12, but they can be adapted to other Linux distributions by following the relevant links provided in each section.

Step 1: Install WSL2 on Windows

On Windows, you can run Polars on the GPU by using Windows Subsystem for Linux version 2 (WSL2). WSL2 allows Windows to run a full Linux kernel, enabling you to execute Linux commands and applications directly on your Windows machine. First, we'll walk you through how to install WSL2. Then, in step 2, we'll explain how to install Ubuntu Linux on top of it.

Windows 11 comes with WSL2 preinstalled. To check if you have it, follow these steps:

1. Press the Windows key (⊞).
2. Type **PowerShell**.
3. Right-click on the PowerShell app and select "Run as administrator."

Once PowerShell is open, enter the following command:

```
PS > wsl --version

WSL version: 2.2.4.0
Kernel version: 5.15.153.1-2
WSLg version: 1.0.61
MSRDC version: 1.2.5326
Direct3D version: 1.611.1-81528511
DXCore version: 10.0.26091.1-240325-1447.ge-release
Windows version: 10.0.26100.2033
```

If the first line showing the WSL version starts with a "2," you're all set. However, it's always a good idea to make sure you're using the latest version. To update, run the following command:

```
PS > wsl --update
```

If it starts with a "1" instead of a "2," you'll need to update WSL from version 1 to 2; please refer to the official Microsoft documentation (*https://oreil.ly/6H9I5*).

Step 2: Install Ubuntu Linux on WSL2

Once you have WSL2 installed, you can install a Linux distribution. The default option, which we recommend, is Ubuntu 24.04:

1. Run the following command in the PowerShell window:

   ```
   PS > wsl --install
   ```

2. After this is done, reboot your system to finish the installation.

When restarted, the WSL application in the Start menu will be available as Ubuntu. This will open up a terminal that you can use to run the Linux commands in the next section.

Connecting Your IDE to WSL2

Modern IDEs, such as VS Code and IntelliJ IDEA, can be connected to WSL2 to provide a seamless development experience. For connecting VS Code to WSL2, follow the instructions in the official Microsoft documentation (*https://oreil.ly/H4Dcg*). For connecting IntelliJ IDEA to WSL2, follow the instructions in the official Jet-Brains documentation (*https://oreil.ly/OLkA1*).

After setting up your development environment and installing WSL2, you can follow the Linux installation instructions in step 3. You can either start the WSL2 application directly or connect your IDE to WSL2 and proceed from there.

Step 3: Install Prerequisite Ubuntu Linux Packages

Before proceeding with the GPU package installation, you need to install some prerequisite packages. These are required to build and run the necessary components. First, update the package index to ensure you have the latest information about available packages:

```
$ sudo apt update
```

Note that the prompt is a dollar sign ($), which means that these commands need to be typed in a Linux terminal, not in PowerShell. Next, upgrade all installed packages to their latest versions:

```
$ sudo apt upgrade -y
```

Finally, install the `build-essential` package, which includes compilers and other tools needed for building software:

```
$ sudo apt install build-essential -y
```

Step 4: Install the CUDA Toolkit

The CUDA Toolkit is a software development kit (SDK) created by NVIDIA for building and running applications that leverage CUDA technology, including the GPU engine for Polars. To install the CUDA Toolkit, you first need to determine the version of CUDA currently installed on your system. This will help you install the correct dependencies.

1. Run the following command to check the installed CUDA version:

   ```
   $ nvidia-smi | grep "CUDA Version"
   ```

   This will return either 11.X or 12.X, depending on the version installed. As mentioned earlier, these instructions assume CUDA version 12. If you're running CUDA version 11, which Polars does support, you can follow these instructions (*https://oreil.ly/qYf8H*).

   For now we will follow the download instructions shown here (*https://oreil.ly/DO9QT*).

2. Run the following commands in a Linux terminal (and note that the URL after `wget` should be on a single line):

   ```
   $ wget https://developer.download.nvidia.com/compute/cuda/repos/ubuntu2404/
   x86_64/cuda-keyring_1.1-1_all.deb
   $ sudo dpkg -i cuda-keyring_1.1-1_all.deb
   $ sudo apt update
   $ sudo apt -y install cuda-toolkit-12-6
   ```

This will download and install the CUDA keyring package, update your package list, and install the CUDA Toolkit.

Step 5: Install Python Dependencies

Now that the prerequisites are installed, you can install the Python dependencies. At the time of writing, dependencies are available for Python up to 3.12. You can check the RAPIDS documentation (*https://oreil.ly/_1Vkz*) for the most up-to-date information.

Install the required dependencies by running the following command from the Unix command line:

```
$ uv pip install polars[gpu]
```

Step 6: Test Your Installation

Run the following code snippet to test if the installation was successful. You can either run this in a Python interpreter in a Linux terminal by running python, or in a Jupyter Notebook:

```
import polars as pl

pl.LazyFrame({"x": [1, 2, 3]}).collect(engine=pl.GPUEngine(raise_on_fail=True))

shape: (3, 1)
┌─────┐
│ x   │
│ --- │
│ i64 │
╞═════╡
│ 1   │
│ 2   │
│ 3   │
└─────┘
```

In this command, you pass the pl.GPUEngine() to the lf.collect() method with the raise_on_fail argument set to True. This means that if the GPU engine cannot execute the query, it will raise an error instead of silently falling back to the CPU engine. By doing this, you can make it transparent when the GPU engine is not able to execute a query, which is what you want to verify here. We'll get into the configuration of the GPU engine in the next section.

If you get the same output as earlier, the installation was successful. If you get an error, check the RAPIDS documentation (*https://oreil.ly/Qa2qY*) to troubleshoot any issues.

Using the Polars GPU Engine

Once everything is set up, using the GPU engine is straightforward. Any lf. collect() call can be easily changed to use the GPU by specifying the engine. To run the query on the GPU, use lf.collect(engine="gpu"). That's it; your query will now be executed on the GPU.

Configuration

If you want to take control of the configuration of the GPU engine, you can specify the engine config by calling the `pl.GPUEngine()` function. This function accepts the following three arguments:

`device`
> In case you have multiple graphics cards on your system, you can specify which one to use. This argument is an integer that represents the ID of the device to run the query on. You can find the ID of the device by running `nvidia-smi` in a Linux terminal.

`raise_on_fail`
> The default behavior is that the GPU engine silently falls back to the CPU engine if it cannot execute the query. When this argument is set to `True`, it will raise an error instead, which stops execution.

`memory_resource`
> This argument allows you to configure the way memory is allocated using the RAPIDS Memory Manager (RMM). We will not elaborate on this advanced use case here, but if you're interested you can consult the RMM documentation (*https://oreil.ly/QbxT6*).

 Tell Me Why

When you run Polars in verbose mode through the config `pl.Con fig().set_verbose(True)`, a `PerformanceWarning` is issued showing that Polars falls back to the CPU, and it shows the reason why.

For example, at the time of writing, inequality joins are not supported by the GPU engine. When you attempt to run a query that is not supported on the GPU engine, you'll get the following warning:

```
PerformanceWarning: Query execution with GPU not supported,
reason: <class 'NotImplementedError'>: IEJoin
```

Unsupported Features

As we've shown throughout the book, the Polars API is very extensive. It's challenging to support every function and method.

For starters, none of the eager operations are supported; you have to use the lazy API. Besides that, at the time of writing, the following features are not supported:

- Reading data from JSON, Excel, and databases
- Operations on Categorical, Struct, and List data types

- Using user-defined functions (UDFs)
- Rolling aggregations and window functions
- Time series resampling and timezones
- Folds and horizontal aggregations

Benchmarking the Polars GPU Engine

We've gone over setting up the engine, how to use it, and what it can be used for. In this section we'll compare the GPU engine to other Polars engines and to other DataFrame packages, both GPU-accelerated and standard CPU versions, for different dataset sizes.

Solutions

The benchmarks were run on the versions listed in Table A-1 for every library.

Table A-1. Benchmarked solutions and their versions

Solution	Version
cuDF	24.12.00
Dask	2024.12.1
DuckDB	1.1.3
pandas	2.2.3
Polars	1.20.0
Polars on GPU	1.14.0
PySpark	3.5.4

Queries and Data

Benchmarking is hard. To try and make the benchmark as fair as possible, the Polars team has created their own Polars Decision Support (PDS) benchmark repository based on the TPC-H benchmark. The TPC-H benchmark is a decision support benchmark that consists of a suite of business-oriented ad hoc queries and concurrent data modifications. You can learn more about the TPC-H benchmark at the TPC website (*https://oreil.ly/2s0Ml*). We forked that repository (*https://oreil.ly/fMmQB*) to be able to run it on our test environment with minor modifications, and we've implemented the missing queries for pandas.

The benchmark consists of 22 queries that are run on a dataset. The datasets are generated by the benchmark itself and are stored in Parquet files. Additionally, the queries are run on different dataset sizes, which is determined by a scale factor. For timing, only the query itself is measured, including the time to read the data from disk. Importing packages is not included in the timing.

To give you an idea of what a query looks, here's query 15:

```
%%time
lineitem = pl.scan_parquet("data/benchmark/lineitem.parquet")  ❶
supplier = pl.scan_parquet("data/benchmark/supplier.parquet")

var1 = pl.date(1996, 1, 1)
var2 = pl.date(1996, 4, 1)

revenue = (
    lineitem.filter(pl.col("l_shipdate").is_between(var1, var2, closed="left"))
    .group_by("l_suppkey")
    .agg(
        (pl.col("l_extendedprice") * (1 - pl.col("l_discount")))
        .sum()
        .alias("total_revenue")
    )
    .select(pl.col("l_suppkey").alias("supplier_no"), pl.col("total_revenue"))
)

query_15 = (
    supplier.join(revenue, left_on="s_suppkey", right_on="supplier_no")
    .filter(pl.col("total_revenue") == pl.col("total_revenue").max())
    .with_columns(pl.col("total_revenue").round(2))
    .select("s_suppkey", "s_name", "s_address", "s_phone", "total_revenue")
    .sort("s_suppkey")
)

query_15.collect(engine="cpu")  ❷
```

❶ Reading files *is* included in the timing.

❷ The default engine is cpu. Change this to gpu in order to use the GPU engine.

```
CPU times: user 17.7 ms, sys: 16.5 ms, total: 34.2 ms
Wall time: 10.9 ms
shape: (1, 5)
```

s_suppkey	s_name	s_address	s_phone	total_revenue
i64	str	str	str	f64
677	Supplier#00000 0677	8mhrffG7D2WJBS QbOGst…	23-290-639-331 5	1.6144e6

Method

We performed the benchmarks on a Dell Precision 5860 Tower (*https://oreil.ly/ OwlbQ*). The specifications of the system are listed in Table A-2.

Standing on the Shoulders of Giants

We are incredibly fortunate to have received support from NVIDIA and Dell Technologies in conducting these benchmarks. They generously provided the hardware necessary for running these tests. See the "Acknowledgments" on page xxv for more details on our partnership.

Table A-2. Benchmark system specifications

Property	Value
Name	Dell Precision 5860 Tower
Processor	Intel Xeon w7-2495X 2.50 GHz
RAM	128 GB (8 x 16 GB), 4,800 MT/s DIMM, DDR5
OS	Windows 11 Pro for Workstations
Version	Version 24H2, OS build 26100.2033, Feature Experience Pack 1000.26100.23.0

We used several different graphics cards in this system in order to benchmark different capabilities (see Table A-3). One graphics card (the A1000) is based on the Ampere architecture, and the other graphics cards are based on the Ada Lovelace architecture. At the time of writing, the Ampere architecture is the previous generation and the Ada Lovelace architecture is the current generation. The listed performance is the single-precision performance.

Table A-3. Specifications of the tested graphics cards

	A1000	2000 Ada	4000 Ada	5000 Ada	6000 Ada
Architecture	Ampere	Ada Lovelace	Ada Lovelace	Ada Lovelace	Ada Lovelace
CUDA cores	2,304	2,816	6,144	12,800	18,176
Performance (TFLOPS)	6.7	12.0	26.7	65.3	91.1
VRAM (GB)	8	16	20	32	48

The code to benchmark the packages is available at our Polars benchmark repository (*https://oreil.ly/aQjfo*). The datasets are based on the TPC-H benchmark.

Every set of benchmarks was run on the scale factors 0.1, 1.0, 5.0, 10.0, 20.0, 35.0, and 50.0. This is effectively the dataset size in GB if the file format were CSV. However, since the data is stored as Parquet files, the actual size is smaller. This does expand to bigger sizes when loaded into memory, but that exact size was not measured in this benchmark. These benchmarks were repeated five times per scale factor to ensure consistent results. The minimum and maximum times were removed to prevent outliers from skewing the results, and the average time of the middle three values was taken as the final result.

Results and Discussion

During initial exploration, running the benchmark with Modin using the Ray back-end caused excessive disk spilling—up to 1 TB—which exhausted the testing environment's storage capacity. For this reason we removed it from the benchmarks.

At the higher scale factors, we only ran the most performant packages—Polars, DuckDB, and cuDF—because of time constraints.

During the benchmarking we found that the specific version we were testing on did not support two queries. Queries 11 and 22 were implemented with an inequality join that was not supported by the GPU engine.

This benchmark allows us to answer a unique set of questions, which we'll go through one by one. We'll walk through the results and discuss the implications of the findings.

Polars GPU engine versus CPU engine

First of all, what is the performance of the GPU engine compared to the CPU engine?

As seen in Figure A-1, the GPU engine is faster than the CPU engine for most queries. Note, however, that for small datasets (scale factor 0.1) the CPU engine is faster. This is because the overhead of moving the data to the GPU is higher than the boost it gets from faster computation time. However, as the dataset size increases, the GPU engine is faster, as can be seen for the rest of the scale factors.

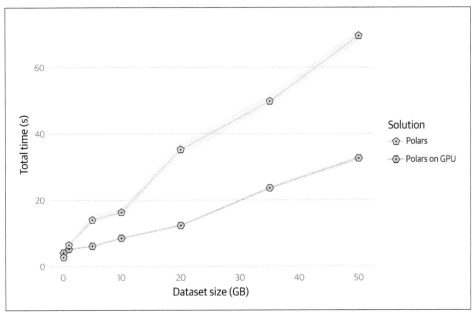

Figure A-1. Comparison of average total benchmark time between Polars' CPU and GPU engines across different dataset sizes on the NVIDIA 6000 Ada Lovelace graphics card

As seen in Figure A-2, compared to the Polars CPU engine, the GPU engine is over 2× faster for the TPC-H benchmark from datasets 5 GB up to the largest tested dataset of 50 GB. This suggests that the GPU engine is a good choice for large datasets.

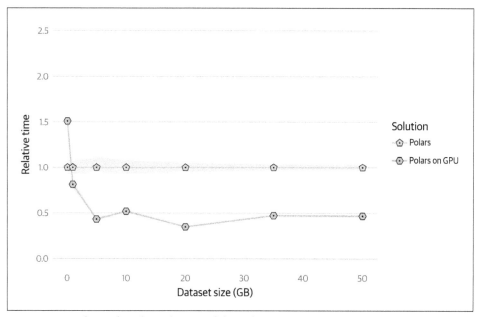

Figure A-2. Relative benchmark time of the Polars GPU engine compared to the CPU engine on the NVIDIA 6000 Ada Lovelace graphics card

Performance on different hardware

The previous results come from the benchmarks that we ran with the powerful RTX 6000 Ada GPU.

How does the performance scale on different pieces of hardware?

As seen in Figure A-3, the total benchmark time is heavily impacted by the type of card.

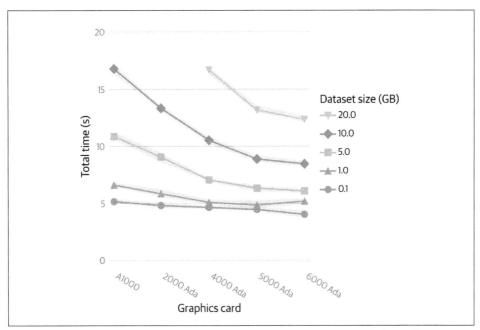

Figure A-3. Comparison of average total benchmark runtime per scale factor between the different GPUs

Even more interesting, however, is the performance per TFLOPS, as seen in Figure A-4.

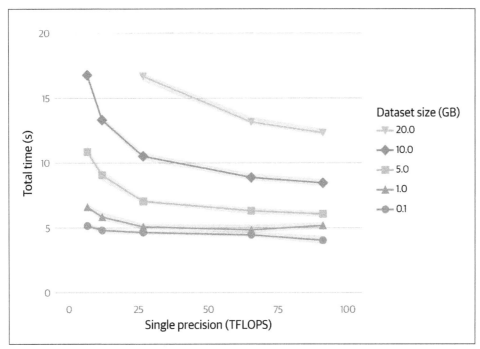

Figure A-4. Comparison of average total benchmark runtime per scale factor per TFLOPS

This shows that as the computation power increases, the additional performance gained decreases. This diminishing return is interesting to note, as it suggests that the performance gain of the GPU engine is not linear with the computational power of the GPU.

For every card we tested, even the last-gen A1000, the GPU engine is faster than the CPU engine starting at about 5 GB, as shown in Figure A-5.

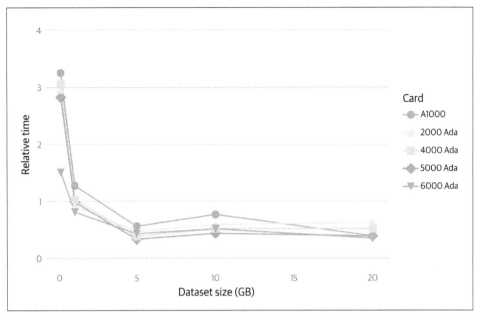

Figure A-5. Runtime compared to the CPU engine per card

Polars GPU engine versus other packages

Now that we've compared Polars to itself, it's time to compare it to comparable packages.

If we compare the GPU engine to pandas and cuDF, we see that both GPU packages are faster than their CPU counterpart, as seen in Figure A-6. With cuDF too, we see the performance gain growing with the size of the dataset.

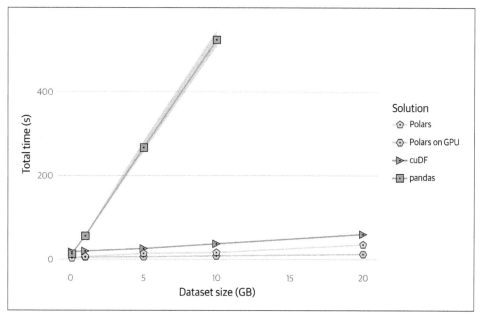

Figure A-6. Comparison of average total benchmark runtime between Polars' CPU in-memory engine and GPU engine with pandas and cuDF on different scale factors

When we scale the results to the Polars CPU engine, we can see that cuDF too has the overhead penalty for moving data to the GPU, outweighing the performance gain for smaller datasets, as seen in Figure A-7.

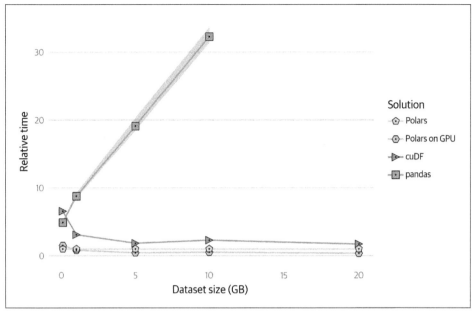

Figure A-7. Comparison of average total benchmark runtime between Polars' CPU in-memory engine and GPU engine with pandas and cuDF on different scale factors, scaled to Polars' CPU in-memory engine

The effect of the Polars optimizer

Another unique question we can answer is what effect the Polars optimizer brings to the table. Because cuDF and Polars' GPU engine are built on the same libcudf package, the only big difference is the optimizer. The optimizer cuts out or rewrites work so that the engine can execute it more efficiently, or better yet, not at all.

As seen in Figure A-8, the Polars optimizer has a significant effect on the performance of the GPU engine. With a consistent 4× speedup over cuDF, the Polars optimizer is a key component in the performance of the GPU engine.

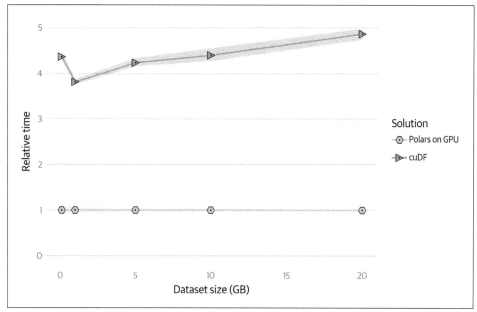

Figure A-8. The effect of Polars' optimizer on the GPU engine compared to cuDF

Conclusion

Based on our benchmarking, you'll see the biggest gains in performance when your queries are computation bound. This means that operations like `lf.join()`, `lf.group_by()`, and `GroupBy.agg()` will benefit the most from the GPU engine. I/O-bound queries, like `pl.scan_parquet()`, which are limited by the speed of reading from disk, will show similar performance on the GPU and CPU, and in the worst case can even be slower on the GPU because of the overhead of moving the data to the GPU. Based on our testing, datasets starting from 5 GB already benefit from the GPU engine, and can be over two times faster than the CPU engine. However, the performance gain is not linear with the computational power of the GPU, and the additional performance gained decreases as the computational power increases.

One thing to keep in mind is that GPUs are usually more limited in memory than CPUs, so very large datasets could fail due to out-of-memory errors.

Although the specifics are always dependent on your use case, we found that for the TPC-H benchmark, datasets from 5 GB and up can benefit from the GPU engine. As long as the data fits into the GPU's VRAM, the performance gain can be substantial. Generally, it is over two times faster than the Polars CPU engine, and multiple times faster compared to most other packages.

The Future of Polars on the GPU

It's important to note that the Polars GPU engine is still in beta; expanded functionality and features are currently in development. Plans for the future include:

- Executing operations that are not (yet) supported by the GPU, on the CPU
- Executing subqueries on both the GPU and CPU simultaneously, to enhance performance
- Executing queries on multiple GPUs, also to enhance performance
- Utilizing CUDA Unified Memory, which optimizes memory utilization of the CPU and GPU, to increase dataset capacity
- Allowing the streaming engine to utilize the GPU, which would enable you to process datasets that are too large to fit into GPU memory

The latter two improvements, in particular, could eliminate the memory limitations of the GPU engine, significantly boosting its power.

Takeaways

In this Appendix we've covered:

- The rationale behind the GPU engine in Polars
- The installation process for the GPU engine
- How to use the GPU engine
- The unsupported features of the GPU engine
- The benchmarks we ran on the GPU engine
- The results and implications of the benchmarks
- The future of Polars on the GPU

You should now have a good understanding of the GPU engine in Polars and how to use it to its full potential.

Index

About the Authors

Jeroen Janssens is a senior developer relations engineer at Posit, PBC. His expertise lies in visualizing data, implementing machine learning models, and building solutions using Python, R, JavaScript, and Bash. He's passionate about open source and sharing knowledge. Previously, Jeroen was at Xomnia, where he first learned about Polars. He is the author of *Data Science at the Command Line* (O'Reilly, 2021). Jeroen holds a PhD in machine learning from Tilburg University and an MSc in artificial intelligence from Maastricht University. He lives with his wife and two kids in Rotterdam, the Netherlands. Learn more on his website (*https://jeroenjanssens.com*).

Thijs Nieuwdorp is the lead data scientist at Xomnia in Amsterdam. His interest in the interaction between human and computer led him to an education in artificial intelligence at the Radboud University, after which he dove straight into the field of data science. At Xomnia he witnessed the birth of Polars as Ritchie Vink started working on it during his employment there and has been using it in his projects ever since. He enjoys figuring out complex data problems, optimizing existing solutions, and putting them to good use by implementing them into business processes. Outside work, Thijs enjoys exploring our world through hiking and traveling and exploring other worlds through books, games, and movies. He lives in Amsterdam with his partner, Paula. Learn more on his website (*https://thijsnieuwdorp.com*).

Colophon

The animal on the cover of *Python Polars* is an Iberian lynx (*Lynx pardinus*). It is one of four species in the genus *Lynx* and is found exclusively in the Iberian Peninsula in southwest Europe. Iberian lynx have tawny fur with dark spots and a lighter belly, with black tufts on their ears and cheeks. They are medium-sized cats, with adults reaching about 32 to 40 inches long. Like bobcats and other species of lynx, they are known for their short tails, which are only 5 to 6 inches long.

Iberian lynx were once widespread throughout Spain and Portugal, but in the latter half of the twentieth century, they lost about 80 percent of their former range through a combination of poaching, habitat fragmentation, and a decline in the population of its main prey species, the European rabbit. By 2000, they were on the verge of extinction, with only 94 individuals in southern Spain. Through conservation efforts, their population has rebounded to about two thousand individuals, and they have been reintroduced into parts of their former range. Thanks to these efforts, their conservation status has been reclassified as vulnerable.

Many of the animals on O'Reilly covers are endangered; all of them are important to the world.

The cover illustration is by Karen Montgomery, based on an antique line engraving from *Natural History of Animals*. The series design is by Edie Freedman, Ellie Volckhausen, and Karen Montgomery. The cover fonts are Gilroy Semibold and Guardian Sans. The text font is Adobe Minion Pro; the heading font is Adobe Myriad Condensed; and the code font is Dalton Maag's Ubuntu Mono.

O'REILLY®

Learn from experts.
Become one yourself.

60,000+ titles | Live events with experts | Role-based courses
Interactive learning | Certification preparation

 **Try the O'Reilly learning platform
free for 10 days.**

www.ingramcontent.com/pod-product-compliance
Ingram Content Group UK Ltd.
Pitfield, Milton Keynes, MK11 3LW, UK
UKHW010745250325
456687UK00003B/5